项目管理资质认证系列

U0748353

# Highly Effective Pass the PgMP® Examination

# 高效通过 PgMP® 考试

于兆鹏◎编著

中国电力出版社
CHINA ELECTRIC POWER PRESS

# 内 容 提 要

本书编写的目的是使你快速掌握项目集管理的体系方法，顺利通过 PgMP®考试。全书共12章，不仅涵盖了 PgMP®的项目集战略一致性、项目集收益管理、项目集相关方参与、项目集治理、项目集生命周期管理，还包括 PgMP®的考试技巧详解、两套模拟题及参考答案。每章都配以秘笈要点、考试重点、章节练习题等，帮助学员能够快速梳理知识点，查漏补缺。

同时，考虑到项目集报考流程的烦琐，以及项目集经验描述的严格审查，本书还提供了项目集报考流程指南、项目集经验描述技巧等，方便读者参考。

最后，本书还增加了 PgMP®标准术语表，助力考生高效通过 PgMP®认证考试。

**图书在版编目（CIP）数据**

高效通过 PgMP®考试 / 于兆鹏编著. —北京：中国电力出版社，2020.12
（项目管理资质认证系列）
ISBN 978-7-5198-5162-0

Ⅰ. ①高… Ⅱ. ①于… Ⅲ. ①项目管理—资格考试—自学参考资料 Ⅳ. ①F224.5

中国版本图书馆 CIP 数据核字(2020)第221348号

出版发行：中国电力出版社
地　　址：北京市东城区北京站西街19号（邮政编码100005）
网　　址：http://www.cepp.sgcc.com.cn
责任编辑：李　静（1103194425@qq.com）
责任校对：黄　蓓　于　维
装帧设计：九五互通　周　赢
责任印制：钱兴根

印　　刷：三河市百盛印装有限公司
版　　次：2020年12月第1版
印　　次：2020年12月北京第1次印刷
开　　本：787毫米×1092毫米　16开本
印　　张：22
字　　数：467千字
定　　价：88.00元

# 前言

1999 年，因一个偶然的机会，我被指派负责一个手机软件开发的项目。自此算来，我从事项目管理领域的管理及相关工作已有 20 年，有幸与中国项目管理发展 20 年同龄。回望这 20 年的项目管理从业经历，有像中国银联、中国联通这样的国企项目经历，也有像惠普这样的外企，像携程、海尔、颐中这样的民企，以及像 NTTDATA 这样的日企等多方面的经历。同时，我也有 12 年项目管理培训咨询的经验，所经历过的行业涉及金融、电商、IT、汽车、旅游、烟草、家电、财会等十几个。

在这 20 年的发展历程中，我观察到中国的项目管理正在经历着一个重要的发展趋势，那就是项目的集群化、大型化发展趋势。

一、项目管理发展趋势三点分析

通过我所亲身经历的企业或行业中项目管理的特点来总结，可以归纳为以下三点。

第一，项目管理在企业和行业中是按层次依次发展的。

开始是乙方最重视项目管理，因为乙方需要更加"多快好省"地完成项目，满足客户需求；甲方则是外企最早开始关注项目管理，因为外企受欧美总部的流程统一化影响，管理理念和流程需要一致；随着中国经济在 2003—2013 这 10 年间的腾飞，民企规模越来越大，民企组织流程化和项目化的程度越来越高，对项目管理的需求也越来越大；最近这几年，国企开始重视项目管理了，一方面因为中国政府对于创新发展的要求，另一方面则是市场化程度的提升，要求自身进行资源整合，快速响应客户。

行业的趋势也是如此，较为新兴的行业最早关注项目管理，比如 IT、互联网，从而带动一些传统行业也在关注项目管理，比如家电、烟草、船舶等。还有行业间的互动也在加速这个趋势，比如金融与互联网及移动电商、通信行业的结合，使得一些行业中的传统成分在发生急速的变化，这种变化使得这些行业中的企业需要找到一种能够横向、快速地进行资源整合、收益集成的方法，从而快速响应客户需求，提升自身流程效率。而项目管理恰恰就是这样的一个领域。

第二，项目的规模越来越大，周期越来越长，复杂度越来越高，企业要求项目经理负责的项目也越来越多。

可能是由于中国经济快速发展的原因，各种企业的项目规模越来越大，项目团队规模从前几年的 3~5 人到动辄几十人、上百人；周期越来越长，现在历时 2~3 年的项目在企业中已经不算周期长的项目；复杂度越来越高，相关方比之前的项目明显增多，市场对企业的不断加大压力直接转嫁到项目上；企业中的项目数量也开始倍增，这也是这几年项目管理办公室（Project Mangement Office，PMO）越来越火的原因吧。这样一来，企业要求项目经理管的项目也越来越多，原来管 2~3 个项目就挺多的了，现在管 20~30 个项目也不是什么怪事。比如前一段时间我与上海的金融行业和手机行业的一些企业交流，就发现像金融行业的浦发银行、手机制造行业的上海华勤这样的企业项目经理管理的项目数量达几十个。

第三，项目管理更加注重价值和集成收益。

这两年与很多行业的项目管理专家和同仁交流过，大家共同得出的一个结论是项目经理不再仅仅关注可交付成果（Deliverable），而是更加关注成果给企业带来的收益（Benefit）。

从某种意义上来讲，可交付成果仅是一个静态的产出，若要体现项目在企业中的价值，就必须考虑我们这个项目究竟能够给企业带来怎样的收益。而且有时不光要考虑自身的，更要把视角拓宽，去看横向的项目有无联系，能否进行收益集成，共同给企业带来"1+1>2"的效果。

综上所述，目前中国的项目管理已经逐步甲方化，更加关注项目的集成收益和整合创新，越来越关注收益层面，而不是单个的可交付成果。

二、项目集管理（PgMP®）的核心思路

（美国）项目管理协会（PMI）推出的 PgMP®认证恰恰是这个发展趋势及市场需求很好的响应，因为 PgMP®的思维角度就是甲方的项目管理。从这个角度理解，整个思路就不一样了。

第一，需要为企业的收益负责。

光有可交付成果已经不够了，需要考虑我们这个可交付成果如何为企业带来价值，如何能够联合其他的成果拼成企业的收益版图，这样的思维乙方一般是不会有的，只有甲方的项目经理才有动机更进一步去考虑这个问题。

第二，五位一体的标准体系适合大项目集的管理实际。

项目集战略一致（Program Strategy Alignment）、项目集收益管理（Program Benefits Management）、项目集相关方争取（Program Stakeholder Engagement）、项目集治理（Program Governance）、项目集生命周期管理（Program Life Cycle Management）这 5 个领域组成了 PgMP®的核心，而且 PgMP®体系标准认为项目集的管理往往不是一种按照 PMP®的输入——

工具—技术—输出（Input-Tools-Technology-Output，ITTO）的顺序流程化模式，而是围绕项目集生命周期综合作用的结果。

笔者非常认同这种体系架构，因为在大型项目集管理中往往是先进行资源的整合，看是否有新的机会进行收益的叠加，从思维方式上是一种开拓性的、跳跃性的，有了局面和路线图后再以一个灵活多变的体系去实现和维持收益，并随时准备着发现机会和收益的叠加。

第三，平台和竞合思维。

通过学习 PgMP®，笔者认为管理大型项目集需要具备两种思维方式：平台思维和竞合思维。

什么是平台思维？我们以前的项目管理思路往往局限于某一个点，而项目集管理则是协调多个项目的收益集成、资源制约和冲突等，因此项目集管理更像是建立一个治理平台，使这个平台成为一个生态圈，项目在这个生态圈中能够更好地发展、互利互惠。要达到这种状态，就需要考虑生态圈中的项目个体如何满足资源和收益供需平衡，如何建立机制使得生态圈内的多边项目市场趋于共赢发展。携程、银联都是平台思维的典型例子，比如银联是连接发卡行、持卡人、商户等多边市场，它的任务就是制定规则让这些在这个平台中的个体互利共赢。项目集也是这样的道理。

什么是竞合思维？以前我们可能会比较静态地看待项目环境中的竞争对手、合作伙伴。现在因为市场环境的复杂多变，竞争对手也有可能成为合作伙伴，合作伙伴在产业链中也有可能成为竞争对手。比如中国银联在国内与支付宝是竞争对手，但对国外的 Visa 和万事达，说不定哪天银联有可能与支付宝联合一致对外，这都是有可能的事情。因此，现在是既竞争有合作的关系，也就是竞合思维。

三、项目管理集群化、大型化的发展前景

单项目管理和项目集管理两者最大的差异在于思维和模式的差异，项目管理因为关注可交付成果更加注重保质、保量地达成既定目标，因此仅仅是完成"1+1=2"；而项目集管理则是因为关注收益更加主动地迎接变化、整合资源从而为企业赢得更多商业价值，是"1+1>2"。

随着中国经济由粗放型到集约型的转变，中国企业会越来越注重集成创新，项目集管理作为实现集成创新的有效手段，将来一定会有非常广阔的应用前景。中国企业也会因为 PgMP®项目集管理体系的推行而获得收益，一个可能预见到的收益就是企业项目间协同作战能力提升，从而可以集成多个项目的产出产生整体的商业价值。

本书编写的目的就是迎合中国项目管理集群化、大型化的发展趋势，普及项目集管理的方法。《吕氏春秋》中说："君子谋时而动，顺势而为。"顺势者事半而功倍，相信阅读本书的你就是这个顺势者。

最后，我要感谢在本书的编写过程中提供过帮助的伙伴：林侃、顾丽、郝德峰、张敏津、张德有、季丽、吴婷、贺伟、杨志专、张丽波。没有他们的辛勤劳动，本书是不可能完成的。另外，十分感谢李静老师，她在百忙之中仍然对我提供了许多帮助，才使得本书顺利出版。

由于作者才疏学浅，加上出版时间很紧，书中还有很多不尽如人意的地方。我诚挚地希望本书能起到抛砖引玉的作用，希望读者对书中不合理或是还要进一步改进的地方提出宝贵意见。我的电子邮箱是 yuzhaopeng@hotmail.com，对您的任何意见或建议，我都会认真回复。

于兆鹏
写于上海
2020 年 3 月

# 目录

# 第 **1** 章

# 概述

## 1.1  考试概述

PgMP®认证考试包含170道单项选择题，每道题有4个选项。你会有4小时时间完成考试，尽可能回答每道题，因为未回答的题目将被认为是错误的。考试完成后，PMI会计算并提供你的分数。

## 1.2  考试内容

PgMP®认证考试包含了项目集管理的5个领域（见图1-1），具体如下。

（1）项目集战略一致性（Program Strategy Alignment）。

（2）项目集收益管理（Program Benefit Management）。

（3）项目集相关方参与（Program Stakeholder Engagement）。

（4）项目集治理（Program Governance）。

（5）项目集生命周期管理（Program Life Cycle Management）。

考题的顺序可能不会按照如上的顺序。但是，每个领域的题目个数是固定的。

根据考试大纲，各领域的考题分布比例如下。

- 15%的题目与项目集战略一致性相关。
- 44%的题目与项目集生命周期管理相关，其中：
  - 6%的题目涉及启动；
  - 11%的题目涉及规划；
  - 14%的题目涉及执行；
  - 10%的题目涉及控制；

■3%的题目涉及收尾。

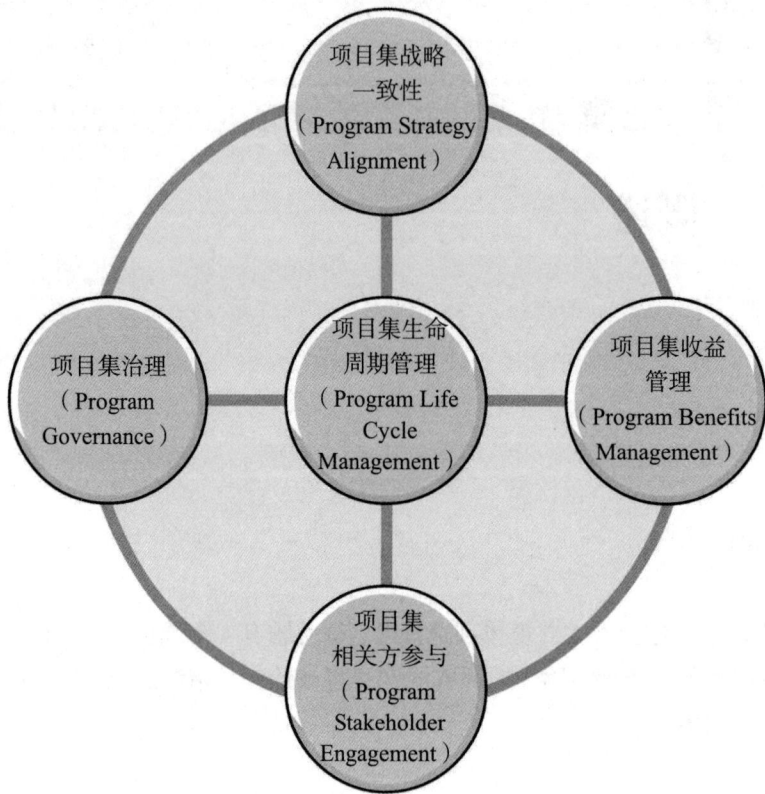

图 1-1 项目集管理的 5 个领域

- 11%的题目与项目集收益管理相关。
- 16%的题目与项目集相关方参与相关。
- 14%的题目与项目集治理相关。

# 1.3 本书的框架

本书分为 12 章，不仅涵盖了 PgMP®的项目集战略一致性、项目集收益管理、项目集相关方参与、项目集治理、项目集生命周期管理，而且还包括 PgMP®的考试技巧详解（第11 章）、两套模拟题及解析（第 12 章）。每章都配以秘笈要点、考试重点、章节练习题等，帮助学员能够快速梳理知识点，查缺补漏。

同时，考虑项目集报考流程的烦琐，以及项目集经验描述的严格审查，本书还提供了项目集报考流程指南（附录 A）、项目集经验描述技巧（附录 B）等，方便读者参考。

最后，本书还增加了 PgMP®标准术语表（附录 C），助力考生高效通过 PgMP®考试。

# 第 2 章

# 项目集战略管理

战略项目集管理在 PgMP® 认证考试的试题中占到全卷内容的 15% 或者是 25 个题目。这些题目涉及《项目集管理标准》（第 4 版）中的项目集战略一致性领域，而这个领域的重点是确保项目集持续支持组织整体的战略目的和目标。

## 2.1　秘笈要点

战略一致性领域发生在项目集立项前，目的是确保该组织认同批准该项目集。这一领域是非常重要的。因此，需要通过定义项目集的目标和需求，来实施项目集的初步评估，目的是确保项目集与组织目的和目标相一致。

在项目集被正式批准之前，应该制定商业论证。而商业论证中需要包含高层级的路线图或时间表。使命陈述应该描述为什么项目集是重要的。此外，关于项目集所需资金的论据阐述也是必要的。考题将重点考查项目集商业论证中的这些关键部分。

在项目集批准之前，发起人必须确定参与和/或受该项目集影响的关键相关方，并与他们协同确保项目集支持组织的目标，确保项目集是可行的，确保项目集与项目组合中陈述的优先级相一致，确保项目集与组织的战略计划相一致。考试的问题可能会集中在关键相关方，以及如何最好地确保他们对该项目集的支持。

即使收益管理是一个单独的领域，项目集收益也应该是商业论证和本领域的一部分。收益是项目集的产出。为了识别收益，应实施成本收益分析、市场分析和其他相关研究，这样就可以同时编写高层级的项目集范围说明和高层级的收益实现计划。

请记住这一点，项目集能立项的首要原因是通过项目集可以获得比独立管理项目、子项目集或项目集中的其他工作的更大收益。收益是指组织运行的改善，收益可以是有形的，也可以是无形的；可以是定量的，也可以是定性的。这两种类型的收益都应该被记录下来，并包含在项目集的商业论证中。项目集的有些收益会在项目集进行过程中就实现，而有些收益直到项目集完成才实现，甚或项目集结束后有的收益仍没有实现。

同时，管理项目集比管理项目有更多的制约因素。这些制约因素（如法规、标准、可持续性、文化考量、地缘考量，政治和伦理问题等）必须在项目集被批准之前加以考虑。问题将集中在各种制约因素给项目集带来的影响，以帮助决策者决定是否批准该项目集。

项目集战略一致性领域引入了项目集路线图。路线图是在项目集进行的过程中渐进明细的，并图形化地、按时间顺序来表示项目集的预期方向。路线图对确定项目集是否应该被批准有帮助。定期审查路线图有助于确定项目集是否与组织战略保持一致。

在项目集战略一致性领域中，需要经常进行环境评估，这包括评估商业论证和初始项目集计划。分析方法包括竞争优势分析、可行性研究、SWOT 分析、假设分析，以及历史信息的利用。其中，企业环境因素需要加以考虑。

项目集战略一致性还包括评估项目集整合机会，这意味着考虑各种项目集活动或非项目工作中的资源需求、设施、财务、资产、流程和系统，这样它们能被跨组织地匹配和整合。

一旦该项目集被批准，那么项目集启动过程就开始了。项目集战略一致性领域涵盖了大量的知识。

## 2.2  重要考点

以下是项目集战略一致性的主要知识点，帮助你锁定考点范围。

1. 项目、项目集和项目组合的定义
2. 项目集管理的定义
3. 子项目集、组件和项目集活动
4. 商业价值
5. 以下三者的关系
- 项目集管理和项目组合管理；
- 项目集管理和运营管理；
- 项目集管理和项目管理。
6. 项目集因素
- 组织过程资产；
- 事业环境因素；
- 环境分析：
  - 比较优势分析；
  - 可行性分析；
  - SWOT 分析；
  - 假设分析；

　　　　■历史信息分析；

　　　　■评估商业论证和项目集计划的有效性。

- 环境评估。

7. 组织战略和项目集一致性

8. 战略规划

- 可行性：

　　■准备就绪；

　　■初步范围；

　　■初步收益实现计划。

- 愿景；
- 使命；
- 项目组合管理；
- 聚焦客户的项目集；
- 内部项目集。

9. 初始项目集评估

- 目标；
- 需求；
- 风险；
- 组织收益：

　　■市场分析；

　　■成本/收益分析；

　　■财务和非财分析；

　　■资金需求。

10. 项目集商业论证

- 成本和收益；
- 问题或机会；
- 业务影响和运营影响：
- 备选解决方案；
- 财务分析；
- 内在和外在收益；
- 市场需求或阻碍；
- 潜在利润；
- 社会需求；
- 环境影响；
- 上市时间；

- 制约因素；
- 授权、意图和商业需要的宗旨。

11. 项目集授权
- 使用商业论证获得项目集批准；
- 高层级章程——成本、里程碑时间表和收益。

12. 高层级项目集计划
- 愿景；
- 使命：
  - ■ 相关方关注和期望；
  - ■ 确立项目集方向。
- 目的和目标。

13. 高层级项目集路线图
- 意图方向；
- 时间顺序的；
- 项目集活动和期望收益之间的关系；
- 依赖关系：
  - ■ 主要里程碑；
  - ■ 商业策略和计划工作的链接；
  - ■ 决策点。
- 终端目标、挑战和风险；
- 高层级视角的基础设施和组件计划；
- 进度间的区别；
- 初步估算；
- 设立项目集定义、规划和执行的基准；
- 帮助项目集执行和收益交付的工具；
- 治理的有效性；
- 执行发起人的确认和批准。

14. 项目集目标
- 规章和法律的制约因素；
- 社会影响；
- 可持续性；
- 文化考虑；
- 政治气候；
- 道德考虑；
- 相关方一致性；

- 项目集可交付性。

15. 整合机会和需要。

- 人力资本和人力资源需求；
- 技能组合；
- 设施；
- 资产；
- 流程；
- 系统；
- 匹配和整合利益；
- 开拓变更的战略机会。

# 2.3　章节练习

1. Assume you are working for an organization, ABC, which has about 500 people in it. Recently, your executives attended a one-day training program that presented an overview of portfolio, program, and project management. When the CEO, CFO, and CIO returned from this session, you were tasked to provide a list of all of the projects under way in the organization for their review. When you reviewed all the projects before giving the list to the executive team, you recommended to them that some of the multiple   projects under way be managed as a program. This is because_____

A.  Deliverables are independent　　　B.  A collective capability is delivered

C.  Resource constraints affect projects　　D.  Greater benefits would result

1. 假设你正就职于一个叫 ABC 的公司，员工约 500 人。最近，你的管理人员参加了一个为期一天的培训项目，简要介绍了项目组合、项目集和项目管理。当 CEO、CFO、CIO 结束培训回来后，交给你一项任务：提供一个清单，列出所有的正在进行的项目供他们审阅。在你把所有的项目列表交给执行团队之前，你向他们推荐一些正在进行的多个项目可以作为一个项目集来管理。这是因为_____

A.  可交付成果是独立的　　　　　　B.  共同能力被交付

C.  资源制约因素会影响项目　　　　D.  将获得更大的收益

2. You met with the members of the Executive team in your company ABC.  They were impressed with your knowledge of program management, and since they had attended the one-day seminar, they told you they wanted to make sure every program they set up supported the organization's strategic goals because_____

A.  The organization's strategy is a result of its strategic planning

B.  The organization's strategy affects how its vision will be achieved

C. Different clients, suppliers, and technologies are included in each program

D. Benefits and outcomes may affect the entire organization

2. 你在你公司 ABC 里遇到了执行团队的成员。他们对你项目集管理的知识留下了深刻的印象，因为他们参加了为期一天的研讨会，他们告诉你，想确保建立的每一个项目集都支持组织的战略目标，因为_____

A. 组织战略是战略规划的结果

B. 组织战略影响其愿景如何实现

C. 每一个项目集包含不同的客户、供应商和技术

D. 收益和成果可能影响整个组织

3. Working to improve the maturity of an organization's work in program management there are a number of items one can do. In the early stage of such an initiative, one recognizes the influence of the program by the needs of the organization's portfolio, an example of which is _____

A. Timelines　　　　　B. Stakeholder expectations

C. Risk tolerances　　　D. Escalated issue

3. 为提高组织在项目集管理工作中的成熟度，有许多事可以做。在一个初始方案的早期阶段，一般认为组织项目组合的需求会对项目集产生影响，其中的一个例子是_____

A. 时间线　　　　　B. 相关方期望

C. 风险容忍度　　　D. 升级的事件

4. Moving into a program environment is a major change for organizations especially in ones in which people are more used to working on projects. Programs have a broader scope, tend to be more complex, and may last for many years. This means it is necessary to_____

A. Focus on benefits management

B. Exploit strategic opportunities for change

C. Recognize the vision reveals the organization's truest intent

D. Focus on market changes

4. 演进到项目集环境是组织的一项重大变革，尤其是在那些人们更习惯基于项目工作的组织。项目集有更广泛的范围，往往更复杂，可能会持续很多年。这意味着必须要_____

A. 聚焦于收益管理

B. 开拓变革的战略机会

C. 认识到愿景揭示了组织最真实的意图

D. 聚焦于市场变化

5. You are one of many project managers working on the new plasma screen development program. Your project has not yet started, but the program manager is anxious to have it begin

as soon as the program starts. But before you can receive the go-ahead to start, it is necessary to

_____

   A.　Create a schedule and identify risks

   B.　Define the expected benefits in the business case

   C.　Have a business case and a program mandate

   D.　Identify the key stakeholders and determine their level of influence

5.　你是在新的等离子屏幕开发项目集的其中一名项目经理。你的项目还没有开始，但项目集经理急于尽快在项目集启动时开始项目。但在你可以接受开始之前，哪一项是必要的_____

   A.　创造进度表并识别风险

   B.　在商业论证中定义期望的收益

   C.　有商业论证或项目集授权

   D.　识别关键相关方并确认他们的影响水平

6.　Assume you are the program sponsor for this new program on the new plasma screen development to replace all existing LCD screens and enhance plasma's screens so they can be viewed in 4D.　As you worked to obtain approval for this program, you decided to contribute to the body of knowledge available to the decision makers so you_____

   A.　Held a focus groups

   B.　Consulted with experts for suggestions based on work on previous programs

   C.　Conducted a customer acceptance review

   D.　Prepared a feasibility study

6.　假设你是一项新项目集的发起人，开发新的等离子屏幕取代所有现有的 LCD 屏幕并升级等离子体屏幕至 4D 观看效果。当你获得这个项目集的批准，你决定给决策者提供可获得的知识体系，所以你_____

   A.　开展焦点小组

   B.　基于之前项目集的工作向专家咨询建议

   C.　实施客户验收审查

   D.　准备可行性研究

7.　Assume you are working in a Fortune 500 company. Recently, your company hired an outside OPM3® Certified Professional to conduct an Organizational Project Management Maturity Assessment of its program management practices in terms of the standardize, measure, control, and continuous improvement areas. Organizational program management relates to program management because it_____

   A.　Has an approach to foster a sustainable competitive advantage

   B.　Has a program management office (PMO)

C.  Has an emphasis to harmonize project and program components

D.  Has a focus on developing and implementing plans toward a common goal

7. 假设你在一家财富 500 强公司工作。最近，你的公司雇用了一个外部 OPM3®认证的专家依据规范、测量、控制和持续改进领域为项目集管理实践进行组织项目集管理成熟度评估。组织的项目集管理与项目集管理有关，因为它_____

A.  有一种形成可持续竞争优势的方法

B.  有项目集管理办公室（PMO）

C.  强调协调项目和项目集组件

D.  专注于制订和实施实现共同目标的计划

8.  As you work to prepare the business case for the new plasma screen program, you recognize it is essential to identify potential benefits that will accrue from establishing this program. You have assembled a team of stakeholders and plan to interview them for their opinions. You want to point out how and when this program's goals will be pursued. It is documented in the_____

A.  Program plan

B.  Benefit realization plan

C.  Business case

D.  Program roadmap

8. 当你在为新的等离子屏幕项目集准备商业论证况下，你认识到识别这个项目集的潜在收益是非常重要的。你已经组建了一个相关方团队，并计划采访他们的意见。你想指出的是，当这个项目集的目标将如何并何时实行。它被记录在_____

A.  项目集计划

B.  收益实现计划

C.  商业论证

D.  项目集路线图

9.  You are preparing the business case to obtain organizational leadership approval for a new program to implement a company-wide customer relationship management system to better manage sales activities and leads. You have been meeting with many people as you work to prepare this business case, and already you have heard a lot of the more than 600 salespeople in your company object to it. Your business plan therefore should clearly address_____

A.  The technical feasibility of the program

B.  Intrinsic benefits

C.  How generally accepted methods of change management will be used

D.  How the return on investment will be calculated to demonstrate success

9. 你正在为一个新的项目集准备商业论证，以获得组织领导批准。该项目集是为实现公司范围的客户关系管理系统，以更好地管理销售活动和超前量。当你准备商业论证时，你已经会见了许多人，你听到了全公司有超过 600 名销售人员在反对它。因此，你的商业计划应该清楚地解决_____

A.  项目集的技术可行性

B. 内在收益

C. 如何运用普遍接受的变更管理

D. 如何通过投资回报率的计算，来证明项目集成功

10. Assume you are working for the Motor Carrier Safety Administration in your government, responsible for the regulation of motor carriers in your country. You are a senior executive in this Administration, and you are getting ready for a meeting with the Administrator of the Agency and the other senior executives to review new programs and projects for the next budget cycle to be part of the overall portfolio. You have suggested that a program be established to consolidate various projects that require overhaul of existing regulations. Such a program is_____

A. One with major resource assumptions

B. Preceded by the development of a roadmap

C. A catalyst for change

D. One with a parent-child relationship with the Agency's portfolio

10. 假设你正在为政府汽车运输安全署工作，负责在你国家的汽车运输公司的监管。你是这个行政机构的高级管理人员，你正在准备与该机构的行政官和其他高级管理人员审查下一个预算周期的新的项目集和项目作为整体投资组合的一部分。你建议成立一个项目集以合并各种需要对现有法规进行彻底检查的项目。这样的项目集是_____

A. 有主要资源的假设

B. 需要先制定路线图

C. 变更的催化剂

D. 与组织的项目组合有父子关系

11. Realizing that before you meet with the Agency Administrator and the other members of the senior staff that funding is limited, especially with your President's mandate to reduce spending at the federal government level by 50%, that you need to estimate the high-level financial benefits of your regulatory overhaul program to ensure it receives approval from your Agency Administrator and the other senior leaders. You need to establish a constant reminder of the objectives and the program's intended benefits so you prepare_____

A. A program vision

B. A financial framework

C. An analysis of the net present value

D. An analysis of the internal rate of return

11. 在会见署长和其他高级职员之前你意识到资金是有限的，尤其是总统下达的指令即减少联邦政府 50%的支出水平，你需要估计你的监管改革项目集的高层次金融收益并确保得到署长和其他高级领导人的批准。你需要不断得到提醒你的目标和项目集的预期利

益，所以你准备了_____

    A. 项目集愿景            B. 财务框架

    C. 净现值分析            D. 内部收益率分析

12. You are a member of your organization's Product Portfolio Committee. The head of your enterprise program management office (EPMO) recommends that a program be undertaken to develop a series of products for the next-generation automobile to be run using helium. In deciding whether or not to approve this program, of the following, which one is the most important for your committee to consider_____

    A. Proposed schedule            B. Benefits

    C. Feasibility studies            D. Key resources

12. 你是你所在组织中的产品项目组合委员会的成员。你的企业项目集管理办公室的主任（EPMO）建议实施一个项目集，即开发一系列可以使用氦运行的新一代汽车产品。在决定是否批准这个项目集时，以下哪一项是委员会需要重点考虑的_____

    A. 建议的进度表            B. 收益

    C. 可行性研究            D. 关键资源

13. You are a member of your organization's Product Portfolio Committee. The head of your enterprise program management office (EPMO) recommends that a program be undertaken to develop a series of products for the next-generation automobile to be run using helium. An important consideration of your committee is_____

    A. Sustainability            B. Regulatory issues

    C. Market analysis            D. Key resources

13. 你是你所在组织中的产品项目组合委员会的成员。你的企业项目集管理办公室的主任（EPMO）建议执行一个项目集，即进行开发一系列可以使用氦运行的新一代汽车产品。你的委员会考虑的一个重要因素是_____

    A. 可持续性            B. 规章问题

    C. 市场分析            D. 关键资源

14. You are a functional manager in your organization, the head of the Department of Engineering, and a member of the Selection Committee for new programs. At the committee meetings, you review potential programs. One key factor that you consider as to whether to approve a program is_____

    A. Who will be the program manager?

    B. What are the funding requirements?

    C. What is the source of program funding?

    D. What are the next steps to get the program started?

14. 你是你所在组织中的一名职能经理——工程部的负责人和一个新项目集的选择委

员会的成员。在委员会会议上，你会审查潜在的项目集。你认为是否批准一个项目集的关键因素是_____

A. 谁将是项目集经理？　　　　B. 资金需求是怎样的？

C. 项目集融资来源有哪些？　　D. 使项目集开始的下一步是什么？

15. As a result of all of your hard work and diligence to get your program started, and based on the business case that you developed, you have received approval form your Portfolio Review Board, which consists of your organization's senior leaders, to proceed to initiate your program. However, you now should_____

A. Define how the program aligns with the strategic plan

B. Define your program mission statement

C. Establish a high-level roadmap

D. Prepare individual plans for components

15. 由于你努力促使项目集开始，并基于开发的商业论证，你已经从项目组合审查委员会收到了批准来启动你的项目集。该项目组合审查委员会包括你组织的高层领导。然而，你现在应该_____

A. 定义如何使项目集战略计划相一致

B. 定义你的项目集使命说明书

C. 确定高层级路线图

D. 为组件准备个体计划

16. You are on the program planning team to develop a program for the next generation of drugs to combat joint disease. The executive sponsor has asked that you prepare a comparative advantage analysis to_____

A. Show "what-if" analysis

B. Proceed with benefit analysis and planning

C. Issue the program mandate

D. Assess feasibility according to constraints

16. 你在项目集规划团队内，为下一代的药物开发一个项目集，以抗击关节疾病。执行发起人要求你准备一份比较优势分析_____

A. 显示"假设"分析　　　　　B. 进行收益分析和规划

C. 起草项目集授权说明书　　D. 根据制约因素评估可行性

17. Assume you are a member of your agency's Program Selection Committee, and the Committee has just met to determine which programs and projects it should pursue. Your program to develop the next generation Air Force radar system was approved. Since you now have the authorization to proceed, your committee then has to_____

A. Develop a program budget

B.  Identify and receive the key resources needed for planning

C.  Establish the rules for subcontractor selection

D.  Identify the feasibility studies that need to be conducted

17. 假设你是你所在机构的项目集选择委员会的成员，和委员会刚刚见面以确定应该开启哪些项目集和项目。你的关于发展下一代空军雷达系统的项目集得到了批准。既然你现在有授权继续进行，你的委员会接下来需要_____

A.  开发项目集预算

B.  确认并接受规划需要的关键资源

C.  建立分包商选择的规则

D.  确定需要实施的可行性研究

18.  As you worked to obtain approval for this Air Force radar program, you realized the necessity of conducting a SWOT analysis. Its analysis then_____

A.  Focuses on factors outside of the program

B.  Assists in benefits identification

C.  Helps to develop the program charter

D.  Helps establish meaningful measures to assess program performance

18.  随着你获得这个空军雷达计划的批准，你意识到进行 SWOT 分析的必要性。这个分析会_____

A.  聚焦于项目集外部的因素

B.  协助识别收益

C.  帮助开发项目集章程

D.  帮助确定有意义的测量方法来评估项目集绩效

19. You are a member of your insurance company's Program Selection Committee. You are considering a number of programs to pursue. Each has identified benefits that support your company's overall strategic plan, but you need to select the one with the shortest payback period. Program A is estimated to cost $100,000 to implement and have annual net cash inflows of $25,000; Program B is estimated to cost $75,000 with inflows of $20,000; Program C is estimated to cost $225,000 with inflows of $80,000; and Program D is estimated to cost $275,000 with inflows of $90,000.  You recommend that your company select_____

| Program A NPV at | Program B NPV at | Program C NPV at | Program D NPV at |
|---|---|---|---|
| 5% = $2,399 | 5% = $2,105 | 5% = $6,400 | 5% = $4,065 |
| 10% = $3,112 | 10% = $1,254 | 10% = $3,275 | 10% = $1,852 |
| 15% = $1,402 | 15% = $1,001 | 15% = $1,679 | 15% = $925 |

Note: NPV = Net Present Value.

A.  Program A                                              B.  Program B

C．Program C　　　　　　　　　　D．Program D

19．你是你所在的保险公司的项目集选择委员会的成员。你正在考虑选择的一些项目集。每个项目集都有被识别的收益以支持你的公司的整体战略计划，但你需要选择一个投资回收期最短的项目集。项目集 A 估计实施成本为 100 000 美元，并有每年的净现金流入 25 000 美元；项目集 B 的估计成本为 75 000 美元，流入 20 000 美元；项目集 C 的估计成本为 225 000 美元，流入 80 000 美元；项目集 D 的估计成本为 275 000 美元，流入 90 000 美元。你建议你的公司选择_____

| 项目集 A<br>净现值 | 项目集 B<br>净现值 | 项目集 C<br>净现值 | 项目集 D<br>净现值 |
|---|---|---|---|
| 5% = 2 399 美元 | 5% =2 105 美元 | 5% =6 400 美元 | 5% =4 065 美元 |
| 10% =3 112 美元 | 10% =1 254 美元 | 10% =3 275 美元 | 10% =1 852 美元 |
| 15% =1 402 美元 | 15% =1 001 美元 | 15% =1 679 美元 | 15% =925 美元 |

注：NPV=净现值。

A．项目集 A　　　　　　　　　　B．项目集 B
C．项目集 C　　　　　　　　　　D．项目集 D

20．You are a member of your manufacturing company's Program Selection Committee. You are considering a number of possible programs to pursue. Each one has identified benefits that support your company's overall strategic plan. Data are available on four possible programs, but you can select only one because of resource limitations.

| Program A IRR | Program B IRR | Program C IRR | Program D IRR |
|---|---|---|---|
| 42% | 40% | 36% | 33% |

Note: IRR = Internal Rate of Return.

Based on this information, you recommend that your company select_____

A．Program A　　　　　　　　　　B．Program B
C．Program C　　　　　　　　　　D．Program D

20．你是你所在的制造公司的项目集选择委员会的成员。你正在考虑一系列可能选择的项目集。每个项目集都有被识别的利益以支持你的公司的整体战略计划。数据来自 4 个可能的项目集，但你因为资源的限制只可以选择一个。

| 项目集 A<br>内部收益率 | 项目集 B<br>内部收益率 | 项目集 C<br>内部收益率 | 项目集 D<br>内部收益率 |
|---|---|---|---|
| 42% | 40% | 36% | 33% |

注：IRR=内部回报率。

基于这些信息，你建议你的公司选择_____

A．项目集 A　　　　　　　　　　B．项目集 B

C. 项目集 C                        D. 项目集 D

## 2.4 章节练习参考答案

1. D 作为一个管理项目的项目集，子项目集和项目集活动的目的就是实现比单独管理它们获得实现更多的收益。

2. D 组织启动项目集来交付收益和完成商定的结果，这可能会影响整个组织。

3. A 当一个组织管理其项目组合，项目集会受项目组合需求的影响，其中之一便是时间线。其他的影响包括组织战略和目标、收益、资金分配、需求和制约因素。

4. B 为了最大限度地为组织实现项目集收益，有必要利用变革的战略机会。

5. C 在制定项目集章程之前，商业论证和项目集授权必须得到组织领导的批准。

6. D 可行性研究建立在商业论证、组织目标和已有的项目上，以评估组织的财务、采购、复杂性和制约因素的配置文件。因此，它有助于为选择项目集的决策者提供信息。

7. C 组织的项目管理是一个战略执行框架，运用项目、项目集、项目组合管理和组织使能来预见并始终如一地为组织战略服务。在项目集管理中，重点是协调项目和项目集组件，并管理依赖关系，来实现收益。

8. A 项目集计划在项目集战略一致性的领域中得以准备，并和其他成果一起定义了在每个项目集组件中，项目集的目标将如何并何时实行。

9. B 题目描述的场景是内部项目集的一个例子。商业论证中包含了若干要素，其中包括内在的和外在的收益。作为一个内部项目集，内在收益应该是商业论证的一部分。

10. C 如同在该问题中描述的内部项目集一样，这是企业范围的过程改进项目集，并由组织作为变革的催化剂来执行。

11. A 愿景描述项目集的将来状态，它也可以不断提醒项目集的目标和其预期收益。

12. B 项目集选择标准可能会不一样，从模糊、非正式的到详细、具体的、正式的都有。项目集的建立将提供比项目、子项目集和其他工作作为独立的活动管理更大的收益。

13. B 当考虑是否选择或批准一个项目集时，规章批准将是必需的。因此，目标必须依据规章和法律的制约因素来进行评估。

14. B 事业环境因素影响选择决策，即使它们是在项目集外部。资金需求就是一个典型的例子。

15. B 使命说明描述了项目集目的，并阐述了项目集存在的合理性。

16. A 竞争优势分析是用来评估商业论证的有效性。商业论证包括对真实或假设工作的分析和比较，包括假设分析以显示项目集的目标和预期收益如何通过其他手段来实现。

17. B 一旦组织领导批准了项目集，识别和评估整合机会和需求就成为必要。这种识别包括人力资本和人力资源的需求，因为启动和规划项目集时需要资源。规划项目集的人不一定最终会在项目集核心团队中。

18. C SWOT 分析是一种环境分析，它在制定项目集章程和计划时提供了有用的信息。

19. C 在使用净现值（NPV）作为选择标准时，一年后的一美元与今天的一美元时间价值不一样。未来贴现率越大（较高的贴现率），该项目集的净现值就越小。如果净现值高，则项目集评级高。在这种情况下，你就会选择 C 项目集。

20. A 内部收益率（IRR）是净现值为零时的贴现率。它没有固定形式的公式。IRR是迭代计算的，产生一个贴现率使得净现值刚好为零。大多数的电子表格软件可以计算IRR。本题中，项目集 A 的 IRR 高于其他选项。虽然 IRR 折现未来价值（期值），它并不考虑一个项目集的大小。

# 第 **3** 章

# 启动项目集

PgMP®项目集管理的考试大纲中有项目集生命周期的部分，包括启动、规划、执行、控制和收尾 5 个部分，而启动部分在 PgMP®认证考试的试题中占到全卷内容的 6%或者是 10 个题目。

## 3.1　秘笈要点

启动部分的考题集中在想办法为项目集获得更大的支持和批准，这个部分专注于确保该项目集的价值和目标与记录在项目集授权书中的组织价值和目标相一致。

在项目集管理标准中，启动是涵盖在"项目集管理支持流程"中。而这个支持流程则是在项目集管理生命周期的定义阶段。它侧重于进一步定义项目集的目的，确保融资，并显示项目集将如何交付所期望的收益。其中的活动包括：指派项目集经理，准备项目集章程，准备财务框架，以及定义详细的项目集路线图。一旦章程被批准，就意味着项目集的开启。

考题可能围绕着项目集经理和核心团队的角色和责任，以及可能的项目集组织结构展开。考题还可能涉及章程的内容和目的，商业论证应该何时更新，以及高层级的项目集范围说明（这个高层级的范围说明会在生命周期的规划阶段演变为更详细的范围说明）。

考题还可能涉及通过使用项目集目的和目标制订高层级的里程碑计划，以确保项目集与相关方期望保持一致（特别是发起人的期望）。随着项目集核心团队的角色和责任的确定，项目集的资源责任分配矩阵也是本阶段的重要考点。与相关方一起召开的项目集启动会议也是一个重点。

## 3.2  重要考点

1. 项目集启动
- 目的;
- 范围,资源和成本估算;
- 初步风险评估;
- 更新商业论证。

2. 主要角色
- 项目集发起人的指定;
- 项目集经理的指定;
- 关键决策者/相关方的识别。

3. 项目集章程
- 目的;
- 启动和设计项目集和收益;
- 合理性;
- 愿景;
- 战略匹配;
- 成果;
- 范围;
- 收益战略;
- 假设和制约因素;
- 风险和问题;
- 时间线;
- 所需资源;
- 相关方考虑;
- 组件成功的测量标准;
- 项目集治理。

4. 项目集路线图明细
- 高层级范围说明;
- 高层级里程碑计划。

5. 项目集成本估算

6. 项目集财务框架
- 目的;
- 融资结构;
- 融资来源;

- 融资目的；
- 付款进度；
- 融资方法；
- 更新商业论证。

7. 资源责任分配矩阵

- 核心团队；
- 项目集和项目资源间的区别。

8. 与相关方一起的项目集启动会议

# 3.3 章节练习

1. Although your program is part of a portfolio with four other programs and 14 separate projects, it has no direct relationship or interdependencies with any of these other initiatives. However, the success of your program will depend on which two areas for which all these other initiatives are competing?_____

A. Physical space and technology assets for team members

B. Funding and executive sponsorship

C. Funding and available resources

D. Available resources and technology assets

1. 虽然你的项目集与其他 4 个项目集和 14 个独立的项目都是项目组合的一部分，但它与其他项目举措没有直接或相互依赖关系。你的项目集的成功将取决于和其他项目举措在以下哪两个领域竞争_____

A. 团队成员的物理空间和技术资产

B. 资金和高层赞助

C. 资金和可利用的资源

D. 可用的资源和技术资产

2. You have recently joined a corporation that is a leader in the development of products for the automotive industry. You are pleased to be selected as a program manager, because you know that this company has established a culture of management by programs. The company operates within a program management structure, and each program manager is responsible for products in certain years. To best align your program with your stakeholders' expectations, this means that_____

A. You should develop a high-level milestone plan

B. In performing a stakeholder analysis, you need to consider the other program managers

C. The way the organization is structured means that there is no need to compete for resources

D.　The roadmap is essential

2.　你最近加入了一家公司，该公司是汽车行业产品开发的领导者。你很高兴能够被选为项目集经理，因为你知道这家公司已经建立了项目集管理的文化。公司在项目集管理结构下运营，每个项目集经理负责一定年限内的产品。为了最好地调整你的项目集与相关方期望保持一致，这意味着_____

A.　你应该制订高层级的里程碑计划

B.　在进行相关方分析时，你需要考虑其他项目集经理

C.　组织结构的方式意味着没有必要争夺资源

D.　路线图是必不可少的

3.　Assume that in your automotive company, you will be appointed as the program manager for the 2016 new line of hybrid cars that only will use gasoline if the vehicle has traveled more than 300 miles. This program is a major change for your company as it has not entered the hybrid market until this past year, and the new line of vehicles is to have an average of 75 miles per gallon. The current hybrid gets 30 miles per gallon. You are going to produce at a minimum five different vehicles: a coupe, a sedan, a luxury SUV, a minivan, and an inexpensive SUV. Finally, your program charter was approved, and you were officially named as the program manager. You were fortunate to work with your sponsor in developing the charter, and you also_____

A.　Used input from all stakeholders

B.　Relied extensively on historical information

C.　Convened a panel to assist in its preparation using the Delphi technique

D.　Sent a draft of the charter to the proposed members of the Governance Board for their input

3.　假设在你的汽车公司，你将被任命为 2016 年混合动力汽车的新产品线的项目集经理。车辆行驶超过 300 英里后才会使用汽油。这个计划是你们公司一个重大的变革，因为公司去年刚刚进入混合动力市场，新的车辆是平均每加仑汽油能跑 75 英里。目前的混合动力仅为每加仑 30 英里。你要至少生产 5 种不同的车辆：跑车、轿车、豪华 SUV、小型货车和经济款 SUV。最后，你的项目集章程被批准了，你被正式任命为项目集经理。你很幸运地与发起人一起合作制定章程，你也_____

A.　使用所有相关方的意见输入

B.　广泛依赖历史信息

C.　召集一个小组，使用德尔菲技术协助准备工作

D.　向治理委员会成员发送章程草案，以获得他们的意见输入

4.　Assume you are working for a dry foods company. For the past five years, all of your projects in this company have met their goals of being on schedule, within budget, and meeting specifications. You are a successful project manager, and you have identified a potential new line of business for your company, which you feel will enhance its sales. You met with your Portfolio Review Board and presented a business case for this new line of work, which would move your firm into the chocolate market building on research that shows that a small amount of dark chocolate can be extremely healthful. You now have a business mandate to proceed into more in depth work to determine whether or not the program should proceed to the planning phase. You now are considering questions such as: "is the program financially smart?", "do the program's benefits align with those of the organization?", and "can the company afford the program?". Answers to these questions basically serve to translate strategic objectives into_____

    A.　The program management plan　　B.　The program's roadmap

    C.　A high-level program scope statement　D.　An accountability matrix

4.　假设你在一家干货食品公司工作。在过去的 5 年里，你在这家公司的所实施的项目都达到了时间目标，并在预算范围内，而且满足规范要求。你是一个成功的项目经理，你已经识别出了一个具有潜力的新业务线，你觉得这个新业务将帮助公司提升销售额。你拜访了项目组合审查委员会，并为这个新业务工作提出了商业论证，这将使你的公司进入巧克力市场。因为研究表明，少量的黑巧克力特别有助于健康。你现在已有商业授权书来进行更多深入的工作，以确定该项目集是否应进入规划阶段。你现在正在考虑的问题有"该项目集财务灵活吗""项目集收益与组织一致吗""公司能负担得起这个项目集吗"。这些问题的答案基本上是将战略目标转化为_____

    A.　项目集管理计划　　　　　　　B.　项目集路线图

    C.　高层级项目范围说明书　　　　D.　责任分配矩阵

5.　You are responsible for a program to develop the next- generation cellular phone. The program includes a number of key products and is set up according to the "father-son" model. Because programs are responsible for delivering benefits, you want to ensure that the targeted benefits are measurable. You now are working in the Program Initiation phase; one purpose is to_____

    A.　Establish and staff the infrastructure that the program will use

    B.　Set up the program control framework for planning, monitoring, and controlling the program

    C.　Expand on the roadmap that provides a chronological representation of the program's direction

    D.　Complete the program team staffing

5.　你负责开发下一代手机的项目集。该项目集包括一些关键产品，并根据"父子"模型建立。因为项目集是负责交付收益，你想确保目标收益是可衡量的。你正处于项目集启

动阶段，该阶段的其中一个目的是_____

    A. 建立和配备该项目集将使用的基础设施

    B. 制定用于规划、监控项目集控制框架

    C. 完善能提供按时间顺序表达项目集方向的路线图

    D. 完成项目团队的人员编制

    6. You have recently been assigned as the program manager on a global drug development project. You have read and thoroughly understand the program's business case and overall objectives. However, you are curious as to the key program outcomes that are required to achieve the program vision. These outcomes are stated in the_____

    A. Program mandate

    B. Preliminary project scope statement

    C. Technical and economic feasibility study

    D. Program charter

    6. 你最近被分配作为一个全球性药物开发项目的项目集经理。你已经阅读并深入了解了该项目集的商业论证和总体目标。你对关键的项目集成果有兴趣，而这些成果又是实现项目集愿景所必需的。这些结果在以下哪个文件有陈述_____

| | |
|---|---|
| A. 项目集授权书 | B. 初步项目范围说明书 |
| C. 技术和经济的可行性研究 | D. 项目集章程 |

    7. Assume you now have obtained approval of your charter for your program in your automotive company for the development of the new line of hybrid vehicles. This program will be extremely complex given its development of the five vehicles and also the goals and objectives to be met. You realize as well that you are going to have a number of issues and risks to resolve. However, you are pleased you are the program manager and that the charter has been issued.　Your next step is to_____

    A. Perform a more detailed analysis of the identified risks in the charter to help in deciding how best to respond to them should they occur

    B. Determine the key benefits to be realized by the program

    C. Describe the program outcomes required to achieve the program's vision

    D. Conduct a program kickoff meeting with key stakeholders

    7. 假设你现在已经获得了项目集章程的批准，即在你的汽车公司开发新的混合动力汽车产品线。考虑到它将开发的 5 种车型，以及需要达到的目的和目标，这一项目集将是非常复杂的。你也意识到，你将有一些问题和风险需要解决。然而，你很高兴你已经是项目集经理，并已发出章程。你的下一步是_____

    A. 针对章程中所识别的风险进行更详细的分析，以帮助决定当风险发生的时候如何最好地响应它们

B. 确定通过该项目集实现的关键收益

C. 描述实现项目集愿景所需的项目集成果

D. 与关键相关方一起，召开项目集启动会议

8. You are the program manager responsible for building a dam that will provide flood control and generate electricity for millions of residents. The dam will have five turbines generating electricity. The program sponsor, the local provincial government, has only enough money to install three turbines. The income generated from those three turbines will then be used to fund the remaining two turbines. As part of your planning, you estimate that in month 26, Turbine No. 4 will be fully operational, and in month 38, Turbine No. 5 will come on line. You and the team document this in the_____

A. Benefits realization plan

B. Roadmap

C. Benefits analysis phase

D. Constraints and assumptions

8. 你是负责修建大坝的项目集经理，该大坝将为数以百万计的居民提供防洪和发电。大坝将有 5 个涡轮机发电。该项目集的发起人，也就是当地的省政府，其资金只够安装 3 个涡轮机。这 3 个涡轮机产生的收入将被用来资助剩下的 2 个涡轮机。作为计划的一部分，你估计在 26 个月后， 4 号涡轮机将全面投入运行，并在 38 个月后，5 号涡轮机将上线。你和团队将这个文件记录在_____

A. 收益实现计划

B. 路线图

C. 收益分析阶段

D. 制约因素和假设

9. You are a program manager working for a conference planning company. Your program has been launched as a component of your company's portfolio. Your organization has been in existence for 10 years; therefore, as you prepare your program charter and roadmap, you should consider the_____

A. How the program will deliver the desired benefits

B. How program components will be unified

C. Authority tolerance levels

D. Program budget baseline

9. 你是一个项目集经理，在一个会议策划公司工作。作为公司项目组合的一部分，你的项目集已经启动。你的组织已成立 10 年，因此当你准备项目集章程和路线图时，你应该考虑_____

A. 项目集将如何交付期望的收益

B. 项目集组件将如何统一

C. 职权承受力级别

D. 项目集预算基准

10. Your company, a major dairy cooperative, has embraced portfolio management. Previously, some projects continued indefinitely, even after their sponsors had left the company, and no one could remember why they had been initiated. Now all programs and projects are part

of the portfolio, which is where investment decisions are made. In response to a growing consumer demand for organic foods, the company is attempting to capitalize on this demand by entering the organic foods market. You are appointed as program manager. Your program is the result of_____

A. Business intelligence

B. The need to remain competitive with others in the field

C. A program mandate

D. A recommendation from your major customer

10. 你的公司是一家主要的乳制品集团，开始尝试项目组合管理。在此之前，一些项目被无限期地拖延下去，即使项目发起人离开了公司，也没有人会记得它们为什么被启动。现在所有的项目和项目集都是项目组合的一部分，这是投资决策的重点。为了应对日益增长的消费者对有机食品的需求，公司正试图通过进入有机食品市场来投资这一需求。你被任命为项目集经理。你的项目集结果是_____

A. 商业智能      B. 在该领域保持竞争力的需要

C. 项目集授权书      D. 来自主要客户的建议

11. You have been appointed program manager for a Motor Carrier Safety Administration program to develop new regulations that avoid the need for highway weigh stations yet ensure that weight restrictions are followed. You must complete the program in two years, and the administration must approve the regulations in one year. You have not started the planning process. At this time, your first step is to_____

A. Secure program funding

B. Assign project managers to each project in the program

C. Plan the program's to-be state

D. Manage each of your stakeholders

11. 你已被任命为一个汽车运输安全管理项目的项目集经理，目的是制定新的法规，以尽可能减少对公路称重站的依赖，同时确保遵循汽车的重量限制。你必须在两年内完成该项目集，并且政府必须在一年内批准新法规。你还没有开始项目集规划过程。在这个时候，你的第一步是_____

A. 获取项目融资      B. 任命项目集中每个项目的项目经理

C. 计划项目集的将来状态      D. 管理每个相关方

12. You work for a company that produces and distributes catalogs focused on luxury items such as jewelry, home furnishings, clothing, and accessories. In addition to the major undertaking of catalog production, several projects are under way to make the catalogs available online; Ease of ordering and faster delivery time are key objectives. Many people in the company support the catalog production initiatives as well as some of the Web-based initiatives.

The company should_____

A. Aggressively pursue the Web and discontinue its print production of the catalogs

B. Assign a program sponsor for these initiatives

C. Appoint a project manager to report directly to the CEO to coordinate activities

D. Implement critical chain scheduling to avoid potential bottlenecks in resource allocation

12. 你服务于一家生产和销售珠宝、家居装饰、服装和配件等奢侈品产品系列的公司。除了主要的产品系列外，还有几个项目也正在进行中，目的是上线产品；易用性和更快的交货时间是关键目标。该公司的许多人支持产品系列生产的方案，以及一些基于网络的举措。公司应该_____

A. 积极开展网络产品，并停止产品系列中的打印产品

B. 为这些产品举措指定项目集发起人

C. 任命一个项目经理直接向首席执行官汇报协调活动

D. 实施关键链法，避免资源分配中的潜在瓶颈

13. Your city is in the early stages of determining whether or not it should construct a new shopping mall. Already, there is a major shopping mall at the northern part of the city, but its location is inconvenient for many residents of the city given the extensive traffic. In the southern part of the city, there is a small mall that lacks large department stores. The city is considering a program to develop a mall in the center of the city, and if it is approved, you will be the program manager. You believe approval is basically guaranteed, and you are looking forward to this challenge. Your funding will largely come from_____

A. The parent organization　　　B. Bonds

C. Equity partners　　　D. Payment from future lease income

13. 你所在城市正处于决定是否应该建造一个新的购物中心的早期阶段。目前在城市北部有一个主要的购物中心，但它的位置对城市的许多居民来说交通很不便利。在城市的南部有一个小商场，但缺乏大型的百货公司。城市正在考虑启动一个项目集，在城市中心开发一个购物中心。如果它被批准，你将是项目集经理。你相信批准基本上是有保证的，你也期待着这个挑战。你的资金将在很大程度上来自_____

A. 上级组织　　　B. 债券

C. 股权合伙人　　　D. 未来租赁收入的支付

14. As the portfolio manager for an aerospace and defense contractor, you recommend that programs be initiated when your company decides to bid on contracts. Given the business development process and the need to focus on capture management, the pre-proposal phase may last several years, especially on major government defense projects. As you work to initiate the program, which of the following is critical_____

A. Statement of Work

B.  Contract program work breakdown structure (PWBS)

C.  Program financial framework

D.  Program outcomes

14. 作为航空航天和国防承包商的项目组合经理,你建议当你的公司决定投标合同时,就要启动项目集。鉴于业务开发过程和聚焦业务机会捕捉管理的需要,提案前期阶段可能会持续几年,在重大的政府国防项目尤其如此。当你开始启动项目集时,下列哪个是关键的_____

A.  工作说明书

B.  合同的项目集工作分解结构（PWBS）

C.  项目集财务框架

D.  项目集成果

15.  You are working in your city to have a new shopping mall that is centrally located.  Your charter is under development, and if it is approved, you will be the program manager. You have not managed a program as complex as this one as in the past; instead, you worked on smaller programs or projects. This program is to have at least seven different projects, and they have been identified so far in the charter. You believe you should prepare_____

A.  A description of the other projects you believe you should add

B.  A business case for a Program Management Office to support this program

C.  A description of the methods you plan to use to procure external resources

D.  A high-level milestone plan

15. 你在所在城市正致力于建设一个位于市中心的新购物中心。项目集章程正在制定中,一旦被批准,你将是项目集经理。你过去并没有管理过如此复杂的项目集,而是在较小的项目集或项目上工作。这个项目集至少包含 7 个不同的项目,而且在项目集章程中已经被识别出来。你认为应该准备_____

A.  你认为应该添加的有关其他项目的描述

B.  用于项目集管理办公室的商业论证来支持此项目集

C.  你计划用于获取外部资源的方法的描述

D.  高层级里程碑计划

16.  Assume you are working for an international training company. It has decided to add several new lines of courses because it tracks its courses now to the Project Management Institute's publications and standards. You will be the program manager for these new courses, and you plan to have a team of people located in different countries to support you as you will want to translate each course into at least four other languages and pilot test them in other parts of the world.  After your program is initiated, you then will work to authorize the various projects within it. Furthermore, it is important to have a high-level plan for the program's

components. This plan is_____

    A.  Used to start initiating the program

    B.  Part of program authorization

    C.  Stated as part of the program charter

    D.  Set forth in the preliminary program scope statement

16.　假设你在一家国际培训公司工作。公司已决定增加几个新的课程，因为课程现在都能跟踪到项目管理学院的出版物和标准。你将成为这些新课程的项目集经理，你计划有一个不同的国家成员组成的团队来支持你，你想把每一门课程翻译成至少4种其他语言，并在世界其他地区的试点进行测试。在你的项目集启动后，你将授权项目集内的各项目。此外，重要的是要为该项目集的组件制订一个高层级的计划，这个计划是_____

    A.　用于启动项目集

    B.　项目集授权的一部分

    C.　作为项目集章程的一部分来启动

    D.　在初步项目集范围说明书中提出

17.　While fax machines are basically considered to be outdated, a number of people still use them to send and receive information. Your company is considering a new line of fax machines as it has specialized in them and wants to make sure fax remains as a way to distribute information. This new line of fax machines would make it easy to send information from one's computer or a tablet to the fax machine and not have to rely on printed documents. It also would enable transmission of printed materials at a far faster speed with immediate confirmation that the recipient received it. As you determine funding methods for your program, you should first consider_____

    A.  Performing a program financial analysis

    B.  Various funding methods

    C.  Payment schedules

    D.  Program funding source

17.　虽然传真机被认为是过时的，但一些人仍然使用它们来发送和接收信息。你的公司正在考虑一个传真机的新生产线，因为公司擅长传真机的制造，并希望确保传真仍然是分发信息的一种方式。这种新的传真机将很容易将信息从个人电脑或平板电脑发送到传真机，而不必依赖于打印的文件。它也将使传输的印刷材料以一个更快的速度，立即确认收件人收到它。当你确定你的项目集融资方法时，你应该首先考虑_____

    A.　执行项目集财务分析        B.　各种融资方法

    C.　付款进度                D.　项目集融资来源

18.　As you prepare your program charter for your new program for your international training company, you have a vision of continuing as the industry leader. However, this is an internal initiative, and funding is a key concern, especially given the economic downturn, and many people do not sign up for the existing courses until the last minute. You are working to initiate the program. This means which of the following peoples should be identified by this time?_____

A.　Program manager and program sponsor

B.　Program manager and core program team members

C.　Program manager and program management office (PMO) director

D.　Program manager and program control officer

18.　当你准备为你的国际培训公司的新项目集制定项目集章程时，你有一个继续作为行业领导者的愿景。然而，这是一个内部项目，融资是一个关键问题。特别是考虑到经济低迷，许多人直到最后一分钟才注册现有的课程。你正在开始启动项目集，这意味着以下哪些人应该在这个时候确定_____

A.　项目集经理和项目集发起人

B.　项目集经理和项目集团队成员

C.　项目集经理和项目集管理办公室（PMO）总监

D.　项目集经理和项目集控制者

19.　Your government agency has been considering adding a new program to its existing portfolio of the development of national parks in your country. You have heard about this possible program through a friend, who is on the agency's Portfolio Review Board.  Once you learned about this possible program, you went to others on the Review Board and requested to be the program manager for it and were pleased to be assigned to manage it. One reason you were selected early is so you can_____

A.　Authorize the program　　　　　　B.　Provide expert judgment

C.　Prepare the strategic directive　　　D.　Guide the initiation process

19.　你们的政府机构一直在考虑在其已有的开发国家公园的项目组合中加入一个新的项目集。你已经通过你所在机构的项目组合审查委员会的一个朋友听说了这个可能的项目集。一旦你了解了这个可能的项目集，你就去找审查委员会，请求成为项目集经理，并很乐意来管理该项目集。你选择在早期被选上的一个原因是因为你可以_____

A.　授权项目集　　　　　　　　　　　B.　提供专家判断

C.　准备战略指令　　　　　　　　　　D.　指导启动过程

20.　You are one of the core team members developing the program charter for the next generation of medical imaging technology. There is significant market opportunity, but the competition is strong, and the wrong technical approach could set the company back several years. To ensure that the program charter is viable, a best practice is to_____

A.　Conduct a SWOT analysis　　　　　B.　Conduct an assumptions analysis

C.  Use the nominal group technique　　D.  Use an influence diagram

20. 你是开发下一代医疗成像技术的项目集章程的核心团队成员之一。现在有明显的市场机会，但竞争是激烈的，错误的技术方法会让公司倒退好多年。为了确保项目集章程是可行的，最好的做法是_____

A.  实施 SWOT 分析　　　　　B.  实施假设分析

C.  使用名义小组技术　　　　D.  使用影响图

# 3.4　章节练习参考答案

1.  C 在一个项目组合内，项目集往往和其他项目集或项目是不相关的，但是，所有的项目集或项目通常会竞争资金和其他资源，在大多数组织资源都是有限的。

2.  A 这样的计划使用项目集的目的和目标、适用的历史信息和其他可用的资源。调整该计划与包括发起人在内的相关方期望一致是有用的。

3.  A 相关方参与章程的制定有助于获得他们的支持和他们对项目集的承诺。

4.  C 基于项目集授权书和项目集的战略目的和目标来构建，高层级项目集范围说明书应与相关方协商来准备。

5.  C 在项目集启动时，项目集章程的路线图是用来沟通整个项目集方向的。

6.  D 项目集章程为项目集的开展提供了基础依据。另外，章程定义了项目集愿景（或最终状态），介绍了项目集将如何对组织产生收益，并介绍了实现愿景的关键项目集成果。

7.  D 一旦团队建立，项目集团队的启动会议是推荐的最佳实践。在项目集章程被批准后，建议与关键相关方在启动阶段一起开会，让组织借此机会更加熟悉项目集，并继续获得相关方对项目集的认可。

8.  B 路线图显示了不同的里程碑、细节、描述和要交付的收益。它建立了项目集活动和预期收益之间的关系。

9.  A 在项目集启动时，目的是定义项目集，获得资金，并展示了项目集将如何交付预期收益。

10.  C 商业论证和项目集授权书是组织领导者对项目集章程许可和授权项目集的关键输入。

11.  A 项目集成本的发生往往早于可实现的收益。因此，我们要确定资金来源，获得资金，并建立起付款和获取收益之间的桥梁。

12.  B 项目集可以包括网络项目，以及聚焦于收益交付的持续活动的方式来构建。应指派项目发起人来监管项目集，确保资金的获取和预期收益的交付。

13.  A 项目集可以不同的方式来获取融资。在这个案例中，城市是上级组织，项目集将由城市来资助。

14.  C 当项目集作为投标决定的结果而启动时，项目集成本将发生于收益实现之前。

因此，项目集的财务框架是必要的，因为能决定项目集持续时间的财务环境。

15. D 该计划使用项目集的目的和目标，以及适用的历史信息和其他可用的资源，如工作分解结构、范围说明书和收益实现计划，从而使包括发起人在内的相关方与项目集保持一致。

16. C 批准章程即授权了项目集的开始。其中包括项目集组件的讨论，来描述项目和其他组件如何被配置来交付项目集收益。项目章程通常包括组件的高层级项目集计划。

17. D 项目集的资金来源是项目集财务框架的一部分。项目集有各种各样可能的资金来源，可以有多种来源支持，其组件也可以有不同的来源资助。

18. A 项目集经理和项目集发起人在项目集启动中被选择和指派。

19. D 项目集经理的任命在项目集启动时应尽早进行，以指导启动活动，并促进过程输出的产生。

20. A SWOT（优势、劣势、机会、威胁）对制定可行的项目集章程和项目计划来说，是一个值得推荐的方法。

# 第 **4** 章

## 规划项目集

规划项目集在 PgMP® 认证考试中占比 11%（19 个考题）。规划几乎涉及项目集管理的方方面面，因此详细而全面的项目集规划是很重要的。

## 4.1　秘笈要点

在项目集生命周期中，项目集定义阶段重点强调了项目集管理计划的准备。每个项目集管理支撑过程都有规划组件，你会在本章习题看到不少关于规划组件的题目。一旦项目集管理计划正式批准通过，就进入了项目集收益交付阶段。注意，项目集收益管理、项目集相关方参与，包括沟通管理及治理涵盖在本书的不同章节里，因此其规划组件在本章中不会深入讲解。

类似于《PMBOK®指南》中工作分解结构对项目规划的重要性一样，在 PgMP® 里也包含了项目集工作分解结构（PWBS）。PWBS 的目的并不是代替项目集中每个项目的工作分解结构，而是提供了项目集的概貌，并展示了项目和非项目工作如何安排在整个项目集的工作结构中。

考试大纲在规划项目集这部分列出了 9 项内容，这都会在本章的章节习题中进行考查。这里的重点是确保项目集的使命、愿景和价值观能够支撑组织的使命、愿景和价值观。规划过程组的特点是迭代、循环的。由于项目集一般时间很长，且包含多个项目，因此在组织的财年和预算规划周期内，当事先没有规划的事件出现时，项目集管理计划及其组件计划需要在组件启动或者结束时重新进行审查和更新。

## 4.2　重要考点

1. 项目集准备
- 制订项目集管理计划；

- 与项目集计划的区别；
- 定义项目集组织；
- 描述替代组件；
- 描述管理计划；
- 优化计划；
- 获得批准以进入项目集交付阶段。

2.　支撑过程组

- 项目集财务管理计划的制订；
- 项目集基础结构计划；
- 项目集基础结构的开发；
- 项目集采购规划；
- 项目集质量规划；
- 资源规划；
- 项目集风险管理规划；
- 项目集进度规划；
- 项目集范围规划。

3.　项目集范围说明书

- 项目集工作分解结构（PWBS）；
- 进度；
- 项目集管理信息系统；
- 识别和管理项目层级问题；
- 制订过渡/整合/收尾计划。

4.　制定关键绩效指标

- 分解/映射；
- 平衡计分卡；
- 实施范围和质量管理系统。

5.　关键人力资源

- 确定项目集和项目角色；
- 包括分包商；
- 团队激励机会。

# 4.3　章节练习

1. As you work to develop a new washer and dryer that will not require any electricity and also will decrease your monthly water bill by 50% assuming you use the washer at least once

per week, you have a complex program to manage. Thus far, even though you are still in the early phases of your program, you have six separate projects in it. Now, you are developing the schedule for your program. Typically the first step is to_____

A. Use the schedules from the six projects

B. Determine the component milestones

C. Determine the interdependencies between the components

D. Use the scope management plan

1. 现有一个复杂的项目集需要你去管理：这个项目集是假设你每周至少使用一次洗衣和烘干机，开发一个不需要电力但同时每月减少 50%用水量的洗衣和烘干机，这个数据的分析对象是每周至少使用一次洗衣机及烘干机的人群。截至目前，尽管你仍处在项目集的早期阶段，该项目集已经有了 6 个独立的项目。现在，你要为你的项目集制订进度计划。通常第一步应该是_____

A. 使用这 6 个独立项目的进度计划

B. 确定组件里程碑

C. 确定组件之间的依赖关系

D. 使用范围管理计划

2. You are Company A's program manager for the development of an online banking system for your community bank, for which your company will receive $20 million. Because the bank would like to implement this system quickly, it has also contracted with Company B. You must implement your system completely in six months to ensure that you beat Company B's schedule. At this point, you have an expense estimate of $2.5 million. You will lose $10 million if you cannot deliver the product in six months, but if you can complete it sooner, you will earn an additional $25 million, for a total of $45 million. Your risk management officer performs a risk analysis and tells you that there is a 70 percent chance that the program will be completed ahead of schedule. Your company has completed similar programs in the past; judging by these experiences, there is a 30 percent chance that your final expenses will increase by $10 million. What is the expected value of your program if it is completed ahead of schedule?_____

A. $29 million      B. $32 million

C. $42.5 million      D. $45 million

2. 你作为公司 A 的项目集经理，为你的社区银行开发一个线上银行业务系统，为此你们公司将获得 2 000 万美元的收益。同时，由于银行想尽快实现该系统，所以它同时和公司 B 签订了合同。你必须在 6 个月内完全实现该系统以确保你能够领先于 B 的进度。当前情况下，你的费用估算为 250 万美元。如果你不能在 6 个月内交付这款产品，你将损失 1 000 万美元，但是如果你能提前完成，你将赢得额外的 2 500 万美元的收入，共计 4 500

万美元。你的风险管理专员进行了风险分析并告诉你有 70%的可能性项目集可以提前完成。你的公司过去曾完成了类似的项目集；以过去的经验判断，有 30%的可能性你最终的费用将会增加 1 000 万美元。如果你的项目集提前完成，它的期望价值是多少_____

A. 2 900 万美元      B. 3 200 万美元

C. 4 250 万美元      D. 4 500 万美元

3. Working as Company A's program manager for the development of an on line banking system for your community bank, you have been asked to provide a list of deliverables and the success criteria for the program and its products, services, and results that must be included in the procurement documentation that is provided to potential suppliers. This list is derived from an analysis of the_____

A. Benefits realization plan      B. Project work breakdown structure (WBS)

C. Contract WBS      D. Program scope statement

3. 作为公司 A 的项目集经理，你正在为你们公司的社区银行开发一个线上银行业务系统，发起人要求你为项目集制作一份采购列表，这份列表包括采购产品、服务和产品的交付成果列表和成功验收标准，用来提供给潜在的供应商。这一列表来源于对以下哪项的分析_____

A. 收益实现计划      B. 项目工作分解结构

C. 合同工作分解结构      D. 项目集范围说明书

4. You are managing a program to establish a new distribution center. The facility's location was selected because labor costs were low, but it is in a remote area. Now gasoline prices have increased 30 percent and are forecasted to rise another 20 percent in the next six months. In planning for the procurement of transportation services, you need to_____

A. Prepare a competitive analysis of service providers

B. Recommend to your sponsor that the program be terminated and the distribution center be moved to a more urban area

C. Prepare a contract management plan

D. Encourage bidders by providing simplified legal requirements in the form of standard terms and conditions

4. 你在管理一个项目集，以建立一个新的配送中心。选定的配送中心位置的主要原因是它低廉的劳动力成本，但它在偏远地区。现在汽油价格提高了 30%并且预计在接下来的 6 月还将涨价 20%。在规划运输服务的采购工作时，你必须_____

A. 准备关于提供服务的提供商的竞品分析

B. 建议你的发起人终止项目集并将配送中心迁到离市区较近的地区

C. 准备合同管理计划

D. 通过在标准条款中使用简化的法定要求来鼓励投标人

5. As program manager, you find yourself repeatedly changing and refining the program management plan as a result of a number of factors, such as changing external conditions, market factors, stakeholder requirements, and currency fluctuations. A member of the program Governance Board stops you in the corridor and asks what is wrong with the program. You remind this person that program planning is_____

A. An inexact science, and so long as the program is within acceptable variance levels, everything is fine

B. An iterative process, and as issues arise and are addressed, the plan will naturally fluctuate

C. Basically a process of elimination, and as work is accomplished, future work is progressively elaborated

D. Only done at predefined intervals to reduce administrative expenses

5. 作为项目集经理,你发现由于一些因素,自己在不断地变更和改进项目集管理计划,这些因素有:变化的外部条件、市场因素、相关方需求和币值波动。一位项目集治理委员会的成员在走廊上叫住了你,并询问项目集出了什么问题。你应提醒该项目集治理委员会成员项目集规划是_____

A. 不精准的预估,所以只要项目集在可接受的变量水平内,一切都还好

B. 一个重复的过程,并且随着问题的出现和解决,这一计划将会随之波动

C. 基本上是一个工作消除的过程,当工作完成时,未来的工作会渐进明细

D. 仅能在预定时间段内完成,以控制管理成本

6. You are Company A's program manager for the development of an online banking system for your community bank, for which your company will receive $20 million. However, the bank is so interested in implementing this system quickly that it also contracts with Company B. You must implement your system completely in six months to ensure that you beat Company B's schedule. At this point, you have an expense estimate of $2.5 million. You will lose $10 million if you cannot deliver the product in six months, but if you can complete it sooner, you will earn an additional $25 million. Your risk management officer performs a risk analysis and tells you that there is a 30 percent chance that the bank will change its requirements, and a 70 percent chance that the program will be completed on time or ahead of schedule. Your company has completed similar programs in the past, and on the basis of these experiences, you know that there is a 30 percent chance that your final expenses will increase by $10 million. If no risks occur, the value of your program will be_____

A. $2.5 million                    B. $17.5 million

C. $29 million                     D. $42.5 million

6. 你作为公司 A 的项目集经理，为你的社区银行开发一个线上银行业务系统，为此你们公司将获得 2 000 万美元的收益。因为银行非常想尽快实现该系统，所以它同时和公司 B 签订了合同。你必须在 6 个月内完全实现该系统以确保你能够领先于 B 的进度。当前情况下，你的费用估算为 250 万美元。如果你不能在 6 个月内交付这款产品，你将损失 1 000 万美元，但是如果你能提前完成，你将赢得额外的 250 万美元的收入。你的风险管理专员进行了风险分析并告诉你有 30% 的可能性银行会改变需求，并有 70% 的可能性项目集可以按时或者提前完成。你的公司过去曾完成了类似的项目集；以过去的经验判断，有 30% 的可能性你最终的费用将会增加 1 000 万美元。如果没有风险出现，你的项目集的价值会是多少_____

    A. 250 万美元            B. 1 750 万美元

    C. 2 900 万美元         D. 4 250 万美元

7. You are conducting a program kickoff meeting for a new accounting system that will affect more than 500 accounting professionals in 10 locations. The preliminary schedule shows that in month 13, the transition of the system to the users will begin. The Director of Accounting is quite concerned about the impact of the new system on the employees. To ensure a smooth transition, you, as program manager, need to ensure that the Director that the program has_____

    A. A sufficient number of people to operate the new system

    B. Enough money in the budget to ensure that the employees receive the appropriate training

    C. The necessary lead time to get people ready

    D. An understanding of the steps needed to move from a development state to an operational state

7. 你正在为一个新的会计系统召开项目集开工会，这一新的系统将会影响到 10 个地区的 500 多位会计专业人士。初步的进度计划显示在第 13 个月，开始将该系统移交给用户。会计主管很关心新系统对雇员的影响。为了确保平滑的移交，你作为项目集经理，向该主管确保该项目集有_____

    A. 足够的人力来开发这个新系统

    B. 足够的资金预算来确保对进行相应的培训

    C. 必要的缓冲期来让用户准备好接受新的系统

    D. 对从开发状态转移到运营状态所需步骤的共同理解

8. Your firm's senior program manager is overwhelmed with stakeholder problems and has asked you to join the team as the program's resource manager. More than 20 people have already joined, and 15 more are expected over the course of the next month. The senior program manager believes that no additional members will be required. However, in casual observation you detect some problems. A handful of people seem to be working extraordinarily hard,

whereas others do not seem to have enough to do. As a program resource manager, your first priority must be to_____

A. Identify the compensation package for each team member that will drive the best performance

B. Determine the people, equipment, materials, and other resources that are needed and obtain them

C. Identify those competencies that are critical to the program but are not possessed by current team members

D. Ensure that program resources are allocated across projects to ensure that they are not overcommitted

8. 你公司的高级项目集经理对于来自相关方的问题应接不暇，并要求你作为项目集资源经理加入这个项目集管理团队。已经有 20 多个人加入了，并且另外 15 个人有希望在下个月能够加入。该高级项目集经理自信不再需要添加其他成员。然而，在平时的观察中，你发现了一些问题。不少成员好像超乎寻常地忙，而其他的一些人好像并没有什么工作。作为项目集资源经理，你的第一优先级必须是_____

A. 确认每一位团队成员的薪资可以与他所提供的工作业绩成正比

B. 确定人力、设备、材料和其他必需的资源，并获取这些资源

C. 辨识那些对项目集来说极为重要但当前团队成员所不具备的能力

D. 确保项目集资源在项目之间进行分配，以确保它们没有过度承诺

9. Assume you are working on a program to review and then update as needed all the regulations in your National Highway Transportation Safety Administration especially since people now are using small helicopters for their travel of distances less than 50 miles in your country. Many of the regulations in your Agency were put in place when the Agency was established over 40 years ago, and therefore, a detailed review is needed. You have a major program to manage and are preparing your program work breakdown structure. You believe a bottom-up approach to preparing it is desirable because_____

A. The top two levels of each project's work breakdown structure (WBS) can be included in the PWBS

B. Project-related artifacts are then part of the PWBS

C. The management and control responsibilities of the project team are determined

D. Earned value reporting is simplified

9. 假设你正在负责某个项目集的工作，这个项目集是为了评审并根据需要对你们国家高速公路交通安全管理局的规章制度做必要的更新，特别是现在在你的国家，在小于 50 英里的短距离旅行时，人们会乘坐小型直升机。很多的规章制度是在 40 年前建立的，由于时间已经很久远了，所以需要详细的评审。你有一个主项目集要管理，并在准备项目

集工作分解结构。你相信利用自下而上的方法来准备这个分解结构是可行的，因为_____

A. 每一项目的工作分解结构中最高两个层级可以包含在项目集工作分解结构中

B. 项目相关的构件是项目集工作分解结构的一部分

C. 项目团队的管理和控制责任是确定的

D. 挣值汇报是简化的

10. You have prepared your program scope statement, your PWBS, and PWBS Dictionary. Now, it is time to develop the schedule for this program. An essential element as you develop it is_____

A. Determining the order and timing of program packages

B. Estimating required resources for each activity

C. Focusing on resource leveling across the constituent projects

D. Adjusting leads and lags

10. 你已准备好你的项目集范围说明书、项目集工作分解结构和项目集工作分解结构词典。现在该为项目集制订进度计划了。在你制订计划时，一项必不可少的元素为_____

A. 确定项目集工作包的顺序和时机

B. 评估每项活动所需的资源

C. 关注在各构成项目间的资源平衡

D. 调整提前量与滞后量

11. You are the program manager on a multiyear, multimillion-dollar transportation program for the provincial government. Funding for your program is allocated on a fiscal year basis, yet your program transcends multiple years. This situation will affect how your costs are_____

A. Estimated      B. Obligated

C. Committed      D. Budgeted

11. 你是负责某个需要若干年才能完成的项目集的项目集经理，项目集的内容是某省几百万美元的交通运输工程。这一项目集的资金是按照每个财年划拨的，你的项目集需要跨越若干年。这一情况将影响你对成本的_____

A. 估算      B. 责任

C. 承担      D. 预算

12. You are the program manager on a multiyear, multimillion-dollar transportation program for the provincial government. Funding for your program is allocated on a fiscal year basis, yet your program transcends multiple years. Because of the challenges in cost estimating and the lack of additional funding to support your program, as program manager in preparing the financial management plan, you should_____

A. Ensure infrastructure and operational costs are included

B. Establish a set amount for the contingency reserve

C. Derive program estimates by using scenario analysis

D. Baseline each estimate

12. 你是负责某个需要若干年才能完成的项目集的负责人，项目集的内容是某省几百万美元的交通运输工程。这一项目集的资金是按照每个财年划拨的，你的项目集需要跨越若干年。由于对于成本估算的困难和缺少额外的资金支持，作为项目集经理在准备财务管理计划时，你应该_____

A. 确保基础设施和运营成本包含在计划之内

B. 建立一定数量的应急储备金

C. 利用情景分析得出项目集各项估算

D. 对每次估算进行基准化

13. You are the program manager for a series of new condominium developments in City A. Each of these condo developments is a separate project, as the City has different zoning requirements. Your company has developed similar condos for a neighboring city, City B. The City B program manager tells you that many different sellers can support the various subcontracts. With respect to awarding contracts, a best practice to follow_____

A. Ask each seller to prepare a detailed proposal so that you can evaluate its technical and managerial approaches

B. Procure the services of a product integrator

C. Review each potential seller's financial capacity as a key evaluation criterion, along with life-cycle costs

D. Base your evaluation criteria primarily on an understanding of need and technical capability

13. 你是城市 A 的一系列新公寓开发项目集的项目集经理。该城市有着不同的区划要求，所以每一个公寓的开发都是一个独立的项目。你们公司曾在附近的城市 B 开发过相似的公寓。城市 B 的项目集经理告诉你很多不同的销售商可能有着各式各样的转包契约。关于授予合同，需要遵循的一项最佳实践是_____

A. 要求每个销售商准备一份详细的建议书，这样你可以评估它们的技术和管理方法

B. 采购可以提供集成产品服务的供应商

C. 将每一家经销商的财务能力作为一项关键评估标准，并结合生命周期成本来评估

D. 你的评估标准应该主要基于对需求和技术能力的理解

14. You are the program manager for a new program in your company that will provide global support services for supply chain integration. This program will support your multi-national corporation, and you have a total of nine countries involved in it; three are in Asia Pacific, one is in Europe, Middle East and Africa (EMEA), two are in Latin America, and

three are in the United States. Your corporate headquarters are in London. You plan to outsource a large portion of proprietary development work to a vendor located in Canada. A key evaluation criterion in selecting the vendor is to assess_____

A. Its technical capability

B. References to see how successful it has been on other contracts of a similar nature

C. The level of compatibility between your company's culture and processes and the vendors

D. The provisions the vendor has in place to protect intellectual property

14. 你是你们公司一个新的项目集的项目集经理，项目集的工作内容是为你们公司的全球业务提供供应链支撑服务。这一项目集将支持你们的跨国企业，共涉及 9 个国家：3 个在亚太，欧洲、中东和非洲各有 1 个，2 个在拉丁美洲，3 个在美国。你们公司的总部在伦敦。你计划将大部分的专有开发工作外包给位于加拿大的厂商。用来选择供应厂商的一项关键评估标准是_____

A. 它的技术能力

B. 参考它曾在其他类似合约上的表现

C. 你们公司和厂商在文化和流程上的匹配程度

D. 厂商现有对知识产权的保护能力

15. As the company's risk expert, you have been requested by the program Governance Board to perform a risk assessment on the Apex program, which includes more than 25 projects. The focus of your assessment should be on_____

A. Analyzing response mechanisms for individual components

B. Ensuring that each project has a risk mitigation plan

C. Interproject risks

D. Stakeholder risk tolerance and thresholds

15. 作为一个公司的风险专家，项目集董事委员会已经要求你就 Apex 项目集执行风险评估，这包含多于 25 个项目。你的评估重点应该是_____

A. 为每个独立的组件分析应对机制　　B. 确保每个项目都有风险减轻计划

C. 项目与项目之间的风险　　　　　　D. 相关方风险承受力和风险临界值

16. As the organization's troubled program recovery specialist, you have been called in to take over a program that has had difficulties from the start. An initial assessment reveals that the project-level requirements have not been completed. This needs to be accomplished before any work can be initiated. One way to reduce the time needed for the requirements-gathering cycle is to_____

A. Use as many business analysts as you can find in the organization

B. Require each project manager to function as a business analyst until such time as the requirements have been gathered

C. Outsource all the requirements activity so each project manager can devote his or her time to the more important parts of the project

D. Apply the use of normalized templates, forms, and guidelines to make the process consistent across all projects

16. 作为组织的陷入困境之后的项目集风险补救专家，你受命去接管一个从一开始就有很多困难的项目集。一项最初的评估报告揭示各个项目层面的需求还没有完成。这项工作在其他任何工作开展之前理论上就应该已经完成了。一个可以减少需求收集周期所需时间的方法是_____

A. 使用你能在组织里找到的尽可能多的商业分析师

B. 要求每一个项目经理完成商业分析工作直到需求收集完成

C. 外包所有需求分析活动，这样每个项目经理可以将全部精力和时间放到项目等重要的事务上

D. 利用标准化的模板、表格和指南来使得在所有的项目上达到流程的一致

17. You are the program manager for a new program in your company that will provide global support services for supply chain integration. This program will support your multi-national corporation, and you have a total of nine countries involved in it. You plan to outsource a large portion of proprietary development work to several companies in a province located in Canada. Looking at procurement planning, it is important to_____

A. Adhere to legal and finance obligations

B. Direct all procurements to be centralized

C. Prepare complete evaluation criteria

D. Set standards for the components

17. 你是你们公司一个新项目集的项目集经理，项目集的工作内容是为你们公司的全球业务提供供应链支撑服务。这一项目集将支持你们的跨国企业，共涉及9个国家。你计划将大部分的专有开发工作外包给位于加拿大的几家公司。看一下采购规划，这里重要的是_____

A. 符合法律和财务规定　　　　B. 所有采购中心化

C. 准备完整的评估标准　　　　D. 为组件建立标准

18. You are the executive sponsor of a program that provides global support services for supply chain integration. The program is experiencing quality problems in the individual projects. After meeting with the program manager to discuss the issues, you suggest that one way to improve quality is to_____

A. Identify alternatives on scope definition methods through inputs from subject matter experts

▶ 42

B. Apply a common approach to the creation of the work breakdown structure across projects for consistency in scheduling, resourcing, and cost control

C. Align acceptance criteria for the deliverables across phases and projects with the program objectives

D. Set standards that are relevant to the entire program

18. 你是一位为供应链集成提供全球支撑服务的项目集的执行发起人。该项目集正受到其中几个独立的项目的质量问题的困扰。在和项目集经理讨论了这些问题后，你建议一个提高质量的方法为_____

A. 通过请求主题专家的帮助，在范围定义方法上，确认可选方案

B. 为了进度、资源和成本控制的一致性，在各项目间，利用通用方法来完成工作分解结构

C. 将各阶段和各项目交付成果的验收标准和项目集的目标保持一致

D. 设定整个项目集相关的标准

19. You and your team have prepared the program work breakdown structure (PWBS) shown below in Figure 4-1. Assume that this program involves the development of products, each of which follows the same sequence.

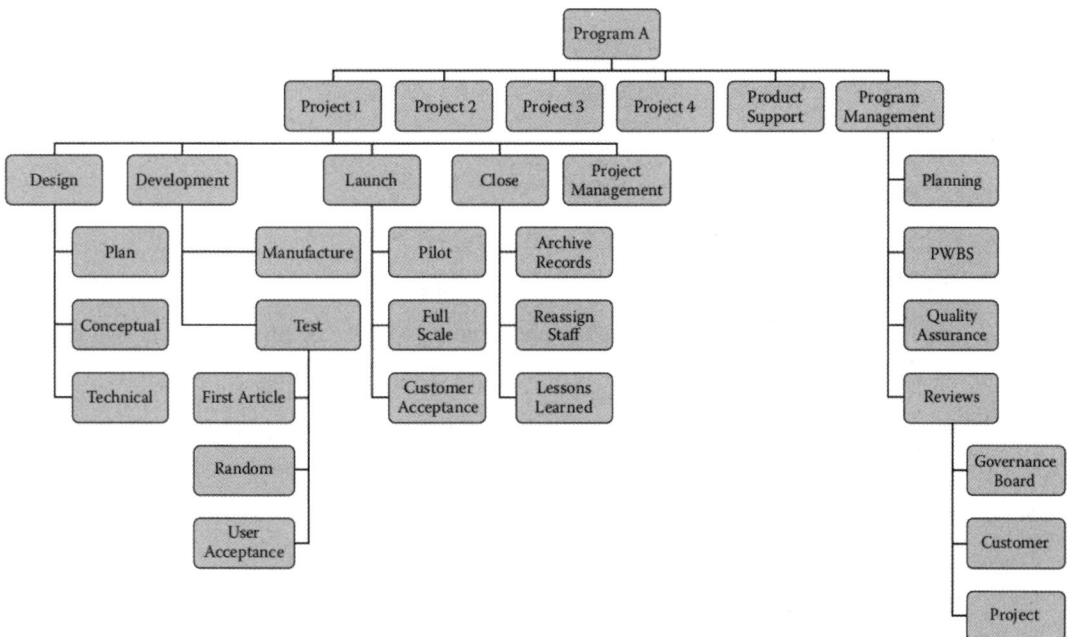

图 4-1 PWBS

In this PWBS, a program package is_____

A. Project 1                              B. Design

C.　Program Management　　　　　　D.　Plan

19.　你和你的团队已经准备了项目集工作分解结构（PWBS），如图 4-1 所示。假设这个项目集包含了各产品的开发工作，每一项工作遵循同样的顺序。

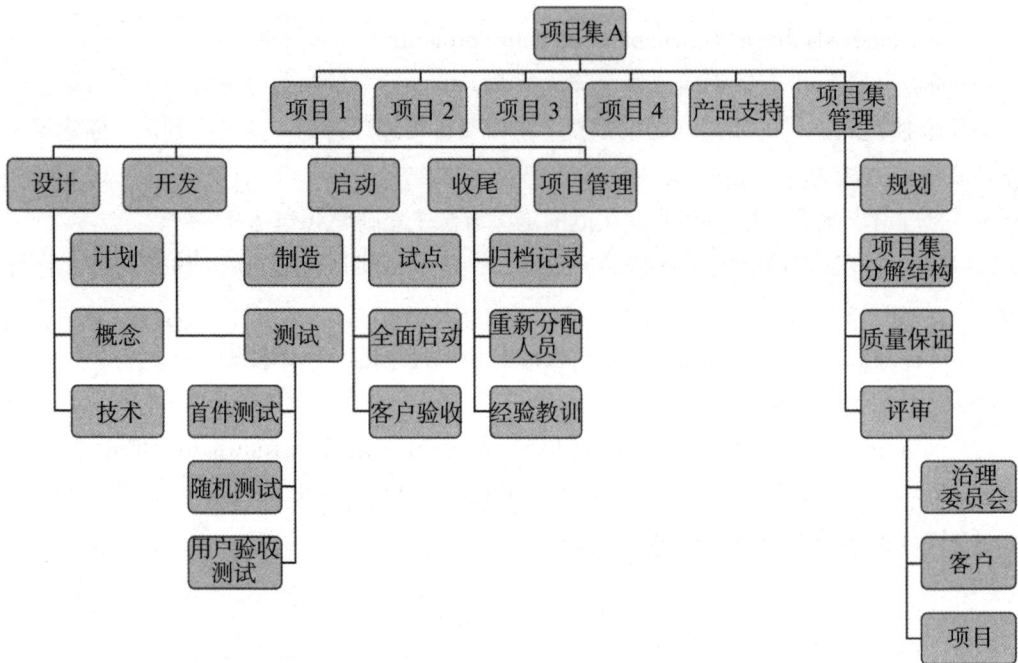

图 4-1　PWBS

在这一 PWBS 里，一个项目集包是_____

A.　项目 1　　　　　　　　　　　　B.　设计

C.　项目集管理　　　　　　　　　　D.　计划

20.　Working for an automotive company and wanting to develop an electric car that can be sold for under $25,000 US and run for 1,000 miles without needing a charge is a major undertaking. Your company is striving to be the first to market. To assess the program regularly, when you became program manager, you were asked to use a strategic performance measurement tool to track execution of the various activities, which means you should develop_____

A.　Key performance indicators　　　B.　A traffic light system

C.　Balanced scorecard　　　　　　D.　Earned value metrics

20.　你在一家汽车公司工作，这家公司想开发一款电力汽车，其定价在 25 000 美元以下，一次充电行程 1 000 英里，这对公司来说是个挑战。你们公司在努力成为第一家将这样的产品投放市场的公司。在你成为这个项目集经理时，你被要求使用战略绩效管理工具来跟踪各活动的执行情况，为了按照正常情况来评估这个项目集，这意味着你应

该开发_____

    A. 关键绩效指标         B. 红黄绿交通灯系统

    C. 平衡计分卡         D. 挣值指标

# 4.4 章节练习参考答案

1. D 在准备项目集进度时，首先要准备范围管理计划和 PWBS，这里确认了可以产生项目集收益的项目集组件。

2. B 你将会获得以下两项之差：2 000 万美元加额外 2 500 万美元的 70%，250 万美元的费用加额外 1 000 万美元费用的 30%，即：

$[\$20m + (0.7 \times \$25m)] - [\$2.5m + (0.3 \times \$10m)] = (\$20m + \$17.5m) - (\$2.5m + \$3m) = \$37.5m - \$5.5m = \$32m$

$[\$2,000 + (0.7 \times \$2,500)] - [\$250 + (0.3 \times \$1,000)] = (\$2,000 + \$1,750) - (\$250 + \$300) = \$3,750 - \$550 = \$3,200$

注意：期望值是可能性百分比乘以风险的货币价值。

3. D 项目集范围说明书是未来项目集决策的基础。它定义和阐述了项目集的范围。它同时包含项目集可交付成果列表和成功标准。在项目集采购规划里，一项最佳实践是去评估项目集范围内的各种采购的共性和差异。

4. A 在项目集采购规划里，项目集经理要考虑所有的项目集组件，以及为满足各项目标而制订的全面的采购计划。考虑一个全项目集的竞争指标是对这一规划的补充。

5. B 为了解决关键因素问题，比如商业目标、可交付成果、收益、时间及成本，这样的问题会随着竞争优先级、假设和制约被确定和解决，这一计划将会随着时间的推移而更新。

6. B 决策树分析被用来展示这一情况和每一可用选项的含义。它同时也为各备选项提供了期望货币价值。如果没有风险发生，你的项目集的价值可计算如下：2 000–250 = 1 750。

7. D 移交规划包括识别所有将项目集转移到运营状态的必要步骤。从可交付成果到能力、收益到组织的移交规划对项目集的成功来说是至关重要的。这一移交计划定义了标准，该标准是为了确保所有管理、商业及合同的责任都能够在项目集完成时得到满足。

8. C 能力是知识、态度和技术，以及其他能够影响其工作的个人特征。第一步是确认那些对于项目集至关重要但现有团队成员所不具备的能力。这确保了能够获得这些关键资源并在需要时可用。能力模型可以协助确定绩效，以及确定在项目集的工作中每个人需要具备的个人能力。

9. A PWBS 通常是对于每个项目工作分解结构的第一或者前两层的拓展。这一自下而上的方法随着 PWBS 的制定能够逐步地去展示这些层级。

10. A 在为项目集层级制订计划的时候，项目集包的顺序和时机及非项目集活动必须确定下来，为了产生项目集收益。这使得调度者可以预见项目集的完成日期及项目集里每一里程碑和每一项目关键交付成果完成的日期。

11. D 部分的成本预算是基于财务制约怎样来影响预算边界的。财政年度预算计划周期会影响到这些边界，导致项目集团队在这一生命周期内可能会使用到不同的技术。项目集财务管理计划应该讨论初始预算，以及拨款进度和里程碑。很多组织也同意需要一份整体财务管理计划和每一治理里程碑里对它当下下一阶段的预算承诺。

12. A 在制订项目集财务管理计划时，它扩展了财务框架。而当组件成本占据了大部分的项目集预算时，运营成本和基础设施成本也会包含在内。

13. B 除了依赖多个承包商，在多个项目集中，项目集经理和团队可能决定外包一个产品集成商的服务，以便将不同项目的产品成果集中在一起。项目集采购的目标是为各组件优化采购系统。

14. D 保护知识产权对于任何公司来说，在外包特别是在外包给一家外国公司时，都是一项重大关切，特别是要考虑法律系统和保护标准的差异。对于项目集经理的执行能力来说，确保项目集里的知识产权被正当的保护是必要的。

15. C 在项目集风险分析的工作里，当站在项目集层面，重点是集成相关组件风险并管理这些风险中的相互依赖关系，以及管理项目集以为项目集和项目提供必不可少的收益。对于项目集经理来说，执行能力是确认关键项目集风险和问题，这包括了确认组件风险之间的相互依赖。

16. D 项目集管理办公室的一项职能就是定义项目集管理需要遵循的流程和程序。通过标准的流程，可以减少需求收集的时间，因为各团队无需首先设计他们自己的收集需求的方法，可以立即开始工作。同时，有效的项目集管理信息系统要包括需求管理活动和工具。

17. A 在采购规划里，要执行许多活动。因为需要优化项目集采购管理，以及遵守法律和财务规定，因此在项目集层面对于采购负责人必须在规划阶段一起工作。

18. D 项目集质量规划的一个关键目的就是确认与整个项目集相关的标准，并且确定怎样满足这些标准。为确保整个项目集的质量，不同的质量保证和质量控制规范需要相互协调，必要时增加其他规范。

19. D PWBS 是面向可交付的对于项目集整体范围的层级描述。项目集包是最低层级的 PWBS。选项 A、B 和 C，都不是在 PWBS 的最低层级。

20. C 平衡计分卡是卡普朗和诺顿发明的，可用作战略绩效测量工具。它跟踪各成员活动的执行情况，以及这些行动产生的影响。

# 第 **5** 章

# 执行项目集

执行项目集在 PgMP®认证考试中占比 14%（24 个考题）。考试内容大纲显示其重点在生命周期的执行阶段。

## 5.1 秘笈要点

执行阶段是启动项目集的组件项目、管理组件的接口，以及产生项目集收益的过程。执行阶段管理项目集计划的各个组成部分，并将组织标准、资源、基础设施、工具进行标准化，并应用流程来保持一致性和关键相关方知情的决策制定。项目集经理的绩效是根据能否最大化实现项目集的目标成果来评审的，并且项目集经理具有人力资源的管理权。考题会涉及人际技巧，以及管理团队和管理相关方期望的能力。而经验教训往往通过沟通反馈流程来获取。评估项目集状态及整合项目集和组件的数据是一项持续的活动。在执行过程中，项目集的某些组件会陆续收尾。

在《项目集管理标准》中，执行和监控阶段是项目集生命周期中的收益交付阶段。所以其重点是信息发布（相关方管理章节）、项目集执行管理、组件成本估算和项目集成本预算（规划章节）、项目集采购、项目集质量保证、资源优先级（本章节）及风险识别、风险分析和风险应对规划（规划章节）。

执行过程的目的是执行项目集工作并产生项目集可交付成果以及预期收益。资源通常都是稀缺的，所以考题可能包括如何在整个项目集生命周期里进行项目集资源的权衡和适应。重点是项目集层级的资源供应以及供应商选择和合同签订。

请注意这一点：因为考试中相关方管理是另外的领域，所以信息发布及和相关方交互相关的考题主要涵盖在相关方管理领域内。同样，大多数收益交付的考题涵盖在本书的收益管理领域内，而治理相关的考题则在治理领域内。

## 5.2 重要考点

1. 项目集收益交付中的执行过程
- 项目集执行管理或项目集交付管理；
- 变更申请；
- 组件启动和转移。
2. 项目集采购
- 建立组件标准；
- 合格卖方名单；
- 预先商定的合同；
- 一揽子采购协议；
- 方案评价标准；
- 采购文档；
- 合同。
3. 项目集质量保证
- 政策和标准符合度；
- 质量保证规范；
- 审计；
- 标准报告；
- 质量控制结果分析；
- 变更申请。
4. 项目集资源优先级
- 资源变更；
- 资源优先级。
5. 项目集收益交付的目的
- 组件规划；
- 组件集成；
- 组件交付；
- 转移申请。
6. 执行项目集管理计划
- 设立项目；
- 授权项目经理；
- 建立统一标准；
- 审计结果；
- 评估状态；

- 使知情的决策制定。

7.　项目集经理绩效

- 完成目标贡献最大化；
- 领导人力资源职能：
  - 培训；
  - 辅导；
  - 教练。
- 团队激励。

8.　领导团队

- 培训；
- 辅导；
- 教练；
- 认可；
- 绩效评审。

9.　获取经验教训

## 5.3　章节练习

1.　As the program manager for the annual construction program for a large government agency, you prepared the program management plan and scope statement that were approved by all stakeholders. Nine months later, a small group of influential stakeholders wants to increase the program's scope by including all maintenance and operations of the buildings. You should_____

A.　Demonstrate the return on investment to the organization for increasing the scope of the program

B.　Reject the proposal because maintenance and operations typically are outside of the scope of programs

C.　Respond favorably because programs have a wide scope that may need to change to meet and exceed the organization's benefits expectations

D.　Ask a sponsor to make the business case to approve this new component

1.　作为一个大型政府机构的年度建设项目集的项目集经理，你已准备了一份项目集管理计划及范围说明书，这两份文档将需要得到所有相关方的批准。9 个月后，一小部分具有影响力的相关方想扩大项目集范围，即增加大楼的维护和运营。你应该_____

A.　向组织展示扩大项目集范围的投资回报之后产生的投资回报

B.　拒绝扩大范围的提议，因为维护和运营通常是不含在项目集范围内的

C.　积极响应，因为项目集有些宽广的范围，可能需要变更来满足，以及超越组织期

望收益

    D. 为批准新的组件邀请发起人做相应的商业论证

2. As program manager for a global payroll application, you have project teams in Bangalore, Singapore, London, and Washington, D.C. Currently, each team is following its own time-reporting process, which seems to be working well. From the perspective of global program management, you should_____

    A. Define and apply a mandatory common time-reporting process

    B. Allow each location to use its own process in consideration of its unique cultural norms and local holiday schedule

    C. Define a common time-reporting process that each location has the option to use

    D. Do nothing because the current approach appears to be working well, and there are other more important issues on which to focus

2. 作为一个开发全球化工资单 App 应用的项目集经理，你的项目团队分散在班加罗尔、新加坡、伦敦和华盛顿。目前每一个团队都是遵循自己的工时报告流程，看上去这样工作挺好的。从全球项目集管理的角度，你应该_____

    A. 定义和应用强制的、统一的工时报告流程

    B. 考虑到文化准则和当地假期计划的唯一性，允许每一地区使用自己的流程

    C. 定义统一的工时报告流程，每一地区来选择是否使用

    D. 什么也不做，因为当前的方法工作得很好，并且还有其他更加重要的事务要处理

3. An audit of your program has just been completed. The audit report claimed that a new process that had been implemented was receiving strong resistance from the users, thus indicating that a change impact review had not been conducted early enough in the program to detect potential barriers to adoption. Ensuring that such a review is conducted is clearly the responsibility of the_____

    A. Program manager            B. Program sponsor

    C. Program office             D. Benefits manager

3. 你的项目集已经完成了审计。审计报告显示一项已经实现了的新的流程招致用户的强烈抵制，这表明变更影响评审在项目集里进行得太晚了，以至于没有发现应用此流程后带来的潜在的障碍。为了确保这种评审的执行，这显然是以下谁的责任_____

    A. 项目集经理             B. 项目集发起人

    C. 项目集办公室           D. 收益经理

4. You are meeting with the team member who is responsible for the program management information system (PMIS) for your program. Because the data that will be captured are of a scientific and medical nature, the PMIS will generate more than eight terabytes (8,000 gigabytes) of data. Given the critical importance of the PMIS, you and the PMIS team member agree that

the first order of business is to_____

    A.　Consolidate existing data to maximize storage capability

    B.　Integrate all financial data

    C.　Produce timely and valid inter-project information

    D.　Define the program data naming conventions

4.　你在和负责你的项目集管理信息系统（PMIS）团队成员开会。因为将要获取的数据是科学性和医学性的数据，所以项目集信息管理系统将会产生多于 8T（8 000G）的数据。鉴于项目集信息管理系统的极其重要性，你和你的项目集信息管理系统的团队成员同意其商业第一要务是_____

    A.　合并现有数据以最大化存储容量

    B.　整合所有财务数据

    C.　产生及时有效的项目内部信息

    D.　定义项目集数据命名规范

5.　Many organizations that practice portfolio management for programs and projects use enterprise resource planning software. Your large program to implement a culture that focuses first on a standardized approach to portfolio management in which every proposed project or program must be justified with a business case and formally approved by a Portfolio Review Board before it can be initiated is using enterprise resource planning software. It is also beneficial at the individual program and project levels. Since you are using it on your program, your best course of action is to_____

    A.　Use your program management office (PMO) for support with this software

    B.　Handle it through the portfolio management office

    C.　Have a core team member work with it throughout the program

    D.　Set it up so that a program control framework is also established

5.　很多在项目集和项目实践项目组合管理的组织都在使用企业资源规划软件。你所在的大项目集正在使用企业资源规划软件，并需要去建立一种文化，它首先聚焦在对项目组合管理标准化的方法上，在这样的文化氛围下，每一项被推荐的项目或者项目集在其可以启动之前，必须经过商业论证以及项目组合评审委员会的正式批准。这对于单个项目集和项目层级来说也是有益的。因为在你的项目集里正在使用该软件，你的最佳行动方案是_____

    A.　利用你的项目集管理办公室来支持使用该软件

    B.　通过项目组合管理办公室来推行该软件

    C.　让一名核心团队成员在整个项目集使用该软件

    D.　搭建这个软件的环境，这样项目集控制框架也就随之建立

6. Your program management plan for your program for new pharmaceutical product to assist people with insomnia without any adverse side effects has been approved. Already, you have three projects in this program, and you have selected the project managers. You also have a core team of four people who report directly to you, and they have been selected and helped in the planning phase. Now, you are ready to assign team members to the various projects in your program. One factor that you should consider in the assignment process is to_____

A. Align pay/compensation to industry norms

B. Align personnel aspirations to available roles

C. Assign to the project managers those persons who will be the best performers

D. Assign team members with similar personalities to the same projects to reduce the risk of team conflict

6. 你的项目集管理计划已经获批。该项目集是关于医药产品的，用来帮助那些失眠的人，并且没有任何不良的副作用。该项目集里已经有 3 个项目，你已为它们选定了项目经理。同时，你有 4 人组成的核心团队直接向你汇报，并且他们早在项目规划阶段就已选定并参与了工作。现在，你已准备好在你的项目集里为各项目分配团队成员。在分配过程中，你应该考虑的一点是_____

A. 将薪酬水平和行业标准保持一致

B. 将员工的愿望与现有的角色保持一致

C. 将那些会成为最佳绩效者的员工安排为项目经理

D. 将具有类似个性的团队成员安排到同一项目，以减小团队冲突的风险

7. Your company is small and has only 90 people. Its annual sales are about 5 million US and have been at this amount for the last three years. Recently, the CEO and the other two senior executives met and prepared a long-term strategic plan for the next three years. The company provides services primarily in the government market and has a high win rate, but a low capture ratio, which has made it difficult for the company to grow. The executives want to focus on improving the capture ratio. You are the program manager to help lead your organization into one that has annual sales in the 15–20 million range in the next two years. Your program management plan has been approved, and you are now in the executing phase. You must concentrate on_____

A. Managing scope, schedule, and cost

B. Finding the right fit between the role and the person

C. Initiating components as planned and indicated on the roadmap

D. Making make-or-buy decisions

7. 你们公司是一家小公司，仅有 90 名员工。其年销售额在 500 万美元，并且过去的 3 年都维持在这一水平。公司在为政府市场提供服务，虽然市场占有率较高但增长率很低，

这使得公司很难成长。公司执行者想重点提高增长率。你是项目集经理，以帮助带领你们组织在未来的 2 年内将年销售额提高到 1 500 万~2 000 万美元。你的项目集管理计划已经获批，并且你现在正处于执行阶段。你必须将精力放到_____

    A.　管理范围、进度和成本        B.　为各角色找到正确的人

    C.　按照路线图的计划启动组件    D.　做出自制或采购的决策

8．With the last Space Shuttle mission completed, you have been selected by the Administrator of the National Aeronautics and Space Administration to plan and execute the next new program at its Cape Canaveral campus. This is a highly classified program, which will take the United States into space throughout the galaxy into the 2030s. It is important to therefore_____

    A.　Ensure that the architecture is consistent across deliverables

    B.　Manage and integrate program components

    C.　Produce cumulative benefits

    D.　Establish the program's organizational structure with a PMIS that is easy to access and use

8．最后一次航天飞机任务完成后，你被选为美国国家航空航天局的主管，在其卡纳维拉尔角校区来计划和执行下一个新的项目集。这是一项高度机密的项目集，可以使美国在 2030 年进入银河系的太空。以下比较重要的一点是_____

    A.　确保所有可交付成果的结构一致性

    B.　管理和整合项目集组件

    C.　产生累积收益

    D.　建立具有易访问和易用的项目集管理信息系统的项目集组织架构

9．Your program has seven projects in it. You have a PMO as well, which will support your program, and a core team of five people who also report to you. However, you are working now to manage the resources of your program, and you need to consider as you do so_____

    A.　Information from status reports

    B.　Preparing a human resource plan

    C.　The program's communications management plan

    D.　Establishing an adequate compensation plan

9．你的项目集有 7 个项目。该项目集有项目集管理办公室来支持你的项目集，并且有个 5 人组的核心团队直接向你汇报。然而，你正在管理你的项目集资源，在你做资源管理的时候你必须要做的事情是_____

    A.　来自状态报告的信息        B.　准备人力资源计划

    C.　项目集沟通管理计划        D.　建立适当的补偿计划

10．You are managing a program to develop a new source of energy that can be used in the northern and southern hemispheres when solar power is not available. Working with your core program team and your Governance Board, you have identified a number of component projects. However, your company has several key projects under way, and resources will be difficult to acquire for this new program. In determining whether to use internal or external resources, one key consideration is_____

A. The ability to coordinate use of external resources

B. Your ability to negotiate with functional managers for the needed staff

C. The availability of external resources

D. The impact on the morale if external resources are used

10. 你在管理一个项目集，来开发一项新的能源，它可以被用在地球的南北极太阳能无法利用的地方。和你的核心项目集团队及你的治理委员会一起，你们已经确认了很多的组件项目。然而，你们公司还有几个关键项目在进行中，所以很难为新的项目集获取资源。在确定是否使用内部或者外部资源时，一项关键的考虑是_____

A. 协调使用外部资源的能力

B. 你和职能经理为所需职员协商的能力

C. 外部资源是否可用

D. 利用外部资源对团队士气的影响

11. You are supported on your program by a variety of contractors who need to work closely together to deliver program benefits. Two of the contractors are blaming each other for missed deadlines. It appears that a critical milestone was missed by Contractor A, the output of which was needed by Contractor B. However, Contractor A alleges that Contractor B provided the wrong specifications. In this situation, your first step should be to_____

A. Seek liquidated damages from both contractors because of the missed dates

B. Alert your attorney to the possibility of litigation and its associated expense

C. Review the termination clause in each contract to see what your options are

D. Ensure there are unambiguous contract management procedures

11. 你的项目集有各类承包商，他们必须紧密地工作在一起以便交付项目集收益。其中的两家承包商在相互指责对方错过了最后期限。很明显承包商 A 在一个至关重要的里程碑上拖期了，而承包商 B 需要这一里程碑点的产出物。然而，承包商 A 辩称承包商 B 提供了错误的规范。在这一情况下，你第一步应该做的是_____

A. 向两个承包商寻求违约金，因为他们都错失了最后期限

B. 就可能的诉讼及其相关费用通知你的律师

C. 查看每一合同的终止条款，看看选择什么样的行动最为合适

D. 确保合同管理程序清楚明晰

12. You are managing a program to develop a new product to protect all workers from

germs in the workplace so everyone is assured that the workplace is clean. They will not have to worry in the future if a co-worker has a transmittable disease. However, you have just learned that there was a failure to adhere to a major element in the work breakdown structure (WBS) of one of the key projects. This problem means that_____

    A.  Interactions and realignment of this project must be managed

    B.  Rebaselining may be required

    C.  A change request has been approved

    D.  New metrics are required

12.  你在管理一个项目集，该项目集的工作是生产一个新的产品，这个产品是用来保护工人在工作场所不被细菌侵害，向每个人保证工作环境是干净的。将来他们不必担心其同事是否有可传播的疾病。然而，你已获知在关键项目之一的工作任务分解结构中漏掉了一个重要项。这个问题意味着_____

    A.  必须管理这一项目的交互和任务分配

    B.  可能需要重新定义基准

    C.  一项变更申请已获批

    D.  需要新的测量标准

13.  You are working on an emergency response program for your city and have realized that you lack the needed resources to support your program. Over the years, your organization's Procurement and Contracts Department has compiled a qualified seller list. This list will be extremely helpful to you when you_____

    A.  Prepare your program procurement management plan

    B.  Issue requests for proposals (RFPs) or requests for quotations (RFQs)

    C.  Plan contract evaluation criteria

    D.  Advertise in the local newspaper for your procurement requirements

13.  你正在为你所在的城市管理一个应急响应项目集，并且你已经意识到你缺少必要的资源来支持你的项目集工作。经过过去的几年，你们组织的采购和合同部门编写了一份合格销售商列表。这一列表在下列哪种情况下对你来说将极为有用_____

    A.  准备你的项目集采购管理计划时

    B.  发布建议邀请书或者报价邀请书时

    C.  规划合同评估标准时

    D.  在当地报纸为你的采购需求做广告时

14. As you work on this emergency response program for your city, you recognize you will need a number of different types of supplies and services to support your program and its component projects. One common approach is to use_____

    A.  Expert judgment

B.  Formalized proposal evaluation criteria

C.  Screening systems

D.  Weighting systems

14. 当你在为你的城市管理应急响应项目集时，你认识到你将需要很多不同类型的供应和服务来支持你的项目集及其组件项目。一个通用的方法是利用_____

A.  专家判断

B.  正式的建议评估标准

C.  筛选系统

D.  权重系统

15.  As a program manager, once your team is in place you need to focus on_____

A.  Providing mentoring

B.  Setting up a team-based reward and recognition system

C.  Promoting integrity in all interactions

D.  Striving to be a role model for the team

15.  作为项目集经理，一旦你的团队已就位，你必须将重点放到_____

A.  提供辅导

B.  建立团队层面的奖励和认可系统

C.  促进所有交互的完整性

D.  努力为团队做个榜样

16.  You have identified seven candidate projects to comprise your program. You also have identified seven capable project managers to manage these projects who have the requisite knowledge, skills, and competencies to do the required work against an aggressive schedule and demanding stakeholders. Before each project can officially begin, it is important that_____

A.  The program's business case is updated

B.  The scope of work is formalized

C.  A component initiation request is approved

D.  Each project has a defined charter

16. 你已确认 7 个候选项目来组成你的项目集。同时你已指定了 7 个有能力的项目经理来管理这些项目，他们都有在紧张的进度下，以及与要求型的相关方一起工作所必需的知识、技术和能力，用来完成所要求的工作。在每个项目正式开始前，以下哪一项是非常重要的_____

A.  确保项目集的商业论证已经更新

B.  工作范围正式确定

C.  确定组件启动申请已获批

D.  每一项目都有一份已定义好的章程

17.  Assume you are the program manager for your pharmaceutical company for a new product designed to cure sleep apnea. As part of your program potential patients will not need to

first go to a hospital to diagnose whether they have this condition and stay the night. You of course must get regulatory approval and conduct numerous clinical trials before your new product is ready so your program will last at least five years. You hope to be the first to market with this product even though your business development manager has said that a competitor is also working in this area. Based on your previous work on long programs, you know it is hard to sustain morale among your team, and many often then volunteer to work on projects that may be in trouble just to see results. Therefore, this time, you are_____

A. Setting up a process where your resources are dedicated to your team and cannot be used on other projects

B. Setting up a master schedule that has some early milestones, which you know you can meet

C. Asking each team member to sign a commitment statement to your program as they join your team

D. Having weekly performance reviews with your project managers, who in turn will have similar performance reviews with their team members

17. 你是你们医药公司的项目集经理，正在为研发一个可以治愈睡眠呼吸暂停症的新产品。你的项目集的部分潜在病人不必到医院住上一晚上来诊断他们是不是有这个症状。当然，在你的新产品上市之前，你必须获得监管批准并通过大量的临床试验，所以你的项目集完成至少需要5年的时间。商务开发经理说过有一个竞争对手也在研发类似的产品，但你希望你的产品第一个上市。根据你过去的在长周期的项目集的工作经验，你知道很难在项目团队中长时间维持高昂的斗志，很多人后来会主动选择那些有困难但曙光就在眼前的项目。所以，这一次你要_____

A. 建立一个流程，以便你的资源专属于你的项目集，不能为其他项目所用

B. 制订一个主进度计划，包含一些你认为可以完成的早期里程碑

C. 要求团队成员在加入你的团队时签署一份对你的项目集的承诺声明

D. 和你的项目经理进行每周的绩效评审，而后他们分别与各自的团队成员进行类似的绩效评审

18. You have decided to use standard Key Performance Indicators for your program and have adopted the Balanced Scorecard approach as well. You want to do so in order to_____

A. Minimize the information that is to be reported

B. Make sure that information is available in a format that has a template so a lot of time is not spent on the reporting process

C. Set up the reports to be provided on a weekly basis to all stakeholders

D. Evaluate the program status while maintaining current program information

18. 你已确定在你的项目集使用标准的关键绩效指标的同时也已采用了平衡计分卡方法。你这样做是为了_____

    A. 最小化需要汇报的信息

    B. 确保信息按照一定的格式可用，这样可以省却很多的花在汇报流程上的时间

    C. 建立向所有相关方汇报的周报机制

    D. 在维护当前项目集信息的同时评估项目集状态

19. Working on a major program to upgrade the software used in your country's airspace system to make it far easier for the air traffic controllers to use and also to avoid incidents of their falling asleep at times when there is limited activity or having tremendous stress when there is a lot of activity, you are facing many challenges in your role as a program manager. You have seven projects on your program and expect to add others. One project is about to close. You need to make sure before it does close that_____

    A. Deliverables are complete, and scope is compliant with the functional overview

    B. Deliverables have exceeded the original requirements, and there is universal agreement upon all stakeholders about the project's success

    C. The detailed administrative procedures for program closure have been followed, which are managed by your Program Management Office

    D. The program manager and team have been reassigned to other projects now that this project is complete

19. 你正在管理一个重要的项目集，来更新国家的空域系统软件，以便它在空中交通控制的工作中更加易用，同时也是为了避免在很少操作的时候陷入休眠状态，而在多线程工作的状态下又压力过大。作为项目集经理，你正面临挑战。在你的项目集里有 7 个项目，你希望增加其他项目。其中一个项目马上就要收尾。在它收尾前，你必须确保_____

    A. 可交付成果已完成，范围符合其功能概览

    B. 可交付成果超出了原始需求预期，并且与所有相关方就项目成功达成一致

    C. 在收尾的时候可以遵循你们的项目管理办公室的针对收尾过程的一系列详细管理程序

    D. 项目完成之后，项目经理和团队都已被安排到其他项目上

20. Program management is new to your company. You are managing the first program as you have taken program management training and have a track record of successfully managing complex and multiple projects. Your team is new to program management, and no one on the team has been exposed to it. Some team members have questioned the new approach, and others have asked why the organization has decided to manage projects as programs rather than as standalone projects. The project managers on your program are concerned they may lack visibility in this concept, limiting their opportunities for advancement and benefits. This shows

that you must_____

A. Persuade them that program management is desirable and becoming a program manager then can be the next step in their career

B.  Set up a training session for your project managers and team members to explain the benefits of program management

C.  Establish an open-door policy and invite anyone who has concerns to meet individually with you or to call you without any fears that in doing so their performance may be criticized

D.  Establish a policy of "no surprises" and provide your team with the same status information that the executives receive

20. 项目集管理对于你们公司来说是新近引入的。因为你参加了项目集管理培训并且有着成功管理复杂多项目的良好记录，所以由你来管理第一个项目集。项目集管理对于你的团队来说也是新的，而且，团队里没有人曾接触过项目集管理。一些团队成员对这一新的方法提出了质疑，并且其他的成员也在问为什么组织决定把项目作为项目集而不是单个的项目来管理。你的项目集的项目经理们很关切他们可能不清楚这一概念，这可能限制了他们的发展和收益机会。这表明，你必须_____

A.  说服他们项目集管理是需要的，并且成为项目集经理可以成为他们职业规划中的下一个目标

B.  为你的项目经理们和团队成员们开设培训课程，宣讲项目集管理的好处

C.  建立门户开放政策，欢迎任何有疑问的人和你单独面谈或者直接给你打电话，而不用担心在他们的绩效评估时为此受到批评

D.  建立稳妥的政策，给你的团队成员提供与汇报给执行者相同的状态信息

## 5.4　章节练习参考答案

1．D　虽然项目集有着宽广的范围，并可能需要变更来满足组织的收益期望，但这个申请是为项目集增加新的组件。所以，它要求组件启动申请要通过商业论证来根据批准的选择标准评估它是否应该被加进来。

2．A　在执行项目集时，每一位团队成员都要依照定义规范的统一的标准来记录他/她的工作时间，这一点很重要。文化准则和国家的假日计划，以及某位员工在本项目集上的工作时长和天数没有什么关联。

3．A　项目集经理必须设定清晰的目标、评估标准、变更计划、监督变更，以及解决那些没有完全同意变更的人的问题。变更管理是项目集经理应具备的一项核心知识和应重点关注的技术领域。

4．D　为了避免混乱和项目间各自增加命名规范，对于所有的信息，项目集应该有一个标准的命名规范，并且这一规范的使用在所有项目中应该保持一致。这将在项目集团队

里提高效率和生产率。

5. A 项目集倾向建立一个支撑性的基础结构，包括具体的流程和程序，以及物理设施。这一基础结构可能包括具体项目集的工具，比如，企业资源规划软件。

6. B 当团队成员为项目工作时，倾向更多的激励，或者委派他们担任他们很感兴趣的角色。所以，一个项目集经理在分配任务时应该总是考虑员工的个人兴趣和愿望。

7. B 没有具体负责执行的人，项目集不可能完成。为各角色找到适合的人是困难的，因为人们会在他们比较擅长的领域才表现出最好的工作状态。价值和能力不可能很快地发生变化，而额外的技能可在短时间内获得。这些角色的职责必须作为一个人如何看待和考虑事情的补充。

8. B 项目集交付管理的目的是在整个收益交付阶段管理和整合项目集组件。所以，组件必须被启动，变更申请一定要执行，并且组件会随之转变。

9. B 在资源优先级里，人力资源规划对于确认、记录，以及给个人和小组分配项目集角色和职责是有用的。资源应该按照满足关键项目集的需要来分配。

10. A 在项目集工作中使用承包商是普遍的，而管理他们的输入和贡献是决定项目集是否可以成功的基本因素。为确保外部资源的增值，在一种无缝的、整合的方式下，有效地协调不同的第三方的输入是必要的。

11. D 如果项目集的团员希望用一个通用的标准来将整个项目集作为整合的项目集来管理，清晰的合同管理程序是至关重要的。比如，每一个承包商都需要一份可比较的验收标准，这一标准适用于促使大家达成一致的项目集流程。如果一个组织拥有标准的供应商合同，为了项目集的效率，他们可能需要些实质性的变化。不要轻易签约，并确保程序没有不明之处，这很重要。成功的买方—卖方关系依赖于这些因素，信任和良好的工作关系在项目集层面很好地得以解决。

12. A 在项目集收益交付阶段，项目集经理负责维护项目集组件的调整，以便交付项目集收益。在项目集层面，和组件的交互对于完成目标、促进项目集的成功是必不可少的。项目集经理必须按照一致的、相互协作的方式管理每一组件，以及监督这一项目集组件的执行。

13. B 在发布建议邀请书、报价邀请书或者信息邀请书时使用合格的供应商列表。他们可以在整个项目集采购管理流程中节省时间，因为他们仅列出了已知的能够提供所需产品和服务的供应商。

14. B 项目集经理有很多可用工具和技术去指导项目集采购，并为项目集组件设立标准。正式的建议评估标准是可以遵循的最佳实践。

15. C 作为 PMI 的成员，根据《项目管理协会（PMI）道德和专业行为规范》，诚实是至关重要的组件，因为一个人必须"理解忠实并在我们的沟通和行动中体现一种忠实的行动方式"。通过在所有的交互中提高整体性，重点是诚实地行动，提供数据，直面不诚实，以及挑战任何鼓吹不诚实或者奖励的系统。道德的行为必须在项目集上进行实践。

16. C 组件规划是在项目集收益交付阶段执行的活动。在组件被授权之前，必须适当地支持项目集产出物。一个新的组件启动申请必须经过提交和批准。

17. B 团队成员很容易失去激励，特别是在大的项目集上。一种方法就是在你的团队里来庆祝胜利，并最大化他们对于完成项目集目标的贡献。如果主进度计划有些早期的可以完成的里程碑，这可以为庆祝成功并组建一个优胜的团队提供机会。

18. D 关键绩效指标在项目集管理中是一项最佳实践，特别是它展示了项目集是怎样维持与战略目的和目标一致性。平衡计分卡在设定绩效目标时是有用的，目的是可以在执行阶段评估项目集状态，以便在维护当前项目集信息的同时监督和控制项目集。

19. A 在申请结束一个项目获批之前，项目集经理必须确保项目的可交付成果已完成。其范围应该和功能概览一致，因此需求和范围说明书里的成功标准都已满足。

20. B 项目集管理的使用是因为通过项目集管理可以获得比单个项目管理方式更多的收益。所以它比项目管理更加强调在战略一致性、收益实现、相关方参与及治理的重要性。一个项目集经理必须通过开设培训带领团队以加强团队的参与并完成对项目集目标的承诺。

# 第 6 章

# 监控项目集

监控项目集的考题占比是 10%，也就是 17 道题。这些题目主要关注考试内容大纲中有关项目集生命周期第四个阶段的内容，尤其是监督和控制项目集及其组件部分。预期收益要与初始计划吻合，风险必须要控制在可接受的水平，以及可接受的最佳实践必须遵从。

## 6.1 秘笈要点

本章节中，考试大纲关注这样一些需求，即如何通过分析成本、进度、质量和风险中的变化因素，来识别由其导致的项目集的纠正措施和新的机会。当纠正措施被实施后，项目集管理计划和其他计划也需要进行相应的更新。需要强调是，在管理项目集的问题时，要识别和选择与项目集的范围制约和所需达到的项目集收益目标相一致的一系列措施。需对各种可能的变更带来的影响进行评估和确认。另外，风险要依据风险管理计划进行监督。

在项目集管理标准中，监督和控制是项目集生命周期中收益交付阶段中的一部分。相关问题涵盖了项目集绩效报告、项目集财务监督和控制、项目集绩效监督和控制、项目集采购管理、项目集质量控制、资源依赖关系管理、项目集风险监督和控制及项目集范围控制。

考试要求你能回答关于挣值方面的问题，并熟悉各种有关挣值的术语和公式。并要求你能回答关于项目集趋势，以及与项目集相关方沟通这些趋势的需求方面的问题。在项目集相关方期望管理的流程中，相关方是一个重点，相关内容包含在本书的相关方有关章节中。其他一些和治理监督及收益管理相关的工作，也被本书的相关章节所涵盖。

由于监督和控制涉及预防和纠正措施，一些问题会涉及诸如项目集经理和核心项目集成员需要决定采取何种最佳措施的场景。因为项目集经理负责管理项目集问题，他会使用到问题登记册，治理委员会则会评审该问题登记册的内容。在贯穿从启动到收尾的整个项目集的生命周期中，上述的很多流程将会发生。此外，项目集范围、进度和预算的监督和控制也非常重要，包括合同签署后的项目集采购管理。

## 6.2 重要考点

1. 项目集收益交付
- 项目集绩效监督：
  - 准备合同和发起人相关的数据报告；
  - 要求用户反馈；
  - 准备定期报告、演示文稿和关键绩效指标。
- 项目集财务监督和控制：
  - 监督项目集财务和协调预算内花费；
  - 管理发生的变更；
  - 向承包商付款；
  - 关闭组件的预算；
  - 更新预算基准；
  - 批复变更请求；
  - 使用挣值；
  - 执行纠正措施。
- 项目集绩效监督和控制：
  - 收集、测量和发布绩效信息；
  - 评估项目集趋势；
  - 提供确定项目集的状态、趋势和重新校准方面的信息；
  - 决定是否需要预防和纠正措施；
  - 准备状态报告；
  - 准备预测。
- 项目集采购管理：
  - 确保预算花在收益交付上；
  - 使用绩效/挣值报告；
  - 使用带有关键绩效指标的由分包商提供的进展报告。
- 项目集质量控制：
  - 监控可交付成果以确认质量需求是否实现；
  - 执行质量变更请求；
  - 使用质量控制检查表；
  - 使用质量测试报告和测量结果。
- 资源依赖关系管理：

- 控制稀有资源的时间表；
- 聚焦于相互依赖的资源。

- 项目集风险监督和控制：
  - 识别，分析和规划新的风险；
  - 跟踪已识别的风险；
  - 重新分析已有的风险；
  - 执行风险响应；
  - 记录经验教训。

- 项目集进度控制：
  - 跟踪和监督里程碑的开始和结束；
  - 管理主进度计划规划的时间表；
  - 识别下滑和机会；
  - 评审项目集主进度计划；
  - 更新路线图。

- 项目集范围管理：
  - 确定有重大影响的范围变更；
  - 建立范围变更控制系统；
  - 确定范围说明和 PWBS 需要更新的时间。

2. 预防和纠正措施

3. 主动式和响应式成本控制

4. 管理和控制变更

- 变更请求；
- 协调变更；
- 变更控制委员会；
- 变更请求日志；
- 影响分析；
- 批复变更请求；
- 偏差分析。

5. 会议和评审

- 演示文稿；
- 状态评审会；
- 经验教训评审。

6. 项目集管理控制

- 标准；
- 政策和程序；

- 项目集计划；
- 绩效报告；
- 预测；
- 项目集绩效分析；
- 问题分析；
- 项目集衡量标准；
- 影响评估；
- 时间和成本报告系统；
- 检查；
- 评审；
- 监督；
- 审计；
- 合同；
- 文档；
- 法规。

7. 挣值

- 进度和成本偏差；
- 进度绩效指标和成本绩效指标；
- 完工估算（EAC）；
- 完工尚需估算(ETC)；
- 完工预算(BAC)。

8. 趋势分析

9. 偏差分析

10. 影响评估

11. 问题登记册

# 6.3　章节练习

1. As a program manager on the next generation nuclear submarine, you have six projects so far in your program, and this is only year one. You know additional projects and non-project work will be added as the program continues since it is scheduled to last for at least seven years. One of your responsibilities is to ensure that common activities among projects are coordinated to maximize the use of resources and achieve results that would not be possible if the projects were managed in a standalone fashion. This is done in_____

A. Program Performance Monitoring　　B. Benefit Management

C. Resource Prioritization  D. Resource Interdependency Management

1. 作为新一代核动力潜艇的项目集经理，你的项目集在第一年有 6 个项目。按照进度计划，完成该项目集至少需要 7 年时间，所以，你知道随着项目集的进行，还会加入其他的新的项目和非项目工作。你的一个职责就是要确保项目之间共同的活动能够被统一协调，最大化利用资源并取得成果，而该成果是无法通过单独管理每个项目的方法获得的，这可通过什么实现_____

A. 项目集绩效监督  B. 收益管理

C. 资源优先级排序  D. 资源依赖关系管理

2. You know from your work on programs, that change is inevitable on both on the overall program and its projects. As a program manager for this nuclear submarine program, you use a change management system as part of the program management information system (PMIS). You do this during part of your work in_____

A. Integrating overall change control

B. Working to deliver incremental benefits

C. Managing scope

D. Monitoring and controlling program performance

2. 你了解自己在项目集的工作中，变更在整个项目集和它的各个项目中是无法避免的。作为核动力潜艇项目集经理，你使用了变更管理系统，并把它作为项目集管理信息系统中的一部分。这些是你在以下哪部分工作中实现的_____

A. 集成整体变更控制  B. 交付增量收益

C. 管理范围  D. 监督和控制项目集绩效

3. Your program, which designs, develops, and manufactures a class of farm equipment that can be used above the Arctic Circle, has been requested to consolidate data and status for a key stakeholder. Part of your work involves maintaining a spare parts inventory and fulfilling spares requests for clients. In consolidating your report, you_____

A. Do not include the spares data because they are really not part of the defined program and do not fit the definition of a project

B. Include the spares data, even though they are non-project work, because they are part of the program

C. Include the spares data because you can reasonably define fulfilling a spares order as a project

D. Ask the stakeholder who requested the report whether he or she wants to see the spares data

3. 你的项目集是设计、开发和制造一种可以用于北极圈内的农场设备，一名主要相关方要求获得该项目集汇总的数据和状态。你的一部分工作涉及维护一张备件库存清单和

执行用户的备件请求。为了汇总你的报告，你会_____

 A. 不包含备件数据，因为这些备件既不是项目集的一部分，也不符合一个项目的定义

 B. 包含这些备件数据，尽管它们是非项目的工作，但它们还是项目集的一部分

 C. 包含这些备件数据，因为你可以合理地把执行备件定单定义成一个项目

 D. 询问提出报告请求的相关方，问他或她是否要看这些备件数据

4.　You have been asked to assume the management of a program to rebuild the water desalinization plant for Haddad, Saudi Arabia.  Much of the equipment on the job is being leased.  The program has been under way for more than five years. You decided to conduct an audit of the hundreds of lease agreements, and you found that you are making payments on leases for equipment that are not being used.   Your next step is to_____

 A. Set up a system to alert your team to this problem on future leased resources

 B. Use a resource register

 C. Recommend corrective actions

 D. Inform your Governance Board because it is focused on the program's financial status

4.　假设你被要求管理一个项目集，为沙特阿拉伯哈达德重建海水淡化工厂，大部分设备是租赁的。这个项目集已经进行超过 5 年了。你决定对成百的租赁协议进行审计，于是你发现在为一些不在使用的租赁设备支付费用。你的下一步是_____

 A. 建立系统，把未来可能有的这个租赁资源的问题警示你的团队

 B. 使用资源登记册

 C. 推荐纠正措施

 D. 通知治理委员会，因为它关注项目集的财务状态

5.　Your program to produce the first polycarbonate city car is making progress. The client is concerned that the cost to manufacture the car will cause the car to be priced at a level that the average consumer cannot, or will not, pay. The client has asked you to see whether you can reduce the cost of manufacturing the vehicle yet still meet the specifications. Such customer feedback requests are helpful and are part of_____

 A. Establishing a cost change management system

 B. Preparing program performance reports

 C. Determining when to take corrective actions

 D. Implementing a lean Six Sigma manufacturing processes

5.　你的生产第一辆聚碳酸酯的城市汽车的项目集获得进展。客户担心这种汽车的制造成本会导致定价高到一般消费者不能也不愿支付的水平。用户要求你评估是否能够在满足要求的情况下降低制造该汽车的成本。这种用户反馈回来的需求对项目集很有帮助，是如下哪个工作的一部分_____

 A. 建立成本变更管理系统　　　　B. 准备项目集绩效报告

C. 确定执行纠正措施的时间　　　　D. 执行六西格玛制造流程

6. You have been asked to assume the management of a program to rebuild the water desalinization plant for Haddad, Saudi Arabia. You are using earned value on your program. The schedule performance index indicates that you will not meet your proposed schedule, and you are only about 20 percent complete to date. You need to_____

A. Issue a revised schedule to your program team

B. Update the program master schedule

C. Update your budget baseline

D. Inform your Governance Board

6. 假设你被要求管理一个项目集，为沙特阿拉伯哈达德重建海水淡化工厂，大部分设备是租赁的。你使用了挣值的方法管理项目集，进度绩效指标显示，你将无法达到计划的进度，比计划落后 20%。你需要_____

A. 给你的项目集团队发布修改的进度表

B. 更新项目主进度计划

C. 更新预算基准

D. 通知治理委员会

7. As program manager for development of a next-generation catalytic converter, you have a core team of six people. So far, you are in the first year of your program, scheduled to last four years, and you have three projects as part of your program. The project manager of the first project to design the converter has raised an issue to you as he feels it has far reaching consequences. You decide to use an issue register. After each issue is identified, your core program team records it in this register. The next step is to_____

A. Subject the issue to analysis by a reviewing authority

B. Appoint a member of the program team to resolve the issue

C. Ask the person who raised the issue to propose a resolution

D. Determine a course of action

7. 作为开发下一代催化剂转换器的项目集经理，你有一个 6 个人的核心团队。该项目集有 3 个项目，计划 4 年完成，到现在为止，已经过了一年。设计转换器的项目经理向你抛出了一个问题，因为他觉得项目集离达到目标还很远。于是，你决定使用问题登记册。在识别每个问题后，你的核心团队将其记录在问题登记册中，下一步你要_____

A. 提供问题给评审部门分析

B. 指派一名项目集人员解决问题

C. 让问题提出者提供问题解决方案

D. 确定一个措施

8. Assume you are managing a program for the judicial branch of your government, and

you are reporting to the Chief Information Officer of the Administrative System of the Courts. The program is the number one priority on the Court's list of ongoing programs and projects in the portfolio. The purpose of your program is to manage a legacy system conversion program, and thus far, your team has identified a number of risks to monitor, which means at the program level, you should_____

A. Determine if the program's assumptions are still valid

B. Appoint a member of your core team to be responsible for risk management on the program

C. Ensure the planned risk responses are executed in a timely way

D. Monitor the effects of the risk responses as they are executed to ensure they were effective

8. 假设你管理一个政府司法分局的项目集，你准备向主信息官汇报有关法庭的管理系统。这个项目集在法院的所有正在进行的项目集、项目和项目组合列表中优先级是最高的。项目集的目标是管理遗产系统转换。因此，你的团队已经识别一定数量的风险，并对其进行监控，这意味着在项目集层面，你要_____

A. 确定项目集的假设是否依然有效

B. 指派一名项目集核心人员负责管理风险

C. 确保计划的风险响应能及时执行

D. 监督风险响应的执行效果，确认他们的执行是有效的

9. It is important to address and control scope changes on programs to ensure successful program completion. These scope changes can originate from many sources including_____

A. Risks                          B. Architecture issues

C. Missed milestones              D. Resource reallocations

9. 提出和控制范围变更，确保项目集能成功完成是非常重要的。导致这些范围变更的因素很多，包括_____

A. 风险                           B. 架构问题

C. 错过的里程碑                    D. 资源再分配

10. One of the issues on your program is difficult to resolve because it concerns serious personality conflicts. Although it was raised by Project Manager A, it affects Projects B and C. Each of the three project managers has a different solution, and there is a stalemate. Therefore, a key performance competency for a program manager in monitoring and controlling the program is to_____

A. Establish an issue analysis process

B. Recognize some of these solutions could be program opportunities

C. Provide issue oversight at the program level

D. Ask an expert for assistance before taking corrective

10. 涉及严重的个性冲突的问题是项目集最难解决的问题之一。尽管问题由项目经理 A 提出，但它也影响项目 B 和 C。3 个项目经理每个人都对这个问题有不同的解决方案，往往会导致僵局。因此，在监督和控制项目集中，对项目集经理来说关键的能力是_____

A. 建立问题分析流程

B. 意识到这些解决方案有可能有新的项目机会

C. 提供项目集层面的问题监督

D. 在采取措施前寻求专家支持

11. You realized in your work on the next generation nuclear submarine that since it will last seven years, you will probably have scope changes. You want to prepare for them and be able to exploit them as much as possible. However, because most scope changes have associated costs, every proposed change requires analysis to determine whether it should be implemented. If change requests are accepted and approved, the next step is to_____

A. Communicate the decision to the stakeholders involved

B. Update the program management plan

C. Revise the work breakdown structure (WBS)

D. Work with the component manager to implement the change

11. 由于下一代核动力潜艇的项目集会持续 7 年，你意识到你在该项目集的工作将有可能发现范围变更。你想尽可能对这些变更有所准备，并能够利用它们。然而，由于大部分范围变更和成本相关，每个提出的变更都需要分析确定是否要被执行。如果变更请求被接受和批准，下一步是_____

A. 与相关方沟通这个决定　　　　B. 更新项目集管理计划

C. 修改工作分解结构（WBS）　　D. 与组件经理一起实施变更

12. A scope change request is approved for your program. It is estimated to require an additional $1 million. Your program Governance Board recommended to the executive sponsor that this scope change be approved to maintain a competitive advantage. Which of the following should you first update?_____

A. Program management plan

B. Budget baseline

C. Program work breakdown structure (PWBS)

D. Scope management plan

12. 在你的项目集中，一个范围变更请求被批准，估计额外需要花费 100 万美元。项目治理委员会向执行发起人建议批准这个范围变更以维持竞争优势。下面内容你最先更新的是_____

A. 项目集管理计划　　　　　　　B. 预算基准

C. 项目集工作分解结构(PWBS)　　　　D. 范围管理计划

13. You are the legacy system conversion program manager in your company. You have a request now to update the company's business development/sales tracking system, which was not in your business case. Your Governance Board recognizes the importance of including this project in your program and asks you to prepare a cost estimate for this new project. The board approves your estimate. You now should_____

A. Update the program budget baseline

B. Revise the cost management plan

C. Prepare a resource management plan

D. Identify staffing needs

13. 你是公司的遗产系统转换的项目集经理,你有一个需求要更新公司的商业拓展/销售跟踪系统,而该需求和你的工作内容无关。治理委员会意识到把这个项目加入你的项目集的重要性,要求你准备一份这个新项目的成本估算。最终这个估算被治理委员会批准了。你现在应该做的是_____

A. 更新项目集预算基准　　　　　　B. 修改成本管理计划

C. 准备资源管理计划　　　　　　　D. 识别成员需求

14. Because of their size, complexity, and duration, programs tend to be more important than projects in most organizations, and program managers tend to interact more with senior management, often through the Governance Board or steering committee that oversees the program. Throughout the program, it is especially important to monitor and control program changes. It is helpful to_____

A. Conduct impact assessments

B. Authorize funding for each change

C. Update the scope statement

D. Influence factors that lead to change with effective program metrics

14. 由于项目集的规模、复杂度和持续的时间等特性,在大多数组织中,相比于项目,项目集有更大的重要性。项目集经理通常通过监督该项目集的治理委员会和董事会更多地和高级管理层互动。在整个项目集过程中,监督和控制项目集的变更非常重要。它有助于_____

A. 执行影响评估

B. 为每个变更授权资金

C. 更新范围说明

D. 影响那些导致有效项目集指标变更的因素

15. You are the program manager on a mergers and acquisition (M&A) team that is responsible for integrating your company with the one it has recently acquired.  The company

you acquired has a history of failure in such mergers; your company is now its fourth owner, and unfortunately, things are not going well. In a meeting with your executive sponsor after the last governance review meeting, he suggested that you set up_____

    A. Key performance indicators     B. A different governance structure

    C. Benchmarking studies     D. A program audit

15. 你是一个并购团队中的项目集经理，该团队负责你们公司和新近并购的一家公司的整合。这家并购的公司有过合并失败的历史，你的公司是它的第四位所有人，不幸的是，事情总是进行得不顺利。在最近的一次治理评审会之后，你的执行发起人在一个会议上建议你建立_____

    A. 关键绩效指标     B. 不同的治理结构

    C. 基准研究     D. 项目集审计

16. In a program performance meeting, you asked the project manager of Project A what the status was on her program. She responded by saying that the total project budget of $600,000 was evenly allocated over the project's six-month life. She has just completed the second month of the project and has finished 50 percent of the work. What earned value method information is available thus far?_____

    A. Earned value     B. Planned value

    C. Actual costs     D. Earned value and planned value

16. 在一个项目集绩效会上，你要求项目 A 的项目经理汇报项目状态。她反馈说整个项目预算的 600 000 美元的预算已经平均分配到项目的 6 个月的执行期中。她已经执行完项目的第二个月工作，完成了 50%的计划。这提供了与挣值方法相关的什么信息_____

    A. 挣值     B. 计划价值

    C. 实际成本     D. 挣值和计划价值

17. Every program is planned on the basis of a set of hypotheses, scenarios, or assumptions. As a newly appointed program manager, you ask one of your core program team members to explore cost and contingency reserves. This is important as part of the_____

    A. Forecasts

    B. Risk monitoring function

    C. Program procurement administration

    D. Program financial monitoring and controls

17. 每个项目集的计划都基于一系列的前提、场景或假设。作为一名新任命的项目集经理，你要求一名核心项目集团队成员研究成本和应急储备。这属于哪部分的重要工作_____

    A. 预测     B. 风险监控功能

    C. 项目集采购管理     D. 项目集财务监控

18. You are a program manager on an international program that relies on contractors for

approximately 75 percent of its work. Some of the contracts apply to a specific project, but five contracts span six of the projects. You have one basic ordering agreement, which enables you to obtain temporary resources as required for this complex program. In terms of Program Procurement Administration, you should review the_____

A. Program reports

B. Procurement register

C. Contract management plan

D. Change requests

18. 你是一名国际项目集经理，该项目集 75%的工作依靠承包商完成。一些承包商合同只使用在某一个专门的项目中，但有 5 个合同在 6 个项目中使用。你有一个基本的订单协议，通过它可以获取这个复杂项目集需要的临时资源。从项目集采购管理的角度上看，你应该评审_____

A. 项目报告

B. 采购登记册

C. 合同管理计划

D. 变更请求

19. Your program is beginning to miss key milestones because of delays by your customer, with whom you have a contract. Your goal is to ensure that corrections are made as quickly as possible, so you decide to conduct a contract performance review earlier than planned. At the program level, it is your responsibility now to_____

A. Prepare a change request

B. Document the causes for the delay and bring it to your attorney's attention

C. Ensure the budget is being spent properly

D. Document the delay and discuss it with the steering committee

19. 由于和你签约客户的延期，你的项目集开始错失关键的里程碑。你的目标是确保尽快能有纠正措施，所以你决定比计划提前执行一次合同绩效评审。在项目集层面，你现在的责任为_____

A. 准备变更申请

B. 记录延期的原因并让你的律师关注

C. 确保预算被正确使用

D. 记录延期并和治理委员会讨论

20. You are preparing for a meeting of your program's Governance Board. On your program, you are using earned value for monitoring, control, and forecasting. The planned value is $30,587, and the earned value is $26,365. You are working on a customer-imposed schedule for the completion of the program. Looking at the schedule variance (SV), you conclude that_____

A. The SV is –$4,222, and the program is behind schedule

B. The SV is 1.16, and it appears that the schedule will be met

C. The program is behind schedule, and the tasks on the critical path are affected

D. The budget at completion is $46,475, but the delays are insignificant

20. 你正在为一个项目集治理委员会的会议做准备。在你的项目集中，使用挣值方法来监督、控制和预测。计划值是 30 587 美元，挣值是 26 365 美元。在项目集完成时间上，你正在执行一个客户施加了影响的进度计划。从进度偏差（SV）角度看，你得出的结论是_____

A. SV 是–4 222 美元，项目进度滞后

B. SV 是 1.16，标明进度到达要求

C. 项目集的进展滞后，关键路径上的任务受到影响

D. 完工预算是 46 475 美元，但进度滞后不明显

# 6.4 章节练习参考答案

1. D 资源必须在项目集内共享，项目集经理控制这些资源共享的时间表。

2. C 范围控制对于确保项目集交付其预期收益是必要的。管理范围必须通过变更管理来实现。

3. B 在项目集层面，准备绩效报告过程中，这些报告汇总了项目集中各个组件的进展。这个汇总同时包含项目和非项目工作的内容。

4. C 为了避免罚款和持续的租赁花费，应该跟踪租赁资源，确保在租赁到期和不再需要使用时归还。基于审计的发现，必须要申请变更或申请推荐的纠正措施。如果一个项目集的成本超过预算，将无法验证商业论证的合理性，甚至微小的超出也需要调整。

5. B 项目集绩效报告协同绩效数据，向相关方提供资源使用信息，供其确定项目集收益交付的有效性。客户反馈需求是这个活动的输出。

6. D 项目集进行到这个时间点，显然将无法达到进度要求。第一步应该是先通知治理委员会，然后决定下一步要执行哪些纠正措施。

7. D 当识别出一个问题，必须将其在问题登记册中记录。这是一个项目集层面的问题的例子，项目集经理必须选择和范围、制约和目标相一致的行动，取得计划的收益。

8. A 在项目集的风险监督中，必须经常评审初始的项目集假设和决定是否依然有效，因为假设是风险的关键来源。

9. B 范围控制是项目集成功的关键。范围变更可能产生于相关方、项目集组件、以往未经识别的需求、架构问题或外部来源。

10. 项目集经理的绩效能力，就是持续识别问题和风险并采取需要的纠正措施。作为这个技能的一部分，要建立问题分析流程，用于评估问题的影响和严重性；同时，必须维护一个问题日志。

11. B 在项目集范围控制中，必须有变更管理活动。当变更请求被接受和批准后，必须更新项目集管理计划和项目集范围说明书。

12. B 项目集财务监控的一个输出就是更新项目集预算基准。监督财务和控制花费

是确保项目集达到资金目标的关键方面。这种量级的变更需要更新预算基准。

13．A 作为项目集财务监控的输出，当重大成本影响发生时，需要更新项目集预算基准。这些更新要向项目集相关方进行合理的沟通。

14．A 当项目集有变更时，必须进行影响评估，目的是根据项目集的治理模型进行决策推荐和获得批复。

15．A 在项目绩效报告中，汇总了项目集的绩效数据并传达给相关方，为其提供项目绩效的信息。因此，必须建立关键的绩效指标。

16．D 项目的挣值（EV），表明工作已经完成了一半，挣值是 300 000 美元。2 个月的计划值（PV）是 200 000 美元。记住，估算是根据 600 000 美元平均分配到 6 个月中（或每个月 100 000 美元）。

17．B 当根据新的和变化的风险进行项目集风险响应的持续监控，风险监控包含评估成本和进度的应急储备需要按照项目集风险的变化进行修正。

18．C 在管理重要采购和收购的合同时，需要使用合同管理计划。它涵盖了整个合同周期的合同管理活动并用来有效管理各种供应商。作为项目集采购的一部分，它要遵从项目集采购管理。

19．C 在项目集采购管理中，当合同被授予后，项目集经理有责任维持采购的可见性，确保预算被正确的使用，从而获得项目集收益。

20．A 进度偏差（SV）通过挣值（EV）减去计划值（PV）获得，即 SV = EV – PV。因此，SV 是–4 222 美元，项目集进度滞后。而且没有其他信息，关键路径的效果是未知的。

# 第 7 章

## 收尾项目集

收尾项目集的考题占比是 3%，也就是 5 道题。根据考试内容大纲中的内容，项目集收尾强调项目集生命周期的最后阶段。这个阶段会正式验收产品、服务或成果，并将结束整个项目集和其中的项目。项目集的工作完成后，还将从项目集中获得收益，组织在将来能够持续获得这种收益。

## 7.1 秘笈要点

在项目集管理标准中，收尾项目集包含在项目集生命周期的收尾阶段，目的是执行可控制的项目集收尾。这个阶段集中关注项目集的移交和收尾，包括财务收尾、项目集移交和收益维持、项目集关闭和项目集采购收尾等。

这个阶段跟踪收益管理生命周期中的收益移交。此时，项目和非项目活动的收益都将被集成，维持收益的责任将根据项目集移交计划转移给运营单位。很多相关的进行中的活动与确保和维持收益有关，而这些活动在每个组织中都不一样。收益相关的问题主要包含在本书的收益部分。

必须要注意，行政收尾会持续进行，不需要等到项目集结束。项目集中的每个项目在不同的时间段收尾，与相关联的合同一样。如果一个项目由于某种原因被终止，它可能早于进度计划或预期时间结束。经验教训在整个项目集生命周期中都要收集。收尾活动因此贯穿于整个项目集，而不仅仅是项目集结束的时候。

## 7.2 重要考点

1. 项目集收尾阶段
- 项目集移交：

■符合项目集收益；

■完成移交工作；

■要求启动新项目集，以监督移交活动。

项目集收尾：

■项目集财务收尾；

■收益维持预算；

■财务关账说明；

■关闭的项目集预算。

- 项目集移交和收益维持：

■确保收益维持。

- 项目集收尾：

■最终报告；

■知识移交；

■资源遣散；

■项目集收尾。

- 项目集采购收尾：

■合同关闭报告；

■经验教训更新；

■关闭合同。

- 项目集绩效分析报告；

- 相关方对收尾的支持；

- 执行项目集和组件的移交和收尾计划。

2. 执行后评审会议

3. 报告经验教训和最佳实践

4. 知识产权要求

5. 项目集结果沟通

# 7.3　章节练习

1. You have been managing a major software program for six years under contract to a Fortune 500 company. You have been helping this company move to Cloud computing. Finally, you completed the last project in this program, and it is time to officially close the program. Although you have completed your program, your customer requires telephone and e-mail support in case an issue arises or a defect is detected.　Such assurance is_____

A.　An activity to be done as part of closing the program

B. Outside the scope of the program

C. An ongoing activity that is part of the program

D. A standard best practice

1. 你已经管理一个软件项目集 6 年了，该项目集是和一个财富 500 强公司签订的合同。你正在帮这家公司实施云计算的迁移。最后，你完成了这个项目集中的最后一个项目，并到了正式收尾这个项目集的时候。尽管你已经完成了你的项目集，你的客户要求万一在问题发生或一个漏洞被检测到时，能有电话和邮件支持，这种保障是_____

A. 作为项目集收尾的一部分，需要将来执行的活动

B. 在这个项目集的范围之外

C. 作为项目集收尾的一部分，是一个正在进行的活动

D. 标准的最佳实践

2. You are managing a program for the first time in your telecom company. It is to convert all the existing phone lines in your city to ones that are underground to prevent outages during hurricanes and tornadoes, which are common to your region of the country. You realize that since you have seven projects in this program that various projects will close at different times during the life cycle of your program. These closing activities are_____

A. Limited to the project's life cycle

B. Covered as you close the program

C. Followed by a certificate of program completion

D. Limited to closure of each project

2. 在你的通信公司中，你是第一次担任项目集经理。该项目集要将你所处城市中现有的电话线转移至地下，防止网络在飓风和龙卷风发生的时候出现线路中断，因为你所在国家该地区这种自然现象非常普遍。你意识到这个项目集包含 7 个项目，会在项目集生命周期的不同时间点收尾。这些收尾活动_____

A. 受到项目生命周期的限制　　　　B. 作为项目集收尾的一部分

C. 遵从项目集完成的认证　　　　　D. 受到每个项目收尾的限制

3. As the closing manager for a program that has been under way for five years in your company, you must ensure that all deliverables were completed and that program objectives and measurable program success criteria were met. You meet with the former program manager, the Governance Board, key stakeholders, and members of the core program team. To further confirm that all the work has been completed, you review the_____

A. Program work breakdown structure (PWBS)

B. Program charter

C. Benefits register

D. Program management plan

3. 你是公司的一名收尾项目经理，正在对一个执行 5 年的项目进行收尾，作为一个贵公司已经进行了 5 年的项目集收尾的项目经理，你必须确保所有可交付成果都已经完成，达到项目集的目标和可以度量的项目集成功标准。你会见了之前的项目集经理，他是治理委员会成员，关键的相关方，也是这个项目集的核心成员。为了进一步确认所有的工作都已经完成，你要复审_____

A. 项目集工作分解结构（PWBS）　　B. 项目集章程

C. 收益登记册　　　　　　　　　　D. 项目集管理计划

4. You are a program manager, and one of your component projects is complete. You work with the project manager to ensure that all closure activities are finished. The project manager has numerous tasks to complete; at the program level, you need to_____

A. Review relevant contract documentation

B. Confirm that the project's benefits have been delivered

C. Assess the project's budget

D. Confirm that project closure has occurred

4. 你是一名项目集经理，该项目集中的一个组件项目已完成。你和该项目经理一起，确认所有的收尾活动都已经完成。项目经理有很多收尾任务要完成，在项目集层面，你需要_____

A. 复查所有相关合同文档

B. 确认项目的收益已经交付

C. 评估项目预算

D. 确认项目的收尾已经发生

5. You are in the closing phase of managing a major program in your company. Your program included 11 separate contracts and was a significant endeavor for your organization. Your Governance Board has asked your PMO to conduct an individual review to make sure all procurement closure activities are complete. It should focus on_____

A. Those contracts that were terminated for convenience or default

B. The procurement management plan

C. The contract management plan for each of the 11 contracts

D. The procurement process for outstanding issues

5. 你正在管理公司的一个重要项目集，该项目集处于收尾阶段。这个项目集有 11 个不同的合同，对你的组织来说，这些合同的收尾需要投入大量精力。项目集的治理委员会要求该项目集的 PMO 执行一个独立的评审，以确保所有采购收尾活动都已完成。这个评审要关注_____

A. 这些合同是由于便利性或缺省条件被终止

B. 采购管理计划

C. 这 11 个合同的每个合同管理计划

D. 突出问题的采购流程

6. You have been managing a program to deliver a new tractor that will use 75 percent less fuel. The program is ready to close, and activities then to sustain the benefits will be transitioned to the product support group. During this transition, you need to make sure_____

A. The operations group has been involved in the program as a key stakeholder

B. Estimates of the cost to sustain the benefits are finalized

C. Stakeholders have signed off on product acceptance criteria

D. Component transition requests have been submitted

6. 你正在管理一个项目集，即生产一种新型拖拉机，仅使用不到原来 75%的汽油。该项目集准备收尾，维持收益的活动将被移交至产品支持组。在这个移交过程中，你需要确保_____

A. 运营组作为一个主要相关方，参与到项目集中

B. 完成维护收益所需要的成本的估算

C. 相关方已经签署了产品验收标准

D. 已经提交了组件移交请求

7. You establish a program support function to provide ongoing product support for the heating, ventilating, and air-conditioning (HVAC) program for the new class of amphibious warfare vehicles. Prior to transitioning your program's work to this group, you need to ensure_____

A. Successful, on-time product delivery

B. The Governance Board is consulted

C. That attention is paid to benefits sustainment

D. That all documented benefits are realized as planned

7. 你建立一个项目集的支撑功能，目的是给一个新型两栖战车的加热、通风和空气调节（HVAC）的项目集提供持续的产品支持。在你的项目集工作移交到新的项目组前，你需要确认_____

A. 成功、准时的产品交付     B. 咨询治理委员会

C. 收益维持受到关注     D. 所有记录的收益都按计划实现了

8. Finally, it is time to close your program. You need to now execute the transition plan to the operations group in your company. When you are executing your transition plan you focus on_____

A. Ensuring the program has satisfied all requirements

B. Managing the redeployment of all project resources

C. Conducting reviews of your suppliers

D. Archiving lessons learned

8. 最后，到项目集收尾的时间了。你需要向公司的运维组执行移交计划。当你执行移交计划时，你关注_____

　　A. 确保项目集满足所有需求

　　B. 管理所有项目资源的重新部署

　　C. 实施供应商评审

　　D. 存档经验教训

9. You work with numerous contractors and suppliers on your program. Your company considers two of the contractors to be valued partners; however, three of the contractors have not worked on any previous programs or projects for your company. Furthermore, one supplier and two contractors have worked with competitors, and one contractor uses a competitor as a supplier. In closing your program, you need to ensure_____

　　A. Each contractor has signed a nondisclosure agreement

　　B. A final performance review is held with each contractor

　　C. A decision is made to determine whether any of the three new contractors should be added to the qualified supplier list

　　D. All deliverables are completed satisfactorily

9. 在你的项目集中，你有很多分包商和供应商。公司考虑将选择 2 个分包商作为有价值的合作方；然而，有 3 个分包商从来没有在公司之前的项目集和项目工作过。并且，1 个供应商和 2 个分包商与竞争对手合作过，1 个分包商使用一个竞争对手作为供应商。在对你的项目集进行收尾时，你需要确保_____

　　A. 每个分包商都签署有保密协议

　　B. 每个分包商都有一个最终的绩效形式

　　C. 3 个分包商是否加入认证的供应商列表，需要做个决定

　　D. 所有可交付成果都令人满意地完成了

10. You are the Business Change Manager on a mobile workforce initiative to decrease the costs associated with office space. As a result of this initiative, 2,000 employees now work in their homes, thereby saving the company millions per year in lease fees. Now that the culture change has been complete, you are working to close this program. You realize program closure activities are distinct from those of other phases of program management because closure activities_____

　　A. Do not require involvement with sellers or suppliers

　　B. Occur at the end of the program life cycle

　　C. Are handled by someone who is appointed as the closing manager

　　D. Occur throughout the program

10. 你是一名移动办公初始方案的商务变更经理，目的是减少和办公场所有关的成本。

作为这个初始方案的结果，2 000 名雇员在家办公，因此为公司节省了数百万美元的租赁费用。现在这种文化的改变已经完成，你正启动项目集的收尾。你意识到，项目集的收尾活动和项目集管理的其他阶段有所区别，因为收尾活动_____

A. 不要求买方和供应商参与

B. 发生在项目集生命周期结束时

C. 由被任命的收尾项目集经理负责

D. 发生贯穿于整个项目集

11. Assume it is time to prepare your final report to close your new product development program. This means you need to describe in it_____

A. Actual work performed

B. Contractors to be added to the qualified supplier list

C. Program documentation archive plan

D. Knowledge transition

11. 假设到了你准备最终报告的时候，以对新产品开发项目集进行收尾。这意味着你要在报告中描述_____

A. 实际完成的工作

B. 被加到合格的供应商列表的承包商

C. 项目集文档存档计划

D. 知识移交

12. Resource Disposition is an important aspect of program closure so the resources can be used elsewhere in the organization. Releasing resources is handled by_____

A. The program manager　　　　　B. The program sponsor

C. PMO Director　　　　　　　　D. Program governance

12. 资源遣散是项目集收尾的一个重要方面，这样，项目集资源可以在组织的其他地方被使用。释放资源由谁来处理_____

A. 项目集经理　　　　　　　　　B. 项目集发起人

C. PMO 总监　　　　　　　　　　D. 项目集治理

13. Lessons learned can be reported in various ways. For consistency and quality, each program should adopt a standard approach. In the closing phase of the program, the program manager should_____

A. Address the advantages and disadvantages of the methods used to gather and report on lessons learned

B. Share lessons learned with team members

C. Survey the customer and the team for overall program satisfaction

D. Report these lessons learned to the chief knowledge officer

13. 经验教训可以用多种方式形成报告。为了保证一致性和质量，每个项目集必须采用一个标准的方法。在项目集收尾阶段，项目集经理要_____

　　A. 说明用来收集经验教训并形成报告的方法的优劣

　　B. 与项目集团队成员分享经验教训

　　C. 调查顾客和项目集成员对项目集的整体满意度

　　D. 向首席知识官汇报经验教训

14. You have been appointed closing manager for a program that has been under way for eight years. You have met with the program manager to talk about lessons learned. You have also met with the core program team members and reviewed the lessons learned that were documented by each of the six projects in this program. Your next step is to_____

　　A. Select the key lessons learned and archive them

　　B. Add any additional lessons learned to the program's final report

　　C. Index each project's records

　　D. Assign metadata tags to the records so they can be easily located using a content management system

14. 你被任命为一个历时 8 年的项目集的收尾经理。你和项目集经理会面沟通经验教训。你也和项目集的核心团队成员会面，审查这个项目集中 6 个项目所记录的经验教训。你的下一步是要_____

　　A. 选择关键的经验教训进行存档

　　B. 在项目集的最终报告中加入任何其他没有被记录的经验教训

　　C. 对每个项目的经验教训进行索引

　　D. 为每个记录标注元数据标签，让这些记录容易被内容管理系统定位到

15. As program manager, you follow a detailed closure process that was developed by the enterprise program management office (EPMO). You have customized this procedure somewhat to fit the unique requirements of your program. Project C is now in its closing phase. This means it is your responsibility to_____

　　A. Conduct a performance review with the project team members

　　B. Reallocate resources to other program components

　　C. Perform a final performance review

　　D. Update personnel records

15. 作为一名项目集经理，你遵从由企业项目管理办公室制定的项目集收尾详细流程。你定制了这个流程的某些地方，以满足你的项目集的独特要求。项目 C 现在处于收尾阶段。这意味着你负责_____

　　A. 和该项目团队成员进行绩效评审

　　B. 将该项目资源重新分配到项目集的其他组件

C. 执行最终的绩效评审

D. 更新项目人员记录

16. You are a program manager for an aerospace company that is developing the C888 aircraft. Each of the component projects is scheduled to end at a different time. Each time a project closes to initiate closeout activities, it is necessary to_____

A. Obtain stakeholder support

B. Ensure all project procurements are closed

C. Meet with your team to discuss lessons learned before team members are released

D. Ensure operations management is ready to handle sustainment activities

16. 你是一家正在开发 C888 飞机的航空航天公司的项目集经理。该项目集的每个组件项目计划在不同时间结束。每当一个项目收尾，就会启动收尾活动，该收尾必须_____

A. 获得相关方支持

B. 确保所有项目的采购都结束

C. 在项目集团队解散前，和项目集团队会面讨论经验教训

D. 确保运营管理部门做好管理维持活动的准备

17. You are managing the development of a series of heating, ventilation, and air-conditioning (HVAC) products. Each product is being managed as a separate project. Because the products will be completed at different times, you have a product support group. Your team has also established a configuration management system as a subsystem of the overall program management information system (PMIS). Changes have been requested to the product that was delivered in Project A. These changes affect the product from Project B, which is in production. You focus on_____

A. Responding to customer complaints regarding the product already delivered from Project A

B. Ensuring that support is properly scheduled for Projects A and B

C. Ensuring that a policy of zero defects is implemented as part of the quality assurance and control activities

D. Conducting a thorough audit and extensive testing of future products before they are delivered

17. 你正在管理加热、通风和空气调节（HVAC）一系列产品的开发。每个产品的开发都通过一个不同的项目来管理。因为每个产品完成的阶段不同，你成立了一个产品支撑小组。你的团队也建立了一个配置管理系统，作为整个项目集信息管理系统（PMIS）的一个子系统。针对项目 A 交付的产品有些变更请求，这些变更将会影响项目 B 的产品，而该产品正在生产过程中。你将关注_____

A. 考虑到项目 A 的产品已经交付，响应客户投诉

B. 确保对项目 A 和 B 的支持能准时安排

C. 确保作为质量保证和控制活动一部分的零缺陷政策被实施

D. 将来产品交付前执行彻底的审计和扩展性测试

18. Each project in your program, Program B, is developing a specific product. Together your program will have eight separate products once it is complete. You establish a product support group to provide ongoing support for all the products in your program. A critical success factor is to ensure that_____

A. Staff members are physically collocated with the project team

B. Support is available on a 24/7 basis

C. Support is properly scheduled when changes are made

D. Knowledge transfer activities are performed

18. 在你的项目集 B 中，每个项目正在开发一个特殊的产品。你的项目集一旦完成，将会有 8 个不同的产品。你建立了一个产品支持组，为你的项目集的所有产品提供持续的支持。该小组一个关键的成功因素是确保_____

A. 工作人员要和项目团队在一起

B. 支持要每周 7 天，每天 24 小时

C. 当执行变更时，支持要准时安排

D. 执行知识转移活动

19. You are the program manager responsible for product development for your company's Class C vehicles. You have six projects in this program. After five years, the program is finally in the closing stage. It is time to begin program financial closure when_____

A. Benefits are delivered

B. A financial closing statement has been prepared

C. All contractors have been paid

D. Budget allocation reconciliation is complete

19. 你是项目集经理，负责公司 C 类汽车的产品开发。在该项目集中有 6 个项目。5 年后，这个项目集到了收尾阶段。什么时候开始进行项目集的财务收尾_____

A. 收益被交付                    B. 准备好财务收尾声明

C. 所有承包商都已经付款          D. 完成了预算分配对账

20. A critical part of program management is managing the intellectual property that is created. One of your senior engineers left the company three weeks before your program was complete. A key scientist departed a year early. For program success you need to ensure that_____

A. Lessons learned are readily accessible

B. Program staff are not able to join competing firms at any time

C. The organization conducts exit interviews with anyone who leaves the program

D. Knowledge assets are transferred into the organization's knowledge repository

20. 项目集管理的一个关键部分是管理项目集创造的知识产权。一名高级工程师在项目集结束前的 3 周离开了公司。一名关键的科学家在更早的一年前离开。从项目集成功的角度，你需要确保_____

A. 经验教训易于获取

B. 项目集人员不能在任何时候加入竞争对手的公司

C. 组织对任何离开项目集的人员实行离职面谈

D. 知识资产被转移到组织知识库

# 7.4　章节练习参考答案

1. A 项目集收尾的活动会导致构件、收益监控和其他组持续的运营等方面的移交。一个通常由合同定义的关键活动，就是在交付后，为客户提供运营支持功能，万一产品出现任何问题，或检测到任何缺陷，都能确保提供指导和维护。

2. B 组件的移交和收尾发生在每个组件收尾的时候。其所有内容都会被评审以确保收益被交付，以及移交给其他项目和维护的工作都已经完成。在授权正式收尾前，将和项目集发起人和治理委员会一起评审最终的组件状态。收尾活动的发生贯穿于整个项目集。

3. B 项目集会在章程被履行或者出现让项目集提早结束的条件时结束。在项目集收尾前，要评审项目集章程。

4. B 项目集组件收尾会关注项目集层面的收尾问题。它涉及确认项目层面的收尾已经发生，但它不能替代正常的项目收尾活动。项目集经理负责执行所有项目集和组件项目计划的移交和收尾。

5. D 在项目集采购收尾要执行一些关键活动，包括确保每个合同都正式关闭，所有可交付成果都已经令人满意地完成，所有款项支付都已经完成，确认是否还有突出的合同问题。

6. B 作为项目集财务收尾的一部分，需要估算确定项目集收益维持需要的成本。尽管在收益交付阶段，当组件被交付时，大部分成本花掉了，但是还有一些剩余的活动需要监控持续的收益。

7. B 在项目集移交前，项目集经理要会见治理委员会，决定项目集是否符合预期收益，移交工作是否成功被执行，是否有维持的活动监督章程中规定的收益。

8. D 在执行项目集移交计划时，项目集和项目计划处于收尾过程。在这个过程中，管理和 PMIS 项目集收尾活动将被执行，项目集文档要存档，经验教训要记录，持续的活动要进行移交以保持收益可维持性。

9. D 在项目集采购收尾时，确认所有可交付成果都令人满意地完成了，每个合同必须正式关闭，所有款项支付都已经完成，没有突出的问题。

10．A　项目集收尾活动不只发生在项目集的结尾，它的发生贯穿于整个项目集。在项目集收尾前，所有组件必须完成，所有合同必须关闭。

11．C　项目集的最终报告包含适用将来项目集、项目的信息，以及高级管理为公司治理而要求的信息。另外，它需要包含一个项目集文件存档计划。

12．D　有效和合适的资源释放非常重要。在项目集层面，项目集治理处理资源遣散，将其作为项目集众多的一系列收尾批复活动中的一部分。

13．B　经验教训是项目集收尾时的知识移交的一个重要部分。作为这个活动的一部分，项目集经理评估总体绩效并和他的团队成员分享经验教训。

14．B　在项目集完成时，必须和团队成员举行一个会议讨论经验教训。如果有项目集经理没有识别到的经验教训，应该被加到项目集的最终报告中。

15．B　在项目集层面，项目的可用资源可以被分配给项目集中其他仍然在进行的项目或者组织中其他的项目集。

16．A　在开始对项目集或其中的项目进行收尾时，如果要相关方支持启动收尾活动，就要确保相关方满意于项目集已经成功交付的收益。

17．B　在一个产品被部署后，必须安排相应的支持，避免客户使用过程中有任何中断以保证有最大的可用性。收益维持可用通过运营、维护、新项目或其他方式来处理。

18．D　当收益被移交到其他组织进行维持时，必须要包含知识移交活动来支持持续的收益维持。它通过提供文档、培训和材料给新的支持组织来实现。

19．A　项目集的财务收尾开始于维持预算完成制定、收益被交付及维持启动时。

20．A　经验教训的识别和文档记录要贯穿整个项目集管理流程中。当人员离开和项目集收尾时，经验教训应该正常地被现在和将来的项目集获取用于持续的学习，以避免任何陷阱。

# 收益管理

收益管理是项目集管理第三大领域，在考试中占比 11%，约 19 道题目。

## 8.1 秘笈要点

项目集设立的目标就是获得比项目集所含项目或者其他工作单独执行更大的收益。因而，早在商业论证阶段项目集作为组织投资组合的候选方案，一直到项目集正式收尾阶段实现项目集收益并移交给组织，都必须重视收益管理。

该部分侧重收益实现计划，以及按照什么标准来确定计划中的收益是否实际完成。收益实现计划要求与相关方保持细致持续的沟通，当该计划在项目集整个过程中发生变更时尤其如此。任何变更，特别是当计划中所描述的收益实现方式或收益需要修改时，就应该与相关方（特别是治理委员会及项目集发起人）进行沟通。

另外，还需要制订相应的收益移交计划和收益维持计划。也就是说，一旦项目集结束，它的收益将移交给客户、最终用户或产品团队、运营支持团队。这些相关方需要参与到项目集中，对项目集收益有细致的理解，并因此在项目收尾及整个项目集收尾后能维持收益。

因而，需要测量指标来监督收益，确保计划中所描述的收益得以实现，并以收益实现报告中的术语与相关方沟通。有些收益是有形的，可以被量化。还有些收益虽然是无形的、难以量化的，但对某些特定项目集同样非常重要。收益必须持续审查，以确保项目集与组织总体战略目标保持一致。

当有风险（威胁和机会两种都要考虑到）和问题出现，或引入新项目，以及项目完成时，就需要对收益实现计划定期进行审查更新，来决定是否需要做相应变更。因此，收益管理在整个项目集周期中持续进行，并需要定期审查。项目集管理标准的项目集收益管理章节着重描述了项目集周期及其与收益管理的联系，同时也描述了在全周期过程中维护收益登记册的重要性，以及登记册中的内容。标准也解释了整个项目集生命周期的成本和收益配置变化。因此，收益管理与项目集路线图之间的关系，以及项目集收益与项目集治理的关系，都在这里得到了解释。请认真学习标准中的该部分内容。

## 8.2　重要考点

1. 项目集收益管理重要性
- 主要活动；
- 收益类型；
- 定义和交付收益。
2. 项目集生命周期和收益管理
- 收益识别：
  - 识别和定性商业收益；
  - 收益识别活动；
  - 商业论证和收益识别；
  - 收益登记册；
  - 目的；
  - 内容。
- 收益分析和规划：
  - 主要活动；
  - 量化收益的增量交付；
  - 贯穿生命周期的成本收益配置；
  - 收益和项目集治理；
  - 收益实现计划；
  - 目的；
  - 内容；
  - 测量标准；
  - 相关方沟通；
  - 收益和相关方路线图；
  - 收益登记册更新。
- 收益交付：
  - 目的；
  - 主要活动；
  - 报告和指标；
  - 监督指标的方法；
  - 收益和项目集组件；

    ■收益实现标准；

    ■实现战略目标；

    ■分析和更新收益实现计划；

    ■收益和治理；

    ■战略一致性；

    ■价值交付。

- 收益移交：

    ■目的；

    ■主要活动；

    ■收益移交规划；

    ■项目集收益的接收者。

- 收益维持：

    ■目的；

    ■主要活动；

    ■流程；

    ■指标；

    ■工具；

    ■规划持续维持；

    ■商业论证；

    ■分析和更新维持计划。

# 8.3　章节练习

1. Assume you are leading a consortium of four other firms. This is the second time your consortium has worked for this specific client, and it seems that the interpersonal relationships between the people on your team and the client's team are positive, and there is trust between the two groups. You hope for future business with this consortium and this client once your program is complete. Your success is measured primarily according to_____

A. Payback period

B. Sustainment of benefits

C. Products delivered according to specification

D. Products delivered on time and without the need for additional funding

1. 假设你负责一家包括 4 个公司的联盟。这是联盟第二次为一个特别客户服务，团队成员与客户团队的人际关系不错，互相信任。你希望在项目集结束后，还能获得这家客户将来的业务。可以依据以下标准来衡量你的成功_____

A. 回收期

B. 收益维持

C. 按规格交付产品

D. 产品按时交付，没有追加资金的必要

2. As you lead this consortium, XYZ, in its program work for company DEF, you have a large team and a large number of stakeholders. Since the consortium is of interest to the senior executives of all four firms, you and your core team seem to be in constant meetings and briefings with the executives and submitting reports to them, not to mention the meetings and briefings with the points of contact in company DEF. The person who is ultimately responsible for delivering the program benefits is_____

A. The program director

B. Your Chief Executive Officer, since your firm leads the consortium

C. The consortium program manager

D. The program sponsor

2. 你领导 XYZ 联盟为 DEF 公司项目集工作，团队规模大，相关方众多。4 家公司的高级总监对该联盟感兴趣，你和核心团队与他们定期开会并汇报情况，也与 DEF 公司联系人开会和报告。最终负责项目集收益交付的人是_____

A. 项目集总监

B. 公司 DEF 首席执行官，因为你的公司对联盟负有领导职责

C. 联盟项目集经理

D. 项目集发起人

3. Working on the next generation of computing since Cloud computing, as the program manager for the G6 program, you believe you have a major innovative, new development product. You are developing this new product for a client, firm MNO, and now you are at a point in your program where one of the projects in this G6 program is complete. You are delivering it to the MNO client representative, who wants to measure now how this benefit has helped MNO. Measuring benefits should focus on_____

A. The degree to which the benefit has been adopted and used by its intended recipients

B. The level of customer satisfaction achieved, as measured by specific surveys

C. The ability of benefits to translate into value

D. The morale of the individual employees who are responsible for executing the new process or operation

3. 你是 G6 项目集经理，项目集目标是云计算的下一代运算平台。你觉得你们新开发的产品具有创新性。产品的客户是 MNO 公司，目前项目集中某个项目刚刚完成，你们正将产品交付给 MNO 客户代表。客户代表打算对收益进行评估，了解产品如何给 MNO

带来益处。测量收益应该侧重在_____

A. 受众群的收益应用度

B. 经调查所获得的客户满意度

C. 收益转换成价值的能力

D. 负责执行新流程的员工士气

4. In your work on the G6 program, which was set up with eight separate projects, since each project in it has inter-relationships with other projects especially in terms of the benefits to be delivered, you decided one best practice to follow was to track the benefits described in your benefit realization plan in a benefit register and make this register visible not only to your entire team but also to your client, firm MNO. In terms of the program benefit management life cycle, this register ends when_____

A. Benefits are delivered incrementally

B. Benefits are transferred to product support

C. Benefits planning is completed

D. The program is terminated

4. G6 项目集包括 8 个子项目，每个子项目之间有着相互关联，特别是在收益方面有很大关联度。你认为将收益计划所述收益记录在收益登记册中，进行跟踪，并让整个团队和客户 MNO 公司能查看，是个不错的做法。从项目集收益管理周期的角度来看，以下什么时候，可以认为这份收益登记册完成了它的使命_____

A. 收益得到持续交付

B. 收益转移给了产品支持部门

C. 收益规划完成

D. 项目集被终止

5. Assume you prepared a benefits register for use on your program. You decide to review it with your key stakeholders to_____

A. Obtain buy in to begin developing the benefits realization plan

B. Determine if benefit achievement is occurring within key parameters

C. Define and approve key performance indicators

D. Determine how best to transition benefits to operations

5. 假设你为项目集制定了收益登记册。你打算与主要相关方审查该收益登记册，以_____

A. 争取启动制订收益实现计划的支持

B. 判断收益实现是否处于关键参数的范围内

C. 确定并审批关键绩效指标（KPI）

D. 确定如何最佳实现从收益到运营的转移

6. Working on your personal helicopter program for company BCD, one of your first tasks as the program manager was to build on the benefits identified and recorded in the benefit register and prepare a benefits realization plan. Now, you are measuring how each benefit is realized, which means you are working in_____

A. Benefits management
B. Executing
C. Monitoring and controlling
D. Benefits delivery

6. 你是 BCD 公司私人直升机项目集经理，你的首要任务之一是识别收益，记录在收益登记册中，并制订收益实现计划。你正在评估每项收益该如何实现，这意味着你正在做_____

A. 收益管理
B. 执行
C. 监督和控制
D. 收益交付

7. Finally, your program, G6, which has taken the concept of Cloud computing to the next level, and your eight separate projects as well as some ongoing work, is complete. As program G6 is closed, now benefit management is focusing on a number of key initiatives, including_____

A. Reporting planned versus actual benefits at the current point in time
B. Ensuring that the benefits delivered are in line with the original business case
C. Ensuring stakeholder agreement on the factors contributing to the benefits
D. Verifying the program has met or exceeded benefit realization criteria

7. 最终，G6 项目集将云计算概念推进到了下一层次，并且 8 个子项目也顺利完成。G6 项目集结束，现在收益管理的重心是一系列关键创新，它们包括_____

A. 报告当前时刻的收益计划值与实际收益的对比
B. 确保收益交付与最初商业论证一致
C. 确保相关方同意那些对收益有贡献的因素
D. 核实项目集达到或者超出收益实现标准

8. Your Governance Board decided to conduct a benefits review on your internal program. During such a review, it is important to analyze_____

A. Reasons for any deviation in the proposed benefits and the ones that were realized
B. How new benefits affect the flow of operations
C. The effectiveness of the transition plan
D. Usefulness of the benefit reports to stakeholders

8. 治理委员会决定对你所负责的内部项目集的收益进行评估。在评估过程中，分析以下哪项是非常重要的_____

A. 计划收益与实现收益差异的原因
B. 新收益将如何影响运营流程
C. 转移计划得有效性
D. 收益报告对相关方的有用性

9. You are the Business Change Manager on a mobile workforce initiative to decrease the costs associated with office space. As a result of this initiative, 2,000 employees now work in their homes, thereby saving the company millions per year in lease fees. Assume you are working to transition the benefits of your program. A key activity is to_____

A. Dispose resources

B. Plan for behavioral changes necessary for the at home employees

C. Monitor performance to evaluate productivity improvements

D. Monitor the need for logistical support for the at home employees

9. 你是某移动办公项目的商业变更经理，目标在于降低办公场所成本。最终，2 000 名员工在家办公，因此每年为公司节省了上百万的租金成本。如果你正在做项目集收益转换，那么你的一项重要工作是_____

A. 遣散资源

B. 在家办公的员工所需的行为变化计划

C. 监督绩效以评估生产率的提高

D. 监督在家办公的员工对后勤支持的需求

10. You have been appointed program manager for Program XYZ. You have assembled your team and have begun work on your benefits realization plan. The person who wrote the plan delivered it to you. After you read it, you told the team member that the plan was missing a key component. It did not describe_____

A. How the potential impact of any planned program change affects the benefits outcome

B. A method to identify interdependencies of benefits within program components

C. A way to link the outputs to the planned program outcomes

D. An assessment of the value and organizational impact of the program

10. 你被任命为 XYZ 项目集经理。你召集了团队进行价值实现计划。负责人做完了计划并发给了你。你读完计划后，告诉团队计划中缺失了一项重要的部分。它没有描述_____

A. 规划的项目集变更是如何潜在影响收益成果的

B. 识别项目集组件收益依赖关系的方法

C. 将规划的项目集产出与输出联系起来的方法

D. 项目集价值及其对组织带来影响的评估

11. Assume you are the program manager for the next generation of parachutes for your Department of the Army. Each of the new parachutes must have a reliability rating of 99.99%, and certain types of parachutes will be deployed in certain conditions given climate and terrain. In total, your program has five projects; all work is to be done in three years. As you regularly report on the status of the benefits of this program, you must measure the benefits that have accrued to date and communicate the information to your program sponsor and the program Governance

Board.　The metrics and procedures you are using for this reporting are stated in_____

A. Program charter
B. Benefits realization plan
C. Program management plan
D. Key performance indicators

11. 假设你是一名项目集经理，制造军方的下一代降落伞。每把降落伞需要有 99.99% 的可靠度，对于某些确定型号的降落伞，还需要在特定的气候和地理条件区域使用。项目集共有 5 个项目，所有的工作需要在 3 年内完成。因为定期汇报项目集收益情况的需要，你需要及时了解截止收益，并向项目集发起人及治理委员会汇报。在报告中，你所采用的指标和过程应该在哪里描述_____

A. 项目集章程
B. 收益实现计划
C. 项目集管理计划
D. 关键绩效指标

12. Assume your government is in serious financial difficulty and may even default on some government issued funds. However, you are managing a program to cut the spending of the National Park Service in your Department of Interior by 50%. You and your team have seven projects in your program. Finally, you have completed this program and have made the spending cuts, which were approved by the Secretary of the Interior. Now that the program is closed, benefits sustainment focuses on a number of key initiatives including_____

A. Facilitating the ongoing realization of benefits

B. Ensuring that the benefits delivered are in line with the business case

C. Reviewing the operational and program process documentation for needed updates

D. Ensuring the capabilities provided continue

12. 假设你的政府面临严重财务困境，甚至会拖欠政府发行的基金。但是，你在负责一个项目集，目标是削减 50%国家公园服务内务部的花费。项目集有 7 个子项目。最后项目集完成了，削减了成本，并获得内务秘书的批准。现在项目集面临结尾，收益持续化可以侧重_____

A. 促使收益的持续实现

B. 确保交付的收益与商业论证一致

C. 审查运营和所需的项目集过程文档的更新

D. 确保提供的能力持续

13. Working in your processed cheese company, project management has been successfully introduced over the past seven years. A member of your PMO recently attained her PgMP®. She has recommended that a new initiative to modernize the process cheese factory be managed as a program because it is so complex and will have a number of projects associated with it that have interdependencies. She needs to_____

A. Follow a repeatable process
B. Identify and qualify benefits
C. Quantify benefits in the business case
D. Focuses first on benefits realization

13. 你在一家奶酪生产公司工作，在过去的 7 年中，项目管理方法得到很好的应用。你的 PMO 团队中某人刚获得 PgMP®证书。她认为目前奶酪生产过程工厂过于复杂，推荐对奶酪生产过程工厂进行现代化改造，并采用项目集方式来对改造进行管理。项目集将包括一批项目，相互间有依赖。因此，她必须_____

A. 遵循重复流程      B. 识别和定性收益

C. 量化商业论证中的收益      D. 首先侧重收益实现

14. Because a program is responsible for delivering benefits to the organization, the program manager, members of the program team, project managers and team members, and other program stakeholders all have key roles and responsibilities in benefits management. These roles are set forth in the_____

A. Benefits register      B. Benefits realization plan

C. Benefits management plan      D. Responsibility assignment matrix

14. 项目集目的在于为组织产生收益。项目集经理，团队中的项目经理和成员，以及其他项目集相关方，都担任着很重要的角色，并承担收益管理中所述的一定职责。这些角色在以下哪个文档中描述_____

A. 收益登记册      B. 收益实现计划

C. 收益管理计划      D. 职责分配矩阵

15. As the manager of a new program to develop the next- generation heating, ventilation, and air-conditioning (HVAC) system, you have three projects in your program, and it is only the first year. You expect the program to last at least three years, and you are hopeful you will have a PMO for support. You also are sure more projects will be added as the program ensues. Therefore, you establish a process to monitor your program benefits. Following the standard benefits management life cycle, you develop this process during the_____

A. Benefits identification      B. Benefits analysis and planning

C. Benefits realization      D. Benefits delivery

15. 你是一个新项目集的经理，目标在于开发新一代制热和空调（HVAC）系统。它包括 3 个子项目，目前正处于第一年。你期望项目集至少持续 3 年，也希望有一个 PMO 来支持。你相信将来会有新项目加入。因此，你设置了一套过程来监控项目集收益。根据标准的收益管理全过程要求，你通过以下哪个步骤来设置收益管理流程_____

A. 收益识别      B. 收益分析和规划

C. 收益实现      D. 收益交付

16. As you move to establish program management in your processed cheese company, you are facing a lot of questions especially from project managers and the other members of the PMO since this is a culture change from the organization. A first step is to_____

A. Define program critical success factors

B. Meet with key stakeholders

C. Establish processes for benefits realization

D. Set up individual project deliverables to ensure that they align with organizational objectives

16. 你正要为奶酪公司建立项目集管理。因为你的行动将改变公司文化，对此，很多人提出质疑，特别是项目集经理和其他 PMO 团队成员。第一步，你应该_____

A. 制定项目集成功因素

B. 与关键相关方会面

C. 确立收益实现流程

D. 建立单个项目交付标准，确保项目集与组织目标保持一致

17. Assume you have just completed a program to design and develop a new Park for your City of 10,000 people. The purpose was to provide benefits to the residents of all ages. You are working to transition the benefits from your program to your City. It Is important to recognize as you do so that these activities are_____

A. One part of program transition

B. Updated in the program roadmap

C. Ones that ensure benefit sustainment

D. Monitored to ensure the benefits provided are those expected

17. 假设你刚完成一个项目集，为你所在的 10 000 城市人口设计和开发新的公园。它的目标是为各种年龄的市民带来收益。你正在将项目集收益移交给城市。在移交工作中，识别以下哪类活动是非常重要的_____

A. 项目集移交的一部分

B. 在项目集路线图中更新

C. 确保收益维持

D. 监督以确保所提供的收益符合预期

18. You are the program manager for a six-year program that is in its second year. You are in the early phases and are working to identify your benefits. A best practice is to prepare a benefits register using the_____

A. Identified and qualified benefits

B. Business case

C. Program's key performance indicators

D. Target dates in the roadmap for benefit achievement

18. 你是一个为期 6 年的项目集的经理，目前处于项目集第二年。在该阶段的早期，你正在为识别收益努力。一次最佳实践是，采用以下哪项来准备一份收益登记册_____

A. 识别和定性收益　　　　　　　　B. 商业论证

C. 项目集的关键绩效指标　　　　D. 收益实现路线图的目标日期

19. Your company is a leader in the pharmaceutical industry. It has received approval from the Food and Drug Administration (FDA) for a new drug that will cure all glaucoma conditions. Although the demand for this product is high, the company has many other drugs to manufacture. You are managing a program to upgrade the manufacturing process. Because you recognize the potential benefits associated with this new product, as the program manager, you should regularly monitor the_____

A. Organizational environment

B. Benefits realization plan

C. Benefits register

D. Extent to which each benefit is achieved prior to program closure

19. 你所服务的公司是一家医药行业领头企业。它获得了食品药品监督局（FDA）对治愈青光眼新药的批准。市场对该新药的需求很大，但是公司还需要生产很多其他药品。你正管理一个项目集，来升级现有生产流程。你意识到了新产品能带来的潜在收益，作为项目集经理，你需要定期监控_____

A. 组织环境

B. 收益实现计划

C. 收益登记册

D. 项目集收尾前，每项收益所实现的程度

20. You have worked hard on your four year program. As it is about to close you want to execute your sustainment plan. It is prepared_____

A. During the performance of the program

B. As a subsidiary plan to the program management plan

C. As part of the benefit realization plan

D. As an activity in benefit transition

20. 你正在为为期 4 年的项目集努力。项目集将要完成，你打算执行维持计划。该计划是_____

A. 在项目集运行期间准备

B. 作为项目集管理计划的附属计划

C. 收益实现计划的一部分

D. 收益移交活动

# 8.4　章节练习参考答案

1. B 虽然所有选项可以衡量成功，项目集设置的目的在于，获得比项目集中项目独

立运营产生收益之和还要高的收益。这些收益在收益实现计划中进行描述，并在项目集收尾时，通过维持的收益实现来衡量。

2. D 项目集发起人是倡导该项目集提议，对所需资源提供支持，并对最终交付收益负责的组织或个人。

3. C 价值交付是收益交付的核心。价值交付关注项目集产生收益，并转化为价值。实现计划收益的机会可能很小，项目集经理、治理委员会成员，以及其他相关方需要确保能抓住这样的机会。

4. D 项目集可能会在没有完成到运营的转化之前终止。特别是当项目集章程得到实现，运营不在收益实现考虑的范围，或者项目集不再对组织有益的情况下，项目集可能提前终止。每个子项目与项目集，作为一个成体，需要是可用的。

5. C 在收益分析规划阶段，更新收益的登记册。收益登记册需要经过相关方的审查，来制定批准关键的项目集指标，以及其他监控项目集绩效的手段。

6. D 在收益交付阶段，重点需要确保项目集交付了在收益实现计划中所描述的预期收益。这还包括为相关方准备一系列报告或指标，用来监督项目集及其相应活动，以确保收益得到成功交付。

7. D 在收益转换阶段，收益向运营转化，并能在转化后保持持续性。一项关键活动是，合适项目集集成、移交，以及收尾达到或者超出收益实现标准，完成项目集战略目标。

8. B 对于内部项目集，收益实现过程衡量了新的收益如何影响组织运营流程。重点是检查变更是如何引入的，以及如何最小化那些因为引入变更所带来的负面影响和潜在干扰。

9. A 收益转化的一项关键活动是，在项目集完成并和其他项目集整合时，释放所有相关资源。

10. C 收益实现计划中有些部分很关键，它们在收益实现计划规划时得到确定。其中之一是，将输出与计划项目集产出关联起来，作为项目集收益规划的一部分。

11. B 收益实现计划在项目集最初阶段草拟，并在项目集所有阶段进行维护。在所有其他事情中，该计划定义了衡量指标，包括关键绩效指标和衡量收益的过程。

12. D 收益维持过程包括一系列活动，其中之一是实施相应变更，确保项目集所带来的能力，在项目集结束并且资源释放之后，还能继续使用。

13. B 收益识别的目的在于分析组织可用信息和商业收益、内部外部影响，以及项目集源动力。这可以通过识别和定性相关方期望项目集能实现的收益来达到。

14. B 收益实现计划中关键的一个部分是，收益管理中对于角色和职责的描述。

15. D 收益监督在收益交付过程中确立，包括监控组件、维护收益登记册，以及汇报收益。

16. A 在收益识别中，项目集经理使用项目集必要和商业步骤。通常首要的关键活动是，确定项目集目标和关键绩效指标。

17. A 收益移交规划非常重要，但它们仅是全部移交过程的一部分。

18. B 收益登记册的制定以商业论证、战略计划和其他相关项目集目标为基础。

19. A 收益交付的主要活动之一是监督组织环境，包括内部和外部因素。它的目标是确保项目集与组织战略目标相一致。

20. A 项目集的持续维持不能等到项目集收尾时才考虑。项目集收益维持由项目集经理和项目经理来规划，并贯穿项目集运行全过程。

# 第9章

## 相关方管理

在 PgMP® 考试中，相关方管理的考题占比 16%，约 27 道题。重点考查在整个项目集生命周期中，对相关方识别、管理、争取重要性的理解。

## 9.1 秘笈要点

本章强调相关方与有效沟通之间的关联，因为沟通力是项目集经理的关键能力之一。项目集过程中，项目集经理大部分的时间要用于与项目集不同相关方的沟通。因此，另一些考题要点是关注沟通规划，以及以恰当的方式、恰当的频率、恰当的详略程度将信息传达给相关方。

整个项目集生命周期的不同阶段，相关方对项目集有不同程度的影响和兴趣度。因此，相关方分析必不可少且持续进行。项目集经理和团队核心成员必须同相关方一起努力工作，以赢得他们对项目集的信心，这些相关方不仅仅是项目集发起人。相关方矩阵是项目集中一个非常有用且需持续维护的工具。

相关方参与对项目集的成功至关重要，这是一种维持项目集可见性的方法。因此，定义并提供针对不同类型的相关方沟通需求，也将提升他们对项目集的支持度。

虽然考试大纲将这一知识领域命名为相关方管理，但在项目集管理标准中，这一知识领域叫作相关方参与。标准认为，项目集相关方不能管理，但相关方的期望值可以被管理。这一领域的标准有 3 个关键活动：项目集相关方识别、相关方参与计划和相关方参与。从标准中可以看出，支持过程中，项目集沟通管理是另一个要点，其中包含沟通规划和信息分发。

## 9.2 重要考点

1. 相关方管理的重要性
- 相关方定义；
- 相关方分类——内部和外部；
- 客户参与管理；
- 桥接当前状态与将来状态的差距；
- 组织变革的必要性。

2. 项目集相关方识别
- 识别项目集相关方；
- 相关方类型；
- 相关方登记册；
- 相关方矩阵；
- 相关方分析；
- 相关方优先级排序列表。

3. 相关方参与规划
- 收集相关方相关信息；
- 相关方参与计划；
- 相关方支持的谈判；
- 相关方参与活动的绩效测量指标；
- 组件指南。

4. 相关方参与
- 确保相关方充分且恰当地参与；
- 产生和维持项目集的可视性；
- 确认相关方支持；
- 相关方评估识别的风险；
- 发展和培养相关方间的关系；
- 捕捉问题和信息；
- 使用沟通、谈判和解决冲突的技能；
- 使用问题日志；
- 优先级机制；
- 解决问题和顾虑；
- 相关方指标。

5. 项目集沟通管理
- 与项目沟通管理的区别；

- 沟通技能；
- 影响技能。

6.　沟通规划
- 确定相关方信息和沟通需要；
- 定义沟通需求；
- 语言和文化差异；
- 虚拟团队；
- 沟通方式；
- 项目集沟通计划。

7.　信息发布
- 提供给相关方及时准确的信息；
- 信息渠道；
- 信息状态；
- 变更请求通知；
- 预算信息——内部和外部；
- 政府和监管机构备案；
- 公告和新闻发布；
- 媒体信息和收益更新；
- 沟通方式的类型。

8.　沟通考虑因素
- 沟通和呈现技能；
- 定义和记录沟通需求的策略。

9.　信息收集和检索系统
- 不同媒体；
- 数据库使用；
- 存储和检索系统。

10.　信息发布方法
- 与相关方及时沟通所需信息；
- 面对面会议；
- 电子通信和网络会议工具；
- 电子系统管理工具；
- 社交媒体；
- 非正式沟通；
- 在项目集控制下保留信息。

11. 经验教训数据库

- 获取经验教训；
- 借鉴经验教训来制订沟通管理计划；
- 更新经验教训；
- 项目管理信息系统（PMIS）；
- 数据归档和检索指令。

12. 项目集绩效报告

- 提供资源利用信息以交付收益；
- 双向沟通；
- 使用信息发布。

# 9.3 章节练习

1. As the program manager to develop a new source of energy that can be used in the northern and southern hemispheres when solar power is not readily available, you have a large number of stakeholders, both internal and external. You also are working with a virtual team, and many team members represent different cultures. You recognize since you are the program manager the importance of keeping all of your stakeholders informed in a timely manner by distributing various types of information. One piece of information that stakeholders need but that is often overlooked by program managers is a_____

A. Receipt of proposals

B. Notification of responses to change requests

C. List of preventive actions

D. Record of training

1. 作为项目集经理，你正在开发一种新能源来源，可以在南北半球太阳能发电不便时使用。该项目集包含大量的内部和外部相关方。你带领的是一个虚拟团队，许多团队成员有不同的文化背景。你意识到，持续及时地且用不同方式来告知所有项目相关方相关信息是很重要的。以下属于相关方需要，但往往被项目集经理忽视的信息是_____

A. 接收的提案
B. 变更请求的响应通知
C. 预防行动清单
D. 培训记录

2. You are working on a complex five-year program that has a minimum of four projects under way at any given time. A major scope change to Project L has resulted in a need to rebaseline its schedule. Consequently, because of dependencies with Project L, Project D also had to revise its schedule. You have informed your Governance Board and key stakeholders about the revisions. Some stakeholders have asked questions regarding the rebaselining. Your

next step is to_____

A. Capture and publish questions and answers

B. Ask the project managers to meet with their key stakeholders

C. Hold meetings with key stakeholder groups to listen to their concerns an answer questions

D. Follow your defined communications strategy

2. 你负责一个复杂的、时跨 5 年的项目集，在任何时间至少有 4 个项目并行。项目 L 的重大范围变更需要重新规划项目进度基准。由于项目 D 与项目 L 存在依赖关系，项目 D 也必须同步修改项目计划。你将此情况通知了项目治理委员会和与变更相关的关键相关方。一些相关方很关心重新设定的项目基准。下一步你将_____

A. 采集和发布问题和答案

B. 让项目经理们与他们的项目相关方会面

C. 与关键相关方群组召开会议，倾听他们关注的问题并回答

D. 按照先前定义的沟通策略

3. The president of your company has selected you to be the head of all elearning and has asked that you launch a program to develop new media for delivering your company's content. The program has a number of stakeholders, some of whom are supportive and some of whom are skeptical, and you anticipate many debates concerning the program's objectives. As the program manager, you recognize that you need to rely on_____

A. Leadership skills

B. Conflict resolution skills

C. Environmental awareness skills

D. Diplomatic skills

3. 公司总裁任命你负责一个项目集并作为在线学习的总负责人，其目的是开发新媒体，并将公司内容发布上去。此项目集有众多相关方，其中一些人持支持态度，而另一些人持怀疑态度，你预见到许多关于该项目集目标的辩论。作为项目集经理，你意识到需要依靠_____

A. 领导力技能　　　　　　B. 解决冲突技能

C. 环境感知技能　　　　　D. 外交技能

4. As program manager for all elearning in your company, BBB, you are launching your program to develop new media for delivering your company's course content. You have a diverse group of stakeholders, and your program has active involvement by BBB's Chief Executive Officer. As the program manager, you must ensure the performance data on your elearning program are consolidated and routed to the intended recipients to provide a clear picture of overall program performance and especially to show how resources, which already

are constrained in BBB, are being used effectively. This is done through_____

    A. Targeted communications messaging

    B. Information distribution

    C. Program performance and status reports prepared in reporting program performance

    D. Stakeholder engagement as identified in the stakeholder management strategy

4. 作为公司负责所有在线学习的 BBB 项目集经理，你正在将公司内容发布到新媒体上。你有群体迥异的相关方，并且公司 CEO 也积极参与其中。作为项目集经理，你必须确保整合你的在线学习项目集绩效数据，并向数据接收者提供整体项目集绩效的清晰画面，尤其要显示在项目集 BBB 中的资源是如何有效利用的。这样做是通过_____

    A. 定向沟通消息

    B. 信息发布

    C. 在报告项目集绩效过程所准备的项目集绩效和状态报告

    D. 在相关方管理战略中所确定的相关方参与过程

5. As the program manager to develop a new source of energy that can be used in the northern and southern hemispheres when solar power is not readily available, you have a large number of stakeholders, both internal and external. You also are working with a virtual team, and many team members represent different cultures. You have eight projects so far in your program and are in the planning phase. This means in regard to project and program communications with your stakeholders you should be_____

    A. Determining who needs to be receiving the communications and when

    B. Distributing communications messages to stakeholders

    C. Implementing the feedback loops developed earlier in the program

    D. Building your communications infrastructure

5. 作为项目集经理，你正在开发一种新能源来源，在南北半球太阳能发电不便时使用。该项目集包含大量的内外部相关方。你带领的是一个虚拟团队，许多团队成员有着不同的文化背景。你迄今为止共有 8 个项目，它们都处于计划阶段，这意味着在项目和项目集与相关方沟通上，你应该_____

    A. 确定谁以及何时需要接受沟通信息    B. 向相关方发布沟通信息

    C. 实施项目集中早期形成的反馈环    D. 搭建沟通基础结构

6. On your program, you have identified over 50 internal and external stakeholders, and have three projects in your program. You are providing regular updates on the status and specific requirements of your program to these stakeholders. A key focus in performance reporting is information on_____

    A. Cost and schedule status

    B. Use of resources to deliver program benefits

C.　Issues to be discussed at program Governance Board meetings for decisions to move to the next phase

D.　Activities to determine whether specific work results have been completed

6.　在你负责的项目集中，你已经识别了超过 50 个内外部相关方，而且项目集包含 3 个项目。你定期向相关方提供更新的项目集状态和具体需求。在绩效报告中的关键点是_____

A.　成本和进度状态

B.　使用资源以交付收益

C.　在项目集治理委员会上有待讨论的，决定是否能进入下一阶段的问题

D.　确定具体工作成果是否完成的活动

7.　Meeting stakeholder expectations is vital to program success; therefore, participation of stakeholders must be monitored to ensure that their expectations are met. You are managing a large program with diverse stakeholder groups. On this program, you have found that you often need to_____

A.　Meet one-on-one with each of the 200 stakeholders on the program

B.　Facilitate negotiation sessions between stakeholders

C.　Have your Enterprise Program Management Office (EPMO) take over responsibility for stakeholder expectations management

D.　Use your stakeholder analysis chart as a key tool and technique to assist in managing expectations

7.　满足相关方期望对项目集成功至关重要，因此必须监督相关方的参与，以确保其期望得到满足。你正在管理一个有着不同相关方群体的大型项目集。在该项目集中，你发现经常需要_____

A.　与项目集 200 个相关方的每个人都会面

B.　协调相关方之间的谈判会议

C.　让企业项目管理办公室（EPMO）接管并负责相关方期望管理

D.　将相关方分析图表作为关键的工具和技术，以协助管理相关方期望

8.　You have been managing a complex and major program in your company, BBB. Your program has 11 separate contracts and also two projects using in-house resources. Your team is a virtual, and because of budget constraints, you could not have a face-to-face meeting. Because of the large number of stakeholders to best address the urgency of their issues, you decide to_____

A.　Hold a focus group

B.　Set up a prioritization mechanism

C.　Conduct an impact analysis

D.　Determine the frequency and rate of communications on the program

8.　你负责公司一个复杂、重大的项目集 BBB。该项目集共有 11 个独立合同，其中 2

个项目使用内部资源。因预算经费有限，团队是虚拟团队，所以无法面对面会议。因为有大量的相关方需要以最佳的方式来解决他们的迫切问题，你决定_____

    A. 召集焦点小组           B. 建立优先级机制

    C. 进行影响分析           D. 确定项目集的沟通频率和速度

9. You are now conducting a phase-gate review with your Governance Board to determine if you can close the program. You and two of the Board members, who are not in the CEO's inner circle, are having a disagreement as to whether the phase has been completed successfully, and your program can now advance to the closing process. One way this can be determined is to_____

    A. Take a vote of the members of the program board

    B. Compare performance to date against the exit criteria for the phase

    C. Try to reach consensus among all stakeholders

    D. Use fact-based decision making

9. 你正在与治理委员会一起进行阶段关口审查，以确定是否可以收尾项目集。两个董事会成员（这两人均不是 CEO 身边的核心人物）在当前阶段是否已成功完成，以及项目集是否可以提前进入收尾过程方面存在分歧。以下哪个方法可对上述情况做决定_____

    A. 项目集委员会成员投票决定

    B. 对阶段的退出标准的绩效进行比较

    C. 尝试在所有相关方之间达成共识

    D. 基于事实的决策

10. In the most recent program performance meeting as part of the program closeout phase, you reported that the earned value data were favorable, that all performance metrics were in line with stated criteria, and that stakeholder requirements were met. Yet several stakeholders reported that the program fell somewhat short of their expectations. You assert that the program is successful because it has met all objective criteria. Your assessment is_____

    A. Incorrect. Expectations are as important as requirements

    B. Incorrect. Although expectations should be considered, they are not as important as requirements

    C. Correct. There is no difference between expectations and requirements

    D. Correct. The stakeholders should have expressed their expectations as requirements during the requirements-gathering phase

10. 在最近一次的作为收尾阶段一部分的项目集绩效会议上，你报告挣值数据是良好的，所有绩效指标与规定标准一致，满足相关方需求。然而，一些相关方报告说该项目集未满足他们的期望值。你断言该项目集是成功的，因为它符合所有既定客观标准。你的评价是_____

    A. 不正确。相关方期望值同需求一样重要

B. 不正确。虽然期望值应该被考虑，但他们并没有需求的重要

C. 正确。期望值和需求之间没有区别

D. 正确。相关方应当在需求收集阶段表达他们的期望需求

11. Recently, your City has been experiencing numerous power outages because of excessive heavy rainfall and numerous hurricanes. Many residents have purchased gas generators, but they tend to not last long enough so people are also purchasing generators that use propane. Your propane company has decided that it should set up a program that would be put in place to use natural gas instead. You are the manager for this program. You also have a large number of interested stakeholders, and they are monitoring your progress to see if this new natural gas approach will be ready before the next hurricane season. Your goal is to_____

A. Assess the degree to which the program satisfies needs and benefits

B. Set clear stakeholder engagement goals

C. Work to turn stakeholders who are negative about the program to be positive or at least neutral to it

D. Communicate actively to your stakeholders as to your progress and your program's benefits

11. 最近，你所在的城市因为大暴雨和长时间的飓风，已经历了无数次的停电。许多居民购买了天然气发电机，但往往并不能持续使用很长时间。他们也同时买了使用丙烷的发电机。你所在的丙烷公司已决定启动一个项目集，提供替代的天然气使用方案。你是该项目集经理。项目集有大量具有利益关系的相关方，他们正在监督项目集的进展，从而看这种新的天然气方法在下一个飓风季节前是否能准备好。你的目标是_____

A. 评估项目集满足需求和收益的程度

B. 设置相关方参与的清晰目标

C. 务求使得对项目集持消极态度的相关方转化为积极的，或至少是中立态度

D. 积极主动地与相关方沟通当前项目集的进展和收益

12. You are the program manager on a highly controversial e-mail retention program for your company, AEI. More than 75 percent of the people in AEI are opposed to the program because they realize all of their e-mail messages will be archived. AEI management has informed everyone someone will review each e-mail to make sure it pertains to company business and is not a personal one. All e-mails are to be written in a professional way and must be ethical. You now have many conflicts as you and your team execute the five projects in your program. This program represents a major culture change for AEI as in the past it was common to discuss anything with anyone. Generally accepted methods of organizational change management are required for this program, and the person in charge of this change is_____

A. The program director               B. The program sponsor

C. The program Governance Board　　D. You, the program manager

12. 你是一个备受争议的"电子邮件保留"的项目集经理，服务于 AEI 公司。超过75%的人对此项目集持反对态度，因为他们认为自己所有的电子邮件都将被存档。AEI 管理层通知大家会审查每一个电子邮件，决定其属于公司业务还是私人邮件。所有的电子邮件都必须以专业格式书写，且须符合职业道德的。现在存在许多冲突，因为你和你的团队正在该项目集中执行 5 个项目。该项目集是一项重要的文化变革，因为在过去随便与任何人讨论什么事都可以。通常情况下，对该项目集需要结合组织变革管理的方法，那么负责该变革的人最好是_____

A. 项目集总监　　　　　　　　B. 项目集发起人
C. 项目集治理委员会　　　　　D. 你，项目集经理

13. As a program manager, you recognize the importance of stakeholder engagement. To support your efforts, especially with key stakeholders whose displeasure might hinder the program's success, you prepare a stakeholder engagement plan You know that stakeholders must see the benefits of the program. Therefore, you need to have strong skills in_____

A. Strategic planning　　　　　B. Leadership
C. Enterprise resource management　　D. Customer relationship management

13. 作为一个项目集经理，你意识到相关方参与的重要性。为了让相关方能支持你的工作（特别是哪些可能对此不满或阻碍项目集成功的关键相关方），你准备了一份相关方参与计划。你知道相关方要看到项目集收益。因此，你需要擅长以下哪种技能_____

A. 战略规划　　　　　　　　　B. 领导力
C. 企业资源管理　　　　　　　D. 客户关系管理

14. Each program has stakeholders. At the time you were appointed as program manager, you and your core team immediately identified 50 key stakeholders. Now the number of stakeholders has increased according to your stakeholder analysis to 88. You seem to feel as if all you do all day is communicate with stakeholders and have meetings with groups of them. As part of stakeholder engagement planning, you need to identify how the program will affect stakeholders in areas such as_____

A. The organization's culture　　B. Management of operations
C. Corporate governance　　　　D. Legal policies, standards, and regulations

14. 每个项目集都有相关方。当你被任命为项目集经理时，你和核心团队立即识别出50 个关键相关方。根据相关方分析，现在相关方的数量已增加到 88 个。你觉得，如果整天与相关方沟通，与相关方群组开大会小会的话，那么你就需要确定项目集在哪些领域如何影响相关方，并将其作为相关方参与计划的一部分_____

A. 组织文化　　　　　　　　　B. 组织管理
C. 公司治理　　　　　　　　　D. 法律政策、标准和法规

15.　When you worked as a project manager, you learned that most project managers spend about 90 percent of their time in communications. Now as a program manager you know you are spending almost 100% of your time in communications. It seems to never end.　You have set presentations now for different groups of stakeholders but then you must continually update them to show progress, and new stakeholders seem to become interested in your progress as the program ensues. Communication planning in program management therefore focuses on_____

A.　Reacting to stakeholder concerns

B.　Taking corrective actions in response to program issues

C.　Determining the information and communications needs of each stakeholder

D.　Identifying suitable technologies for distributing program information

15.　你知道，多数项目经理 90%的时间用于沟通。而现在作为一名项目集经理，你几乎将 100%的时间都用于沟通，而且好像无休无止。你向不同的相关方呈现和更新项目集进展，新的相关方似乎也对你的项目集进展感兴趣了。因此，在项目集管理的沟通计划中，应关注_____

A.　回应相关方的顾虑

B.　采取纠正措施来应对项目集问题

C.　确定信息和每个相关方的沟通需求

D.　识别发布项目集信息的合适技术

16.　You are the program manager responsible for implementing salesmagic.com, a highly complex but powerful tool for customer relationship management. You and your team have spent three days identifying the metrics against which you will measure stakeholder engagement activities. Your next step is to_____

A.　Meet with key stakeholders to gain agreement

B.　Include the metrics in the stakeholder register

C.　Test the effectiveness of the metrics through a focus group

D.　Include the metrics in the stakeholder engagement plan

16.　你是负责"魔力销售"网站的项目集经理，这是一个高度复杂、功能强大的客户关系管理工具。你和团队已经花了 3 天的时间来识别衡量相关方参与活动的指标。下一步将是_____

A.　与关键相关方会面以达成共识

B.　在相关方登记册中包含这些指标

C.　通过焦点小组测试指标有效性

D.　在相关方参与计划中包含指标

17.　You are a program manager for a city transit authority. Your program has a number of projects under way to upgrade the infrastructure to current technologies and to implement a process improvement program. The transit authority's Chief Financial Officer (CFO) has left to assume a position in a different city, and a new person has been appointed CFO. You should_____

A. Update your stakeholder inventory

B. Appoint one of your core team members to interact with the new CFO

C. Meet with the new CFO to explain the importance of the program

D. Update the stakeholder register

17. 你是一个城市交通局的项目集经理。该项目集有许多正在进行的项目，其目的是将基础设施升级为当前最新技术，并实施过程改进计划。交通局的首席财务官（CFO）已升迁为另一个城市的 CFO，一个新人被任命为 CFO。此时你应该_____

A. 更新相关方目录

B. 指派一名核心团队成员与新 CFO 互动

C. 会见新 CFO 说明该项目集的重要性

D. 更新相关方登记册

18. You are a program manager for a new line of children's toys called The Destroyer. Your stakeholders—especially the members of your program Governance Board—have requested an analysis of any opportunities that can be leveraged as you collect and analyze performance on your program. Also, you want to identify any adverse impacts that must be corrected. After you prepare this information and consolidate it, you_____

A. Meet with your key stakeholders to inform them of your program's progress according to their specific areas of interest

B. Make the information available through the information distribution activity

C. Follow the process outlined in your communications management plan

D. Contact your Governance Board about any adverse trends that require immediate action to meet the required delivery date

18. 你是一名项目集经理，负责一个名叫"驱逐舰"的新儿童玩具产品线。相关方（特别是项目集治理委员会的成员们）要求你在收集和分析项目集绩效的同时也要做机会分析，从而识别任何能利用的机会。此外，你也要识别任何必须纠正的不利影响。当你准备并整合了这些信息，你需要_____

A. 与关键相关方会面，并依据他们特定的领域兴趣告知项目集的进展

B. 通过信息发布活动，使信息随时可获取

C. 参照沟通管理计划中的过程概述

D. 联系项目集治理委员会关于任何不利趋势，需要立即采取行动，以满足所需交付日期

19. Stakeholders play a critical role in the success of a program or project. As program manager for development of a next-generation motorcycle to be available in 2030, you know it

is a best practice to determine a strategy to engage stakeholders. This should be done_____

 A. During overall program planning

 B. While the business case for the program is made

 C. As the program is being initiated

 D. After the projects and other ongoing components of the program are determined

19.　相关方对项目集或项目的成功起着至关重要的作用。作为一名开发 2030 年上市的新一代摩托车的项目集经理，你知道确定相关方参与的策略是最佳实践。这应该在何时完成_____

 A. 在整个项目集规划中

 B. 当项目集商业论证完成时

 C. 当项目集正处于启动时

 D. 在项目和其他正在进行的项目集组件确定后

20.　You are managing a program under contract with a major motion picture studio. The Statement of Work noted that you needed to interface with ten different groups of people within the studio. After your company, KSI, won this contract, you and your team recognized the importance of performing a detailed stakeholder analysis based on the Statement of Work. To conduct such an analysis, you plan to hold interviews, use focus groups, and perhaps conduct a survey. This approach enables you to_____

 A. Develop a stakeholder communications strategy

 B. Prioritize stakeholders in terms of their ability to influence the program

 C. Develop a stakeholder register

 D. Identify stakeholders'attitudes toward the program

20.　你正在负责与一家重要电影工作室客户合作的项目集。项目集工作说明书（SOW）声明，你需要在工作室与 10 个不同群组的人工作对接。当你所在的公司 KSI 赢得这份合同后，你和团队认识到基于 SOW 做详细的相关方分析是很重要的。要进行这样的分析，你计划采用访谈、焦点小组或是问卷调查的方式。这种方法能使你_____

 A. 制定相关方沟通策略

 B. 依据相关方对项目集的影响能力来进行优先级排序

 C. 创建相关方登记册

 D. 识别相关方对项目集的态度

## 9.4　章节练习参考答案

1.　C　信息发布包括项目集、项目团队的变更请求及请求响应的通知。

2.　A　使相关方参与并与相关方互动沟通是非常重要的。由于一些相关方会对项目集好奇并提问，其中一个最佳实践就是捕捉问题、回答他们，并以恰当的方式发布信息，让众多相关方从中受益。

3．B 在相关方参与中，项目集经理需要具有解决冲突技能，不同的相关方群组将对项目集产生不同的利益和影响。项目集经理必须定义如何将管理相关方之间的冲突，以及升级路径，确保不出现僵局。

4．B 信息发布的目的是向项目集相关方传递提供他们所需的状态信息和可交付成果信息。使用有效的方式为相关方提供及时和准确的信息。

5．A 作为沟通规划的一部分，确定相关方信息及沟通需要。这些需要包括：谁需要什么信息、何时需要、他们将如何接收、谁将向相关方提供信息等。

6．B 项目集绩效报告的目的是整合绩效数据，向项目集相关方提供关于收益交付的资源使用信息。这是关于项目集整体绩效的信息。

7．B 谈判技巧是项目集经理管理相关方参与必备的技能。这些技能有助于缓解相关方对项目集的反对情绪，以及影响项目集的可能收益。在大型项目集中，当项目集产生冲突，项目集经理需要协调相关方群体之间的谈判协商。

8．C 相关方问题及其关切点将涉及项目集各个方面，需要从不同层面来解决。而影响分析技术在理解相关方问题的紧迫性和可能性方面是有效的，这也决定了这些问题在项目集是否要被列为风险。

9．D 通常，尽可能使用客观衡量成功的方法，而不是依靠人们的主观意见。因此基于事实的决策是必需的，从而确保所有项目集工作的完整性和预期收益的顺利达成。相关方有相互冲突的意见时，实事求是也利于更好地决策。

10．A 相关方期望同需求一样重要。成功的项目集经理们要关注相关方期望的满足，因为相关方期望值就等同于满足他们的需求。

11．B 成功的项目集经理了解相关方参与的重要性。他们使用优秀的领导力技能，为项目集设定明确的相关方参与目标，以解决项目集过程中可能发生的变更。

12．D 项目集经理是组织变革的倡导者。每个项目集都代表了某种类型的变革，项目集经理必须与这些相关方一起克服积极变革的阻力。项目集经理必须首先期待变化，并准备管理这些。

13．B 相关方对项目集能否成功起到至关重要的作用。因为他们可以起到积极推动的作用，也可能阻碍项目集的进展，因此项目集经理需要有很强的领导力，与相关方一同推动项目集的进展。

14．A 在相关方分析和参与规划方面，组织文化和变更接受度是相关方参与计划的两个关键点。

15．C 沟通规划的重点在于清晰地定义沟通需求，以便将信息传达给每个相关方，因此就有必要确定相关信息和每个相关方的沟通需求。

16．D 相关方参与计划定义了用于衡量相关方参与活动绩效的指标。它包括会议的参与情况，诸多类型的沟通方式，以及相关方参与并达成目标的有效性等。

17．C 在项目集中，CFO 是一个重要相关方，因为项目集的资金通常都是有限的。作为一个新 CFO，他/她可能不了解这个项目集，因此项目集经理需花时间和精力与这位新 CFO 一起解决他/她关切的问题，尤其是涉及项目集收益、目标或成果相关的问题。

18．B 在报告项目集绩效过程中，绩效信息被收集、测量和整合。测量指标和趋势需要进行评估，以便不断改进。整合如何使用资源为项目集交付收益的信息，并通过信息发布活动将这些信息传达给项目集相关方，以便随时获取。

19．C 相关方是与项目集有利益相关性，或对项目集有影响的人。他们可能来自组织内部或外部，他们的期望需在项目集开始到收尾整个过程中被管理。相关方关切的问题需陈述在项目集启动过程所制定的项目集章程中，并包括初步的相关方参与策略来管理他们。

20．C 相关方登记册在相关方识别阶段就要准备。相关方分析过程将创建相关方登记册，其中包括相关方清单、相关方与项目集的关系、相关方影响项目集成果的能力、相关方的支持程度，以及其他可能影响项目集成果的相关方特征和态度。

# 项目集治理

项目集治理是项目集管理的第五个领域，考题占比 14%，约 24 道题。考试大纲中的治理就对应标准中的项目集治理领域。治理超越了项目集管理的范畴，从项目集开启时它便被批准作为项目组合管理的一部分，直到项目集收尾一直对项目集产生监督作用。

## 10.1　秘笈要点

在项目集管理中，治理结构分为以下几种类型：一种用于项目集批准，一种用于项目集的关口监督和定期进展审查，一种用于项目集经理监督项目集中的项目。这些治理委员会也常被称为指导委员会、监督委员会或董事会。无论称谓是什么，为提高效率，以及在项目集和相应的项目之间保持一致性，都需要一个明确的结构。在较小的组织内，高层管理者通常履行这个职能。其中一个最佳实践是通过项目集治理计划来描述治理委员会遵循的政策、流程、标准，以及关口审查的做法和每个关口的要求。

问题升级流程也是一个最佳实践。因为项目集经理希望把一些风险和问题升级到治理委员会以寻求解决方案，项目经理也希望通过同样的方法得到项目集经理的支持。

关键绩效指标（KPI）对测量项目集的成功非常有用，也有助于在整个生命周期中监督收益。KPI 包括风险、财务、合规性、质量、安全、和相关方满意度等方面。项目集管理信息系统有助于跟踪这些 KPI。可借鉴的一个最佳实践是定期评价新的和已有的能影响战略目标的风险，并且按照要求更新风险管理计划，提交治理委员会批准。同时，为确保项目集与组织战略目标相一致，也应实时监控商业环境。

进一步来说，我们应重点关注与项目集相关的经验教训、过程和文档相关的信息储备库或知识储备库，以支持组织的最佳实践。这些经验教训会进一步被识别和应用于支持与影响现有和将来的项目集，或者用于组织的不断改善。

## 10.2　重要考点

1. 治理的重要性

- 治理和项目集生命周期；

- 实践和程序；

- 对项目集成功的支持；

- 不同层级的治理；

- 关口审查和生命周期；

- 项目集目的与战略目的和组织目标相一致；

- 确保项目集承诺的价值得以实现，收益得以交付；

- 确保有效的相关方沟通；

- 建立遵循政策的测量指标；

- 确保项目集使用适当的工具和过程。

2. 项目集治理委员会

- 人员配置；

- 治理模型；

- 定位好委员会以解决问题和疑问；

- 单一项目集治理委员会的作用；

- 对多个治理委员会的需要。

3. 项目集治理委员会责任

- 项目集治理与组织的愿景和目的；

- 项目集批准、背书和启动；

- 项目集融资。

4. 制订项目集治理计划

- 项目集目标总结；

- 委员会结构；

- 角色和职责的定义；

- 规划的会议；

- 阶段关口评审；

- 启动、收尾或移交的标准；

- 定期健康检查；

- 问题和风险的升级过程；

- 成功标准、沟通和背书；

- 关键绩效指标；

- 批准计划和项目集的方法；

- 项目集绩效支持；
- 报告和控制过程；
- 质量标准和规划；
- 监督进展和决定变更；
- 其他决策审查；
- 批准组件启动和移交；
- 项目集收尾。

5. 项目集治理和项目集管理

- 协作关系；
- 分享的责任；
- 项目集管理标准和项目管理标准。

6. *个体治理角色*

- 项目集发起人；
- 治理委员会成员；
- 项目集经理；
- 项目经理；
- 项目集团队成员。

7. *组件治理*

- 组件治理；
- 项目集经理责任。

8. *其他治理活动*

- 项目管理办公室（PMO）；
- 项目管理信息系统（PMIS）；
- 项目集知识管理（PMKM）；
- 识别和应用经验教训；
- 审计支持；
- 评估新的和现有的风险；
- 教育和培训；
- 监督商业环境；
- 开发和支持整合计划。

# 10.3　章节练习

1. Within the Acme Bearing Company, management uses the terms project management and program management interchangeably, and there is no consistency across programs.

Furthermore, there is no executive support to facilitate issue resolution, no direction or leadership provided to program teams, and little control over work initiatives. As an external consultant, you have been asked to provide recommendations for improvement. You prepare a report with a prioritized list of actions for Acme management. Number one on your list is to establish_____

A. A portfolio management information system

B. Enterprise project management across all divisions

C. A program governance model

D. A program delivery model with supporting competencies

1. 在"顶点方位"公司，管理层混用项目管理和项目集管理这两个术语，并且在项目集之间没有一致性。另外，高层对问题的解决几乎不提供支持，对项目集团队也不提供指导和领导，因此对工作举措有微乎其微的控制力。作为一名外部咨询师，你被请来提供建议方案，改善这一情况。你准备了一份报告，按照优先级顺序列出了"顶点方位"公司应该做的工作。排在这份列表中的第一件事情是要建立_____

A. 项目组合管理信息系统

B. 横跨所有部门的企业项目管理

C. 项目集治理模型

D. 有支持能力的项目集交付模型

2. As the program manager for a new curricula of training products, you will need to work with numerous divisions within your company, many of which are located in other countries. Additionally, other projects and programs in the organization are linked to your program at various levels. Because you realize the importance of gate reviews and health checks, you need to develop a(n)_____

A. Interface management plan　　　B. Integration plan

C. Governance plan　　　D. Program roadmap

2. 你是一名项目集经理，开发培训产品的新课程。你将与公司内多个部门合作，而很多部门分布在其他国家。另外，你组织中很多其他的项目和项目集与你的项目集在各个层面都有关联。由于你意识到阶段关口评审和健康评审的重要性，你需要制定_____

A. 接口管理计划　　　B. 整合计划

C. 治理计划　　　D. 项目集路线图

3. As your organization's troubled program recovery specialist, you have been called in to take over a program that has had difficulties from the start. An initial assessment revealed that the project-level requirements had not been completed nor had those at the program level. Of course, they need to be finalized before work can be done. You also found that even though your program management methodology requires a Governance Board for a program of this

magnitude that it had been set up. You realize this is a necessity, and stage-gate reviews must be conducted. The governance processes, procedures, and templates for programs are defined and managed by the_____

A. PMO
B. Program office
C. Program manager
D. Program Governance Board

3. 作为一名组织的"问题项目集救治"专家，你被指派去接管一个起初就不顺的项目集。初步评估表明，项目集和项目级别的需求都没有完成。按理说，需求本应该在工作开始前就完备的。按照项目集管理方法论，如此大规模的项目集需要建立治理委员会。而且必须要执行阶段关口评审。项目集治理的过程、程序和模板由以下哪一个来定义和管理_____

A. 项目管理办公室
B. 项目集办公室
C. 项目集经理
D. 项目集治理委员会

4. Assume you now have a Governance Board set up for this troubled program that has had difficulties from the start. You worked with your core team and developed program-level requirements. When you inherited the program, you learned it already had three projects, so you have had your project managers define the project-level requirements succinctly. You have been working with the project managers now on overall program planning and also on planning for their projects. You are scheduled now to meet with your Governance Board in two weeks to see if you can pass Gate Review 3 and officially begin the executing process. You realize these gate reviews are a necessity to_____

A. Obtaining customer support for your work to date

B. Ensuring the customer acceptance criteria for the end products of the program will be met as planned

C. Delivering benefits according to the benefits realization plan

D. Assuring the ability to sustain program benefits in the long term

4. 假设你现在已经针对这个起初就不顺的项目集建立了治理委员会。你与核心团队一起制定出项目集层级的需求。当接手这一项目集时，你获知该项目集当前存在 3 个项目，所以你要求项目经理们简明扼要地定义项目层级的需求。你与项目经理们一起制订项目集整体规划，也一起规划项目工作。计划两周后与治理委员会一起开会，会议将决定项目集能否通过第三个关口的评审，并正式开启执行过程。你意识到阶段关口评审的必要性是_____

A. 获得客户对你目前工作的支持

B. 确保按照计划满足项目集最终产品的客户验收标准

C. 按照收益实现计划交付收益

D. 确保长期维持项目集收益的能力

5. The program Governance Board on your program is considered to be the best in the organization because of its approach to monitoring performance. Not only do its members monitor progress reports on a routine basis, but they also specifically employ the best practice of_____

A. Meeting with you quarterly to discuss status

B. Conducting client satisfaction surveys to determine whether quality is being achieved

C. Hiring an outside consultant to monitor progress reports to get an objective view

D. Providing support when changes are needed in the program's approach

5. 你所在项目集的治理委员会被认为是组织中最优秀的，因为它在监督绩效方面有非常好的方法。它不仅按照常规做监督进展报告，而且还专门采用了哪一方面的最佳实践_____

A. 与你每季度开会讨论进展情况

B. 做客户满意度调查，以决定是否达到了质量要求

C. 为获得客观的评价而聘请外部咨询师监督进展报告

D. 在项目集方法需要变更的时候提供支持

6. You have been managing a program to run the clinical trials for a new class of drugs that will forever eliminate prickly heat in the subtropics. Partway through the trials, you discovered that a competitor had already achieved regulatory approval to begin manufacturing and selling an identical class of drugs that will be sold at half the cost of the drug that you are developing. You met with your Governance Board to discuss the situation. The next step is to_____

A. Prepare a program closure recommendation

B. Conduct an audit

C. Prepare a performance report

D. Terminate the program

6. 你在管理一个为某类新药进行医疗试验的项目集，这一类药物旨在消除亚热带地区的痱子。这个试验还在进行中，你发现一个竞争对手已经获得了官方批准并且已经开始制造和销售与你完全相同的药物，且他的售价是你拟售价格的一半。你与治理委员会开会商议这一情况，下一步是_____

A. 准备项目集收尾建议　　　　B. 实施审计

C. 准备绩效报告　　　　　　　D. 结束项目集

7. You are working on a complex five-year program that has a minimum of four projects under way at any given time. A major scope change to Project L has resulted in a need to rebaseline its schedule. Consequently because of dependencies with Project L, Project D also had to revise its schedule. These two revisions required that your overall program schedule be revised as well. The program schedule change has been approved, and the program and its

components' schedules have been updated. As a result of these schedule changes, your original estimate is now totally out of date. Your program Governance Board now asks you to prepare revised_____

    A. Forecasts                  B. Estimate at completion

    C. Approach to pursue goals        D. Earned value scorecard

7. 你正在做一个复杂的、持续 5 年的项目集，该项目集任何时候都至少有 4 个项目在并行中。项目 L 的一个大的范围变更导致项目进度计划需要重新设定基准。接下来，因为项目 L 和 D 之间的依赖关系，项目 D 也不得不重新制订进度计划。这两个进度计划的变更将使得项目集整体进度计划也要变更。项目集进度计划的变更得到了批准，项目集和组件进度计划都被更新。进度计划更新的结果之一就是你原来的估算完全不适用于当前的情况。项目集治理委员会现在让你准备重新制定_____

    A. 预测                  B. 完工估算

    C. 达成目标的方法          D. 挣值计分卡

8. Finally, your program to rebuild the water desalinization plant for Haddad, Saudi Arabia is complete. You asked your Governance Board to approve a recommendation to close this program. To do so, the Board confirms that conditions warranting closure are satisfied as possibly defined in the_____

    A. Business case              B. Benefit realization plan

    C. Program charter             D. Closure procedures

8. 最终，你在沙特阿拉伯哈达德重建水处理工厂的项目集已经完成。你请治理委员会批准收尾项目集。为此，委员会需要确认保证收尾的条件是否满足，这些条件可能记录在哪一文件中_____

    A. 商业论证                B. 收益实现计划

    C. 项目集章程             D. 收尾采购

9. You are preparing for a meeting of your Governance Board. This meeting is a decision point review based on the need to_____

    A. Approve initiation of a component

    B. Confirm stakeholder satisfaction with current performance

    C. Confirm that a component has satisfied its business case

    D. Determine if benefits are being realized as stated in the benefit realization plan

9. 你正在为治理委员会的会议做准备。这个会议是一个基于什么需要的决策点审核_____

    A. 批准组件的启动

    B. 确认针对当前绩效的相关方满意度

    C. 确认组件满足了商业论证

D.　决定收益是否按照收益实现计划得以实现

10.　You are the program manager for your city's initiative to put all electrical, cable, and telephone lines underground to prevent outages during tornados and hurricanes. You have a number of subcontractors working for you, and you also have a small core team of five people. So far, you have four projects in your program, but given its complexity, you expect to have more as the program ensues. You are getting ready for a review by your Governance Board for your program. One purpose of this review is to_____

A.　Request approval to initiate another project into the program

B.　Manage the program resources

C.　Identify needed training for your program team members

D.　Prepare for an external audit by the City's Finance Director

10.　你是一名项目集经理，其举措是把城市所有的电力线、信号线和电话线都埋进地下，以防止台风和飓风带来的损失。你有很多分包商，也有一个由 5 名成员组成的小核心团队与你一起工作。项目集有 4 个项目，尽管复杂度已经比较高了，你仍期待随着项目集的推进，会有更多的项目。你准备好治理委员会对项目集开展审查。审查的目的之一是_

A.　请求批准启动另一个项目进入该项目集

B.　管理项目集资源

C.　识别项目集团队成员所需的培训

D.　准备请城市的财务部长来进行外部审计

11.　You are the program manager on a highly controversial e-mail retention program. More than 75 percent of the organization is opposed to the program because it means that all their e-mail messages will be archived and reviewed for inappropriate, unethical, or illegal statements. You know that there will be many conflicts as you and your team execute the component projects. You inform your team that, in the case of any conflict, the first point of escalation is_____

A.　The program director　　　　　　B.　The program sponsor

C.　The program Governance Board　　D.　You, the program manager

11.　你是一个备受争议的"电子邮件保留"项目集的经理，组织内 75%以上的人员反对这一项目集，因为该项目集能够让所有人的电子邮件信息都将被归档和审查以判定是否适当、符合道德和法律规定。你知道你和团队在执行组件项目的时候会有大量的冲突。你通知团队：一旦冲突产生，第一个问题升级点是_____

A.　项目集总监　　　　　　　　　　B.　项目集发起人

C.　项目集治理委员会　　　　　　　D.　你，项目集经理

12.　Although your company has been active in project management for many years, it is relatively new to program management. One of the executives knew about the usefulness of governance and stage-gate reviews from his previous work in new product development, and he recommended all programs have a Governance Board. Since the company is following the Project Management Institute's guidelines, this Governance Board approves each program's approach. To do so it_____

A. Approves the business case

B. Ensures the PMO sets up consistent process that each program follows

C. Approves the roadmap

D. Follows the governance plan

12. 尽管你的公司积极采用项目管理的方法很多年，但最近才接触项目集管理。一名高管从他之前的新产品开发工作中了解到治理与阶段关口评审的效用，所以推荐所有的项目集都要有治理委员会。因为公司遵循的是项目管理协会的指导原则，治理委员会批准每一个项目集的方法。这么做是为了_____

A. 批准商业论证

B. 确保 PMO 建立每个项目集都遵循的一致过程

C. 批准路线图

D. 遵循治理计划

13. Although your company has been active in project management for many years, it is relatively new to program management. You became certified as a PgMP® and suggested to your supervisor that two of your current projects would be better managed as a program. Your supervisor in turn met with some members of the executive team, and collectively, they realized a number of the existing projects in the company would be better handled through a program structure. One of the executives recommended all programs have a Governance Board. The recommended governance structure is stated in the_____

A. Program charter B. Program management plan

C. Benefits realization plan D. Business case

13. 尽管你的公司积极采用项目管理的方法很多年，但最近才接触项目集管理。你是 PgMP®，向你的上司建议你当前的两个项目应该作为项目集来管理会更为有效。你的上司与高层管理人员进行了逐一会谈。总的来说，他们意识到公司一些现有的项目通过项目集结构来管理会更好。其中一名高管推荐所有的项目集都要有治理委员会。这个推荐的治理结构会写进_____

A. 项目集章程 B. 项目集管理计划

C. 收益实现计划 D. 商业论证

14. Your program to develop the next-generation helium automobile has been completed. Your Governance Board suggested that audits be held throughout the program, and while you realized the audits were time consuming for you and your team, you found they were_____

A. A best practice B. An indicator of benefits realized

C. A measure of program quality  D. A way to take proactive actions

14. 你的开发下一代锂电池汽车的项目集已经完成。治理委员会建议审计应该在整个项目集过程中都要执行。而你认为，对你和团队来说，审计是一件非常耗时的工作，审计是_____

A. 最佳实践  B. 收益实现的指标

C. 项目集质量的测量指标  D. 主动开展活动的方式

15. Your program is part of a company portfolio that includes two other programs as well as three projects that are not part of any specific program. The portfolio also includes additional ongoing work. You will have a number of phase-gate reviews of your program's initiatives. These reviews will be_____

A. Carried out within the context of the corresponding portfolio

B. Held at the key go/no-go decision points of your program

C. Used to assess periodic project performance

D. Held when you request them in your role as program manager

15. 你的项目集是公司一个项目组合的一部分，这个组合里有 2 个项目集及 3 个不属于任何项目集的项目。组合也包括一些其他的日常工作。你的项目集会有不少阶段关口评审。这些评审将_____

A. 在相应项目组合的环境中执行

B. 在项目集的做/不做关键决策点上执行

C. 用于评估定期的项目绩效

D. 在你以项目集经理的身份要求的时候再执行

16. You are the program manager for a new version of a MP3 player. The players are manufactured by third-party companies operating plants in five countries. You have a project manager on site in each of these five countries and a total of seven projects in your program to date. Your company is working diligently to be the first to market with these new players as they are using the latest technology, and it differs significantly from that of the competition. You have a Governance Board for your program and it supports program success by_____

A. Ensuring goals are aligned with the strategic vision

B. Setting key performance criteria for the program and project managers

C. Setting up a PMO for direct program support

D. Establishing the benefits the program is to deliver

16. 你是一个新版本 MP3 播放器的项目集经理。这一播放器由在 5 个不同国家的第三方公司生产。你在这 5 个国家各有一名项目经理开展现场工作，目前项目集里有 7 个项目。你的公司正在为将应用最新技术的全新播放器率先推出市场而努力，这将为公司带来非常明显的竞争优势。你的项目集有治理委员会，它通过什么来保障项目集的成

功_____

    A. 确保项目集目的与战略愿景相一致

    B. 为项目集经理和项目经理设置关键绩效指标

    C. 建立项目集管理办公室，指导支持项目集

    D. 确立项目集将要交付的收益

17. You are the program manager for the development of a new slot machine for the Sand Dunes casino in Macau. Your company is using program management more frequently as it realizes the benefits associated with it but operates with a balanced matrix structure. You meet regularly with members of your Governance Board for periodic health checks, which provide the Board an opportunity to_____

    A. Formally review program performance

    B. Assess progress toward benefit realization and sustainment

    C. Focus on the phase that was just completed to determine whether the next phase should begin

    D. Review and approve required program changes

17. 你是一名项目集经理，负责为澳门金沙娱乐场开发新角子机。因为你的公司认可项目集管理的收益，所以经常使用项目集管理，其执行过程采用平衡型矩阵结构。你按期与治理委员会成员开会，执行定期的健康检查，这为委员会提供了怎样的机会_____

    A. 正式审查项目集绩效

    B. 评估在收益实现和维持方面的进展

    C. 聚焦于刚刚完成的阶段，以决定是否开始下一个阶段

    D. 审查和批准所需的项目集变更

18. You are a program manager under contract to a government agency that is responsible for issuing visas and passports. You have been working on this program for eight years and are responsible for all the information and telecommunications functions for the agency. Your company realizes this program is essential to its success, and this is the first time it has worked for this agency. Therefore, it established a Governance Board to oversee the process. You helped prepare a governance plan and a key part of it is_____

    A. A summary of the program's goals

    B. An overview of the business case

    C. Schedules for audits

    D. A description of the knowledge management system

18. 你是一名项目集经理，与某一政府机构签订了一份合同，负责发布签证和护照。你已经在此项目集中工作了 8 年，负责为此机构提供信息与电信功能。这是你公司首次为此机构工作，你的公司认为此项目集必须成功。因此，建立了治理委员会用于监督过程。

你帮助准备一份治理计划，其中一个重要的部分是_____

A．项目集目标的汇总　　　　　　B．商业论证概览

C．审计排期　　　　　　　　　　D．知识管理系统的描述

19．You are preparing for a major review by your program's Governance Board．They are especially interested in progress on Project A, because it sets the stage for two other projects．Your program control officer informs you and the Board that Project A has a pessimistic estimate of being completed within 136 days, a most likely estimate of 121 days, and an optimistic estimate of 116 days．They are concerned that the pessimistic estimate will occur and are therefore considering_____

A．Recommending that this component be terminated since it cannot meet its schedule

B．Adding resources to Project A

C．Working collaboratively with the program manager to provide support for needed changes

D．Requesting a program audit

19．你正在为项目集治理委员会的一次重要审查做准备。他们对项目集的项目 A 特别感兴趣，因为项目 A 为另两个项目搭建平台。你的项目集控制专员通知你及委员会说，项目 A 完成日期的悲观估算是 136 天，最可能估算是 121 天，乐观估算是 116 天。他们担心悲观估算结果有可能发生，因此需要考虑的事情是_____

A．推荐中止本组件，因为它无法按期完成

B．给项目 A 增加资源

C．与项目集经理协同工作，为所需变更提供支持

D．要求项目集审计

20．You are the program manager for a manufacturing program．This program has been under way for three years．You are using a virtual team to manage the program, and you are unable to have face-to-face meetings of your team because of the financial situation．You have five projects in your program thus far．You just learned you needed to take immediate action in response to a quality metric．This metric indicated that the manufacturing process, Project A, exceeded parameters and therefore would affect Projects B, C, and D and the entire program．You decided you needed to meet with your program's Governance Board because of the severity of this issue．Your next step should be to_____

A．Issue a change request

B．Use the governance decision register

C．Update the quality management plan

D．Allocate to the program a resource who is a certified Six Sigma Black Belt

20．你是一个制造项目集的项目集经理。该项目集已经开展了 3 年了。你正在使用一

个虚拟团队进行项目集管理，并且由于财务成本的原因，你无法与你的团队进行面对面的会谈。目前该项目集有 5 个项目。你刚得到消息，为了应对某一质量指标，必须立即采取行动。这一指标显示作为制造过程的项目 A 超标，并且将对项目 B、C、D 甚至整个项目集都将产生影响。你考虑到此事的严重性，所以决定与项目集治理委员会召开会议。你的下一步将是_____

A. 发布变更请求

B. 使用治理决策登记册

C. 更新质量管理计划

D. 给该项目集分派六西格玛黑带认证的专家资源

# 10.4 章节练习参考答案

1. C 在项目集或项目组合的环境中，有 5 个主要的治理功能：促进决策，为项目集团队提供领导力和指导，执行项目集/项目控制，确保一致性，以及为问题的解决提供支持。也就是说治理是为了提高项目集的效率和一致性。

2. C 治理计划描述了目的、结构、角色和职责，以及治理过程的组织工作。

3. A 作为监督的一部分，PMO 为组织内项目集提供支持，包括它的治理功能。它经常执行的任务是提供集中的和一致的项目集管理专家意见。

4. C 阶段关口评审是按照每一阶段已有的标准开展的客观评估，目的是决定项目集是否能够进入一下阶段。这些评审也评估项目集当前目的实现情况，并确保按照收益实现计划交付了收益。

5. D 项目集治理委员会的职责之一就是监督项目集进展和对变更的需要。治理委员会建立了项目集经理能够自行批准变更的界限，并且与项目集经理一起在需要变更时支持项目集既定方法与活动的执行。

6. D 这个情境是治理委员会终止项目集的例子，因为环境的变化，项目集继续下去的必要性已经没有了。

7. C 治理委员会批准单个项目集实现目的的整体途径。在此情境中，这些变更意味着得到批准的途径需要被治理委员会更新与批准。

8. C 项目集收尾是生命周期中的最后一个阶段。在提出收尾项目集意见之前，治理委员会要尽可能地通过审查项目集章程来确定必要性。

9. B 治理委员会能够在各个决策点评审项目集，也能通过要求最新的项目集进展来评审项目集。这些评审可以出于各种各样的原因并进行各种事项的讨论，包括相关方对当前项目集绩效的满意程度。

10. A 在项目集进行下一阶段或启动新的项目进入项目集前，治理委员会的评审对于公司高层来说是一次评估项目集绩效的机会。相应的标准在治理计划中有所定义。

11．D 项目集经理是来自组件经理和团队的问题、变更、风险、界面和依赖关系的第一个升级点。

12．A 通过批准商业论证，治理委员会确认了项目为项目集交付的价值，也确认了资源分配的合理性。

13．A 项目集启动的一个重要输出是项目集章程。与其他选项相比，它包括推荐的用于管理、控制、和支持项目集的治理结构，以及项目集组件的治理结构。

14．C 正因为审计是很耗时的工作，说明审计也恰恰是对于项目集质量很有价值的方法，可以帮助项目集经理和团队避免后续的引正行动的必要性。

15．B 既定的阶段关口评审在项目集治理计划中被描述。治理委员会根据它批准项目集从一个重要阶段进入下一个阶段。

16．A 项目集治理通过很多方式支持项目集的成功，其中之一是确保项目集的目的与战略愿景、运营能力和发起组织的资源承诺保持一致。

17．B 定期的健康检查在阶段关口评审之间进行，并且使得治理委员会能够按照收益实现和维持来评估绩效与进展。

18．A 治理计划的这一部分列出了项目集的目的、各组件的目的，还有收益交付的计划。此部分还描述了治理委员会如何监督和测量目的的实现。

19．C 治理委员会在监督项目集进展和变更需要中具有独特的地位。通过与项目集经理协作，治理委员会能在需要变更时按照项目集既定的方法提供支持。

20．B 治理委员会决策应该正式归档，因为这些决策是改进项目集和组件结果的重要反馈。

# 第 **11** 章

## 怎样通过 PgMP® 考试

一次性通过 PgMP®考试并不是靠运气，而是充分准备及正确运用考试策略的结果。

本书中的其他章节都是关于考试内容的，这一章的重点放在了考试策略上。本章介绍的考试技巧能使你尽量避免考试中由于粗心造成的错误。

## 11.1 关于 PgMP®考试

在深入讨论 PgMP®考试的各项细节之前，我们先介绍一下标准化考试。即使你以前曾参加过一些标准化考试，现在回顾一些要点，也是极好的。

标准化考试是一种为了实现统计相容性而设计的考试。PgMP®考试是一项标准化考试，这基本上说明了以下两点问题：

- 同一个考生在两个不同版本的 PgMP®考卷中的表现应该差不多。
- 所有参加考试的人的成绩应该呈正态分布，这意味着成绩分布图会形成一个钟形曲线。

要知道 PgMP®的考试试题是从大量题库中提取出来的。我们讨论考试策略前，首先来看一下 PgMP®考卷的组成会对考试有所帮助。考试包括 170 道试题，但如第 2 章里说的，只有 145 道试题对你能否通过考试有影响，但问题是你不知道哪道题算分而哪道题不算分。考题由招募的志愿者编写，考题在加入考卷之前都会经过审查、提炼和测试。

25 道试验题看起来与试卷上的其他试题类似。当这些试验题的答题结果在通过评估时，其评估结果和其他试题一致：太难或者太简单的试题都会被系统过滤掉。

每个问题的主题都可能涵盖商业分析的某一个方面，涉及不同的知识点。

标准化考试的试题基本上分成简单题、中等难度题和难题三类。这些问题会随机分布在考卷里。

（1）简单题。大多数考生对回答简单题都不成问题。这些题目集中于非常基本的概念，或是要求你在某个领域的基本活动中做出选择，如可能让你选择哪些子计划涵盖在项目集管理计划中。考试中大约有 55 道简单题。如果你读过本书，答对这些题目应该不成问题。

做这种题目最好的方法是认真阅读几遍试题，那个明显与众不同的最有可能是正确的答案。

（2）中等难度题。中等难度题是考试中最普遍的试题。你大概会遇到 72 道此类的题目。这些题目会包括一些更有挑战的主题来测试你对项目集管理的理解程度。为了答对这些题目，你需要反复阅读本书，确保你理解了一些重点的内容。如果你准备充足，你会发现这类题目基本可以凭直觉来回答。

辨别中等难度题的方法是它通常会更加深奥，建议你认真阅读这类题目，从而不断缩小正确答案的选择范围。

（3）难题。难题将区分出谁能通过考试而谁不能通过考试。考试中大概有 43 道这样的题目。这些题目聚焦在一些模棱两可的实践上或者角色的细微差别上（比如谁将会解决一个特定的问题）。考试中设置难题的目的是让那些准备充分的考生才能答对。

当你辨认出难题时，你应该找出其中的陷阱并先过滤掉，然后再比较剩余的答案哪个更准确。

花些时间多做做本书每个章节后面的测试题及后面的模拟试题，它可以帮助你积累更多的 PgMP®考试经验。

## 11.2　PgMP®考试策略

### 1. 充分利用草稿纸

当你走入考场时，会收到几张草稿纸和一支铅笔。你不能把自己的纸带入考场。当坐下来开始考试时，你可以写下任何记得的内容，例如项目集治理结构等（如果你忘记这个代表什么可以在术语表里找到）。

### 2. 考试时间管理

在一开始你应该花几分钟时间过一遍考试说明。可能在考试说明中你不会发现太多有价值的内容，即便如此，你也应该去阅读考试说明，这将给你时间梳理你的思路并写下想要记下的要点。

### 3. 控制时间

你应该有比较充足的时间来完成考试，但时间绝对应该很好地规划。这里有个建议的时间控制策略，很多人照此安排通过了 PgMP®考试，详述如下：
- 坐下看考试说明，在草稿纸上记下你想写下的任何信息。
- 开始考试，先做前面 85 道题，控制时间不要超过 85 分钟。

- 第一次休息，花 5 分钟时间放松一下。
- 继续做接下来的 85 道试题，同样控制时间在另一个 85 分钟以内。
- 休息 5 分钟（充分放松一下心情，因为你已经完成了所有的题目）。
- 在这个时间点，时间基本上还是被控制在 3 个小时之内。
- 用 15 ~ 20 分钟的时间复查你标记的题目。
- 从头开始全面复看所有的 170 道试题。控制这段时间在 30 ~ 40 分钟。

假如你有一个步骤用了比预计更长的时间，这个计划还给了你一定的缓冲时间。

### 4．阅读试题

通过 PgMP®考试的关键步骤就是阅读和理解每一道题目。PgMP®考试试题比 PMP®考试的题目更复杂。你会发现长题干的题目比较多，对付长题干题目最好的办法就是快速跳读到最后一句去理解这个题目究竟是在问什么，然后再通读整个题干会事半功倍。大多数此类题目的最后一句都比较简短，并且总结了实际要问的问题。但是要确保至少阅读一遍整个题目，而不是仅仅抓住最后一句。

阅读 4 个答案和仔细阅读题干一样重要。在找到一个你喜欢的答案前你应该一遍一遍地阅读 4 个备选答案。记住在你做出选择之前一定要阅读全部的 4 个备选答案。

### 5．猜题策略

如果你能认真阅读本书内容，你就能立即知道如何回答考卷中的很多问题。对于其他的内容，你可以凭直觉来猜测。如果你把这本书反复看了几遍，理解各章节内容的话，你有充足理由相信那种直觉。它并非偶然产生，是你平时的勤奋培养造就的，直觉会引导你找到正确答案，即使你还没有意识到这一点。

### 6．识别骗局和陷阱

PgMP®考试确实有一些特别偏门的题。这些题目是为了对付那些仅有很少的正式项目经验或者那些仅看过少量商业分析书籍就相信他们已经做好考试准备的人。这些人只是试着依靠他们的工作经验来做判断的，但和 PMI 提倡的做事方法不一致。结果是他们一般都通不过考试。

有的时候，这些特别偏门的题可能也会欺骗经验老到的人。你可以使用下面的一些技巧来避免掉入陷阱。

（1）追随《项目集管理标准》的思维。这是永远正确的做法。考试中会有这样的试题，提供一个常识性的场景，设置一条让你看起来很不经意的路绕开或者否定标准。这几乎肯定是个陷阱了。正确的答案是退回到指南及其支持观点上，不要被任何引诱所欺骗。

（2）理解术语表。在你考试之前多花些时间复习术语表。进考场之前最后一件事情就是多读几遍术语表。

（3）不要纠结。考试中你应该会遇到一些不知道该怎么回答的试题。你看着它们感觉有三四个答案都是正确的，没有办法选出其中的一个。在这种情况下，不要感到痛苦。即使是使用最好的技巧，你仍然不得不对一些问题做些有根据的猜测。如果有一个这样的问题让你为难了，请简单地做个记号留待复查，然后快速移到下一题。除非你已经答完所有试题，否则千万不要花 15 分钟盯着某一道题目看。一道题目仅仅值得花整个考试时间的百分之一。所以当你不知道答案的时候，千万不要纠结于此。

你可能甚至会发现有一连串的题目看起来都特别难。这种情况可能会让你感到沮丧，并打击你的自信心。遇到这种情形，千万不要惊慌，给它们做上复查的记号，然后快速移到下面的题目直到遇到你熟悉的领域。你可能会发现试卷中后面的题目会给你一些提示甚或敲醒了你的记忆，从而帮助你回答一开始觉得困难的那些题目。

### 7．管理复查

当你全面复查试卷时，你会遇到第一遍做题时错过的但是这一遍看起来很明显的题目。这个很平常，你应该毫不犹豫地修改你能看到的没抓住的答案。很多人在复查时会修改多达 10%的答案。但是如果你改了更多的答案，你就要小心了！你可能在重新怀疑你自己的判断，实际上这个是有百害而无一利的。

在复查试卷时，不要把试题全部重新做一遍。相反，可以采用以下 3 个快速的步骤：
- 第一遍的时候你认真阅读试题了吗？
- 你选择了与问题匹配的答案了吗？
- 在为数不多的几道计算题里做完整的检验计算。

### 8．如何应对最难的题目

每个人都想知道考试中最难的题目是什么样的，这是个很难回答的问题，但通常这种题目是提出一种情形或一个问题，然后问应该由谁来解决。你可以较快地把正确答案圈定在两个以内，但是接下来就很难了。还是之前提到的，最重要的是熟悉方法和角色！

### 9．管理焦虑

如果参加考试对你来说一直是充满焦虑的话，有一个简单的方法能够帮助你管理身体的焦虑症状，而使你的想法和记忆不受到干扰。这个方法就是深吸一口气。这个可能听起来有点幼稚，但这是依据于可靠研究的。压力管理领域的研究表明焦虑的感觉与升高的肾上腺激素水平及某种脑部化学成分有关。把你的大脑化学成分拉回平衡的一种方法就是进行一次深吸气，保持大概 6 秒钟的时间，再慢慢呼出来。不管何时你开始对一些特定问题感到恐慌时，就重复这种呼吸模式，这将帮助你减缓心跳，以及集中精力关注手中的任务。

# 第 **12** 章

## PgMP®模拟试题及参考答案

## 12.1　PgMP®模拟试题一及参考答案

1. Assume you are working to change the culture of your organization to one that views its programs and projects as strategic assets and critical to overall success. You have been working on a team to define the long-term objectives of the organization and to set forth vision and mission statements for employees that are meaningful and informative. In your efforts you recognize and your team has agreed that one of the indicators of the organization's risk tolerance is found in its_____

    A.　Program management office

    B.　Portfolio

    C.　Strategic plan

    D.　Program charter

1. 假设你正在致力于改变你的组织文化，使其将所有的项目与项目集视为战略资产及整体成功的关键。你一直在团队从事定义组织的长期目标，以及阐述对于员工来说有意义的愿景与使命陈述的工作。在工作中，你和团队已经认识到并达成共识：组织的风险承受力的指标之一可以在哪里找到_____

    A.　项目集管理办公室

    B.　项目组合

    C.　战略计划

    D.　项目集章程

2. Your team is located on three continents. Many team members are struggling to use the new project and portfolio management (PPM) system, and training is required. You have a PPM expert on your staff, and the PPM vendor also offers training courses. Team members work six days a week. In this circumstance, the most appropriate training approach is to_____

    A.　Dispatch your PPM expert to each site for individualized training

    B.　Conduct synchronous webinar training so that everyone receives information at the same time

C. Have your vendor prepare eLearning modules that team members can access at their convenience

D. Provide audio recordings of training sessions that team members can download to their MP3 players

2. 你的团队分布在三个大洲。许多团队成员不熟悉使用新的项目和项目组合管理（PPM）系统，并且需要培训。你的团队里有一名 PPM 专家，PPM 供应商还提供了培训课程。团队成员每周工作 6 天。在这种情况中，最好的训练方法是_____

A. 委派你的 PPM 专家到每个地域进行针对性的培训

B. 举行同步的网络研讨培训，以便在同一时间接受培训

C. 联系供应商准备 eLearning 课程模块，团队成员可以在方便的时候学习

D. 提供团队成员可以下载到 MP3 播放器的培训音频文件

3. You are managing a program to develop a new source of energy in the extreme northern latitudes when solar power is not available. You have a core team and a Program Management Office to support you and the nine projects that are under way. However, your power company, DCE, is resource constrained. You are finding it difficult to obtain the key subject matter experts you need for this important program. You have been working diligently with your stakeholders to gain their support as you know stakeholder engagement is critical to program management. Your approach is to have effective and ongoing communications with your stakeholders. You have prepared a communications management plan for your program, and it has been approved by your sponsor and Governance Board. To complement this plan, you should prepare a(n)_____

A. Stakeholder register　　　　　　B. Information distribution plan

C. Communications log　　　　　　D. Knowledge management plan

3. 你正在管理一个用于北部高纬度地区新能源开发的项目集，以便在太阳能不能使用的时候提供能源。你有核心团队和项目集管理办公室，来支持你和正在进行中的 9 个项目。你所在的电力公司——DCE 资源受限。你发现很难获得关键领域专家，来帮助你管理这个重要的项目集。你一直与相关方勤勉合作，你知道这些相关方的参与对项目集管理非常关键。你的方法是与相关方保持有效、持续的沟通。你已经为项目集准备好了沟通管理计划，并已被发起人和治理委员会批准。要补充这个计划，你应当准备_____

A. 相关方登记册　　　　　　B. 信息分发计划

C. 沟通日志　　　　　　D. 知识管理计划

4. Assume your organization submitted its proposal to government agency ABS. One requirement was that the program manager be certified as a PgMP®. You were listed in the proposal as the program manager and plan to take the exam in three weeks; there is plenty of

time as it is June 1, and the contract is not to be awarded until July 1. Your company is convinced it will win this opportunity, and you are working on the charter. You passed the exam, and the company won the contract. But, you just learned you did not pass the MRA. You should _____

    A.  Complete the charter so the program can commence

    B.  Hold a kick-off meeting with your team

    C.  Inform your sponsor about the MRA issue

    D.  Inform the ABS point of contact about the MRA issue

4.　假设你的组织把建议提交给政府机构 ABS。其中一个必要条件是项目集经理必须具有 PgMP®认证。你被列为候选人，并要在 3 周内考试；现在还有时间，因为现在是 6 月 1 日，而合同要 7 月 1 日才签署。公司对赢得此次机会充满信心，你也努力准备项目集章程。你顺利通过了考试，公司也赢得合同。但是，你刚听说自己没有通过 MRA（注：PgMP®笔试通过后的多方面试评估）。你应该_____

    A.　完成章程，以便项目可以开始

    B.　在团队里发起启动会

    C.　通知你的发起人关于 MRA 的问题

    D.　向 ABS 接口人通知关于 MRA 的问题

5.　You are preparing for a meeting of the Governance Board for your program. Board Member A told you in a pre-meeting that she believes some recent issues were not in line with your benefits realization plan. She also says that the level of risk in your program is unacceptable. She plans to request a change during the Board meeting. Your best course of action is to_____

    A.  Review your benefits register and resolve any issues

    B.  Update your benefits realization plan and present the revised version at the Governance Board meeting

    C.  Proceed as planned with your meeting, as other Board members have not expressed any concerns

    D.  Consider her proposed change may be an opportunity to respond adaptively

5.　你正在为项目集准备治理委员会的会议。委员会成员 A 在会前告诉你，她认为最近一些问题与收益实现计划不一致。她还说目前你这个项目集的风险水平是不能接受的。她计划在会议期间要求变更。你下一步最该做的是_____

    A.　审查收益登记册，并解决问题

    B.　更新收益实现计划，并在治理委员会上提出修订版本

    C.　按原计划开会，因为其他委员会成员没表达任何顾虑

    D.　将她的建议变更视为机会，拥抱变化

6. Assume you are on a selection committee to determine which programs and projects your organization should undertake in the next year. Resources in terms of both people and funding are major constraints. One program is for an organizational change program in which for one project in this program, its output is a new personnel information system, with an outcome a new resource management and compensation policy, which is documented in the_____

A. Benefits realization plan

B. Business case

C. Program goals and objectives

D. Program management plan

6. 假设你正在选拔委员会成员，主要用来决定你们的组织明年开展哪些项目与项目集。人和资金方面的资源是目前主要的制约因素。其中一个项目集是推动组织变革，其中包含一个项目，成果是新的人事信息系统，以及新的资源管理和补偿政策，它将被记录在哪里_____

A. 收益实现计划

B. 商业论证

C. 项目集目的和目标

D. 项目集管理计划

7. You are excited because upon achieving your PgMP®, you have been assigned to manage a program in your motorcycle company, BCD, to design the 2025 program of vehicles to be produced. Each motorcycle is to be able to be used without helmets. Also, the motorcycles must have other safety features to make sure even in heavy traffic or inclement weather that the rider is protected, and the motorcycle must be able to travel for at least 500 miles without the need to refuel. You just prepared your benefits realization plan for this program. It will be helpful because_____

A. Your performance plan is tied to the benefits realization plan through the balanced scorecard approach

B. The benefits realization plan will involve all the key stakeholders in the program to get their buy in to each specific project

C. You and your team can monitor the agreed-upon benefits until the program is completed

D. It will define how and when benefits will be delivered

7. 你最近获得了 PgMP®认证，非常兴奋。你被指派去管理你所在摩托车公司 BCD 的一个项目集，完成 2025 年汽车生产的计划。每辆摩托车可以在没有头盔的情况下使用。摩托车必须有众多安全特性，即使在拥挤交通或恶劣天气中也可以确保骑手的安全，摩托车必须能够骑行至少 500 英里而无需加油。你刚刚制订完项目集的收益实现计划。它有用是因为_____

A. 你的绩效计划通过平衡计分卡的方法与收益实现计划联系在一起

B. 收益实现计划会涉及这个项目集里所有关键相关方，以便得到他们对于每一个具体项目的支持

C. 你和团队会监督商定的收益，直到项目集完成

D. 定义收益如何及何时交付

8. On your motorcycle program, you and your team are actively tracking the benefits identified in your plan. Your Governance Board asked you to revise your plan after they saw that there were so many intangible benefits and asked you to also include more tangible ones that were easier to track and then report to your stakeholders. You made a strong case for retaining your intangible benefits as you also felt the plan was useful as it_____

A. Served as a baseline for the program with the existing metrics in it

B. Was prepared through a brainstorming session with some of the key stakeholders who then would question why some of the intangible benefits were omitted

C. Helped to better define the specific project deliverables

D. Was set up in a fashion that all the benefits would be realized at the end of the program

8. 在你的摩托车项目集上，你和团队正在积极跟踪在计划中确认的收益。治理委员会看到了有过多的无形收益后要求你修改计划，让你做一个更切合实际的、更易于跟踪的计划报告给你的相关方。你进行了强有力的论证，力主保留无形收益，你认为计划是有用的，因为_____

A. 这是项目集的基准，里面包括现有指标

B. 计划是经与一些关键相关方的头脑风暴会议后准备形成，并且后续这些关键相关方又对某些无形效益的省略而提出质疑

C. 帮助更好地定义具体的项目可交付成果

D. 计划建立在所有收益都会在项目结束时得以实现的基础上

9. You are the program manager for your city's initiative to put all electrical, cable, and telephone lines underground to prevent outages during tornadoes and hurricanes. As program manager, you will select subcontractors to support your program. You prepare criteria for the make-or-buy decisions, as well as the criteria to select the subcontractors to_____

A. See how much cheaper it is to buy rather than to make

B. See how much cheaper it is to make rather than to buy

C. Outsource as much as possible in accordance with company policy

D. Determine the optimal supply chain strategy based on a wide variety of factors

9. 你是一名项目集经理，负责城市的电力、电缆，以及电话线路的地下铺设工作，以防在龙卷风和飓风期间服务的中断。作为项目集经理，你会选择承包商来支持你。你准备了一份自制或购买的决策标准，以及选择承包商的标准，以便_____

A. 确定采购比自制有多便宜

B. 确定自制比采购有多便宜

C. 根据公司政策尽可能多地外包

D. 基于广泛的因素考虑，确定最佳的供应链策略

10. Because your program has the highest priority in the organization's portfolio, your Governance Board meets each month, and each member receives a weekly status report. The executive sponsor requests these reports to enable him to stay current on program activities and assist you with any issues that need resolution. Your customer also requests monthly meetings and a weekly teleconference. To ensure that your list of these meetings and communications is up-to-date, you should develop a(n)_____

A. Communications log
B. Information distribution plan
C. Communications capability matrix
D. Communications strategy

10. 因为你负责的项目集在组织的项目组合中有最高优先级，治理委员会每个月召开例会，每个成员都会收到一份每周状态报告。执行发起人要求看到这些报告，从而能紧跟项目集进展，并在需要解决问题的时候帮助你。客户也要求召开月度会议和每周的电话会议。为确保你的会议和沟通列表保持更新，你应该开发_____

A. 沟通日志
B. 信息分发计划
C. 沟通能力矩阵
D. 沟通策略

11. Assume your executive management team has requested that a standard process be put in place for a business case for new programs and projects to pursue in the organization. You are the leader of a cross-functional team that is designing this process. Your executives have stressed they wish to analyze each proposal from multiple business perspectives and want a balanced view of the business opportunity to be realized as well as the business risk to do so. The first step in this generic process should be to_____

A. Determine the key milestones in the program
B. Define the high-level requirements
C. Establish authority, intent, and philosophy
D. Analyze program complexity and strategic alignment

11. 假设高管团队要求你制定一个标准流程，用于选择组织新项目集和项目的商业论证。你是这个跨职能团队的领导者，负责设计这个流程。高管强调，他们希望从多个业务视角全方位分析每个提案，并获得商业机会和商业风险的平衡分析。这一通用流程的第一步应该做的是_____

A. 确定项目集的关键里程碑
B. 定义高层级需求
C. 确立职权、意图和思想体系
D. 分析项目集的复杂性和战略一致性

12. You are managing a program with a long duration for the water management district in your county. At this time, it is scheduled to last nine years, but you believe the timeline could even be longer. You have seven projects in your program at this time, and you are only in year

two. You and your program management team need to analyze any environmental or legislative changes during execution that may affect your program. This is a key activity to perform during the_____

    A.  Benefits Identification phase

    B.  Program Financial Monitoring and Control

    C.  Program Setup phase

    D.  Program Risk Monitoring and Control

12.  你正在管理县区的一个水资源管理长期项目集。此时已制订了一个 9 年计划，但是你认为工期过长。项目集中有 7 个项目，而现在仅仅是第二年。你和项目集管理团队要分析在项目集执行期间可能影响项目集的环境或法律的变化。需要执行的关键活动是_____

    A.  收益识别阶段        B.  项目集财务监督和控制

    C.  项目集建立阶段        D.  项目集风险监督和控制

13.  You are a program manager for a software services company. This new software will bring your company into Cloud computing. It also will replace your company's legacy finance and accounting systems. You are to complete your program in two years. Your sponsor has asked you to develop metrics for program success. This is done as part of the development of the_____

    A.  Program charter        B.  Program roadmap

    C.  Program plan        D.  Program management plan

13.  你是一家软件服务公司的项目集经理。这个新软件将把公司带进云计算领域。它也会取代公司过去的财会系统。你将在两年之内完成项目集。发起人已经邀请你为项目集的成功制定指标。这是哪项工作的一部分_____

    A.  项目集章程        B.  项目集路线图

    C.  项目集计划        D.  项目集管理计划

14.  You are a program manager for a software services company. This new software will bring your company into Cloud computing. It also will replace your company's legacy finance and accounting systems. To formalize scope, you should use the_____

    A.  PWBS        B.  Program charter

    C.  Business case        D.  Financial framework

14.  你是一家软件服务公司的项目集经理。这个新软件会把公司带进云计算领域。它也会取代公司过去的财会系统。要正式确定范围，你应该使用_____

    A.  项目集工作分解结构        B.  项目集章程

    C.  商业论证        D.  财务框架

15.  As executive sponsor of a major program to restore coral reefs off the coast of the

Maldives, you have observed conflict between the program manager and her project managers, stakeholders, and peers. Although the conflict is manageable, you are concerned about her long-term future with the organization. She is a very bright and talented individual, and you want to keep her in the organization. Therefore, you_____

A. Tell her to take a well-deserved vacation to reduce her stress level

B. Send her to a training class on conflict management

C. Have her go through a 360-degree feedback analysis

D. Assign her a personal coach to uncover the causes of conflict

15. 作为马尔代夫海岸恢复珊瑚礁项目集的执行发起人，你发现项目集经理和她的项目经理、相关方、同事们有冲突。虽然冲突是可管理的，但是你担心组织的长期发展会受影响。项目集经理是一个非常聪明和有才能的人，你想留她在组织中。所以，你会_____

A. 要求她去度假来减轻她的压力

B. 送她去上冲突管理的训练课程

C. 对她进行 360° 反馈分析

D. 为她安排一个私人教练，帮助她发现冲突的原因

16. On your motorcycle program, you and your team are actively tracking the benefits identified in your benefit realization plan. You found, though, that employee satisfaction, which was in the first plan, was not really useful so you decided to delete this benefit and not track it. Now, you have a new plan in place. Your next step is to_____

A. Begin a process to revise your benefit report and benefit register

B. Update the roadmap

C. Discuss the new plan at your upcoming, regularly planned program status meeting with your Governance Board in two weeks

D. Distribute your plan to your key stakeholders

16. 在你的摩托车项目集中，你和团队正积极跟踪收益实现计划中所确认的收益。不过你发现，虽然员工们对第一个收益满意，但它并不是真正有用，所以你决定删除这个收益并不再跟踪它。如今你有了一个新的计划。你的下一步是_____

A. 启动修改收益报告和收益登记册的过程

B. 更新路线图

C. 在两周后即将到来的定期项目集状态会上，与治理委员会讨论新计划

D. 把你的计划分发给关键相关方

17. Assume your company has fully embraced program management. It has recognized its value and has changed its Project Management Office into an Enterprise Program Management Office. You are the Director of this Enterprise Program Management Office and report directly to the CEO. You have a program life cycle, which is followed, and you and your team

developed a standard but scalable program management methodology. You also have set up a process where each program has a Governance Board with stage-gate reviews. Such an approach_____

- A. Is focused on control
- B. Ensues the program sponsor makes all final decisions
- C. Enables a focus on changing strategies
- D. It requires monthly meetings for increased effectiveness

17. 假设你的公司已全面接受了项目集管理理念，认可它的价值，并把企业项目管理办公室转变成企业项目集管理办公室。你是企业项目集管理办公室的主任，并且直接向总裁汇报。你有一套正在遵循的项目集生命周期方法，你和团队也开发了一套标准的但也可扩展的项目集管理方法。同时，你又制定了一个标准流程，要求每个项目集都有阶段关口评审的治理委员会。这样的方法_____

- A. 致力于控制
- B. 确保发起人能做所有的最终决策
- C. 聚焦变更策略
- D. 要求召开月度例会，以提高效率

18. Assume you are the sponsor for a program for helping your government become a member of the Asian Union, which will be set up like the European Union. You know this will take some time to achieve so you have_____

- A. Prepared a funding framework
- B. Prepared a roadmap
- C. Assessed costs and benefits
- D. Focused on business value

18. 假设你是帮助政府加入亚洲联盟的项目集的发起人，像欧盟那样的亚盟即将建立。你知道这会花些时间实现，所以你已_____

- A. 准备了融资框架
- B. 准备了路线图
- C. 评估了成本和收益
- D. 专注于商业价值

19. Working as the program manager for the Asia Union program has proved to be a challenging assignment to say the least. Not only do you have a number of stakeholders located in many different countries, you now have seven projects in your program and fortunately a PMO for support. You find it is necessary to_____

- A. Differentiate between the resources assigned to the program and those at the project level
- B. Implement a team-based reward and recognition system
- C. Prepare a team charter and present it to the team
- D. Establish one person to be the sole contact with each of the different stakeholders

19. 亚洲联盟项目集经理的工作至少被证明是一项挑战性任务。因为不仅有大量位于

众多不同国家的相关方，而且项目集中有 7 个项目。幸运的是，你得到了 PMO 支持。你发现有必要_____

    A. 分配给项目集和项目的资源区别对待

    B. 实施基于团队的奖励与认可体系

    C. 准备团队章程并将它展示给团队

    D. 设立单点联系人机制，负责与每个不同的相关方联系

20. On your program, you are continually spending the majority of your time communicating with stakeholders at all levels and in varying locations and coordinating activities. You also are preparing a number of status reports for different stakeholder groups and also for your Governance Board with its numerous program reviews and more rigorous stage-gate reviews. Working as a program manager, you recognize the key distinctions between a project life cycle and a program life cycle. One of these distinctions is_____

    A. Some projects may need to be integrated with others to provide program benefits

    B. The life cycle assists in the control and management of the project deliverables

    C. Programs have a distinct life cycle that is not extended

    D. The way the life cycle is set up means that project benefits cannot be realized immediately

20. 你正在持续花费大量时间与来自各地的、各层级的项目集相关方沟通，并协调各项活动。同时你也准备众多的状态报告，发给相关方及负责大量项目集评审和尤为严苛的阶段关口评审的治理委员会。作为项目集经理，你认识到项目生命周期与项目集生命周期之间的显著区别。其中一个是_____

    A. 某些项目可能需要与其他项目整合以获得项目集收益

    B. 生命周期有助于项目可交付成果的控制和管理

    C. 项目集有截然不同的生命周期，且不能延长

    D. 生命周期建立的方式意味着项目收益不能立即实现

21. As one of the industry's leading program management consultants, you have been asked by the Global Financial Corporation to help establish a program governance structure and then to put in place a management-by-program culture in the organization. You now are establishing your core team and your first step it to_____

    A. Negotiate with functional managers for key resources

    B. Identify competency requirements for each role and responsibility

    C. Establish a training program for core team members to address skill gaps

    D. Conduct a 360-degree assessment on each team member to better understand his or her strengths and weaknesses

21. 作为一名行业翘楚的项目集管理顾问，你应全球金融公司之邀，来帮助建立一套

项目集治理结构，然后在组织里构建基于项目集的管理文化。你正在建立核心团队，第一步是_____

    A. 和职能经理们谈判关键资源

    B. 确定各个角色的能力要求和职责

    C. 为核心团队成员开展培训项目，填补技能差距

    D. 为每个团队成员进行 360° 评价，以便更好地理解他/她的优势和劣势

22. Assume as you continue with this program to put in place a management-by-program culture into the Global Financial Corporation, you realize there are not that many in this worldwide corporation that possess actual experience in program management. But, your first program will be in the area of portable financial transactions by any type of device—a phone, PDA, tablet, eReader, or computer. You recognize that with this program an expert in your corporation will be needed by two of the projects in the program at approximately the same time. Both project managers have included this person in their project management plans, resource assignment matrices, and project schedules. This is an example of_____

    A. An assumption

    B. A constraint

    C. Critical chain analysis

    D. An issue to be resolved by the Governance Board

22. 假设你继续管理这个项目集，在全球金融公司中基于项目集的管理文化。你发现，这个世界性企业中拥有项目集管理方面实际经验的人并不多。你的第一个项目集是涉足各种移动设备上进行便携式金融交易的领域，这些移动设备包括电话、PDA、平板、电子阅读器及计算机等。你发现在这个项目集中，有两个项目大概会在同一时间需要你公司的一位专家支持。两个项目经理都已经将该专家的资源纳入他们的项目管理计划、资源分配矩阵和项目进度计划中。这个例子是关于_____

    A. 假设               B. 制约因素

    C. 关键链分析      D. 治理委员会需要解决的问题

23. One of the projects in your program has reported actuals to date of $1 million against a planned value of $500,000. You suspect that the project will run out of money soon. If it runs out of money, it will place financial constraints on your other projects and also on the entire program. Therefore, as the program manager for this program, you should_____

    A. Prepare a program operational cost estimate

    B. Issue a request to terminate this project

    C. Hold a status review

    D. Calculate the schedule performance index (SPI) to see how far behind schedule you are

23. 在你的项目集中，有一个项目到目前为止已经花费了 100 万美元的金额，这相对

于 50 万美元的计划价值已经大大超支。你怀疑这个项目将很快耗尽资金。如果这个项目的钱花完了，就会对其他项目及整个项目集产生融资方面的制约因素。所以，作为项目集经理，你应该_____

A. 准备项目集运营成本估算

B. 请求终止这个项目

C. 举行状态评审会议

D. 通过计算成本绩效指数（SPI），判断晚于进度计划多长时间

24. You work as a program manager for a medical device company. Extensive clinical trials are typically managed as individual projects during and after product development. This is done to assess any flaws in the products before they are submitted for regulatory approval. As a program manager, you recognize that_____

A. You must define the life-cycle phases for each of these projects

B. The major project life-cycle phases and the activities in them will remain similar

C. The purpose of your program life cycle is to produce deliverables

D. Each project should have a different life cycle to ensure that there are no problems with the devices that are being manufactured

24. 你是一家医疗设备公司的项目集经理。大量的临床试验在产品开发期间和期后通常是作为单个项目分别管理的。这么做的目的是，在提交监管审批前，评估产品的所有可能的问题。作为项目集经理，你意识到_____

A. 你必须定义每个项目的生命周期阶段

B. 这些重要项目的生命周期阶段和活动都是类似的

C. 你的项目集生命周期的目的是生成可交付成果

D. 每个项目都应该有不同的生命周期，以确保正在制造的设备没有问题

25. You are managing a business process management program for a large insurance company. After six months of effort, you have noticed that the key stakeholders seem to be losing interest in the effort and that friction has surfaced between your key staff members and key client contacts. You look into the root causes to uncover the reasons for these apparent issues. You advise your deputy program manager to have lunch with her client counterpart at least once a week; likewise, you will start taking the client's vice president out to dinner every month. This activity can be viewed as_____

A. Positive, because you will be building stronger relationships with your client

B. Positive, but bordering on being unethical

C. Negative, because it is a calculated attempt to gain information that could be obtained through more direct means

D. Ineffective, because clients can see through such actions

25. 你正在管理一家大型保险公司业务流程管理的项目集。经过 6 个月的努力，你注意到主要相关方似乎对项目集工作渐渐失去兴趣，核心员工和关键客户联系人之间的摩擦日益显现。你在努力找出这些问题的根本原因。你建议项目集副经理与客户至少每周吃一次午饭；同样，你也会每个月与客户的副总裁共进晚餐。这一活动可以被看作_____

A. 积极的，因为你将与客户之间建立更加稳固的关系

B. 积极的，但是近乎是不道德的

C. 消极的，因为这些活动是精心安排的，完全可以通过其他更直接的途径获取信息

D. 无效的，因为客户可以看穿这些行动

26. You are the executive sponsor for a proposed program to be presented in two weeks for approval from your Portfolio Review Board in your automotive company, ABC. Your program is to develop a next generation vehicle that will not require gasoline, ethanol or electricity. In your presentation in your business case, you want to differentiate this product. To do so, you should first_____

A. Demonstrate an understanding of the needs of the customer

B. Define the program success criteria

C. Describe the business opportunity

D. Analyze program risk

26. 你是汽车公司 ABC 的一个建议项目集的执行发起人，这个项目集会在两周内向项目组合评审委员会报告申请批准。该项目集目的是开发新一代汽车，这款汽车不需要汽油、乙醇或电力。在你的商业论证中，你想展示这款产品的差异化优势。为了达到这一目的，你首先应该_____

A. 展示对客户需求的理解        B. 定义项目集成功标准

C. 描述商业机会              D. 分析项目集风险

27. Assume you are managing a program for the National Oceanic and Atmospheric Agency (NOAA) in your country. Scientists in NOAA have been doing extensive research on global warming and have noted that the current warming of the world's oceans can cause serious diseases in the next three years. You and your team prepared a benefit realization plan. This plan is one of the key documents that now are being used by your Governance Board members in NOAA to_____

A. Determine specific projects to pursue in the program

B. Present the business case for the program to the Agency Administrator

C. Determine whether changes are required to components

D. Determine the Governance Board's roles and responsibilities

27. 假设你正在管理所在国家海洋和大气局（NOAA）的一个项目集。大气局的科学家对全球变暖进行了大量的研究，并指出目前全世界的海洋变暖现象在未来 3 年内可能引

发人类严重的疾病。你和团队准备了一份收益实现计划。这个计划是关键文档其中之一，NOAA 治理委员会成员都在使用这些关键文档，以便_____

　　A．确定项目集所开展的具体项目

　　B．将项目集的商业论证报告给 NOAA 局长

　　C．确定是否要对组件进行变更

　　D．确定治理委员会的角色和职责

28. Assume a new program to increase the use of social media in your engineering company was approved by the Portfolio Review Board. A number of people have expressed interest in managing this program. The program manager should be_____

　　A．The person with the knowledge, skills, and competencies best suited for the position

　　B．An individual who has attained the PgMP® and has excellent interpersonal skills in engaging stakeholders

　　C．Appointed by the Portfolio Review Board members

　　D．Assigned by the program sponsor

28. 假设在你所在的工程公司里，有一个提升社交媒体使用率的项目集已经得到了项目组合评审委员会的批准。一些人也表示对管理这个项目集感兴趣。项目集经理应该是一位_____

　　A．最具有适合这个职位的知识、技能和能力的人

　　B．已经获得 PgMP®认证，并具备与相关方沟通卓越能力的人

　　C．由项目组合评审委员会成员任命的人

　　D．由项目发起人任命的人

29. In your program to manufacture a new series of hybrid vehicles for the 2021 year, you initially thought you would have seven projects. As you worked to develop your program charter, however, you now know you will need instead 15 component projects. You have prepared a business case for each of these projects. However, you have not been successful in recruiting the specific team members you want for your program. People have been assigned to your team by other managers who contend that these people have the necessary skills for the job. Your first step is to_____

　　A．Complete a skill set inventory

　　B．Conduct a kickoff meeting

　　C．Have an informal meeting to get to know the team members

　　D．Align personnel aspirations to available roles

29. 你的项目集目的是生产 2021 年混合动力新型系列汽车。一开始你预想将会有 7个项目。而当你开始写项目集章程的时候，你发现将有 15 个组件项目。你已经为这些项目准备了商业论证，但并没能招到所有你想要的人员。职能经理表示已经把具备必要技能

的合适人选都派到了你的团队。你的第一步工作是_____

    A. 完成技能集清单　　　　　　B. 召开启动会

    C. 通过非正式会议了解团队成员　　D. 按照个人意愿分配角色

30. So far, you have three projects identified in your program to manufacture the new series of hybrid vehicles. However, you are only in year one of this program. You recognize that at the program level, your role involves exploiting and embracing change. Also, at the program level, analysis of change requests involves identifying, documenting, and estimating the work that the change would entail. In addition, as program manager, you must_____

    A. Document the rationale for the decision

    B. Meet with the program Governance Board for approval, rejection, or deferral of the request

    C. Convene a meeting of the project's configuration control board

    D. Prepare a status report

30. 到目前为止，你在新型系列混合动力汽车制造的项目集中已确定了 3 个项目。然而，项目集刚刚进展了一年。你认识到，你在项目集层面的角色职责包括开拓和拥抱变更。同时，变更请求分析涉及识别、记录，以及估算变更引入的工作量。此外，作为项目集经理，你必须_____

    A. 记录决策依据

    B. 与项目集治理委员会会面，决定请求的批准、拒绝或延迟

    C. 召集项目配置控制委员会的会议

    D. 准备状态报告

31. Finally the hybrid vehicle program is almost complete. As an experienced program manager, you know it is a best practice in program management is to identify and document lessons learned throughout the program as it moves through the various phases of its life cycle. The next step in this process is to_____

    A. Formally document these lessons learned in the knowledge management system

    B. Have experts examine each one to determine whether it should be included in the organization's process asset library

    C. Make them readily accessible for continuous learning

    D. Appoint one of the core program team members as a knowledge broker to pass on these lessons learned

31. 最后，混合动力汽车项目集就要完成了。作为一名有经验的项目集经理，你知道识别和记录贯穿项目集生命周期的各个阶段的经验教训是一项最佳实践。这一流程的下一步工作是_____

    A. 在知识管理系统中正式记录这些经验教训

B. 让专家检查每一个经验教训，以确定是否可以放入组织过程资产库中

C. 使经验教训随时可获取学习

D. 安排核心项目集团队的一名成员作为知识经纪人，以利于经验教训的传承

32. You are responsible for developing a new line of printers using advanced laser jets for the consumer market. The customers for your products are large retail outlets and certain online outlets. As program manager, it is critical that you have a good understanding of the needs of the end user. Therefore, you_____

A. Meet with customers to obtain a profile of the buying habits of their shoppers

B. Meet with customers to understand the wants and needs of their clients with respect to printer capability

C. Conduct market research to see what your competitors are offering

D. Meet with as many end users as is feasible to understand what features they would like in a printer

32. 你负责为消费者市场开发先进的激光打印机产品线。该产品线的客户是大型零售渠道商和某些在线经销商。作为项目集经理，充分理解终端用户的需求是非常重要的。所以，你_____

A. 与客户会面，从而形成购物者购买习惯的资料

B. 与客户见面，从而理解客户关于打印机性能的需要和需求

C. 开展市场调研，从而分析竞争对手提供什么样的产品

D. 与尽可能多的终端用户沟通，了解他们对于打印机最喜欢什么功能

33. Assume you are working as a program manager under contract to the company developing the advanced laser jet printers for the consumer market. Even though you believe you have a good working relationship with the program manager at the printer company, your client has not paid its last invoice of £500,000, and it is now more than 90 days overdue. Your company's accounting policy states that any invoice that is more than 90 days late becomes bad debt. You now need to_____

A. Rebaseline your budget　　　　　B. Update your cost management plan

C. Take corrective action　　　　　D. Issue a change request

33. 假设你是一家打印机公司的签约项目集经理，在为消费者市场开发一款先进的激光喷墨打印机。虽然你觉得自己和打印机公司的项目集经理保持着良好的合作关系，但客户依然没有支付 50 万英镑的尾款，并逾期了 90 天。公司的会计政策声明，超过 90 天后的账单将成为坏账。你现在需要_____

A. 重新设定预算基准　　　　　B. 更新成本管理计划

C. 采取纠正措施　　　　　D. 提出变更请求

34. Risk management is continual in program management. It is important in the early

stages, even when approval to authorize a program has not yet been obtained.  Assume you are the sponsor of a possible new program in which all asphalt on your nation's highway system would be totally replaced with a new product that would never require any maintenance. However, obviously there are going to be risks with such a new product to be developed, and you need to identify some of them to obtain approval to proceed.  Therefore, a key question to be able to answer when you request approval to proceed is_____

A．What are the assumptions that are part of your analysis?

B．How much do we need to set aside for contingency in our budget should the risks occur?

C．How will these risks affect the ultimate sustainability of the product?

D．What is the probability of success for this program?

34．风险管理在项目集管理中是持续进行的。初期阶段尤为重要，即便是项目集尚未获批。假设你是一个可能立项的新项目集的发起人，该项目集是将国家所有公路系统中的沥青全部替代成新产品，这种产品永远不需要维护。开发这样的新产品显然存在风险，你需要识别其中的一些风险，从而让项目集得以批准。所以，决定你是否可以继续项目的关键问题是_____

A．你的分析做了哪些假设？

B．我们预算里需要预留多少风险应急储备？

C．这些风险将会如何影响产品最终的可持续性？

D．项目集成功的概率是多少？

35．Working to prepare the business case for your proposed program to develop a new product to replace asphalt on your nation's highways so maintenance will not be required, you realize the members of the Portfolio Review Board will be interested in a cost/ benefit analysis, which means, you should_____

A．Identify tangible benefits as they can be easily quantified

B．Identify direct benefits to your nation that will result from this program

C．Identify tangible and intangible benefits, expressing the intangible benefits in quantifiable terms

D．Identifying the tangible and intangible benefits showing the intangible benefits through market analysis techniques

35．你正在为提议的项目集准备商业论证，该项目集是为开发一款用来替代国家高速路沥青的新产品，它不需要维护。你意识到，项目组合评审委员会成员对成本/收益分析感兴趣，这意味着你应该_____

A．识别有形收益，因为它们容易量化

B．识别这个项目集会带给你的国家的直接收益

C. 识别有形收益和无形收益，并将无形收益量化

D. 识别有形收益和无形收益，通过市场分析技术显示无形收益

36. As manager of a program for the Federal Trade Commission that involves changes to existing regulations throughout the agency concerning mergers and acquisitions, you have a number of key stakeholders—both internal and external—because these regulations have not been reviewed for more than 20 years. The Commission has established a Governance Board, and you meet with this Board monthly to review progress. Because the Commission practices government in the "sunshine," each meeting is open to the public to attend.  This means that_____

A. Public announcements concerning the program do not need to be prepared

B. Board meeting minutes can substitute for any notifications to the public concerning the program

C. Public announcements should be prepared

D. A member of the core team should interface regularly with every public interest group

36. 你是联邦贸易委员会一个项目集的经理。该委员会涉及所有关心兼并和收购的机构的现有法规的变更，而这些法规已超过 20 年没有被审查过了。这个项目集有大量内部和外部的关键相关方。联邦贸易委员会已经成立了治理委员会，并且你需要每月与治理委员会一起审查项目集进展。因为联邦贸易委员会奉行政务公开政策，所以每一次会议都会向公众开放。这意味着_____

A. 与项目集有关的公告不需要准备

B. 治理委员会议可以代替任何公众对项目集关切的通知

C. 仍然需要准备公告

D. 一名核心团队的成员需要定期与每一个公共利益集团沟通

37. You are pleased to be appointed as the Program Manager for the development of a new ballpoint pen program. This pen will never need replacement and is to be physically appealing and available in a variety of colors. It also is to be fun to use but practical for those in a business setting. Therefore, you are developing a series of these pens and so far the program is considered to be on track. Your only key issue is that each of the stakeholders on this next-generation ballpoint pen program has different communications needs. To ensure each stakeholder receives the appropriate information he or she need in a useful format and in a timely manner, you ask a core team member to prepare a(n)_____

A. Lessons-learned process    B. Stakeholder register

C. Information-retrieval system    D. Information-gathering system

37. 你很高兴被任命为开发新款圆珠笔的项目集经理。这款圆珠笔永远不需要替换，并且在外形上极具吸引力，有多款颜色可供选择。此外，它具备使用的趣味性，在商业环境下也很实用。你正在开发这样的圆珠笔系列产品，整个项目集目前被认为是处于正轨。

你的唯一的重点问题是，这款下一代圆珠笔项目集的每个相关方有不同的沟通需求。为了确保每个相关方都能及时地、按照适用的格式得到所需的合适信息，你要求一名核心团队成员准备一份_____

A. 经验教训总结流程      B. 相关方登记册

C. 信息检索系统      D. 信息收集系统

38. As the program manager for a new line of children's toys, called The Destroyer, because your requirements tend to be constantly changing and because some key subject matter experts have been reassigned, you realize that you already are in a position in which a portion of your budget may be depleted, and you are not yet to the halfway point of your program. Some of the toys do not pass inspection. You are becoming concerned. You need to therefore consider _____

A. Submitting component transition requests to your Governance Board

B. Requesting a quality assurance audit

C. Formalizing a quality policy

D. Reviewing and updating the financial management plan

38. 你是为"驱逐舰"的新系列儿童玩具的项目集经理。因为你的需求经常在变化，并且一些关键领域主题专家已被重新安排，目前项目集尚未完成一半，而部分预算已经耗尽。而且一些玩具还无法通过检验。你开始有些担心了，目前你需要做的是_____

A. 提交组件移交请求给治理委员会

B. 请求质量保证审计

C. 使质量政策正式化

D. 审查且更新财务管理计划

39. One of your project managers (Project Manager A) has identified an issue that has implications for three projects (A, B, and C). You met with this project manager and concurred with her estimate of the importance of the issue. You then convened a meeting of your Governance Board to determine the best way to resolve it. The Governance Board decided that proposed Project B is not required and that existing Project C should be terminated. It decided to add Project D. Your next step should be_____

A. Revisit and update your program documentation as required

B. Inform the client of this issue and its impact

C. Meet with all the project managers and the core program team to discuss next steps

D. Officially recognize and reward Project Manager A for bringing this issue to your attention

39. 你的一个项目经理（项目经理 A）识别出一个对 3 个项目都有影响（A、B 和 C）的问题。你与该项目经理进行了沟通，并且同意她对于问题重要性的预估。然后你召开了治理委员会会议，希望研究一个最好的方法来解决它。治理委员会决定不再需要项目 B，并且终止项目 C。他们决定引入项目 D。于是你下一步的计划是_____

A. 按照要求重新审查并且更新项目集文档

B. 将这个问题及其影响通知客户

C. 与所有的项目经理和核心团队讨论下一步计划

D. 官方认可和奖励项目经理 A，因为她及时上报了这个问题

40. Assume you have a Governance Board overseeing your program in your government agency. It is comprised of the top executives and political appointees as the program is ranked in the top five in the portfolio. You have had to reduce some of the features originally planned for your program deliverables because of funding cuts. The Governance Board must determine_____

A. How corrective actions were applied

B. Whether the window of opportunity was compromised

C. Actual resource use versus that projected

D. The number of issues escalated to you, as the program manager, and their effect on other aspects of the program or other programs in the agency

40. 假设治理委员会在监督你所在政府机构的项目集。该项目集排在项目组合中的前五位，所以治理委员会包含了高层管理人员和政府任命人员。由于经费削减，你不得不减少最初针对项目集可交付成果所规划的一些功能。治理委员会必须确定_____

A. 如何采取正确的措施

B. 机会窗口是否已经做出让步

C. 实际资源的使用与资源预估的对比

D. 作为项目集经理，升级到你这里的问题数量，以及他们在其他什么方面对本项目集和该机构中其他项目集的影响

41. You are the program manager for a sixth-generation cell phone product. A number of component projects are associated with this program. You were on the core program team for the fifth-generation phone, so you can apply the lessons learned from that program. The schedule is the dominant constraint, and there is a chance that you will miss the user-acceptance test milestone even though it is six months away. Your next step is to_____

A. Implement your plan

B. Inform the executive team that you will miss this critical milestone unless preventive action is taken

C. Revisit the program master schedule

D. Ask your program steering committee for additional resources to ensure that you can meet the milestone

41. 你是第六代手机产品的项目集经理。大量的组件项目与这个项目集有关。你曾经在第五代的核心项目集团队中工作过，因此你可以将那个项目的经验教训应用到本项目集。进度是主要的制约因素，而且虽然还有 6 个月的时间，有可能你不能按期完成用户验收测试的里程碑。你的下一步是_____

A. 实施你的计划

B. 通知高管团队，除非做好预防措施，不然会无法达成关键里程碑

C. 重新查看项目集主进度

D. 向项目集指导委员会请求额外资源，以确保你能够达成里程碑

42. In your role as program manager for your country's food safety department to ensure the safety of imported food in your country, you are facing a number of challenges. It seems as if more imported food is arriving rather than producing the food domestically. You lack the needed number of inspectors who have expertise in some of the exotic food that now is being imported, and you are implementing a Hazard Analysis Critical Control Program approach as part of this important program. You are working hard to keep your stakeholders, internal and external, informed of your progress and upcoming milestones in a timely manner, and you distribute a variety of different reports based on the category of stakeholders and their information requirements. However, one type that often is overlooked is_____

A. Needed corrective actions

B. Notification of change requests

C. List of preventive actions

D. Resource prioritization decisions

42. 你担任国家食品安全部门的项目集经理角色，目的是确保国家进口食品的安全。目前面临许多挑战。似乎更多的食品都依赖进口而不是在国内生产食品。你现在缺少在进口食品检验方面有经验的人员，作为本项目集的一部分，你正在实践"危害分析关键控制计划"的方法。你正努力与内外部的相关方保持沟通，及时报告项目集进展和下一个里程碑的完成情况，并且你基于相关方分类和信息需求来进行汇报。然而，经常容易被忽略的一项是_____

A. 所需的纠正措施

B. 变更请求的通知

C. 预防措施的列表

D. 资源优先级决策

43. Your company has been the leader in Segway® production since they were first made available to consumers. However, their popularity has increased tremendously since the product was first made offered, and they are less expensive to manufacture. Therefore, sales have increased dramatically. However, recently your company has been getting a large volume of customer complaints as the battery life is only 20 miles. You have been appointed as the program manager to develop a new line of Segway® products in which the battery life will be 100 miles, yet the production process still will be one that focuses on lean manufacturing so the products can be offered to customers at a reasonable price. To document the relationship

between the program activities and expected benefits, you have prepared a_____

    A.　Roadmap

    B.　Charter

    C.　Benefits realization plan

    D.　Statement of the program's goals and objectives

43.　自从产品第一次上市以来，你们公司就被认为是在赛格威®生产方面的领导者。自从产品第一次被消费者接受以来，产品声望大幅增加，价格也不贵，因此销售额有明显增加。然而，最近公司收到电池续航能力仅仅只有 20 英里的客户投诉。你已被任命为赛格威®新产品的项目集经理，该新产品电池续航寿命将达到 100 英里；你们将采用精益生产的工作模式，因此给到客户的仍然是相对合理的价格。要记录项目集活动和预期收益之间的关系，你已经准备了一份_____

    A.　路线图　　　　　　　　　　B.　章程

    C.　收益实现计划　　　　　　　D.　项目集目标说明书

44. Assume your company has fully embraced program management. It has recognized and has set up a process where each program has a Governance Board with phase-gate reviews. Working with program managers, members of the Governance Board can monitor progress to maximize program success. Obviously changes will occur. The most significant requests involve_____

    A.　Program issues　　　　　　B.　Resource use

    C.　Quality　　　　　　　　　　D.　Program benefits

44.　假设你的公司完全接受了项目集管理，认识到了其重要性并且建立了流程：每个项目集都配备治理委员会进行阶段关口评审。治理委员会成员可以与各项目集经理一起监督项目集进展，以便最大可能获得项目集的成功。很明显变更不可避免。其中最重要的请求涉及_____

    A.　项目集问题　　　　　　　　B.　资源使用

    C.　质量　　　　　　　　　　　D.　项目集收益

45. As the program manager for the development of the next-generation catalytic converter, you have several major challenges. First, it is the first program in your company, second, it is highly complex, and third resources are limited.　To handle these challenges you plan to_____

    A.　Assign program roles and responsibilities

    B.　Establish an easy to use and comprehensive program management information system

    C.　Set up a program control framework

    D.　Use enterprise resource planning tools

45.　作为下一代催化式排气净化系统研制的项目集经理，你有几项重要挑战：第一，它是你公司的第一个项目集；第二，高度复杂；第三，资源有限。为了迎接这些挑战，你

将_____

    A. 分配项目集角色和职责

    B. 确立易于使用和全面的项目集管理信息系统

    C. 建立项目集控制框架

    D. 使用企业资源规划工具

46. You have had several issues on your next- generation catalytic converter program. But, finally it is in the closing stage. You want to make sure there is operational sustainability from your program that is ongoing. To do so effectively, you should_____

    A. Update the program document repository

    B. Document lessons learned

    C. See if residual activities are required

    D. Hold a final meeting with key program stakeholders

46. 你的下一代催化式排气净化系统项目集面临一些问题。但是，到最后它还是迎来了收尾阶段。你想确保项目集具备运营的可持续性。为了高效，你应该_____

    A. 更新项目集文档资料库

    B. 记录经验教训

    C. 确认剩余的工作是否还需要继续进行

    D. 与关键的项目集相关方举行最终会议

47. You manage a program to develop a new e-commerce program for automotive parts distributors. Your organization has established this program to keep up with competitors and to increase market share, but it has recently acquired a competitor that already has a highly regarded e-commerce program in place. Your next step is to_____

    A. Convene a meeting of your Governance Board to terminate your program

    B. Meet with each of your project managers to discuss an orderly transition to redeploy resources

    C. Revisit and update your program plans

    D. See if you can learn from the competitor

47. 你在管理一个项目集，目的是为汽车配件经销商开发新的电子商务贸易系统。你的组织确立这个项目集是为了紧跟竞争对手，同时也可以提高市场份额；公司最近收购了一个竞争对手，它已经有一个受到高度重视的电子商务项目集。你的下一步是_____

    A. 召集治理委员会议，终止你的项目集

    B. 与每一个项目经理沟通，对现有资源进行重新部署

    C. 更新你的项目集计划

    D. 考虑一下是否可以向竞争对手学习

48. Your professional association in business development is increasing in terms of its membership. You have a core team of people to help you in your program to certify its members, but other team members are volunteers. Recently the Executive Director authorized you to hire some consultants to help on a full-time basis. The stakeholders, who are volunteers and members of the association, knowledge and expertise are vital to the outcome of this program. However, especially since so many volunteers are involved, you have had to reach negotiated compromises with some of these stakeholders to respond to their concerns. They are part of_____

   A. The stakeholder engagement strategy

   B. Stakeholder analysis and planning

   C. The communications log

   D. Stakeholder engagement

48. 你所负责的专业协会会员正呈现增长趋势。在你的项目集中，有一个核心团队来协助你认证协会会员，其余的团队成员则是志愿者。最近执行董事授权你可以去招聘一些全职的咨询顾问。这些志愿者和协会成员的知识和经验对于这个项目集的最终结果来说非常重要。特别是志愿者数量众多，你不得不与这些相关方谈判并做妥协，来回应他们的关切问题。这是以下哪项工作的一部分_____

   A. 相关方参与策略　　　　　　　B. 相关方分析和规划

   C. 沟通日志　　　　　　　　　　D. 相关方参与

49. You are sponsoring a program to digitize all of the records in your nation's archives. Some of these records are extremely important but are difficult to digitize, because they are ones when your country was established, approximately 500 years ago. However, it is essential that they be preserved, and the effort of your undertaking is far larger than originally anticipated. But, now your government is in financial difficulty, and you wonder if your program will be able to be funded. You must_____

   A. Prepare an impact analysis to show the results if the program does not receive needed funding

   B. Conduct a benchmarking study to see how other countries have handled this type of project

   C. Estimate the high-level financial and non-financial benefits

   D. Perform a SWOT analysis

49. 你要发起一个项目集来完成国家档案的数字化。有些记录是非常重要的，但是很难数字化，因为它们大多数是 500 年前国家创建的时候保留下来的。然而它们又有必要保留下来，你所要做的工作量远远大于最初的预期。但是现在政府正面临财政困难，你不确定自己的项目集是否可以得到资助。你必须_____

   A. 准备影响分析，显示如果资金不能如期到位的结果

B. 开展标杆对照，研究别国是怎么处理这个问题的

C. 评估财务和非财务的高层级收益

D. 进行 SWOT 分析

50. You have been managing a program to restructure your department within your government agency. The head of the agency informed your sponsor that she wants to change the scope of the program so that you will be working to restructure the entire agency instead. This means you_____

A. Are working on a strategic program

B. Must resubmit a new business case and receive approval from the Portfolio Review Board

C. Should terminate work to date following the standard closure process

D. Submit a formal change request as your next step

50. 你在管理一个重组你所在政府机构部门的项目集。该机构负责人通知你的发起人她想改变项目集范围，这样的话你将重组整个政府机构。这意味着你_____

A. 正致力于战略项目集

B. 必须再提交新的商业论证，并得到项目组合评审委员会的批准

C. 应按照标准收尾过程来终止当前工作

D. 下一步提交正式的变更请求

51. Assume you are in charge of reorganizing your government agency because its funding has been cut by 50% based on the shortfall of the overall available funds in your government. To cut the funds, a number of projects and programs were terminated, and in doing so, many staff members lost their jobs. In making the decisions as to which programs to terminate, one of the considerations was_____

A. The number of staff members involved

B. The overall schedule status

C. The funds already allocated

D. The benefits report

51. 假设你负责重组你们的政府机构，原因是政府资金削减了 50%；由于削减资金，大量的项目和项目集被终止，这样一来许多工作人员失去了他们的工作。在做出终止哪些项目集的决策时，必须要考虑的一个问题是_____

A. 涉及的工作人员人数　　　　B. 总体进度状态

C. 已经划拨的资金　　　　　　D. 收益报告

52. Your company established a Governance Board, and it meets at least monthly to review progress to date on your program, not just at stage-gate reviews. You and your team worked to identify stakeholders who may have an interest in or an influence over your program and to

analyze them to see if they are positive or negative. Your next step is to_____

A. Develop a stakeholder engagement strategy

B. Prepare an interest/power stakeholder map

C. Prepare a stakeholder register

D. Develop a project stakeholder engagement plan

52. 你的公司建立了治理委员会，它主要负责至少每月审查项目集的当前进展，而不仅仅是阶段关口评审。你和团队识别了与项目集有利益相关性或会影响到项目集的相关方，并对他们进行分析以确定他们的支持态度是积极的还是消极的。你的下一步工作是_____

A. 制定相关方参与战略　　　　　B. 准备相关方利益/权利矩阵图

C. 准备相关方登记册　　　　　　D. 制订项目相关方参与计划

53. You are the program manager for the development of a new slot machine for the Sand Dunes casino in Macau. Your organization operates with a balanced matrix organizational structure, and you have resources supporting your program from a variety of functional departments. Some of these people report to you as well as to their respective departmental managers. You should_____

A. Work with the functional managers so you can provide input into the performance of these individuals

B. Set up a team- based reward and recognition system

C. Ask the team to develop a team charter to serve as their commitment to the program

D. Release resources when they are no longer needed

53. 你是一名负责为澳门沙丘赌场开发新款老虎机的项目集经理。你的组织是以平衡矩阵的组织结构来运行的，你需要从各个职能部门中找到可以支持项目集的资源。其中的一些人同时向你及其职能经理汇报工作。你应该_____

A. 与职能经理紧密合作，这样可以对这些员工的绩效提供你的意见

B. 建立团队奖励和认可系统

C. 与团队共同定制团队章程来完成项目集

D. 当你不再需要某个成员的时候，可以释放资源

54. Assume you have been appointed as a program manager for an internal restructuring of your government agency. It has not been reorganized for 10 years, and many new programs and projects are under way. Also, some of the existing Divisions do not seem to relate to the new five year strategic plan the agency issued six months ago, and on the surface, without detailed analysis, it is questionable that they remain necessary. As you initiate the program, you want to reveal and explain any gaps; therefore, it is important to_____

A. Prepare a benefits analysis plan

B. Perform an initial identification of program risks

C. Develop a financial framework

D. Develop a program roadmap

54. 假设你已被任命为政府机构内部结构调整的项目集经理。这个机构已经 10 年没调整过了，而且有许多新的项目和项目集正在进行中。此外，6 个月前机构发布了一个新的 5 年计划，现在有些部门和新的 5 年计划表面看起来没有关系。虽然没有做详细的分析，但是对于它们是否参与项目集是有待商榷的。在你的项目集启动时，你想搞清楚所有问题。因此，现在重要的是_____

A. 准备收益分析计划

B. 执行项目集风险的初步识别

C. 制定财务框架

D. 制定项目集路线图

55. Assume your organization has approved an internal improvement program and has identified key stakeholders. It is now deciding whether or not it should focus on the Software Engineering Institute's Capability Maturity Model for Integration (CMMI) to obtain Level 3 and have the opportunity to bid on more U.S. Federal Government projects. The other option is to establish a program to pursue best practices in portfolio, program, and project management using the Project Management Institute's Organizational Project Management Maturity Model (OPM3®). Since the area to be addressed is understood, the next step is to_____

A. Qualify the business benefits

B. Conduct a feasibility study

C. Use the voice of the customer (VOC) approach for a market analysis

D. Prepare a high-level approach

55. 假设你的组织已经批准了一个内部改进计划，并已确定了关键相关方。目前正在考虑是否应该关注软件工程协会的软件集成能力成熟度模型（CMMI），并且获得 3 级资质，这样一来就有更多的机会可以竞标美国联邦政府项目。另一个使用项目管理协会所推行的组织项目管理成熟度模型（OPM3®），并将其最佳实践应用到项目组合、项目集和项目管理过程中去。由于需要关注领域已经确定，下一步工作是_____

A. 量化商业收益

B. 进行可行性研究

C. 使用客户心声（VOC）方法来做市场分析

D. 准备高层级方法

56. Assume your organization selected OPM3®, and you hired an external consultant to perform the assessment. The consultant prepared an assessment report and an improvement report. As there are 488 Best Practices in OPM3®, your company is so new to program

management and portfolio management, it only achieved 75 of these Best Practices. You are now leading an internal program to address the consultant's prioritized improvement program. You have seven projects now in your program. As each project manager begins to identify the work to be done on their projects, you want to make sure the program's scope encompasses all benefits to be delivered so you should_____

A. Follow the PMO's project management standard

B. Make sure the context and framework are documented is a scope statement

C. Use a program work breakdown structure

D. Prepare a benefits realization plan

56.　假设你的组织选择使用 OPM3®，同时你们雇用了一个外部顾问来进行评估。这名顾问准备了一份评估报告和改进报告。由于 OPM3®包含 488 项最佳实践，你们公司在项目集管理及项目组合管理这项工作上刚起步，只达成了其中的 75 项最佳实践。你正在管理内部项目集，以配合顾问高优先级的改进项目集。在你的项目集中有 7 个项目。各个项目经理开始确定项目所需要做的工作，而你希望确认项目集的范围及所有要交付的收益，那么你应该_____

A. 遵从 PMO 的项目管理标准

B. 确保内容与框架都记录在范围说明书里

C. 使用项目集 WBS

D. 准备收益实现计划

57.　As the contract program manager to integrate the back office components of your customer's system into a single system that contains data on accounting, finance, sales, business development, personnel, and portfolio, program, and project management, you have a core team of six people and six project managers. You are working to obtain information from stakeholders to better understand the organizational culture and decide to_____

A. Use questionnaires and surveys　　　B. Hold a focus group

C. Conduct interviews　　　　　　　　D. Use open-ended questions

57.　作为签约的项目集经理，你需要将客户系统的后台组件整合到一个单独系统中，包含会计、财务、销售、业务开发、人员，以及项目组合、项目集和项目管理等方面的数据，你有一个 6 人的核心团队及 6 个项目经理。你正在致力于从相关方处获取信息，以更好理解组织文化，你决定采取以下行动_____

A. 采用问卷调查　　　　　　　B. 召开焦点小组会议

C. 进行面谈　　　　　　　　　D. 使用开放式问题

58.　You and your core team have identified within the organization 17 key stakeholders, and there are approximately 33 that have a peripheral interest in your program. You know you will have other stakeholders to add to this list as program progresses. The person, or group, who is responsible for providing project resources on this program is_____

A. Program director

B. Program manager

C. Program sponsor

D. Governance Board

58. 你和核心团队已经识别出组织里的 17 个关键相关方，另外还有约 33 个对你们项目集感兴趣的外部相关方。你知道随着项目集的进行，你将还会有别的相关方被识别出来并且加入相关方列表中。负责为这个项目集提供资源的是_____

A. 项目集总监

B. 项目集经理

C. 项目集发起人

D. 治理委员会

59. Because of extreme droughts in Ferguson, Jordan, water restrictions have been imposed. Your company is awarded a contract to eliminate the need for these restrictions. The program includes a project to formulate and implement policies and procedures that ensure continuity of operations and performance of associated equipment. Another project will oversee improvements and modifications to existing treatment methods and facilities. A third project will design modifications to increase productivity and effectiveness. You expect other projects to be added later. Your company has a Governance Board in place for your program, which conducts phase-gate and other periodic reviews. You meet regularly with this board, and these meetings are necessary because they_____

A. Are program performance reviews

B. Assess performance against the need to realize and sustain program benefits for the long term

C. Approve required changes to the program

D. Assess performance of the program against expected outcomes

59. 由于约旦弗格森的极度干旱，那里已经开始了限水工作。你的公司被授予合同以消除对这些限制的依赖。项目集中的一个项目就是去制定和实施一系列政策和过程以确保相关设备的操作和性能的可持续性。另一个项目将监督改进和修改现有的处理方法和设备。第三个项目将为提高生产效率和有效性设计修改方案。你预计后期会增加其他项目。你们的公司为你的项目集成立了治理委员会，以便对项目集进行阶段—关口和其他定期的审查。你与委员会定期开会，这些会议是必要的，因为它们_____

A. 是项目集绩效评审

B. 针对是否需要长期实现和保持项目集收益进行绩效评价

C. 批准项目集所要求的变更

D. 针对预期结果对项目集进行绩效评价

60. Finally, after three years of planning, your detailed design for the next- generation missile system of your country is complete. You were appointed the program manager for this program, and you now have also prepared your program management plan and schedule, as well

as your subsidiary plans. Last week, your program's Governance Board approved your program management plan. The next step is to_____

A. Assign project managers and appoint your core team

B. Prepare charters for component projects

C. Set up your PMO

D. Authorize components

60. 最终，在 3 年的规划之后，你完成了你们国家下一代导弹系统的详细设计。你被指派为这个项目集的经理，你现在也准备了项目集管理计划和进度计划，以及附属计划。上周，项目集治理委员会批准了你的项目集管理计划。下一步是_____

A. 指定项目经理并且任命核心团队　　　B. 为组件项目准备章程

C. 设置 PMO　　　　　　　　　　　　D. 授权组件

61. Assume you are managing a high visibility program that is global with stakeholders located on four continents. You have performed a thorough identification of your program's benefits with your team and have set up a benefits register. In order to develop appropriate performance measures for these benefits, you should_____

A. Review the business case

B. Meet with stakeholders

C. Take the qualified benefits and turn them into ones that can be measured quantitatively

D. Assign each benefit to an owner and empower the owner to set up metrics and discuss them at the scheduled core team meeting

61. 假设你在管理一个高能见度项目集，其相关方来自全球的 4 个大洲。你和团队已经对项目集收益做了彻底的识别，并建立了收益登记册。为了给这些收益制定适当的绩效考核标准，你需要_____

A. 审查商业论证

B. 与相关方面谈

C. 将合格的收益进行量化处理

D. 为每一项收益安排一名负责人，并授权该负责人建立验收标准，并在核心团队会议上对其进行讨论

62. You are pleased to be the first program manager in your company to manage a virtual team. While the company has managed programs for several years, in the past, it tended to hire subject matter experts or ask people from its offices in four other continents to meet in one place in order to work as a collocated team. It also relied extensively on contactor support. Finally, your executives have recognized that it will be cost beneficial to use a virtual team for your new program to develop a new product that combines the capabilities of a smart phone, an eBook reader, and a tablet in a single device that is less expensive with a higher quality of resolution

than possible with the existing products on the marketplace. Such an approach is one in which you should consider_____

    A.  Using focus groups to obtain a picture of the various attitudes of your stakeholders

    B.  The cultural backgrounds of the team members

    C.  Changing culture

    D.  Using market analysis

62. 你很高兴成为你们公司第一位项目集经理来管理一个虚拟团队。你们公司过去多年来都在从事项目集管理,公司更倾向聘请主题专家或者安排另外 4 个大洲的人员聚集在某地作为一个联合团队工作。同时,它还广泛依赖于承包商的支持。最后,你的执行官意识到,你的新项目集使用一支虚拟团队会降低一些成本。该项目集是为了开发一款集智能手机、电子书和平板于同一设备的产品,它比市场上现有产品具有更高的分辨率质量,且更便宜。如果这样做的话你需要考虑_____

    A.  使用焦点小组来收集各相关方的不同态度

    B.  团队成员的文化背景

    C.  变化的文化氛围

    D.  采用市场分析的方法

63.   Your company has a career path in program management and has established standard competencies for the various positions. You were a project manager on the company's virtual team in which your program developed a new product combining the capabilities of the smart phone, eBook reader, and a tablet in a single device. You managed the integration project in your program, and you were commended by the executive team and the program manager for outstanding work. Now, you are transitioning into your first program management position. The guiding rule in your new job is to_____

    A.  Provide as much support as needed to project managers in their daily activities

    B.  Training, coaching, mentoring, and recognizing your team

    C. Actively manage each project until you have confidence in the project manager's ability to do so without your continual involvement

    D.  Mentor project managers in their roles by working with them throughout their projects

63. 你们的公司在项目管理这方面有自己的职业轨迹,并且已经为各个岗位建立了标准的能力要求。你是一支虚拟团队的项目经理,你们团队主要集中力量开发新产品,将智能手机、电子书及平板电脑集成在单一设备上。你负责管理这个项目集中的集成项目,工作出色并且得到了领导的赞许。你现在正在晋升到项目集管理职位,你的新岗位的指导原则是_____

    A.  在项目经理日常活动中需要帮助的时候提供协助

    B.  对你的团队进行培训、教练、指导并认可你的团队

C. 积极管理每个项目，直到在没有你参与的情况下，对项目经理的能力仍有信心

D. 整个项目过程中，与项目经理一起工作来指导他们的工作

64. As the program manager for the new landfill program for your county, you are facing a number of challenges. You have identified a large number of stakeholders, mostly in the county and the residents who have this "not in my backyard" syndrome about the landfill program, along with environmental activists. However, you recognize you need to engage each stakeholder group, even if they are negative, to ensure overall success. Recently, at some key meetings, you and your team realized some of the active stakeholders were missing. You realized some also missed the previous meeting. To identify and assess causes of nonparticipation, as a program manager, one tool to use is_____

A. Root cause analysis                    B. Cause-and-effect diagrams

C. Variance analysis                       D. Conflict resolution strategies

64. 作为你们县一个新建垃圾处理场地的项目集经理，你正面临许多挑战。你已经识别了大量的相关方，他们大部分都是你们县的居民，还有些是"邻避效应"的居民，同时还有环保人士。然而你认识到你需要与每一类相关方接触，以确保整个项目集的成功，即使他们的态度是消极的。最近在一些关键会议上，团队发现一些活跃的相关方没有参加。你同时发现他们之前的一些会议也没有参加。为评估不参加的原因，作为项目集经理，你需要使用的工具是_____

A. 根本原因分析                           B. 因果图

C. 偏差分析                               D. 冲突解决策略

65. Assume you have decided to sponsor a new program to develop a new way to determine whether or not an organization should bid on any opportunity, and the steps it should follow to predict whether the submitted proposal will be selected. This will be a quantitative model that basically can transform the way business development is handled. It will show areas of strength, areas in need of improvement, and an approach to improve an organization's chances of winning the opportunity. As the sponsor, you received approval to move to the initiating phase from your Portfolio Review Board. It now is appropriate to_____

A. Define the program's scope and benefit strategy

B. Identify the program's benefits

C. Quantify business benefits

D. Prepare a program governance plan

65. 假设你已经决定发起一个新的项目集，这个新的项目集是为了建立一种新的方法，以确定组织是否要对某一机会进行竞标，以及组织应遵循的步骤，以确定提交的提案是否会被选中。这将是一个可以改变业务发展处理方式的定量模型。它会显示出优势领域，需要改进的领域，以及提高组织赢得机会的方法。作为项目集发起人，你收到了项目组合评

审委员会的批准进入项目集启动阶段。现在应该做的是_____

A. 定义项目集范围和收益策略　　B. 识别项目集收益

C. 量化商业利益　　D. 准备项目集治理计划

66. Your company has established a program to manage the development of new pet food products, and you have been appointed manager of this program. It is the first program of its kind in your company; its structure was set up because numerous projects in the planning stage have dependencies and require some of the same resources. You realize that there are some commonalities among the benefits in the projects. Your program will be the first in your company to have a Governance Board throughout its life cycle. It has led to the company establishing program governance as a standard process, and it then addresses_____

A. Endorsing or approving recommendations for programs

B. Aggregate performance of components of the program

C. Value indicators for program components

D. Models to ensure that the portfolio makes the best use of resources

66. 你的公司已经启动了一个项目集以管理开发新的宠物食品产品，你已被任命为这个项目集的经理。它是你们公司的第一个这种类型的项目集，目前这个项目集的结构已经事先确定好了，事先确定的原因是在规划阶段有众多的项目之间存在依赖关系并且很多都需要相同的资源。你意识到这些项目中的收益中有一些共性。你这个项目集将会是你们公司第一个在其整个生命周期内设置治理委员会的项目集。这个项目集已经为公司的项目集管理引入了项目集治理作为其一套标准体系过程，下一步需要处理的是_____

A. 背书或者批准项目集的建议

B. 整合项目集组件的绩效

C. 项目集组件的价值指标

D. 建立确保项目组合充分利用资源的模型

67. You are the program manager for the International Air Traffic Association (IATA). The executives, representing all the airlines in the world, want to set up a global program for loyalty to airlines rather than the myriad of separate reward programs that now exist. They have built a business case for this program that shows in doing so benefits will accrue as there will be fewer disruptions to passengers and to the airlines if a flight is canceled, and the passenger could have taken a non-stop flight from his or her home airport rather than needing to travel to another airport just for the loyalty program. You have been asked to document thresholds for evaluating achievement of key performance indicators. This should be in_____

A. The business case　　B. The benefit register

C. The benefit realization plan　　D. The benefit report

67. 你是国际航空运输协会（IATA）的项目集经理。协会执行官，代表着世界上的所有航空公司，想要为提升乘客忠诚度建立一个全球性的项目集，而不是现存的独立的奖励项目集。他们已经做了商业论证，表明这样做将会带来收益的增加，因为在航班取消的情况下，这将会减少对乘客和航空公司的影响。乘客可以搭乘他的原驻机场另一般直达飞机，而不是一定要去另外的机场转机。你已经被要求针对这个项目集做关键绩效指标的评估以及定义关键指标。这应该放在以下哪里_____

A. 商业论证　　　　　　　　　　　B. 收益登记册
C. 收益实现计划　　　　　　　　　D. 收益报告

68. Your organization has a defined process that it follows to determine which programs and projects should be in the portfolio, and this process is followed before leadership approval is received officially to authorize a program or project. In the past 10 years, your company, XYZ, has focused on projects. It has set up a project management methodology, which project managers are to follow, and it also has a Project Management Office. However, you recently attended a conference, and you realize since you are a member of the XYZ's Portfolio Review Board that many of the projects you are considering at your next meeting might be better managed if they were a program. After this conference, you met with other members of the Portfolio Review Board and explained how many of the existing projects in XYZ might be better organized as a program so they could then obtain more benefits than if the projects were managed in a standalone fashion. Now, with the upcoming Portfolio Review Board meeting, of the following possible key initiatives, which one would benefit by being managed as a program?_____

A. Expanding a ski area

B. Setting up a career path for people in the project management profession

C. Upgrading the nation's airspace system

D. Introducing a new project planning tool in a large organization

68. 你的组织定义了一个管理流程，用于确定哪个项目或者项目集应该放到项目组合中。在领导正式审批授权这个项目集或项目之前都要遵循这个过程。在过去的 10 年，你的公司——XYZ 一直在集中精力做项目。公司已经建立了一套项目经理都需要遵循的项目管理方法，并且也有自己的项目管理办公室。然而，因为你是 XYZ 公司的项目组合评审委员会成员，所以在你最近参加完一个会议后，你发现一些在下一次会议要考虑的项目作为项目集来管理可能会更好。会后，你与其他的项目组合评审委员会成员进行了沟通并解释了 XYZ 公司中有多少现有项目可以作为单独的项目集来管理并可能获得更多的收益。现在，随着这个即将到来的项目组合评审委员会会议，下面这些可能的关键活动中，哪个可能将会受益于作为项目集来管理_____

A. 扩大项目集影响范围　　　　　　B. 为项目管理专业人员建立职业发展路径
C. 升级国家空间系统　　　　　　　D. 在大型组织中引进新的项目规划工具

69. You are managing a program under contract with a major motion picture studio. Your contract is for three years with annual renewal possible if the program is completed on schedule. Payment terms in your contract are 60 days. You need to hire several subcontractors to assist with the program. To protect your financial position and cash flow on the program, you should set the payment terms for your subcontractors at_____

A. 30 days

B. 45 days

C. 60 days

D. 90 days

69. 作为一个主要电影工作室的签约项目集经理，你正在管理一个项目集。如果项目集按计划完成，你的 3 年期的合同就能得到年度更新。你的合同的付款周期是 60 天。你需要雇用几个承包商以支持这个项目集。要在项目集上保护你们的财务状况和现金流，你应该为你的承包商设置的付款周期是_____

A. 30 天

B. 45 天

C. 60 天

D. 90 天

70. On your program, two key members of your Governance Board are not attending any meetings. The three other members are pleased with your progress, but you are concerned because these Board members are not participating, sending substitutes, or communicating with you when you send status updates. To avoid incorrect assumptions about their lack of participation, you should_____

A. Request a face-to-face meeting

B. Ask a core team member to meet with some of their staff members

C. Talk with the other Board members about their lack of participation

D. Conduct a thorough analysis of the situation

70. 在你的项目集中，有两名治理委员会的关键成员从不出席任何会议。其余 3 名成员对你们的进展表示很满意，但是你很担心因为那两名成员没有参与，没有委派代理甚至在你提交状态报告时都没有和你沟通。为了避免对于他们缺乏参与而做出的不当假设，你应该_____

A. 请求面对面交流

B. 要求一名核心团队成员会见一些他们的工作人员

C. 与委员会的其他成员讨论他们没有参与的问题

D. 对情境进行深入分析

71. Although each program has its own Governance Board, there are times when issues arise that a program manager may need to interface with executive management and external stakeholders. If this needs to be done_____

A. Escalate the issue first to the Governance Board before going elsewhere

B. Obtain needed information to inform the Governance Board

C. Follow the issue escalation process explicitly

D. Ensure the issue is one that has major implications outside of the program

71. 尽管每个项目集都有自己的治理委员会，但是当项目集经理与高管和外部相关方对接时，就可能出现一些问题。如果这些问题需要处理，则应该_____

A. 在寻求他处前，首先将问题升级至治理委员会

B. 为了向治理委员会汇报，收集所需信息

C. 明确遵循问题升级流程

D. 确认问题是否与项目集外部有关联

72. As your government agency moves toward performance-based management, the senior executives issue a five- year plan with a number of initiatives. Each program and project will have key performance indicators (KPIs). Programs and projects will not be pursued without a detailed business case that is approved by a Governance Board composed of senior managers from each of the functional units. You are appointed as program manager to develop processes for these initiatives and are working on your charter. But, the agency now has undergone a 50% reduction in its budget, and no changes are expected in the near future. As the program manager, you should_____

A. Seek guidance from your sponsor

B. Complete the charter

C. Update the business case

D. Expand your roadmap so initial milestones will not be met for at least two years

72. 当你的政府机构推行基于绩效的管理，高管发布了针对 5 年计划的一系列举措。每一个项目集和项目都有关键绩效指标（KPI）。如果没有治理委员会（由来自各职能单位的高级经理组成）批准的详细商业论证，项目集和项目就不能立项。你被任命为项目集经理为这些举措制定流程，现在正在制定项目集章程。但是，该机构目前已将预算减少 50%，并预计近期不会有变化。作为项目集经理，你应该_____

A. 向你的项目集发起人寻求帮助

B. 完成章程

C. 更新商业论证

D. 扩展路线图，这样初步的里程碑至少应两年内达成

73. Your program to develop a 7G phone is being terminated early because your competition already has a 7G phone model on the market. This early closing has resulted because of_____

A. Poor performance　　　　　　B. Inability to deliver benefits

C. A technology change　　　　　D. Realignment of strategic goals

73. 你所负责的开发 7G 手机的项目集被提早终止，原因是竞争对手已经有一款 7G

手机在市场上销售。该项目集提前终止的原因是_____

A. 不良绩效 　　　　　　B. 无法带来收益

C. 技术变革 　　　　　　D. 战略目标调整

74. Your company is a worldwide leader in Six Sigma and the ISO 9001. Because of the importance of quality management, you appoint a member of your core program team to be responsible for quality planning on your program. At Governance Board meetings, he will often describe whether quality standards for the program are being met. The Governance Board is interested because_____

A. It approved the quality plan

B. Quality issues are covered in reporting and control processes

C. It ensures consistency in program management

D. These standards must be met before approving component transition

74. 假设你所服务的公司是一家在六西格玛和 ISO 9001 领域领先的全球性公司，由于质量管理的重要性，你指定了一名核心项目团队成员负责对项目集进行质量规划。在治理委员会会议上，他经常提到是否达到项目集质量标准。治理委员会对此感兴趣，因为_____

A. 质量计划得以批准

B. 报告和控制流程涵盖了质量问题

C. 它确保了项目集管理的一致性

D. 在批准组件移交前，必须满足这些标准

75. You are the program manager for an updated enterprise resource planning system that also will include business development and knowledge management modules. Time to market is critical, and as the program manager you know other competitors' products tend to take an extremely long time to implement so with your new products you also are emphasizing ease of implementation and training end users. You will be using external contractors for part of the work. As you administer procurements, your company's program management methodology requires you to follow which of the following_____

A. Contract management plan 　　B. Contract administration plan

C. Procurement management plan 　D. Contract procurement plan

75. 假设你是一名负责更新企业资源规划系统的项目集经理。该系统包括业务开发和知识管理模块。快速抢占市场先机至关重要，你知道其他竞争对手的产品开发周期非常长。同时对于新产品，你将重点实施和培训最终用户的易用性特点。对于部分工作，你打算寻求外部承包商。对于采购管理，公司项目集管理方法应该遵循_____

A. 合同管理计划 　　　　　B. 合同行政计划

C. 采购管理计划 　　　　　D. 合同采购计划

76. You are Company A's program manager for the development of an online banking system for your community bank, for which your company will realize $20 million in US dollars. To track the various stakeholders, you and your team set up a stakeholder register and prepared a stakeholder engagement plan. The individual or organization responsible to ensure program goals are achieved is_____

A. Executive sponsor
B. Governance Board
C. Program sponsor
D. Program manager

76. 假设你是 A 公司负责社区银行的网上银行系统开发的项目集经理，此项目集将为公司盈利 2 000 万美元。为了跟踪各相关方，你和团队建立了一份相关方登记册，并准备了相关方参与计划。以下哪一个人或组织负责项目集目标得到实现_____

A. 执行发起人
B. 治理委员会
C. 项目集发起人
D. 项目集经理

77. You are the program manager for a water-alleviation program in Ward, Florida, that requires extensive equipment. Some of this equipment represents new technology. As the program manager, you are preparing regular program performance reports, and each one discusses this equipment. In these reports, they should include_____

A. Risk analysis
B. Resource use
C. Approved change requests
D. Audit recommendations

77. 假设你是沃德·佛罗里达州的一个水净化项目的项目集经理。此项目集需要大量的设备。其中一些设备采用了新技术。作为项目集经理，你正在准备定期的项目集绩效报告，每一份报告都与该设备相关。在这些报告中应该包括_____

A. 风险分析
B. 资源使用
C. 批准的变更请求
D. 审计建议

78. Your water alleviation program in Ward, Florida, is progressing. You have a core team of six people, and you have seven project managers. You were fortunate this year in that while Ward got a lot of heavy rain during the rainy season, it did not get any hurricanes. However, the Lake levels are still low, and residents cannot water more than two hours once a week until your program is complete. The City also is limited to watering only once a week as well but for four hours. You have a number of key stakeholders in the City government as well as the residents plus your own company. Therefore, you realize the importance of influencing throughout the program but especially as you work to_____

A. Manage program resources
B. Negotiate with stakeholders
C. Lead with stakeholders
D. Maintain program strategic alignment

78. 在沃德·佛罗里达州，你负责的水净化项目正在进行中。你有一个 6 人的核心团队及 7 位项目经理。幸运的是虽然这一年的雨季沃德下了很多场大暴雨，但没有任何飓风。湖的水位仍然较低，在项目完成前，当地居民每周最长可以得到 2 小时供水。城市居民用水也受限制，每周一次不超过 4 小时。项目的一些关键相关方包括市政府、居民及你的公司。以下哪项工作，最能让你意识到整个项目集的重要性及影响力_____

A. 管理项目集资源      B. 与相关方协商

C. 引领相关方      D. 维护项目集战略一致性

79. As a program manager for the 888 series of aircraft being produced by your company, you are preparing for an important meeting of your Governance Board to assess progress in coordinating deliverables. Because of an acquisition by your company, the Board includes two new executives. This will be their first Board meeting. The other organization did not follow governance processes. To explain the governance approach, you need to_____

A. Aggregate performance information about your program for these new members

B. Personally provide a copy of the governance plan to these new members

C. Ask your sponsor to meet with these new members to discuss their roles and responsibilities

D. Meet with these two new Board members to discuss your program prior to the Board meeting

79. 作为一名负责 888 系列飞机制造的项目集经理，你准备组织与治理委员会的重要会议，以评估可交付成果协调的进度。因为公司的一项收购活动，董事会新来了两个高管，他们将第一次参加公司的董事会会议。目前尚无其他组织遵循治理流程。为了说明治理方法，你需要_____

A. 为新成员汇总项目集绩效状况

B. 为这些新成员提供一份治理计划副本

C. 要求项目集发起人与这些新成员见面，明确他们的角色和责任

D. 在董事会会议开始前，与两位新董事会成员碰面沟通项目集现状

80. You are a member of your company's Program Selection Committee, which is trying to decide which one of four programs to launch. Your company prides itself on superior quality in the automobile parts field. Each program has prepared its business case. Proposed Program A will overlap and combine its phases, milestones, and activities. Proposed Program B will delay its schedule if necessary in a trade-off situation to ensure that quality is achieved. Proposed Program C will have a flexible structure to ensure innovative features at a minimal cost. Proposed Program D will focus on the technical features, cost, and schedule in its metrics. You select_____

A. Program A      B. Program B

C. Program C      D. Program D

80. 假设你是公司的项目集甄选委员会成员，该委员会将决定启动 4 个项目集中某一

个项目集。公司在汽车零部件领域以品质卓越著称。每个项目集准备了商业论证。项目集 A 草案将项目集的各阶段、里程碑和活动进行重合归并。项目集 B 草案为了确保质量，会考虑计划延期。项目集 C 草案提出了灵活的结构，以达到以最低成本创新。项目集 D 草案侧重技术功能、成本及进度的指标。你会选择_____

A. 项目集 A
B. 项目集 B
C. 项目集 C
D. 项目集 D

81. When your program is complete, it will generate more than 80 percent of the revenue earned by the company. Thus, it will have a major impact on the balance sheet. To assist you in your work, you prepared a program financial plan and established a budget baseline. Now you are tracking, monitoring, and controlling funds and expenses. Not to be overlooked in this process is_____

A. The profit the company earns

B. The balance between profit and loss

C. The operational costs

D. A summary of the revenue, direct cost, indirect cost, operating profit, and net profit of a company at a given point in time

81. 当你的项目集完成，它将为公司带来超过 80%的现金流收入。它将对公司的资产负债表产生重大影响。你准备了项目集的财务计划，并制定了预算基准。假设现在你正在跟踪、监控和控制项目集的资金和费用。以下哪项是不容忽视的_____

A. 公司赚取的利润

B. 盈亏平衡

C. 运营成本

D. 关于特定时间点的项目集收益、直接成本、间接成本、运营利润和净利润的概要

82. You are the program manager for the International Air Traffic Association (IATA). You also are about to complete a project to determine how many points will be transferred from people in existing programs to the new loyalty program. You have just prepared a request to close this project to present to your Governance Board. The Governance Board members and your sponsor have indicted before approving the transition, they want to review_____

A. Sign offs on completed deliverables　　B. Business case

C. Delivery and transition of benefits　　D. Project management plan

82. 你是国际航空协会（IATA）的一位项目集经理。你将要完成一个项目，以确定有多少积分需要从现有项目迁移到新的忠诚度项目。你刚准备好了关闭此项目集的申请，并打算展示给治理委员会。在批准切换之前，治理委员会成员和你的项目集发起人提出要检查项目集的_____

A. 已完成可交付成果的认可签署　　　　B. 商业论证

C. 交付和转移的收益　　　　　　D. 项目管理计划

83. Your company is noted for its maturity and excellence in program management. It has received awards for its successes in program and project delivery. Last year, it received the Project Management Office of the Year Award, even though it really calls its PMO a Program Management Office, which it established about 12 years ago. One reason your company is a leader in the field is the PMO provides support in_____

A. Recognizing the use of environmental enterprise factors

B. Defining quality standards

C. Ensuring alignment to organizational strategy

D. Adhering to standards of professional conduct and responsibility

83. 你所服务的公司以项目管理成熟度和卓越性闻名，并已在项目和项目集交付上获得嘉奖。去年，公司获得了年度 PMO（项目管理办公室）大奖。尽管在公司内部，它其实是成立了 12 年的 PMO（项目集管理办公室）。你的公司之所以能成为该领域中的佼佼者，是因为 PMO 提供了以下哪项支持_____

A. 识别事业环境因素的用处　　　B. 定义质量标准

C. 确保与组织战略一致　　　　　D. 坚持职业操守和责任标准

84. You meet with your Governance Board on the 888 aircraft series program. Your program is on schedule, but the Board wants to accelerate production to beat a competitor's 480 aircraft to market. The Board provides you with an additional 100 aerospace engineers to perform concurrent engineering in the design phase. This shows the importance of the Governance Board in_____

A. Conducting periodic health checks

B. Setting program success criteria

C. Program funding

D. Program performance support

84. 你与 888 系列飞机计划治理委员会见面。你的项目集正在按计划进行，但董事会要求加快生产，以在市场中击败竞争对手 480 飞机。董事会为你额外提供了 100 名航空航天工程师来实施设计阶段的并行工程。这显示了治理委员会在哪方面的重要性_____

A. 定期进行健康检查　　　　　　B. 设置项目的成功标准

C. 项目资金　　　　　　　　　　D. 项目集绩效支持

85. You have been a program manager for three years. You realize that a common understanding of program scope among the stakeholders leads to greater program success. Throughout the past three years, you have communicated extensively with your stakeholders and believe you are meeting most of their expectations, but some still have some doubts as to overall success. Therefore, in your last program review with your Governance Board, you noted

this concern and now want to document a common understanding of the overall scope and have the key stakeholders sign off on it. This understanding is best documented as part of the_____

    A.　Stakeholder management plan　　　　B.　Program scope statement

    C.　Program scope management plan　　　　D.　Program charter

85.　你是有 3 年工作经验的项目集经理。你意识到，相关方对项目集范围达成一致认识将提高项目集的成功率。在过去的 3 年里，你与项目相关方沟通非常充分，并认为你最大限度地达到了他们的期望，但还是有部分相关方对项目集的成功有些疑虑。因此，在最近一次与治理委员会开展的项目集审查中，你注意到该问题，并打算将对项目集范围的共识记录下来，并请关键相关方进行了签字确认。该共识应该记录在哪个文件中_____

    A.　相关方管理计划　　　　　　　　　B.　项目集范围说明书

    C.　项目集范围管理计划　　　　　　　D.　项目集章程

86.　For your program, you prepared a detailed stakeholder analysis. Stakeholder A thought that the program objectives were to deliver a detailed plan for your city's growth and development over the next 10 years; Stakeholder B thought that the purpose was to design a water- retention process to ensure that each citizen would have adequate water in the future; Stakeholder C thought that the program was to provide services to the city for its overall management by outsourcing its information technology (IT) services, personnel, and procurement functions; and Stakeholder D thought that the program was to provide a detailed workflow for all the city's functions. In the face of this lack of common understanding of the requirements, you need to prepare a_____

    A.　Feasibility study　　　　　　　　　B.　Stakeholder management plan

    C.　Benefits realization plan　　　　　　D.　Program scope statement

86.　你为项目集准备了详细的相关方分析。相关方 A 认为，项目集的目标是提供你所在城市未来 10 年发展的详细计划；相关方 B 认为，项目集的目的在于设计一个水保留流程，确保未来每一个市民有充足的水资源；相关方 C 认为，项目集旨在通过外包信息技术（IT）服务、人员管理和采购职能，为城市提供整体管理服务；相关方 D 认为，该项目集为城市的所有功能提供了详细的工作流程。针对如此多样缺乏共同性的需求理解，你应该准备_____

    A.　可行性研究　　　　　　　　　　　B.　相关方管理计划

    C.　收益实现计划　　　　　　　　　　D.　项目集范围说明书

87.　In a meeting with your program's Governance Board, you discussed ongoing and completed risk responses. You have been working to minimize risks, and a member of your core program team is responsible for overall risk management as her primary activity. You recently held a risk review meeting for your program, and many risks have occurred that were not identified and analyzed.  This was followed by a meeting with your Governance Board, which directed you to prepare a comprehensive update on all risks. This decision by the Governance Board in its role in_____

    A.  Establishing an issue escalation process

    B.  Program reporting and control

    C.  Program performance support

    D.  Monitoring progress and determining if changes are needed

87. 在与项目集委员会的会议上，你和大家讨论了已完成及正在进行中的风险措施。你一直在努力尽量减少风险，并指派了一名核心项目团队成员来负责总体风险管理。最近你召开了一次项目集风险审查会议，分析了一些已发生但未曾识别和分析的风险。在随后与治理委员会的会议上，委员会指示你去准备一份包含所有风险的最新全面报告。治理委员会的这一指示表示治理委员会是在_____

    A. 建立问题升级流程        B. 项目集报告和控制

    C. 项目集绩效支持          D. 监督进度和变更决策

88.   You are a member of your insurance company's Program Selection Committee, which is considering a number of potential programs. Program A is estimated to cost $100,000 to implement and will have annual net cash inflows (ANCI) of $25,000. Program B is estimated to cost $250,000 to implement and have ANCI of $75,000. Program C is estimated to cost $600,000 to implement and have ANCI of $125,000. Program D is estimated to cost $125,000 to implement and have ANCI of $50,000. Your selection criteria are based on the shortest payback period. You recommend that your company select_____

    A.  Program A            B.  Program B

    C.  Program C            D.  Program D

88. 你是保险公司的项目集甄选委员会成员，正在评估以下项目集。项目集 A，预计完成需花费 100 000 美元，将带来年均 25 000 美元的净现金流入（ANCI）。项目集 B，预计完成需花费 250 000 美元，将带来年均 75 000 美元 ANCI。项目集 C，预计完成需花费 600 000 美元，将带来年均 125 000 美元 ANCI。项目集 D，预计完成需花费 125 000 美元，将带来年均 50 000 美元 ANCI。采用最短投资回收期方法，你会建议公司选择_____

    A. 项目集 A           B. 项目集 B

    C. 项目集 C           D. 项目集 D

89.  As an energy company "upstream" program manager, you use your program work breakdown structure (PWBS) to build your schedule. You have seven projects in your program, and it is to be completed in three years. The best approach is to_____

    A. Hold an off-site meeting in which project managers and your core program team work together to complete the schedule

B.　Have the project managers build the detail for their projects and then roll it up into the control points and PWBS program packages

C.　Work with your core program team to develop the program schedule and then ask the project managers to use this schedule as they prepare more detailed project schedules

D.　Have the first draft of the program schedule identify the start and end dates of the components

89.　作为一家名叫"上游"能源公司的项目集经理，你按照项目集工作分解结构（PWBS）来构建进度计划。此项目集有 7 个项目，将在 3 年内完成。据此，制定进度表的最佳方法是_____

A.　组织召开场外会议，让所有项目经理和核心项目集团队共同合作完成进度计划

B.　让项目经理们先分别为各自项目创建详细进度，然后再整合成控制点和 PWBS 项目集工作包

C.　与核心项目集团队一起制定进度表，然后让项目经理们基于这份进度计划制订他们的更详细的项目进度计划

D.　草拟项目集进度计划的初稿，并确定开始和结束日期

90.　Your molecular biology program is scheduled to last three years. Project A has been under way since the program began and is scheduled to be complete at the end of year 2. Project B is scheduled to begin in year 2.　Project C has just begun and requires some domain- specific resources in molecular biology from both Projects A and B. Project Manager A is concerned that Project Managers B and C will require some of her key scientists; If these resources are reassigned, then the end date for Project A will slip. She has been practicing a philosophy of "no secrets" with the client and has informed Project Managers B and C that she is not willing to let any of her molecular biologists leave Project A until it is officially closed.　You receive a call from the client requesting a meeting to discuss resource issues and the status of Project A.　At this point, you_____

A.　Meet with Project Manager A and tell her to first talk with you before she informs the client of any concerns in the future

B.　Tell Project Managers B and C that you support Project Manager A's decision not to release any of her key scientists

C.　Meet with all three project managers and inform them that you will manage any resource redeployment issues

D.　Meet with all three project managers and empower them to reach consensus on how the resources should be redeployed before you meet with the client

90.　你的分子生物学项目集预计将持续 3 年。项目 A 已进行一段时间，并计划第二年结束。项目 B 计划于第二年开始。项目 C 刚刚开始，并需要项目 A 和 B 中的一些分子

生物学领域专家。项目经理 A 担心项目经理 B 和 C 都需要她的一些关键科学家；如果这些专家被重新分配到其他项目，那么项目 A 的结束日期将会出现问题。秉承与客户"肝胆相照"的理念，他知会项目经理 B 和 C，并称在项目 A 正式结束前，她不愿意让分子生物学家离开。作为项目集负责人，你收到了客户的电话，要求召开会议讨论资源问题及项目 A 的状态。此时，你应该_____

A. 与项目经理 A 会面，并告诉她，在她向客户提供任何有关未来的顾虑之前先和你谈谈

B. 告诉项目经理 B 和 C，你支持项目经理 A 的决定，不放走关键科学家资源

C. 与 3 个项目经理会面，并告知他们，你将管理任何资源调配问题

D. 与 3 个项目经理会面，在你与客户见面之前，促使他们达成如何重新分配专家的共识

91. You are managing Program BBB for your manufacturing firm. You have one subprogram and seven projects thus far, and the program is just beginning. You need to set up a governance structure for these components. You have your PgMP® and have managed successfully two other programs for your firm. The best approach to follow is_____

A. Use the same governance structure as that for your program

B. Ask your PMO to provide the governance function

C. Manage a component Governance Board

D. Have your sponsor provide oversight and determine when the program Governance Board should be consulted

91. 你正在为所服务的一家制造企业管理项目集 BBB。该项目集刚开始，包括 1 个子项目集和 7 个项目。你需要为这些组件建立治理结构。你获得了 PgMP®认证，并已成功地为公司管理了其他 2 个项目集。以下哪种是最佳的管理项目集的方法_____

A. 使用相同的治理结构作为你当前项目集的方法

B. 请求项目管理办公室（PMO）提供治理功能

C. 管理组件治理委员会

D. 由发起人提供监督，并决定何时向治理委员会咨询

92. You are managing a program whose budget at completion (BAC) is €420,000. The program is 10 percent complete and has an earned value of €42,000. The actual costs (AC) are €50,000. This means that_____

A. Although the program is over budget, the overrun is insignificant at this time

B. The program is over budget by €8,000, which is a major problem

C. You need to calculate a new estimate to complete (ETC)

D. The CV is €378,000, and immediate action is necessary

92. 你所负责的项目集完工预算（BAC）为 420 000 欧元。目前该项目 10%完成，实

现 42 000 欧元挣值，实际成本（AC）达到 50 000 欧元。这表明_____

    A.　尽管该项目集超出预算，超限在此时是微不足道的

    B.　该项目集超出预算 8 000 欧元，是个大问题

    C.　需要计算新的完工估算（ETC）

    D.　CV 成本偏差是 378 000 欧元，需要立即采取行动

93.　You are managing Program BBB for your manufacturing firm. Program EEE is experiencing severe resource shortfalls. The executive sponsor is the same for both programs. Your Governance Board holds an emergency meeting to decide what you can do to assist Program EEE. The Board asks you to transfer seven of your manufacturing engineers to Program EEE and gives you the authority to contract with an outside firm for the engineering support that you need. With the change in your program BBB to use contractors for much of the manufacturing engineering work, you should_____

    A.　Notify your stakeholders

    B.　Update your roles and responsibilities matrix

    C.　Prepare a contracts administration plan

    D.　Approve a change to the outsourcing company's contract

93.　你正在为所服务的一家制造企业管理项目集 BBB。另外一个项目集 EEE 目前出现严重的资源短缺情况。两个项目集由相同的人发起。为此，治理委员会组织召开紧急会议，决定如何帮助项目集 EEE。治理委员会要求你将 7 名制造工程师移到 EEE 项目集，并授权你与一家外部公司联系获得所需的工程支持。随着项目集 BBB 改用很多承包商进行生产工程工作，你应该_____

    A.　通知相关方　　　　　　　　B.　更新角色和职责矩阵

    C.　准备合同行政计划　　　　　D.　批准外包公司合同的变更

94.　Your company is new to program management, but it has practiced a management-by-projects culture for many years. Many people now have their PMPs® as well as advanced degrees in project management. Recently, you took a seminar at a PMI conference on program management and suggested to your manager that the company should consider adopting program management because of its benefits to the organization. Before proceeding to take this idea to the Executive Committee, he asked you to perform an initial assessment as to why a focus on program management would add benefits. You need to therefore_____

    A.　Define the vision statement

    B.　Show the link to organizational program management

    C.　Identify integration opportunities

    D.　Define the objectives

94.　公司刚开始采用项目集管理，但它拥有实践多年的项目化管理的公司文化。很多

人都获得了 PMP®专业认证及项目管理的高级学位。最近，你参加了一个关于项目集管理的 PMI 研讨会，并向你的老板建议，公司应考虑采用项目集管理，因为这样可以带来组织收益。在将这个想法提交给执行委员会前，他要求你初步评估一下，为什么专注于项目集管理会增加收益。因此你需要_____

    A. 定义愿景声明        B. 展示组织项目集管理的关联性

    C. 确定整合机会        D. 确定目标

95.  You manage a program in the Ministry of Education. Your seven-year program is designed to ensure mandatory testing requirements for high school students throughout the country. Your program receives funding soon after the start of each fiscal year. Funds that are not spent during a fiscal year cannot be allocated to other programs or agency activities; rather, they revert to the general fund.  As a program manager, you ensure that_____

    A.  Your program focuses on reserve analysis

    B.  You spend all the money allocated in each fiscal year

    C.  All available financial information and all income and payment schedules are listed in detail as the budget is prepared

    D.  You add at least a 10 percent margin to the budget in anticipation of the reductions by the Ministry's budget office

95.  你负责一个教育部的项目集。该历时 7 年的项目集旨在对确保全国各地的高中生必要测试的需求。在每个财年开始之后不久，该项目集将收到资金。财年内尚未花完的资金不能被分配到其他项目或活动，而是转成普通基金。作为项目集经理，你应确保_____

    A.  项目集专注于储备分析

    B.  花光每个财年的分配资金

    C.  制订预算计划时，详细列明所有可用的财务信息和所有收入和付款进度计划

    D.  为应对教育部预算办公室可能减少预算的情况，你增加了至少 10%的边际预算

96.  Assume you are a member of a program team that is working to provide a better way to notify citizens in your City about the possibility of tornadoes. Now, the warning allows them only minutes to seek safety, and everyone believes a system such as that available for hurricanes and cyclones is necessary. As a resident of this city, you are pleased to be on the core team. Your program manager has asked you to be responsible for ensuring the program's stakeholders, of which there are many, receive information in a timely manner. Among other things, you must_____

    A.  Show "what's in it for me"

    B.  Collect stakeholder feedback on information timeliness

    C.  Be proactive in terms of both preventive and corrective actions

    D.  Prepare a stakeholder engagement plan

96. 假设你是某个项目集团队的成员，你们正在努力为市民改善针对龙卷风的预警机制。现在，预警只给了他们几分钟的时间去寻求安全避难，并且人们相信，一个可用于飓风和龙卷风的系统是必要的。作为这个城市的居民，你很高兴能成为核心团队的一员。项目集经理要求你负责确保该项目集的相关方（人数很多）能及时获得信息。除此之外，你必须_____

A. "设身处地"考虑问题

B. 收集相关方有关信息时效性的反馈

C. 积极主动地预防和纠正

D. 准备相关方参与计划

97. Your organization is embarking on a program to establish a culture of knowledge management. You established a lessons-learned register on your last project. The Enterprise Program Management Office (EPMO) was impressed and suggested to the CEO that a program focusing on knowledge management is needed. The CEO concurred, and you were appointed program manager. Two people from the EPMO have been assigned to the core program team. This is important because_____

A. The organization lacks available resources

B. The two members from the EPMO have expertise in this field

C. The EPMO Director is the program sponsor

D. The EPMO provides knowledge management support

97. 你的公司启动了旨在为公司建立知识管理文化的项目集。你为最近的项目建立了一份经验教训登记册。企业项目管理办公室（EPMO）对此印象深刻，并向 CEO 提议，建立项目集知识管理的必要性。CEO 表示同意，并任命你为项目集经理。EPMO 的两个成员也被分配到该核心项目集团队。知识管理很重要，是因为_____

A. 该组织缺乏可利用的资源

B. EPMO 的两个成员在这一领域有专长

C. EPMO 总监是这个项目集的发起人

D. EPMO 提供知识管理支持

98. Assume you are managing a program in your country which now allows people to buy in each state a pass to enable them to avoid the need to stop at toll booths on highways and bridges. However, each state in your country has a different type of pass so if you are in a different state, you cannot use it. As the program manager, your program's goal is to have an identical pass that every state can use on its highways and bridges. Additionally, your program will enable the pass to be used as well in airports at parking lots and garages. As you work on your program, you find there are a number of issues involved as states are reluctant to change to a new system, and various stakeholders have different concerns and issues. You are working to

identify, track, and close each issue as it arises. It is important to select a course of action consistent with_____

A. Resource control  B. Program scope

C. Risk management  D. Organizational strategic goals

98. 假设你正在负责国家的一个项目集，允许人们在各州购买通行卡，避免在公路桥梁收费站停留。然而，每个州都有不同类型的通行卡，所以如果你的卡在不同的州将无法使用。作为项目集经理，你的目标是让统一的通行卡在每个州的公路桥梁都能使用。此外，该项目集也希望该通行卡适用于机场的停车场和车库。在项目集进行过程中，你发现有一些问题，一些州不愿采用新系统，各相关方有不同的顾虑。你正在努力处理查明，跟踪和解决每个出现的问题。综上，选择与以下什么相关的措施是非常重要的_____

A. 资源控制  B. 项目集范围

C. 风险管理  D. 组织战略目标

99. You are an executive with a major recording studio. Four new groups have auditioned for a record contract, but you can select only one. The program to launch any group consists of Web site development, music videos, a nationwide tour, T-shirts, and a fan cluB. Your head of Marketing has done a net present value (NPV) for each group. Which do you choose?

| Group A NPV at | Group B NPV at | Group C NPV at | Group D NPV at |
|---|---|---|---|
| 5% = 5,243 | 5% = 2,320 | 5% = 6,400 | 5% = 3,000 |
| 10% = 2,841 | 10% = 1,254 | 10% = 3,275 | 10% = 2,755 |
| 15% = 1,563 | 15% = 688 | 15% = 1,679 | 15% = 700 |

You recommend that your company select_____

A. Group A  B. Group B

C. Group C  D. Group D

99. 你负责一家唱片公司。目前有 4 个新演唱组完成了试音，但你只能选用其中一个。推出演唱组，作为一个项目集，包括网站开发、音乐视频制作、全国范围内巡演、制作 T 恤和组建粉丝俱乐部。你的市场营销负责人为每组做了如下净现值（NPV）分析。你会选择哪一个？

| 组合 A NPV | 组合 B NPV | 组合 C NPV | 组合 D NPV |
|---|---|---|---|
| 5% = 5 243 | 5% = 2 320 | 5% = 6 400 | 5% = 3 000 |
| 10% = 2 841 | 10% = 1 254 | 10% = 3 275 | 10% = 2 755 |
| 15% = 1 563 | 15% = 688 | 15% = 1 679 | 15% = 700 |

你建议公司选择_____

A. 组合 A
B. 组合 B
C. 组合 C
D. 组合 D

100. You are the program manager for development of a next- generation personal digital assistant (PDA) that can be used on computers, airplanes, trains, and phones. You are in the early stages of your program, but it is ranked number 5 on your company's portfolio list. You have been asked to determine the organization's overall financial environment for the program and are doing so as part of_____

A. Developing your charter

B. Establishing the program's financial framework

C. Developing the program's financial plan

D. Developing the infrastructure for the program

100. 你是一名项目集经理，开发可以在计算机、飞机、火车和电话上使用的新一代个人数字助理（PDA）。项目集目前处于初期，但它在公司的投资组合列表中排名第 5。公司要求你确定项目集的总体财务环境，因此你需要_____

A. 制定项目集章程
B. 建立项目集财务框架
D. 制订项目集财务计划
D. 搭建项目集基础结构

101. You now have five projects in your next- generation PDA program. So far, you are pleased with your core team and its progress, and you have a Governance Board in place to oversee your progress. They also are responsible for gate reviews. You have just completed the PWBS for this program. Your next step is to_____

A. Generate the program schedule

B. Develop the issue resolution process for Governance Board Involvement

C. Negotiate for project team members

D. Identify key milestones

101. 你负责的新一代 PDA 的项目集包含 5 个项目。迄今为止，你对核心团队及其进展很满意。同时，项目集治理委员会也在监督项目集进展。他们还负责阶段关口评审。你刚刚完成对该项目集的 PWBS。你的下一步是_____

A. 生成项目集计划时间表

B. 制定治理委员会参与的问题解决流程

C. 与项目团队成员协商

D. 确定关键里程碑

102. You are the program manager for the International Air Traffic Association (IATA). The executives, representing all the airlines in the world, want to set up a global program for loyalty to airlines rather than the myriad of separate reward programs that now exist. A number of benefits

were identified in the business case and then in the benefits realization plan, which was approved by the Governance Board. You have a core team member who is maintaining a benefits register to track the status of each benefit, and you have assigned a person on your team to be the owner of each benefit. In a way, you have set this register up so it resembles the risk register you are using on your program. You found this has been a useful approach because_____

A. You need to regularly review your transition plan

B. Some corrective actions may be required as a result of risk mitigation activities

C. The same person who owns the benefit tends to also be a risk owner to minimize the responsibilities of your team members

D. It is then easier to communicate benefit status to your Governance Board

102. 你是国际航空协会（IATA）的项目集经理。该高管代表全球所有航空公司，希望启动一个有关对航空公司忠诚度的全球性项目集，改变现有的各式各样的单独奖励方案。能带来的好处已在商业论证中进行了描述，并包括在收益实现计划中。收益计划也得到了治理委员会的批准。某位核心团队成员负责维护收益登记册，跟踪每个收益的状态；同时，你为每项收益指派了负责人。在某种程度上，你设置了登记册，与你所使用的项目集的风险登记册一致。你发现此方法很有用，因为_____

A. 需要定期审查你的移交计划

B. 风险消除活动要求采取一些纠正措施

C. 负责收益的人往往也是风险负责人，减少团队成员的责任

D. 向治理委员会传达收益情况变得更容易

103. Assume your county government decided to move into program management as it found that a number of projects under way had inter-relationships and interdependencies in terms of the benefits they were to deliver to the citizens in the county. While the county has a project management methodology, it did not have one for program management so it decided to build on the best practices in the Project Management Institute's Standard for Program Management. As you reviewed the guidelines in The Standard for Program Management, you noted some activities are performed throughout the course of the program; an example is_____

A. Program Schedule Control

B. Benefits Realization

C. Program Performance Monitoring and Control

D. Manage Program Issues

103. 假设你的县政府决定采用项目集管理，因为他们意识到，从一些在建项目给市民带来的收益来看，项目之间有相互依赖性。该县目前采取项目管理机制，却没有项目集管理机制，因此他们决定建立一套项目集管理机制，遵循项目管理协会的项目集管理标准的最佳实践。当你回顾项目集管理标准准则时，你注意到一些贯穿整个项目集过程中进行

的活动，以下哪项是活动的例子_____

A. 项目集进度控制　　　　　　B. 收益实现

C. 项目集绩效监控　　　　　　D. 管理项目集问题

104. As the program manager, you have prepared your stakeholder register. However, you want to have a deeper understanding of the impacts of your program concerning your stakeholders' attitudes about it so you decide to use_____

A. Interviews　　　　　　　　B. Focus groups

C. Questionnaires and surveys　　D. Brainstorming

104. 作为项目集经理，你已经完成相关方登记册。然而，你希望更深了解相关方的态度对项目的影响，所以你决定使用_____

A. 访谈　　　　　　　　　　　B. 焦点小组

C. 问卷和调查　　　　　　　　D. 头脑风暴

105. You are managing a program that comprises new systems applications development and maintenance activities. These applications are critical to your company, as they involve access to proprietary data.  The systems must be available to your clients on a 24/7/365 basis. Much of the work is to be outsourced.  From a strategic perspective, your primary concern regarding this program is that_____

A. The contractor has systems capable of accommodating the applications and that all hardware and software has been updated

B. Your legal team has reviewed all the contract's terms and conditions to ensure that your company is protected in case of default

C. Your organization has the necessary levels of skill and expertise to manage and administer a contract of this magnitude

D. The contractor has the appropriate tools and techniques to safeguard your intellectual property

105. 你正负责一个项目集，包括新系统应用软件开发和维护活动。这些应用程序对你们公司至关重要，因为它们涉及访问专有数据。该系统需为你的客户提供全天候的服务。大部分工作打算外包。从战略角度看，你对这个计划主要关注的是_____

A. 承包商的系统能容纳所有的现有应用程序，并且所有的硬件和软件都已经更新了

B. 你的法律团队已经审查了所有合同的条款和条件，以确保公司在违约时获得保护

C. 你的组织拥有相应水平级别的技能和专业知识来控制和管理这种规模的合同

D. 承包商拥有适当的工具和技术来确保维护你的知识产权

106. Working as the program manager for a standard toll pass system, since there are about 30 such systems in existence now in your country to avoid the need for toll booths if people elect to buy these passes, you realized you needed to take the best practices of the various pass

systems already in existence and incorporate them into your program. You found that one State, Virginia, had a quality plan for its pass program, while most of the other states instead were only focusing on inspection as a quality tool and technique. Your emphasis is to perform quality activities throughout the program. As you focus on quality control, you should ensure_____

A. Checklists are completed

B. Quality audit recommendations are implemented

C. Perform health checks are performed

D. Service level agreements are established

106. 你的国家当前存在大约 30 个类似的自动通行系统，人们可以购买通行卡享受快速通行，减少了设置收费岗亭的需要。作为一个标准化收费站系统的项目集经理，你认为应该吸取采纳现有各系统的成功之处，融入新的系统中。你发现弗吉尼亚州对通行项目设有质量计划，而大多数其他州仅仅将检查作为质量工具和技术。你的重点是在整个项目中执行质量控制。对于质量控制，你应该确保_____

A. 检查清单是完整的

B. 质量审计建议是落实的

C. 执行了健康检查

D. 建立了服务等级协议

107. The program sponsor for a new customer-focused program in your organization submitted a business case to the Portfolio Review Board, which was approved. Then, your company merged with Company ABC, and it already has a comparable product in its pipeline. No one has done an inventory of Company ABC's programs and projects to see if there are any overlaps with ones in your company, but you worked for ABC part-time last year before joining Company MNO. You should_____

A. Inform the sponsor in MNO

B. Work with the sponsor in MNO to revise and resubmit the business case

C. Introduce the program manager in ABC to the MNO sponsor

D. Inform the Portfolio Manager in MNO

107. 公司的一个客户相关项目集发起人提交了一份商业论证给投资组合审查委员会并获得批准。最近，公司与 ABC 公司合并，两家公司拥有同类产品。目前没有人针对 ABC 公司的项目集和项目做过总结清单，无法获知两家公司的产品是否存在重叠。去年在加入 MNO 公司之前，你在 ABC 公司曾经兼职过。据此，你应该_____

A. 告知 MNO 公司发起人

B. 同 MNO 公司发起人合作，修订并重新提交商业论证

C. 介绍 ABC 公司项目集经理给 MNO 公司发起人

D. 告知 MNO 公司的组合经理

108. Members of your program Governance Board are complaining about performance information from your program. They claim that your reports are too detailed, are too many in

number, and are produced on a shifting schedule. You met with each person on the Board early in the program and thought you were meeting their information requirements. You then asked your organization's Enterprise PMO for assistance. The Enterprise PMO Director recommends the development and use of_____

    A.　A program dashboard

    B.　Standard metrics used in your industry

    C.　A more comprehensive software tool

    D.　The organization's standard financial reports

108.　治理委员会抱怨你负责的项目集的绩效信息。他们声称，你的报告过于详细，数字过多，进度计划多变。在项目集早期，你与董事会每个人沟通，并认为他们的信息需求得到满足，然后你向企业项目管理办公室（EPMO）求助。EPMO 总监建议开发和使用_____

    A.　项目集仪表盘　　　　　　　　B.　所在行业使用的标准指标

    C.　更全面的软件工具　　　　　　D.　组织标准财务报告

109.　For seven years, you have managed a program that involved breakthrough scientific research. You are now in the closing stage. You have already met with each scientist involved in the program at the time his or her work was finished.　You have also met with a member of your enterprise program management office (EPMO) who specializes in knowledge management to ensure that the intellectual property developed in the program is captured and documented for future reuse. You are_____

    A.　Ensuring legal protection of this valuable asset

    B.　Promoting collaboration in the scientific community

    C.　Recognizing individual efforts as well as the efforts of the entire project team

    D.　Officially releasing each scientist to his or her functional organization

109.　7 年来，你负责一个具有突破性科学研究的项目集。现在已进入项目集的完工阶段。在项目集每位科学家完工时，你都和他们碰了面。你也和一位企业项目管理办公室（EPMO）成员碰面，他在知识管理有专长，以确保项目集所开发的知识产权被记录下来以备未来使用。这样做，你是在_____

    A.　确保这个有价值资产的法律保护

    B.　提倡科学社区协作

    C.　认可个人贡献以及整个项目团队的贡献

    D.　正式遣散每个科学家回到他们的职能部门

110.　Recognizing the importance of benefits realization and management, as a program manager, it has been noted that a best practice to follow is to be able to quantify as many benefits in your benefits realization plan as possible and also to be able to communicate their status as required quickly to stakeholders. You and your core team decided that a best practice to follow in your program to develop a new drug to cure bone cancer with limited if any side effects and to beat your competitors to market even with all the federal regulations was to_____

A. Use tangible benefits in your benefit realization plan

B. Have each stakeholder sign off on your benefits realization plan indicating his or her concurrence with it

C. Invite each stakeholder to regularly scheduled benefit reviews, which are included in your program's roadmap

D. Maintain a benefits register

110. 作为一个项目集经理，应该能意识到收益实现和管理的重要性。大家注意到，尽可能量化收益，同时按照需求将项目集状态快速传达给相关方，是值得采取的一个最佳实践方法。你和核心团队决定开发一种新药物治疗骨癌，具有很小的副作用，以击败市场上的竞争对手，并满足所有联邦法规要求。为此，作为一项最佳实践，你们决定_____

A. 在收益实现计划中采用实际收益

B. 每个相关方签署同意实现方案

C. 作为项目集路线图一部分，邀请各个相关方参与定期收益评估

D. 维护收益登记册

111. As the program manager working on the development of an advanced polymer chemical for raincoats, you are in the process of initiating your program. You were selected as the program manager because in past program work, you excelled in some key performance competencies in initiation, one of which is_____

A. Identifying high-level risks

B. Ensuring alignment of program objectives with organizational strategic goals

C. Preparing a plan to initiate the program

D. Engaging stakeholders in ensuring strategic benefits are understood

111. 作为项目集经理，你的项目集目标是开发用于雨衣的高聚合物。当前项目集处于启动阶段。因为在过去工作的表现，你被任命为该项目集经理。你擅长于启动阶段的关键绩效方面，其中之一是_____

A. 识别高层级风险

B. 确保项目集目标与组织战略目标保持一致

C. 为启动项目集准备计划

D. 和相关方紧密合作，确保他们了解战略收益

112. Finally, your program to develop the advanced polymer chemical for raincoats is near to completion. You have had seven projects in your program, and the last one should finish in two months. You have been involving the people in your operations support group to be part of

your program team meetings now for the last year and earlier included them on the distribution list for your status reports so they felt they were part of the team for success as you recognize transition planning is the key to benefits sustainment in program management. As a program manager, you also recognize the importance of ensuring that component transition requests are prepared. It is especially important during_____

A. Transition Planning

B. Direct and Manage Program Execution

C. Develop Program Management Plan

D. Program Benefit Delivery

112. 你所负责雨衣先进高聚合物的开发项目集已接近尾声。在这个项目集中，有 7 个项目，最后一个应在两个月内完成。你邀请运营支持小组参与项目集小组会议，而且从去年及今年早些时候，你都将项目集状况报告发送给他们，让他们觉得自己是团队成功的一部分。你认识到成功的过渡计划是项目管理的收益维护的关键。作为项目集经理，你也认识到确保组件转换请求准备的重要性。这些在以下哪个阶段尤为重要_____

A. 过渡规划　　　　　　　　　B. 指导与管理项目集执行

C. 制订项目集管理计划　　　　D. 项目集收益交付

113. As you work on your program to design, develop, and manufacture a class of farm equipment that can be used above the Arctic Circle, you are also maintaining a spare parts inventory and are fulfilling spares requests for clients in addition to the new work in this program. You met today with the spare parts project manager, and he had a change to his project that affected his scope dramatically. When you reviewed this change with him, you realized it also would affect the scope of the manufacturing project manager's project in your program. As a result of your work in Program Scope Control, this means you should_____

A. Authorize funding for these changes　　B. Issue an approved change request

C. Convene your CCB　　　　　　　　　D. Update the PWBS

113. 在项目集中，你负责设计、开发和制造一类可以在北极圈内使用的农业设备，同时维护备件库存和满足客户的备件请求。今天你会见了副项目经理，他有一个变更将极大地影响项目范围。当你和他一起审查这个变更时，你意识到它同时也将在整个项目集内影响负责制造的项目经理的项目范围。对于项目集范围控制，你应该_____

A. 为项目变更授权提供资金　　　B. 发出批准变更请求

C. 召集变更控制委员会　　　　　D. 更新项目集工作分解结构

114. On your program to design, develop, and manufacture a class of farm equipment for use above the Arctic Circle, you want to make sure that the benefits from the program will be sustainable ones. Your sponsor is interested in having regular status reports about the progress of your program especially since she is located below the Arctic Circle and rarely makes on site

visits given the weather conditions to assess progress herself. To provide a clear picture of your program's performance as a while, you must_____

A. Forecast information on the significant project components

B. Aggregate information across projects and   non- project activity

C. Provide detailed reports on component projects at regular intervals

D. Monitor the status of the key deliverables

114. 在项目集中，你负责设计、开发和制造一类可以在北极圈内使用的农业设备，要确保项目集的收益是可持续的。发起人对项目进展定期状况报告感兴趣，尤其是她住在位于北极圈之外，因为天气寒冷，她很少进行实地考察和亲自评估。为了给你的项目集提供清晰的绩效状况，你应该_____

A. 预测重要的项目组件信息        B. 汇总跨项目和非项目活动信息

C. 定期提供组件项目的详细报告      D. 监督主要可交付成果的状态

115. You are sponsoring a new program in your company. You have identified the benefits and objectives and submitted the documentation to the Portfolio Review Board two weeks before its next meeting. You are competing with two other possible programs, so you decide to contact the Board members to see if they have any questions about your program. Board Member A is very supportive; Board Member B has concerns about the competitive attributes of your program versus those of other programs in the pipeline; Board Member C is supportive but not enthusiastic; Board Member D is not available to talk to you; and Board Member E is skeptical about the overall program strategy. To try to increase the support of Board Members B and E, you_____

A. Align the elements of your program more closely with the company's strategy

B. Refine your net present value (NPV) and internal rate of return (IRR) analysis

C. Meet with the Enterprise Project Management Office director to obtain support

D. Enlist greater support from the executive sponsor who personally knows the Board members

115. 在你公司，你发起了一个新项目集。你确定了效益目标，并在下一次会议前两周向投资组合审查委员会提交了文档。你与其他两个可能项目集竞争，你决定联系董事会成员，看看他们是否有关于你的项目集的任何疑问。董事会成员 A 非常支持；董事会成员 B 关心你的项目集与其他项目集之间的竞争特点；董事会成员 C 是支持的，但积极性不高；对于董事会成员 D，你无法获得与他谈话的机会；董事会成员 E 对总体项目集战略持怀疑态度。为了提高董事会成员 B 和 E 对项目集的支持，你应该_____

A. 将项目集各要素与公司战略保持更紧密的一致性

B. 优化项目集的净现值（NPV）和内部回报率（IRR）分析

C. 与企业项目管理办公室总监会面并获得他的支持

D.　争取执行发起人更大的支持，他与委员会成员私交不错

116.　You manage the development of an off-shore liquefied natural gas facility. Several contractors will be used in the component projects, and you are creating specific procurement strategies. After you determine which program work breakdown structure (PWBS) elements can be handled internally and which can be contracted, your next step is to_____

A.　Follow the program scope statement

B.　Determine the program requirements

C.　Prepare a procurement management plan

D.　Make sure contractors have comparable acceptance criteria

116.　你管理一个海上液化天然气设施的开发项目集。子项目将对外征召承包商，为此你正在创建具体的采购策略。当你确定完哪些项目集工作分解结构（PWBS）元素可在内部进行运作，哪些可以外包，下一步你将_____

A.　遵循项目集范围说明书　　　　　　B.　确定项目集需求

C.　准备采购管理计划　　　　　　　　D.　确保承包商有可比性的验收标准

117.　Assume you are leading a program in your gas company to promote more use of natural gas by customers. You have identified a number of benefits to the use of natural gas, and one of them is environmental since it is much cleaner. It also is more cost effective. However, everyone resists change, and people are having trouble understanding the benefits of this program and how to best present these benefits to consumers, especially when the natural gas production facilities in your company are fully operational. This means that as the program manager you need to convince stakeholders that the risks associated with natural gas are low. As you do so, it is important therefore to concentrate on_____

A.　Solely financial benefits

B.　Both direct and tangible benefits

C.　Intangible benefits and tangible benefits

D.　Measurable benefits

117.　假设你负责一家煤气公司的一个项目集，此项目集旨在推动促进消费者更多地使用天然气。你已识别了一些使用天然气的好处，其中之一是环保，因为它更加干净，同时性价比也更高。但是每个人抗拒改变，人们无法理解这个项目的好处，尤其是当你们公司天然气生产设施目前全面运作良好时，如何最好地展示这些好处给消费者非常有挑战。这意味着，作为项目集经理，你需要说服相关方，与天然气相关的风险是很低的。如果你打算这样做，需要着重强调以下哪个方面_____

A.　单纯财务收益　　　　　　　　　　B.　直接收益和有形收益

C.　无形收益和有形收益　　　　　　　D.　可衡量的收益

118.　You have set up measurement criteria for each of the benefits you identified in your benefit realization plan. You now want to establish a baseline for the benefits in the plan. As you establish your baseline, you have collected some key organizational, financial, and operational metrics against which you can measure improvements. A key task to consider as you establish the baseline is to_____

A. Devise a strategy to collect baseline data such as using questionnaires and interviews

B. Review your cost estimates

C. Assess process interdependencies

D. Determine the appropriate infrastructure needs

118. 在收益计划中，你已经为每个已识别的收益建立衡量标准。你现在要为收益计划建立基准。当你建立基准时，你收集了一些关键的组织、财务和运营指标，用以衡量改进效果。建立基准的其中一项非常重要的任务是_____

A. 制定策略以收集基准数据，例如使用问卷调查和访谈

B. 查看成本估算

C. 评估过程间的依赖关系

D. 确定合适的基础设施需求

119. Finally after four years of planning, your program management plan to convert customer relationship management software, supplier management software, human resource software, and telecom systems from legacy systems to an integrated platform was approved. At last, you are working to execute your plan, and you have four projects in your program thus far. Approved change requests are being implemented_____

A. Under the supervision of the individual project managers

B. By the program manager, based on his or her scope of authority

C. After approval by the program's Governance Board

D. As directed by the program management methodology

119. 经过 4 年的规划，你的项目集管理计划获得批准。该计划旨在将旧系统升级集成到新的平台，包括客户关系管理软件、供应商管理软件、人力资源软件和电信系统。你正在努力执行你的计划，目前你的项目集中有 4 个项目。批准的变更请求正在实施，应该_____

A. 在各个项目经理的监督下

B. 由项目集经理在他/她的职权范围内来执行

C. 先获得项目集的治理委员会批准

D. 以项目集管理方法论为指导

120. Finally after four years of planning, your program management plan to convert customer relationship management software, supplier management software, human resource software, and telecom systems from legacy systems to an integrated platform was approved. At

last, you are working to execute your plan, and you have four projects in your program thus far. As you build individual and group competencies to enhance the performance of your program, you should also_____

　A. Conduct performance assessments and place reports in the Human Resources files

　B. Communicate personnel performance to each team member's line manager

　C. Communicate personnel performance to the Vice President for Human Resources

　D. Rely on the Chief Learning Officer to conduct competency assessments

120.　经过 4 年的规划，你的项目集管理计划获得批准。该计划旨在将旧系统升级集成到新的平台，包括客户关系管理软件、供应商管理软件、人力资源软件和电信系统。你正在努力执行你的计划，项目集中目前有 4 个项目。为提高个人和团体的能力以增强项目集绩效时，你应该_____

　A. 进行绩效评估，并将报告存放在人力资源档案中

　B. 与直属经理沟通相应团队成员的绩效

　C. 与人力资源副总裁（VP）沟通团队成员的绩效

　D. 依靠首席学习官（CLO）进行能力评估

121.　You are preparing for a meeting of your program's Governance Board. Your program coordinator is using earned value (EV) to track and monitor performance and to forecast future performance. On your program, the planned value (PV) is $30,587, and the EV is $26,365. At this point, your program is 70 percent complete, so you can tell your Governance Board that your schedule performance index (SPI) is 0.86. The Governance Board therefore recognizes_____

　A. You are not experiencing any schedule problems

　B. You will have problems meeting your scheduled end date but are able to allocate additional resources

　C. There are problems, but it is easy to recover from this performance

　D. It will be difficult to recover from this performance, and a decision now is needed to terminate the program

121.　你正准备一个与项目集治理委员会的会议。你的项目协调员正在使用挣值（EV）来跟踪和监督绩效，并以此来预测未来的绩效。在你的项目集中，计划价值（PV）为 30 587 美元，而挣值（EV）为 26 365 美元。此时项目集已完成 70%，你告诉治理委员会，项目集的进度绩效指数（SPI）为 0.86。因此，治理委员会认为_____

　A. 项目集目前没有任何进度问题

　B. 你将面临无法按预定日期结束的问题，但这能通过增拨资源的方式来解决

　C. 存在问题，但能很容易从目前绩效恢复过来

　D. 很难从现在的绩效恢复，并应该当即决定终止此项目集

122. You are assuming a position in a company that has not had much experience with program management. You will be leading the program team and performing a business function for your program. The business case has already been made, and the program is scheduled to move into the Program Initiation phase. As the program manager, one competency that is embedded in your job is_____

A. Communication
B. Political skills
C. Strategic visioning
D. Leadership

122. 假设当前你服务于一家公司，该公司缺乏项目集管理经验。你将负责项目集团队并运营相应的业务部门。目前商业论证已完成，项目集正按计划进入了启动阶段。作为项目集经理，你的工作要求你具备的软技能是_____

A. 沟通能力
B. 政治技巧
C. 战略愿景力
D. 领导力

123. Assume you are managing a program at your University to establish a Master of Science degree in Program Management. Already, the University's Master of Science degree in project management is well recognized, and it has been accredited by leading organizations. Your business case for this program was approved by the University's trustees, and they asked for a benefits realization plan, which you prepared, and they signed off on and approved. However, they felt for reporting purposes to a Governance Board that it would be helpful to prioritize the benefits you have identified and will report on during meetings of the Governance Board. One approach to consider is to ensure_____

A. The identified benefits support best practices
B. The benefits are aligned with the University's strategic objectives
C. A benefit owner is assigned
D. Realistic measures of these benefits can be prepared

123. 假设你在大学负责建立项目集管理的科学硕士学位项目集。目前，该大学的项目管理科学硕士学位已被公众认可，并被鉴定为业内领先。该项目集的商业论证已获得大学理事会批准，他们要求你准备一份收益实现计划，并签署批准。然而，对于向治理委员会汇报而言，应确定各项收益优先级，并在治理委员会会议上进行报告。值得考虑的方法的目的是确保_____

A. 识别的收益为最佳实践提供支持
B. 收益与大学的战略目标保持一致的
C. 指派收益负责人
D. 准备如何实际衡量收益

124. Working on this program to establish a Master of Science degree in Program Management, assume you have a meeting coming up with your Governance Board in two

weeks. You need to demonstrate at this stage-gate review how you will report and track the benefits from your program. However, in your work in planning, you have identified a number of key factors external to your program that affect the proposed benefits, one of which is that your leading competitor in this field and located in your state also is looking into such a program and plans to offer it in an on-line fashion; your University only operates in a face-to-face mode. You know how important it is to track benefits and learning about this other University's plans to offer the degree on line is a key benefit that you had not planned for but now feel it is essential. The new benefit actually represents a_____

A. New project

B. Risk opportunity

C. Major issue

D. New program

124. 假设你负责建立项目集管理科学硕士学位项目集，并且在两周内将与治理委员会开会。你需要在这个阶段关口评审你将如何报告和跟踪项目集收益。然而，在规划中，你已经识别了一些项目集外部对未来收益有影响的关键因素。其中之一是，同一领域的同州首要竞争对手（相同州）也正在考虑类似的项目集并计划以在线发布的形式推出。你的大学只能在面对面的线下模式下运作。你现在知道了跟踪收益并了解其他大学计划提供的在线学位是多么重要，但你之前没有计划去做。新收益实际上是_____

A. 新项目

B. 风险机会

C. 主要问题

D. 新项目集

125. As a program manager, you recognize the importance of effective risk management. You want to maximize any risks that may be opportunities that can benefit your program and the organization. As you prepare your program risk management plan, you define risk profiles, which_____

A. Are collected through surveys

B. You brainstorm with your team and other stakeholders

C. Are expressed in policy statements

D. You determine through interviews

125. 作为一个项目集经理，你认识到高效风险管理的重要性。你想将任何有利于项目集和组织的机会最大化。准备项目集风险管理计划时，你定义了风险配置文件，它是_____

A. 通过调查来收集

B. 通过与团队和其他相关方的头脑风暴来获得

C. 通过政策声明来表述

D. 通过访谈来决定

126. As program manager for the development of a new drug, you are pleased that it has finally received regulatory approval, and you can move on to the manufacturing and distribution phase. You have been managing this program now for eight years, and you had six projects in it.

As this program has been under way for eight years, it is a best practice to_____

A. Organize program knowledge as a reference

B. Obtain a license for exclusive distribution

C. Work to ensure a positive reception for the product from end users and the medical field using skills in customer relationship management

D. Sign a nondisclosure agreement with the government

126. 作为新药物的研发项目集经理，你很高兴终于获得监管机构的批准，并且可以进入生产和销售阶段。你管理这个项目集至今已 8 年，它包含 6 个项目。作为进行了 8 年的项目集，一个最佳实践是_____

A. 整合项目集知识作为参考

B. 获得独家经销的许可证

C. 确保获得用户对产品和医疗领域客户关系管理技巧的肯定反响

D. 与政府签署保密协议

127. As the program manager for a new pipeline system that has as its goal no potential incidents of any type, you have a major challenge as your company in the past has had a poor safety record. This program is complex, and this goal will be difficult to achieve. However, after working to plan the program for three years, your Steering Committee met and approved your program management plan. As you move to approve components to be part of your program, you need to review the_____

A. Component charter      B. Change requests

C. Business case          D. Component initiation requests

127. 作为一个新管道系统的项目集经理，此项目集的目标消除任何类型的潜在事故。鉴于公司过去不佳的安全记录，这对你而言是个大挑战。该项目集复杂且目标较难实现。但是，在规划项目集 3 年后，指导委员会召开会议并批准了该项目集管理计划。在批准审查子项目之前，你需要审查_____

A. 组件章程              B. 变更请求

C. 商业论证              D. 组件发起请求

128. Your program management plan has been approved. So far, three projects have been chartered and authorized to be part of your program, and others may be added later. You have staffed your program team with a variety of in-house staff members, selected consultants, and several new full- time employees. It is now time to_____

A. Prepare your team development plan

B. Update your program resource plan

C. Prepare your resource management plan

D. Update your staffing management plan

128. 你的项目集管理计划已获批准。到目前为止，3 个项目已有项目章程并且已授权成为你的项目集的一部分，其他子项目也会在未来添加进来。你已经配备项目集团队，包括很多内部员工，特选顾问和几个新的全职员工。此时应该_____

A. 准备团队发展计划
B. 更新项目集资源计划
C. 准备资源管理计划
D. 更新人员配备管理计划

129. Assume you are working for a leading training company. Your leading competitor has just announced that it will launch in one month a new training approach using videos. Your CEO realizes such an approach will be highly beneficial and is superior to the on-line training your company offers, which is only asynchronous with people looking at slides, as the instructor discusses each slide. In fact, the CEO has had complaints about the boring nature of your firm's on line training. You have been selected as the program manager for this new video approach, and you need to have it available for all of your courses by the end of the year so you are not lagging that much behind the competition. You are working on your communication plan. You have found which of the following to be especially useful to you in this regard_____

A. Communications strategy
B. Communications requirements analysis
C. Lessons learned database
D. Program charter

129. 假设你正服务于一家领先的培训公司。你的主要竞争对手刚刚宣布，将在一个月内推出使用视频的新培训方法。你的 CEO 意识到，这种新方法非常有价值，比公司现有的联机培训更好。现有的在线培训仅仅提供了异步的方式，学员一边看幻灯片，老师一边讨论每页幻灯片。事实上，CEO 已经收到了关于公司的在线训练枯燥性的投诉。你被任命为该新的视频方式项目集经理，并需要在今年年底实现所有课程上线，这样就不会过于落后竞争对手。你正在做沟通计划。对于下列哪一项，你认为在这方面对你尤其有帮助_____

A. 沟通策略
B. 沟通需求分析
C. 经验教训数据库
D. 项目集章程

130. Finally, you Governance Board approved your communications plan for this program, and you now are addressing the best way to handle performance reporting and how to communicate this information to provide stakeholders with needed information. As you work in this area, you should consult the_____

A. Program management plan
B. Program Work Breakdown Structure (PWBS)
C. Governance plan
D. Organizational communications strategy

130. 治理委员会批准了你的项目集沟通计划。现在你正在研究如何最好地作绩效报告，以及如何与相关方沟通，为他们提供所需的信息。对于目前你所需要的工作，你应该查询_____

A. 项目集管理计划

B. 项目集工作分解结构（PWBS）

C. 治理计划

D. 组织沟通策略

131. You are a member of your organization's Program Selection Committee, which is conducting an off-site meeting to review the company's five major strategic goals, all of which are weighted equally. Goal 1 is to produce the highest possible quality products; goal 2 is to provide outstanding customer relationship management; goal 3 is to reduce reliance on external supply sources and maximize internal resources; goal 4 is to reduce manufacturing costs; and goal 5 is to maximize productivity. You are considering four programs and will recommend one to the CEO. Program A partially supports goal 1, fully supports goals 2, 3, and 4, and does not support goal 5; Program B fully supports goals 1, 3, 4, and 5, but does not support goal 2; Program C fully supports goals 1 and 2, partially supports goals 3 and 4, but does not support goal 5; Program D partially supports goals 1, 2, and 5, and fully supports goals 3 and 4. Considering this information, your recommendation should be to select_____

A. Program A

B. Program B

C. Program C

D. Program D

131. 你是公司项目集甄选委员会的成员，并正在参加一个场外会议，审查公司的 5 个主要战略目标，它们的权重相当。目标 1 是生产最高品质的产品；目标 2 是提供卓越的客户关系管理；目标 3 是减少对外部供应源的依赖，最大限度地发挥内部资源的价值；目标 4 是降低制造成本；目标 5 是最大限度地提高生产力。你正在考虑 4 个项目集，并会最终推荐其中之一给 CEO。项目集 A 部分支持目标 1，完全支持目标 2、3、4，不支持目标 5；项目集 B 完全支持目标 1、3、4、5，但不支持目标 2；项目集 C 完全支持目标 1 和 2，部分支持目标 3 和 4，但不支持目标 5；项目集 D 部分支持目标 1、2、5，并且完全支持目标 3 和 4。考虑到这些信息，你建议应选择_____

A. 项目集 A

B. 项目集 B

C. 项目集 C

D. 项目集 D

132. You are preparing for a major Governance Board review of your program. The program sponsor is especially interested in progress on Project A, as it provides the foundation for two other projects, and at the last meeting it was behind schedule. You want to ask the Board to approve the initiation of a new project. However, it is the Board's responsibility to_____

A. Request an audit of Project A

B. Focus on overall performance at this meeting and convene another meeting to determine if the new project should be initiated

C.　Ask for data on Project A's performance to date and especially its use of resources

D.　Determine minimal acceptance criteria

132．你正在为治理委员会审查你的项目集做准备。该项目集发起人对项目 A 的进度特别感兴趣，因为它是另外两个项目的基础，并且根据最近一次会议的汇报，它落后于原计划进度。你请求董事会批准启动其他新项目。然而，董事会的责任是_____

A.　申请项目 A 的审计

B.　会议上专注于整体绩效，并召集另外会议以决定是否启动新的项目

C.　询问关于项目 A 的目前绩效，特别是资源的使用情况

D.　确定最低验收标准

133．As a program manager, you consider the interests and concerns of all your stakeholders for program success. You manage communications to ensure that your stakeholders are informed about what is happening on your program and so that you can resolve any issues of importance to them. This is done as part of your responsibilities in_____

A.　Communications Control　　　　B.　Information Distribution

C.　Stakeholder Engagement　　　　D.　Communications Planning

133．作为项目集经理，你考虑的是所有相关方对项目集成功的兴趣关注。通过沟通管理，你以确保项目相关方了解项目集的状况，以便能解决一些对他们而言非常重要的问题。这里描述的是你哪方面的职责_____

A.　沟通控制　　　　　　　　　　B.　信息发布

C.　相关方参与　　　　　　　　　D.　沟通计划

134．Assume you are managing a program so your organization, a Fortune 500 company, has a standard program management system (PMIS) that all programs in all of its 90 business units will use. Such a common PMIS is a major internal program, and as a result, you have a limited budget to work with to make sure it is a success and is adopted by the heads of the business units and its program managers. You are following guidelines in the Project Management Institute's Standard for Program Management as you prepare this PMIS. You find as you monitor and control the program's finances you need to be both proactive and reactive. An example of being proactive is_____

A.　Identifying impacts to the components from overruns or under-runs

B.　Responding to necessary but unplanned activities that negatively affect the budget

C.　Responding to necessary but unplanned activities that positively affect the budget

D.　Using cost forecasting techniques on a regular basis

134．假设你正在为一家财富 500 强公司管理一个项目集，目标是建立标准的项目集管理体系（PMIS），应用到所有 90 个业务部门的项目集。作为一个公共的 PMIS（一个主要的内部项目），其结果是你的预算有限，PMIS 系统已被业务部门负责人和项目集经理们

采纳。在准备 PMIS 的过程中，你遵循项目管理协会的项目集管理标准准则。你发现你需要主动和被动地监督该项目集的财务情况。以下哪项是主动的例子_____

　　A. 识别超支或低于预算对子项目的影响

　　B. 对于那些必须但属于计划外的，对预算有负面影响的活动作出响应

　　C. 对于那些必须但属于计划外的，对预算有正面影响的活动作出响应

　　D. 定期使用成本预测技术

135.　You are Company A's program manager for the development of an online banking system for your community bank, for which your company will receive $20 million.Your management at the highest level is totally committed to this program, and it is the number one program in Company A's portfolio. Your Governance Board is dedicated to its success. As a result, the chairperson of the Board is_____

　　A.　The program sponsor　　　　　B.　The CEO

　　C.　The Portfolio Manager　　　　D.　The Director of the Enterprise PMO

135.　你是 A 公司的项目集经理，负责社区银行的网上银行系统项目集，此项目将为公司带来 2 000 万美元的收益。公司最高层完全致力于该计划，它也是 A 公司投资组合中的头号项目集。治理委员会为此项目集的成功全力以赴。因此，委员会主席是_____

　　A.　项目集发起人　　　　　　　　B.　CEO

　　C.　组合经理　　　　　　　　　　D.　企业项目管理办公室（EPMO）总监

136.　As a program manager in your country's food safety department, you are managing a program to ensure the safety of imported food in your country. This program resulted from many people becoming sick because of imported shrimp, poultry, and beef. This program is using public money and will last for several years; therefore, as the program manager, you need to_____

　　A.　Have a thorough understanding of the financial environment

　　B.　Develop a plan for each of the components in your program

　　C.　Have your project managers use earned value management to track all expenses

　　D.　Set up a project management information system to track resource plans and use

136.　作为你们国家食品安全部门的项目集经理，你负责管理一个项目集，确保你的国家进口食品的安全。这个项目集的发起原因是许多人因为食用进口虾、禽肉、牛肉而生病。此项目集使用公共资金并将持续数年；因此，作为项目集经理，你需要_____

　　A.　对财务环境有透彻了解

　　B.　制订项目集中每一个组件的计划

　　C.　让你的项目经理使用挣值管理，跟踪所有费用

　　D.　建立项目管理信息系统来追踪资源计划和使用情况

137.　Each of the projects in your program prepares a project risk management plan to describe how risk management is structured.  Each project manager also prepares risk response plans for each of the key identified risks. As program manager, you review the risk response plans to_____

A.  Establish triggers for the project risks

B.  Determine actions that could affect other components

C.  Identify intra-project risks

D.  Establish a contingency reserve

137.  在你的项目集中，每个项目都准备了项目风险管理计划用来描述风险管理的构成。每个项目经理也准备了针对每个关键已识别风险的应对计划。作为项目集经理，你检查这些风险应对计划是为了_____

A.  建立项目风险触发器

B.  确定可能影响其他部件的动作

C.  确定项目内的风险

D.  建立应急储备

138.  Your organization is ISO 9001 certified.  As program manager, you have arranged for a member of your company's Quality Assurance Program (a Black Belt in Six Sigma) to support your program. This team member reports directly to you and by dotted line to the manager of the Quality Assurance Department. In his first audit, he finds that one of the projects includes several key service management activities that have not met quality requirements. Your next step is to_____

A.  Facilitate an off-site meeting of your core program team to determine how best to handle this deficiency

B.  Convene a meeting of your program Governance Board to request that an additional resource be added to serve as a project manager for these activities

C.  Prepare a quality assurance change request

D.  Revisit the program's quality management plan and update it

138.  你的组织有 ISO 9001 认证资质。作为项目集经理，你已经安排了公司的质量保证项目集的成员之一（黑带六西格玛）来支持你的项目集。该团队成员直接向你汇报同时也间接向质量保证部经理汇报。在他的第一次审计时，他发现其中一个项目中有几个关键的服务管理活动没有达到质量要求。你的下一步将是_____

A.  召开核心项目集团队场外会议，以决定如何最好地解决这方面的不足

B.  召开项目集治理委员会会议，请求额外的资源作为项目经理来管理这些活动

C.  准备质量保证变更请求

D.  重新回顾和更新项目集质量管理计划

139.  You are Company A's program manager for the development of an online banking system for your community bank, for which your company will receive $20 million. One of your first tasks was to work with your sponsor and specify the purpose of the phase-gate

reviews and when they will be held on this program. One goal of these reviews is to_____

A. Monitor the business environment for changes

B. Assess strategic alignment of the program

C. Ensure the program charter remains viable

D. Identify the key decision makers and stakeholders associated with this program

139. 你负责 A 公司的一个为社区银行的网上银行系统开发的项目集，为此公司将获得 2 000 万美元的收益。你的一个首要任务之一是与发起人协作，并详细规定了阶段关口评审的目的。这些审查的目标之一是_____

A. 监督商业环境的变化

B. 评估项目集与战略的一致性

C. 确保项目集章程仍然可行

D. 识别出与该项目集相关的主要决策者和相关方

140. You manage a program for the Occupational Safety and Health Administration (OSHA) to make all the agency's regulations performance based and applicable to any industry group. You identify 50 external stakeholders who are active participants in this process, and 30 who are interested but not active, along with 75 interested internal stakeholders. Initially, when you and our team identified these stakeholders, you used_____

A. Brainstorming          B. Documentation reviews

C. Questionnaires          D. Interviews

140. 你负责职业安全与健康管理局（OSHA）的项目集，为所有机构的监管规定建立绩效基础，并适用于任何行业领域。你识别出了 50 个积极参与的外部相关方，30 个感兴趣但不活跃的外部相关方，以及 75 个感兴趣的内部相关方。你和团队识别出这些相关方，所采用的方法是_____

A. 头脑风暴          B. 文件评审

C. 问卷调查          D. 访谈

141. As manager of a program for the Federal Trade Commission that involves changes to existing regulations throughout the Commission, you have a major challenge as the majority of the regulations have not been reviewed for more than 20 years. Others of course have been added. Your role is to make sure in your program that all of the regulations are current and also are easily accessible by all stakeholders. You have a total of seven projects in your program, and since your program is a government mandated one, you have a Governance Board for your program that meets at least monthly and at key stage gate reviews. The person who is responsible for ensuring program success is the_____

A. Program director

B. Commission Chairman

C. Program sponsor

D. Director of the Enterprise Program Management Office

141. 你是一名联邦贸易委员会的项目集经理，该项目集涉及整个委员会的现有法规的变化，你的一大挑战是大多数法规在超过 20 多年里都没有审查过。而且这期间还有新的法规增加进来。你的角色是确保在项目集中，所有的法律都是最新的，并能很容易被所有相关方访问。项目集中共有 7 个项目，因为你的项目集是政府授权发起的，项目集有治理委员会，至少一个月开一次会，并开展重要的关口审查工作。确保项目集成功的个人是_____

A. 项目集总监　　　　　　　　B. 委员会主席

C. 项目集发起人　　　　　　　D. 企业项目集管理办公室主任

142. Assume you are working in a company, CDE, which specializes in new product development. The CDE executives are concerned because its last two products in the on-line music industry were late to market, and by the time they were on the market, competitors had products out with more attractive features to customers. As a result, CDE is in jeopardy of losing its market share in on-line music for mobile phones and tablets and also in games for these phones and tablets. You are now in process of working with your R&D team to determine a new product to propose to CDE's executives. Given the last two experiences, you believe you should include all of the following items in your business case but you especially need to focus on a_____

A. Existing work under way　　　　B. High-level net present value analysis

C. High-level roadmap　　　　　　D. Competitive analysis

142. 假设你在一个叫 CDE 的公司工作，公司专门从事新产品的开发。CDE 高管最近非常焦虑，因为在线音乐行业的最新两款产品的上市时间都晚于预期。而当这两个产品进入市场的时候，竞争对手的产品具有对于客户来说更有吸引力的性能。所以，CDE 存在失去手机和平板电脑端在线音乐，以及手机和平板电脑端游戏市场份额的风险。你正在和研发团队一同工作，开发 CDE 高管提出的新产品。鉴于上述最新两个产品得经验，相信在商业论证中，你应该包括所有下列内容，而且应特别强调_____

A. 现有工作　　　　　　　　　　B. 高层级的净现值分析

C. 高层级路线图　　　　　　　　D. 竞争分析

143. You are managing a program to develop a new source of energy in the extreme northern latitudes when solar power is not available. Working with your core program team and your Governance Board, you have identified a number of component projects. Your company has several key projects under way, and resources will be difficult to acquire for this new program. A key consideration is_____

A. The availability of key staff members

B. Your ability to negotiate with functional managers for the needed staff

C. Previous work by the staff as a successful team

D. The availability of off-shore employees to drive down costs

143. 你正在管理一个项目集，目的是北极地区没有太阳能的情况下开发新的能源。你与核心项目集团队和治理委员会一起工作，识别了一些组件项目。你的公司正在执行几个关键项目，很难为你的项目集分配资源。一个关键的考虑因素是_____

A. 关键员工的可用性

B. 你与职能经理谈判争取所需员工的能力

C. 员工先前在成功团队中的工作表现

D. 境外员工是否可用，以便降低成本

144. In your role of program manager for this Masters of Science degree in Program Management, your benefit realization plan includes both tangible and intangible benefits. You recognize the demand for the degree, and it in turn will lead to new income to the University. It also will enhance customer satisfaction with the University and will demonstrate to the overall project management community that it is following the trends in the profession. You expect a large number of people to enroll in the program based on the interest now in obtaining the PgMP® credential. You have seven projects in your program and are fortunate to have a PMO, and it is determining an easy but meaningful way to report on the realization of benefits from your program and then to provide this information to your stakeholders—both internal and external. By tracking the benefits during the program rather than after the degree is in place and students have enrolled offers a number of benefits in itself, one of which is_____

A. Provides an opportunity to publicize the program

B. Encourages ownership of the solution

C. Ensures funding limits are not exceeded

D. Ensures the available information is of the highest quality

144. 你正担任一个项目集经理，而该项目集有关理学硕士学位。项目集的收益实现计划包括有形和无形的收益。你认识到客户对学位的需求，这将给大学带来新的收入，也将提高客户对大学的满意度，并且会向整个项目管理社区表明这一课程遵循行业的发展趋势。你期望会有很多人感兴趣而报名参加 PgMP®考试。你的项目集中有 7 个项目，幸运的是还有 PMO 的支持。PMO 制定了收益实现报告及向所有内外部相关方提供信息的方式，这一方式虽然简单，但非常重要。在项目集过程中跟踪收益，而不是学位拿到和完成注册后再跟踪收益，这样做的好处是_____

A. 提供发布项目集的机会      B. 鼓励解决方案责任制

C. 确保不超出融资限制      D. 确保可用信息具有最高质量

145. As you work on your program to improve the economic growth of your country, you

are following a program management methodology that your agency's Center of Excellence in Program Management prepared. Your organization therefore in defining all program management activity as well as that for every deliverable and service realizes the importance of_____

    A. Program infrastructure development    B. Benefit sustainment

    C. Stakeholder engagement    D. Quality management

145. 在你执行改善所在国家经济增长的项目集中，你所遵循的项目集管理方法论是由卓越中心机构制定。因此，你的组织在定义所有的项目集管理活动及每一个可交付成果和服务的时候，会意识到如下哪一项的重要性_____

    A. 项目集基础结构开发    B. 收益维持

    C. 相关方参与    D. 质量管理

146. As the program manager for a multinational program headquartered in Sweden, you have adopted English as the common language for use on the program. However, most of your team members are located in Asia, and many of them do not speak English as their primary language. You have decided, therefore, to adopt the common English vocabulary of 4,000 words to facilitate the communication process. This decision should be stated in the_____

    A. Communications requirements    B. Program management plan

    C. Communications plan    D. Program scope statement

146. 作为一个总部设在瑞典的跨国公司的项目集经理，你已经采用了英语作为通用语言的项目集上使用。然而大多数团队成员都在亚洲工作，英语并不是他们的母语。因此，你决定采用 4 000 个单词的常用英语词汇表来促进交流。这个决定应记录在以下哪个文件中_____

    A. 沟通需求    B. 项目集管理计划

    C. 沟通计划    D. 项目集范围说明书

147. Working on your program to improve the economic growth of your country, you know from the business case there are many risks and issues. However, the business case only presented a high-level view of them. You then held a risk planning meeting with your stakeholders to help prepare a risk management plan, and you have set up a process to track issues. Now, you and your core program team are working to identify risks that could affect your program building on those in the business case. You and your team are clarifying the definition of each risk and grouping them by cause. This means you are using which of the following techniques?_____

    A. Flowcharts    B. Influence diagrams

    C. Root cause identification    D. SWOT analysis

147. 在执行改善所在国家经济增长的项目集中，你从商业论证中得知有很多的风险和问题。然而商业论证只是高层级的表述，所以你召集相关方开了一个风险规划会议，以制订风险管理计划，并建立了问题跟踪过程。现在你和核心项目集团队成员正在识别影响项目集的风险。你和团队正在定义每个风险，并根据其原因进行分类。这意味着你正在采用以下哪种技术_____

A. 流程图

B. 影响图

C. 根本原因识别

D. SWOT 分析

148. However, as you work on this program to improve the economic growth of your country, now you have another problem. A key member of your program staff has been complaining lately of the company's vacation policies. He would like to take more time off but has not yet accrued enough time to do so. You are concerned that he is going to leave the company, so you monitor his e-mail, in accordance with company policy, to see whether he is sending his resume to other companies. The act of sending out his resume would be called a_____

A. Risk trigger

B. Risk event

C. Misuse of the company's e-mail policy

D. Violation of the company's code of ethics

148. 在执行改善所在国家经济增长的项目集中，你正面临另一个问题。项目集团队中一个关键成员抱怨公司最新的休假规定。他想得到更多的假期，却不被批准。你担心他会辞职，因此你按照公司的相关规定监控了他的电子邮件，看他是否向外投递了简历。如果他对外投递了他的简历，这一行为被认为是_____

A. 风险触发因素

B. 风险事件

C. 违反公司电子邮件政策

D. 违背公司职业道德规范

149. You have a total of seven projects in your program, and since your program is a government mandated one, you have a Governance Board for your program that meets at least monthly and at key stage-gate reviews. You and your core team have prepared a governance plan that you will present at the Board's next meeting in two weeks. As you prepared this plan, it was beneficial to review the_____

A. Governance structure and composition

B. Gate review requirements

C. Commission's quality standards

D. Program charter

149. 你的项目集中共有 7 个项目，因为项目集是政府授权的，因此项目集有治理委员会，他们至少一个月开一次会，并开展重要关口的评审工作。你和核心团队制订了治理计划，将在两周后的委员会会议上提交审议。你制订这一计划，对于审查如下哪项有利____

A. 治理结构和组成部分

B. 阶段关口评审需求

C. 委员会质量标准

D. 项目集章程

150. As part of your stakeholder engagement activities, your core program team meets with each of the stakeholders you have identified as critical to program success. During these meetings, the team members assigned to work with specific stakeholders try to gauge their attitudes toward risk, identify their perceptions, and better understand how they might respond. This approach is especially useful to you as you_____

A. Analyze risks

B. Prepare the program's risk management plan

C. Determine stakeholder issues that may lead to risks

D. Prepare the stakeholder engagement plan

150. 作为相关方参与活动的一部分，你的核心项目集团队与每一位识别出的重要相关方会面。会面中，团队成员被指派与具体相关方一起去衡量他们对风险的态度，确定他们的看法，更好理解他们的可能反应。这一方法对于你在从事如下哪项工作特别有帮助_____

A. 分析风险　　　　　　　　　B. 准备项目集风险管理计划

C. 决定会引发风险的相关方问题　　D. 准备相关方参与计划

151. You are sponsoring a new program that will focus on a new product in which educators can immediately determine whether or not a student is plagiarizing, whether the student has cited the reference correctly, or whether it is an entirely new idea. The program will have a number of components, and the planned components have interdependencies between them. In this program you want to evaluate its program objectives, and you realize you need to address a number of concerns to satisfy all the involved and committed stakeholders. One of these considerations in this situation is_____

A. Cultural considerations　　　　B. Ethical concerns

C. Sustainability issues　　　　　D. Technological changes

151. 你发起了一个新项目集，关注开发新产品。该产品可以帮助教育工作者很快确定学生是否存在抄袭，是否正确地引用参考文献，是不是学生自己的原创等。此项目集有很多的组件，而且组件之间存在依赖关系。在此项目集中，你要评估其目标，以及需要解决一些问题，以满足所有涉及和承诺的相关方。这种情形下，你需要考虑_____

A. 文化考虑　　　　　　　　　B. 道德关注

C. 可持续性问题　　　　　　　D. 技术变化

152. Your government program to review and update existing regulations is to be completed in a year and a half, and you are now at the half-way point. You have three projects in your program plus a Governance Board for oversight. As you have been managing this program, it has been extremely helpful to you to_____

A. Have a program management information system

B.  Use your benefit delivery plan

C.  Have a change management specialist as a member of your core team

D. Use benchmarking with other government agencies who have already conducted similar programs to update regulations

152.  你审查与更新现有法规的政府项目集将在一年半后完成，目前正完成了一半。项目集现在有 3 个项目，而且还有起到监督作用的治理委员会。在你管理项目集的过程中，如下哪一项特别有用_____

A.  具有项目集管理信息系统

B.  使用收益交付计划

C.  核心团队中有变更管理专家

D.  使用标杆对照技术，以已建立类似项目集的政府机构为参考来更新相应规定

153.   You have completed five of the seven projects in your program so far to establish a Master's Degree in Program Management. In the last meeting with the Governance Board, when it was time to transition one of the projects, this meant it was then time to hire the program director and a couple of people for supporting roles. This project had outlined all the support tasks that needed to be done and included items such as the job descriptions for the program director and his or her staff members, the criteria to use to select the program director and staff, and methods to evaluate their performance. Now the director has been hired.  You therefore should as a best practice_____

A.  Involve the new director in all meetings with all stakeholders

B.  Ensure the new director understands the benefits of this program and how they will be sustained

C.  Ask the director to serve as the project manager for the two remaining projects on the program

D.  Ask the Governance Board to add the new director to be a member to oversee the remaining projects on the program

153.  目前，你已完成了项目集共 7 个项目中的 5 个，并确立了硕士学位。在最近一次与治理委员会的会议上，决定将一个项目移交，这意味着需要任命项目集总监和其他几个人作为支持角色。该项目概述了所有需要做的支持任务，包括项目集总监和工作人员的岗位职责说明，选择项目集总监和工作人员的标准，以及评估他们绩效的方法。现在总监已经被任命。你现在应做的一个最佳实践是_____

A.  所有与相关方的会议都约请新总监参与

B.  确保新总监理解项目集收益和收益维持方法

C.  请新总监担任项目集中两个未完项目的项目经理

D.  请治理委员会接纳新总监成为成员，以监督项目集中未完的项目

154. Finally, your program to rebuild the water desalinization plant for Ferguson, Saudi Arabia is complete. This program has been under way for more than five years. You had a number of leasing agreements on the program, and you are confident all of them have been closed successfully. You also had several subcontractors, and you have had reviews with each of them. You are meeting with your Governance Board, to obtain approval for the final phase of the program. You have made a recommendation to the Board to close the program. The person who will make the official decision is_____

A. Executive director　　　　　　B. Program sponsor

C. Governance Board　　　　　　D. Head of the PMO

154. 最终，你在沙特阿拉伯弗格森重建水处理工厂的项目集已经完成。该项目集已经执行了 5 年了。项目集中有很多租赁协议，你对这些合同都已成功关闭充满信心。你还有几个分包商，你对他们的工作都已经审核过。你正会见治理委员会，目的是得到项目集最后阶段的批准。你建议委员会收尾项目集。哪个人对此做正式决定_____

A. 执行总监　　　　　　　　　B. 项目集发起人

C. 治理委员会　　　　　　　　D. PMO 主任

155. Your organization has just announced that funds will be cut by 10 percent. Even though you are still in the planning phase of your program life cycle, and your program is considered a high priority in your company's portfolio, unfortunately, your program is not exempt from these budget cuts. But, you do have an advantage because your executive team is interested in your program because it is required for your company's continued viability in its product line of sport utility vehicles. Your executive team has mandated certain delivery dates, which you felt were feasible until these budget cuts were announced.　Still, you must meet them so you have prepared a new program roadmap and a new master schedule. You now must communicate these changes to your stakeholders. As the program manager, you_____

A. Are the champion for change

B. Should meet individually with your key stakeholders

C. Must provide consistent messages to all stakeholders

D. Empower the person listed in the stakeholder register to contact his or her stakeholders

155. 你的组织刚刚宣布将削减 10% 的资金。虽然你仍处在项目集生命周期的规划阶段，你的项目集在公司项目组合享有高优先级。不幸的是，你的项目集并未逃脱这一预算削减。但你有一个优势，高管团队对你的项目集感兴趣，因为它是公司多功能运动车 SUV 产品线的持续生产能力所必需的。高管团队已经规定了确定的交付日，而这些预算削减宣布前，你觉得是可行的。不过，你必须达成高管的要求，所以你准备了一份新的项目集路线图和新的主进度计划。你必须将这些变更传达给相关方。作为项目集经理，你_____

A. 是变更的倡导者

B. 应与关键相关方分别会面

C. 必须向所有相关方提供一致信息

D. 授权相关方登记册上的责任人与他/她的相关方进行联系

156. You have been working on a new product development program for your company, which specializes in farm equipment. Your product is to combine an easy-to-use tractor with a more complex crawler so the customer does not have to purchase two separate items and can use the combination product to meet a number of unique needs. You just found out from your portfolio manager that the company plans to acquire a competitor that specializes in riding lawn mowers. You have now suggested to your Governance Board that you add a project to your program to also combine a mower into the new product of your program. You believe such an improvement will_____

A. Increase the benefits to be realized by the product

B. Result in a longer timeline but will be one that customers should find of use

C. Can position your company well in the marketplace

D. Will lead to improved customer relationship management

156. 你一直致力于为你公司从事新产品开发的项目集，你公司专门从事农业设备制造。产品是将易于使用的拖拉机与更复杂的履带结合，这样客户不必购买两个单独的设备，而是使用组合产品便能满足他们特定需求。你刚从项目组合经理处获知，该公司计划收购竞争对手的专业化骑乘式割草机。现在你向治理委员会建议将一个项目添加到项目集中，将割草机结合到项目集的新产品中。你相信这一改进将会_____

A. 增加产品将要实现的收益

B. 导致更长的时间线，但这会让客户了解使用价值

C. 让你的公司更好在市场定位

D. 将导致客户关系管理的改善

157. You are ready to close a contract for a program-level contract that was set up to cover the requirements for any procurements by the components in you program. Before closing this contract, you should_____

A. Meet with each component manager

B. Hold a meeting with this contractor for a performance review

C. Document results according to the program plan

D. Prepare a contract closeout report

157. 你准备收尾一个项目集层级的合同，此合同涵盖了所有组件项目的采购需求。在关闭此合同之前，你应该_____

A. 与每一个组件经理会面

B. 与这个分包商会谈，进行绩效审查

C.　按照项目集计划记录结果

D.　准备合同关闭报告

158.　Your program communications management plan shows the various items to be distributed to your stakeholders; their purpose, frequency, and format; and the person responsible for each. As you work on your program, you follow this plan for formal communication of program information. You now have your process in place to distribute information to your stakeholders at the time and frequency they require. It is important not to overlook the need to_____

A.　Update the communications requirements analysis

B.　Update the lessons learned data base

C.　Prepare standard information requests

D.　Update the communications log

158.　你的项目集沟通管理计划确定了发布给相关方的众多信息、目的、频率、格式及责任人。随着项目集的进展，你遵循此计划就项目集信息进行了正式的沟通。你现在有相应的流程以更好地按照要求的频率和时间来向相关方发布信息。以下哪一项是重要而不能忽略的_____

A.　更新沟通需求的分析　　　　　　B.　更新经验教训数据库

C.　准备标准的信息请求　　　　　　D.　更新沟通日志

159.　You are a program manager under contract to a government agency that is responsible for issuing visas and passports. You have been working on this program for eight years and are responsible for all the information and telecommunications functions for the agency. Your company realizes this program is essential to its success, and this is the first time it has worked for this agency. Therefore, it established a governance structure to oversee the process. A best practice to follow as approvals for program changes are made is to_____

A.　Update the governance plan based on decisions made

B.　Record the outcome in the knowledge management repository

C.　Meet with your core team and project managers and inform them of the results of the Governance Board meeting

D.　Meet with your program sponsor to discuss your next steps

159.　你是一名项目集经理，与某一政府机构签订了一份合同，负责发布签证和护照。你已经在此项目集中工作了 8 年，负责为此机构提供信息与电信功能。你的公司认为此项目集必须成功，并且这也是你公司首次为此机构服务。因此，建立了治理委员会用于监督整个过程。批准项目集变更的一个最佳实践是_____

A.　根据所做的决策来更新治理计划

B.　将成果记入知识管理库中

C. 与核心团队和项目经理会面，并且告诉他们治理委员会会议的结果

D. 与项目集发起人会面，讨论下一步工作

160. Assume you have been maintaining a benefit register once your program's benefit realization plan was prepared. Because of the importance of benefits management on programs, you are fortunate that a member of your core team has expertise in this area and have appointed her to serve as the business benefits manager of your program, working closely with the PMO in your company. She will work closely with you and the other core team members as she will be maintaining the register, preparing the benefit reports, and also conducting benefit reviews. One of the key purposes of the benefit reviews is to_____

A. Create benefit ownership

B. Address the risk of operational areas that fail to commit to the benefits

C. Establish an approach to prioritize benefits that are in the realization plan

D. Review the benefits realization plan and implement improvements based on lessons learned to date

160. 假设你从项目集收益实现计划一准备好，就一直维护收益登记册。收益管理在项目集管理中很重要，幸运的是一名核心团队成员在这方面有专长，因此你任命她为项目集的商业收益经理，与公司的项目管理办公室（PMO）密切合作。她将与你和其他核心团队成员密切合作，因为她会持续维护收益登记册、准备收益报告和收益审查。收益审查的主要目的之一是_____

A. 创建收益责任制

B. 解决运营方面不能实现收益的风险

C. 收益实现计划中确立收益优先级排序的方法

D. 审查收益实现计划，并基于当前经验教训而进行改善

161. Your company, a member of the Fortune 500, is well known around the world as it is the leading producer of the top selling cereal. The cereal is nutritious, is one that both adults and children both enjoy, and has been on the market for over 40 years. Your company, though, is interested now in moving into the ice cream market. This will be a major change, and you have been asked to be the program manager for a new line of 12 different ice cream types. The development of this product is in your company's strategic plan, but it is so radically different from the cereal products for which you company is well known. Before going further and finalizing your charter, you feel it is important to talk with organizational leaders to address the program's_____

A. Attractiveness　　　　　　B. Readiness

C. Vision　　　　　　　　　　D. Funding methods

161. 你的公司是财富 500 强之一，作为最畅销谷物的主要生产商而享誉全球。公司

谷物是成年人和儿童都喜欢的营养物，并在市场上销售超过 40 年。你的公司现在打算进入冰淇淋市场。这将是一个重大变革，你已被要求担任一个新的、有 12 个不同冰淇淋类型产品线的项目集的经理。这个产品的开发已经列入了公司战略计划，公司上下都非常清楚地认识到它们与谷物产品有根本不同。要正式确定章程及开展项目集前，你认为与组织领导人会谈并处理好如下哪项情况是重要的_____

    A．吸引力                    B．准备就绪度

    C．愿景                       D．融资方法

162. Assume that your ice cream product line has been officially approved, and you are the program manager for this new program in your company. Because it is considered to be such a breakthrough program, it is ranked number three in your company. It has the support and visibility of the executive team. You are now helping to guide the initiating activities and are working on the financial framework. You have determined there will be a larger negative cash flow in the beginning than originally anticipated. This financial framework is useful for a number of reasons including_____

    A．Preparing program funding schedules

    B．Serving as a cost baseline

    C．Determining constraints

    D．Describing management of risk reserves

162. 假设冰淇淋产品线已被正式批准，你是公司新项目集的经理。因为它被认为是一个突破性的项目集，因此在公司排名前三。它有来自高管的支持和可视度。你正协调项目集的启动活动，并在制定财务框架。你已经确定，与原来预期不同，在开始阶段将有更大的负现金流。为什么说财务框架是有用的，其中的原因包括_____

    A．准备项目集融资进度          B．作为成本基准

    C．决定性的制约因素           D．描述风险储备的管理

163. You are working to plan your ice cream program for your Fortune 500 company, which is so well known around the world for its cereal products. Because it is venturing into ice cream, all resources are being provided internally, and everyone on the team is signing a confidentiality agreement so competitors are not aware of this new program. However, already resources are scarce although when you prepared your schedule you assumed the needed resources would be available. Now you realize you will need to do a lot of negotiating for resources. You decided since this program is ranked number three on the priority list that you should use_____

    A．Market analysis              B．Critical chain

    C．Resource leveling            D．Resource optimization

163. 你正在为你的财富 500 强公司规划冰淇淋项目集，你的公司作为最畅销谷物的

主要生产商而享誉全球。它进入冰淇淋市场是冒险的，因此所有资源都将内部提供，团队中每个人都签署了保密协议，所以竞争对手还没有意识到这个新项目集的存在。然而，组织资源已经是很紧张了。你已经在假设所需的资源可用的前提下制订好了进度计划。你现丰发现你要努力争取，才能得到所需的资源。因为这是一个在公司排名第三的项目集，所以你决定应使用如下哪项技术_____

A. 市场分析      B. 关键链

C. 资源平衡      D. 资源优化

164. You are enjoying your work as the program manager for the new ice cream program for your Fortune 500 company, which is so well known around the world for its cereal products. All resources are being provided internally, and everyone on the team is signing a confidentiality agreement so competitors are not aware of this new program. However, already resources are scarce in the organization working on cereal products. You have prepared your schedule and in doing so assumed the needed resources would be available. However, in a meeting with your Governance Board, you now realize you will need to do a lot of negotiating for resources. Fortunately, you have been successful and have three experienced project managers so far assigned who are supporting the three projects thus far in the program. It is important now since these project managers have been assigned that you evaluate their performance according to the_____

A. Project plan      B. Program management plan

C. Benefits realization plan      D. Resource plan

164. 你正在愉快地担任项目集经理，为你的财富 500 强公司执行冰淇淋项目集。你的公司作为最畅销谷物的主要生产商而享誉全球。它进入冰淇淋市场是冒险的，因此所有资源都将内部提供，团队中每个人都签署了保密协议，所以竞争对手还没有意识到这个新项目集的存在。然而，组织中的资源已经很紧张了。你已经在假设所需资源是可用的前提下制订好了进度计划。你发现你要努力争取才能得到所需资源。幸运的是，你成功地拥有了 3 位经验丰富的项目经理，分别被任命组织项目集中现有的 3 个项目的工作。项目经理已经任命，重要的是你应依据以下哪项来评价他们的绩效_____

A. 项目计划      B. 项目集管理计划

C. 收益实现计划      D. 资源计划

165. You are working to plan your ice cream program for your Fortune 500 company, which is so well known around the world for its cereal products. Because it is venturing into ice cream, all resources are being provided internally, and everyone on the team is signing a confidentiality agreement so competitors are not aware of this new program. However, already resources are scarce in the organization working on cereal products. You have prepared your schedule and in doing so assumed the needed resources would be available. Because of your

work in program management, you recognize changes occur on programs, especially given that programs represent a change of some type. Therefore, you and your core team prepared a change management plan. You find it is especially helpful in terms of which of the following types of changes_____

    A. Benefits

    B. Stakeholder expectations

    C. Market conditions

    D. Rewards

165. 你正在为你的财富 500 强公司规划冰淇淋项目集，你的公司作为最畅销谷物的主要生产商而享誉全球。它进入冰淇淋市场是冒险的，因此所有资源都将内部提供，团队中每个人都签署了保密协议，所以竞争对手还没有意识到这个新项目集的存在。然而，组织中已经很紧张的资源都被用在了谷物产品上。你已经在假设所需资源是可用的前提下制订好了进度计划。因为你的工作是项目集管理，你意识到项目集要发生多种变更的，因此，你和核心团队准备了变更管理计划。你发现这个计划在如下哪类变更中尤其有帮助_____

    A. 收益

    B. 相关方期望

    C. 市场条件

    D. 奖励

166. You are working to plan your ice cream program for your Fortune 500 company. All resources are being provided internally, and everyone on the team is signing a confidentiality agreement so competitors are not aware of this new program. However, already resources are scarce in the organization. You have prepared your schedule and in doing so assumed the needed resources would be available. However, in a meeting with your Governance Board, you now realize you will need to do a lot of negotiating for resources. Now you are in year two of your program, and you have four projects. However, now, you have some new members of your Governance Board, and they have been working in different business units of the company. New member E believes the program is too risky, and new member F is also a risk avoidance person. You realize the next meeting of your Board could be quite contentious, and you decided to evaluate the risks of your stakeholders. It is especially important as you perform this evaluation to consider the views of your_____

    A. Sponsor

    B. Head of the Governance Board

    C. Enterprise PMO Director

    D. Portfolio Manager

166. 你正在为你的财富 500 强公司规划冰淇淋项目集。所有资源都将内部提供，团队中每个人都签署了保密协议，所以竞争对手还没有意识到这个新项目集的存在。然而，组织中的资源已经很紧张了。你已经在假设所需资源是可用的前提下制订好了进度计划。然而在与治理委员会会谈后，你发现你要努力争取才能得到所需资源。现在你处于项目集的第二年，有 4 个项目。项目集治理委员会中有一些新的成员，他们在公司不同的事业部工作。新的成员 E 相信此项目集风险很高，新成员 F 也是风险规避型的人。你意识到委员会的下一次会议可能会有很大的争议，你决定评估相关方风险。这是特别重要的，因为

你是站在什么角度来执行这个评价的_____

    A. 发起人               B. 治理委员会负责人

    C. 企业 PMO 总监        D. 项目组合经理

167. You are responsible as the program manager for the development of a new gas transmission pipeline that will span three countries. You are in the early phases, and one of the countries involved has major concerns that the pipeline will impact areas detrimental to the environment. It wants additional information about the program before it will provide the needed permits and approval. Your managers recognize that such approval is paramount for the program to proceed and have asked you to prepare a_____

    A. Feasibility study          B. Roadmap

    C. Mission statement     D. Vision statement

167. 你作为项目集经理，负责一个将跨越 3 个国家的新天然气输送管道。现在处于早期阶段，其中一个国家非常关心管道是否不利于地区环境。该国在许可和批准该项目集前需要更多的信息。你的上司意识到该国的批准对于此项目集是极为重要的，所以要求你准备如下哪一文件_____

    A. 可行性研究         B. 路线图

    C. 使命说明书        D. 愿景说明书

168. Although your company has been active in project management for many years, it is relatively new to program management. You became certified as a PgMP® and suggested to your supervisor that two of your current projects would be better managed as a program and discussed why program management was more appropriate. One of the executives knew about the usefulness of governance and stage-gate reviews from his previous work in new product development, and he recommended all programs have a governance structure. Such a process now has been implemented. The effectiveness of the governance process is best handled through_____

    A. Regularly scheduled reviews

    B. Program performance reports

    C. Formal gate review decision requests

    D. Use of your program management plan

168. 尽管你的公司积极采用项目管理方法很多年，但最近才接触项目集管理。你是获得认证的 PgMP®，向上司建议当前两个项目应该划为项目集来管理会更为有效，并向他解释了原因。一名高管从他之前的新产品开发工作中了解到治理与阶段关口评审的效用，所以推荐所有的项目集都要有治理委员会。这一过程现在已经得以实施。治理过程的效果可以通过以下哪项得以最好地实现_____

    A. 定期计划的审查       B. 项目集绩效报告

C. 正式的关口审查决策请求　　　　D. 使用项目集管理计划

169. You are a program manager in your agency. Your enterprise program management office (EPMO) has a program management information system (PMIS) and a methodology for projects that are undertaken in your agency programs. You will be contributing to the PMIS as you_____

A. Distribute information

B. Monitor and control risks

C. Use the lessons learned data base

D. Perform financial monitoring and control

169. 你是你机构内的一名项目集经理。你的企业项目集管理办公室（EPMO）有一套项目集管理信息系统（PMIS），也有一套适用于你所在机构项目集的项目方法论。当执行如下哪项工作时，将对 PMIS 有贡献_____

A. 发布信息　　　　　　　　　B. 监控风险

C. 使用经验教训数据库　　　　D. 实施财务监控

170. Finally your program to establish the Masters of Science degree in Program Management is complete. You have completed the transition plan to the program director and his staff, and people at the University are pleased with how you managed this program and achieved the benefits in your benefit realization plan. To help future programs at the University, they asked you to identify what you believe is the value of benefits management. As a first step you suggest that_____

A. Each program has an individual on the core team that is responsible for the program's business benefits

B. Involving as many stakeholders as possible, both internal and external to the program, in the benefits identification process to help secure their buy-in to its goals and objectives

C. The program be set up with a viable business case that has a list of initial benefits to be achieved

D. Establish from the start of the program methods to use to measure each identified benefit and ways to track its achievement

170. 最后，你的"项目集管理理学硕士学位"的项目集已经完成。你已经将移交计划完成并提交给了项目集总监和他的团队，大学相关人员对你项目集管理方式及按照收益实现计划所实现的收益非常满意。为帮助大学未来的项目集，他们请你识别在收益管理方面有价值的东西，你建议第一步是_____

A. 每个项目集的核心团队都有人负责项目集的商业收益

B. 请尽可能多的内外部相关方参与项目集的收益识别过程，以便得到他们对项目集目的和目标的支持

C. 项目集建立在可行的商业论证基础上，商业论证有初步的待实现收益清单

D. 从项目集方法使用开始，来确立每个识别收益的测量机制和跟踪收益实现的方法

# PgMP®模拟试题一参考答案

1. B 项目组合是来确定投资决策、资源分配及排定优先级的。因此，它是对组织的意图、方向、风险承受能力及进展的最真实的措施之一。项目集组件必须与组织战略保持一致以清晰的展示为什么要执行这些组件。

2. C 考虑到你的团队成员的地理位置和工作安排，最好的选择是在他们可以自由支配的时间段来进行学习。虽然 MP3 录音也可以随时去听，但是对帮助员工学习使用一个软件系统来说，音频录音和在线学习模块相比，效率要低得多。

3. A 相关方参与和沟通管理是密切相关的。在准备你的项目集沟通计划时，相关方登记册是沟通规划时的另一个输出物，用来记录相关方的信息需求。

4. D 如果你没有通过 MRA，你在一年内不能再次考试。你没有拿到 PgMP®证书，并且这是一项合同要求，所以你必须通知客户。作为《项目管理协会（PMI）道德和专业行为规范》的一部分，按照真实资质进行工作是一项义务，并且本着公平的原则，我们一定要把与利益相关的真实或者潜在的冲突通知给合作方。

5. D 项目集经理、团队成员、治理委员会成员及其他相关方可能因为种种理由提出变更请求。从项目集的工作来看，变更的请求可以视作一次机会。它使项目集经理能够适应不断变化的环境，并且确保项目集可以把它的应有收益和价值交付给该组织。对于项目集经理及治理委员会来说最好的办法是去接受变更需要并且在审核变更时通力合作，以确保收益的交付。

6. C 目的是被明确定义的项目集要达到的成果，而目标是各项目要获得的最终结果、输出和可交付成果。在项目集和战略管理中他们项目集计划的一部分。

7. D 收益实现计划目的是记录为完成项目集计划的收益而进行的活动。它因此定义了收益在何时及如何交付。

8. A 收益实现计划是通过项目集的执行来指导收益交付的基线文档。当制订计划时，把验收标准包含在内，那么它就是一个项目集基准，并且就此和相关方，包括发起人，进行沟通。

9. D 对任何组织来说自制或购买决策是具有深远影响的商业决策。比如说，一个外包一项运营的决策就有可能导致企业在那一个领域核心能力的匮乏。自制或外购决策确定了哪些项目集元素会使用内部资源来完成交付，哪些又会从外部供应商处获得。

10. D 因为项目集经理要和各种级别的受众进行沟通，并且是项目集的关键沟通者，所以有一份定义和记录完备的沟通策略，他/她会从中受益。

11. B 业务和需求概要需要被制定、记录和交付。当准备商业论证时，需求概要作

为这个初始项目集评估的一部分，必须确定下来才能进入下一阶段。

12．B 环境变化是极为重要的，因为它们可以影响项目集财务管理活动。确保项目集的财务和支出是在预算范围内并且可控是必要的；这些环境的变化可能造成对预算基准的变更。

13．C 项目集计划是在确定项目集战略一致性期间进行准备的，它是衡量项目集成功与否的参考并且还包括了成功的度量标准。项目集管理计划是在项目集准备阶段准备的，并且会根据项目集的各种输出进行细化。

14．A 项目集工作分解结构将项目集范围拆分为交付成果及必须要完成的工作。然后它被用于建立切实的进度计划、开发成本估算，并被用来组织协调工作。

15．C 360°反馈分析是一个非常好的方法，可以多面地考察一个人的管理能力、领导力及人际交往技能。这可以为这个经理人的未来发展提供很好的基础，同时也提供了日常与她一起工作的人认识她的机会。

16．B 规划是一个迭代的过程。在收益实现计划被更新时，项目集路线图也应该被更新，特别是因为相对于其他项目集事项，路线图描述了可行的增量收益交付。

17．C 项目层面的治理主要关注点在于控制，以确保项目符合三角约束。不像在项目层面的治理，项目集层面的治理则是寻求授权和支持的一种方法，以便为应对新出现的情况动态的变更项目集战略或者计划。

18．B 这个项目集将会持续很长时间。路线图是以时间顺序图形化地展示出这个项目集的目标方向，并且在每一个时间节点都有一个成功的标准。

19．A 对于项目集来说，一个责任矩阵是非常有用的。为了建立核心团队，它可以识别和指定项目集角色和责任。责任矩阵对于区分项目集资源和项目资源也是有益的。

20．A 在项目集中，某些项目可能产出可以立即实现的收益，而其他项目则可能交付某些能力，以便和另外的项目集成起来实现收益。当其中的一些项目处于过渡期而其他的一些开始的时候，整个项目集的生命周期可能会扩展。

21．B 在能力要求被确认之后，下一步是与团队成员进行协商，评估他们各自的优势和劣势，并且制订培训计划。核心团队的分配是在制定项目集基础架构时确定下来的。

22．A 假设被认为是真正的、真实的或者确定的。这里的情况是，两个项目经理都已经假设这个关键资源届时将是可用的。项目集经理必须解决这个问题。

23．C 作为项目集绩效报告的一部分，在整个项目集的过程中都是需要的。有关状态和进度的信息必须与相关方进行沟通。需要定期准备报告并及时汇报。这样的评审会应当定期进行，以确保符合合同及成本和进度基准。

24．B 虽然这类项目集会影响项目生命周期，但这些主要生命周期阶段及其活动都是类似的，这是因为生命周期管理的目的是管理项目集定义、项目集收益交付和项目集收尾的相关活动。

25．A 假设客户的道德规范并不禁止这样的娱乐活动，政治活动是成功的项目集经理必须要有的技能和能力。在这种情况下，这样的活动对发现潜在的问题可能是有用的。

26. A 商业论证必须展示对需要、商业收益、可行性及项目集合理性的理解。为此，可行性分析与市场营销技术都是必需的。商业环境及客户需求信息对建立商业论证来说是必要的。

27. C 收益实现计划被项目集治理所使用，原因有很多。治理委员会对确定收益成果是否在按计划进行或者是否有必要对这些组件或者项目集进行变更非常有兴趣。

28. D 在项目集启动期间，选定了项目集发起人，然后他任命了一名项目集经理来执行和管理项目集启动工作。

29. A 无论别的经理们给你们团队的成员做了什么样的说明和肯定，你要明白每个成员拥有什么技能，这才是至关重要的。在完成技能需求详单之后，就可以为团队分配工作了。

30. A 在项目集范围控制工作中，要建立变更管理活动。作为管理活动的输出物，变更请求得以处理，并且决策依据得以记录。

31. C 项目集经理应该整理一份经验教训集并且与团队进行讨论。然后，作为知识移交的一部分，经验教训集应当被建立并且保留下来，这样现有或者未来项目集可以随时访问，以便团队的持续学习，避免他们可能碰到的一些问题。

32. D 在这道题中，项目集经理面对两个客户：签订打印机订单的零售商店和那些实际使用产品的终端用户。为了确保制造最好的产品，以满足市场需求，项目集经理应该切合实际的与尽可能多的终端用户沟通。

33. C 坏账是指不被计入账内并且因此而不产生价值的账。因此，它被视为商业损耗而不是收入，因为虽然产生了服务或产品却没有收到相应的费用。你必须采取纠正措施来应对这个问题，这种纠正措施是项目集财务监督和控制的输出物。

34. A 即使是在项目集被授权之前，风险就必须被识别和分析。假设分析是一种风险识别工具和技术，在环境分析中，假设分析也作为项目集战略分析的一部分来进行。

35. C 商业论证可以评估在成本与收益之间的项目集平衡。成本收益分析应该解决诸如需要多少成本可以完成该项目集、需要投入多少工作量来完成项目集，以及就完成具体的商业目标而言这个项目集是否值得投资。这包括有形的和无形的两种收益。无形的收益需要用一种量化的形式表达出来，比如说挣得或者节约了多少美元，节约了多少小时，以及增加了多少毛利率。

36. C 分发的关于项目集的信息应该使用有用的模板和适合的媒体发布。应该适当地准备对大众有用的公告沟通信息。

37. B 相关方登记册是沟通规划的输出物，用来记录各个相关方的信息需求。同样在项目集相关方识别中也会提供一些信息。相关方登记册在整个项目集过程中都会被维护和更新。

38. B 当一款产品没有通过审查的时候，开展一次质量保证审计也许对评估组件的质量控制结果，以及考察在质量保证计划里所陈述的整体项目集质量是否可以交付，是有用的。

39．A　规划是一个迭代的过程。当启动或者终止组件时，所有项目集层次的与组件相关的文档都需要做相应的更新以反映这些变化。

40．B　项目集收益与项目集治理是紧密相连的。较之其他成员，治理委员会则更专注于收益交付及确保项目集交付所承诺的收益。它和项目集经理及其他的一些关键相关方一起来确定机会窗口是否因实际项目集事件而做出让步，其中的一个事件就是功能的减少。投资具有时间价值，在组件进度中的调整可能会产生额外的财务影响。

41．C　项目集主进度计划需要被评审来评估组件变更的影响，比如说没有完成其他组件上的一个关键里程碑，甚至对项目集本身产生影响。为了达到目标可能会有加快或者减慢组件进度的需要。对于像这样的一个下滑的早期识别就是非常关键的。

42．B　在信息发布活动中，发布的信息包括项目项目集及项目团队通报变更请求，以及最终的变更请求应对的通报。

43．A　路线图是一个重要的文件，在整个项目集过程中都会用到。在项目集战略一致性中，它为各种情况做好准备，其中之一是建立项目集活动和预期的收益之间的关系。

44．B　变更请求会因为各种各样的原因发生。由于多数组织在资源上有所限制，最重要的请求往往是资源使用、战略或计划方面的。

45．A　排列资源优先级对于项目集经理来说是其一项关键职责，必须要优化资源在组件间的使用。一份人力资源计划对于识别、记录及项目集角色和责任的分配是很有用的。

46．C　在关闭一个项目集之前，可能需要评估来确定维持项目集收益的成本。为了监督持续的收益剩余的活动也许是需要的。

47．C　并购和合并是计划外的事件。在它们出现时，需要对现有项目集计划进行一系列评审活动来确定是否需要更新以确保其持续有效。规划是一项迭代活动，它作为一项核心的工作必须放在优先级较高的地方。

48．D　在相关方参与中，项目集经理在工作中需要掌握谈判技巧。通常在相关方间的期望有冲突的时候，经理需要把相关方组织起来召开协商会议。

49．C　为了获得融资及维持融资授权，评估项目集财务和非财务概要收益是非常重要的。这个方法在项目集中也决定了项目的优先级顺序。

50．A　这是一个战略型项目集的案例，并且被用来支持组织战略目的和目标，能够帮助组织达到愿景和使命。

51．D　项目集是用来提供收益的。定义好的收益报告或标准必须好好准备并向项目集管理办公室、治理委员会、发起人及其他相关方汇报，以便评估项目集的整体健康状况，确保收益的成功交付。

52．C　在进行项目集相关方识别工作时，项目集经理需要识别这些相关方并且准备一份相关方登记册。登记册需要进行详细的相关方分析，因为登记册包含：相关方列表，他们在项目集中的利益和参与等级，他们对项目集的支持程度，以及其他相关信息。

53. D 通过资源依赖管理，项目集经理会为稀缺资控制日程安排。在所有的项目集中，尤其是这里提到的这个，项目集经理必须确保当前项目集已经不需要这些稀缺资源时，必须释放他们。

54. D 在项目集的启动阶段，路线图是被精心制作的。较之其他的一些文档，它揭示和解释了差距，以及可以作为按照时间顺序来展现的项目集的目标方向。

55. D 在组织战略和商业一致性中，由于要解决的问题已经是大家有所理解的，下一步是制定一个方法概要或计划，通常是以路线图形式来定义的。

56. C 由于 PWBS 反映项目集的整个范围，它包括项目集所要交付的所有的收益（产品和服务），其中包括由组件产生的可交付成果。

57. D 不论是使用什么技术，最好的方法就是使用开放式的问题来尽可能获得更多的信息，以及索取更多的相关方反馈意见。

58. C 项目集发起人是单个执行高管或一组执行高管，他们支持发起项目集，有责任提供项目资源，确保最终交付项目集收益。

59. C 项目集阶段关口评审有很大的作用，而且应该在整个项目集过程中都要开展。阶段关口评审使得治理委员会能够针对能否从一个重要阶段进入下一阶段做出决议，同时审批一些必要的项目集变更。

60. D 因为项目集管理计划已准备好并且被正式批准了，项目集现在处于项目集收益交付阶段。在这个阶段期间，组件需要规划、整合并且被用来促进收益的交付。首先，组件必须通过治理委员会授权。

61. B 收益登记册完成之后，需要关键相关方的评审以便为每项收益制定出合适的绩效考核标准。这些关键绩效指标就是项目集收益登记册的一部分。

62. C 这是这样一个案例：第一次使用虚拟团队并且组织人员散布在 4 个大洲。这种组织文化的变革是需要花时间的。

63. B 一个高绩效的团队对于每个项目集的成功都非常重要。领导力是每个项目集经理在整个生命周期中都需要拥有的能力。这些项目集经理领导项目集团队提高整个团队的项目参与度，并且达到承诺的项目集目的。

64. A 相关方矩阵包含在相关方参与计划中。项目集经理需要经常评审这个矩阵以识别由缺乏相关方参与所引起的潜在风险。可以使用趋势和根本原因分析的方法。

65. A 在项目集正式地被授权之前，项目集启动过程帮助在项目集章程里定义项目集的范围及收益战略。

66. A 项目集治理包括组织定义、授权、监控和支持项目集及其战略的系统和方法。这可以确保项目集被有效地管理和一致性。治理委员会有权去认可或者批准对一个项目集的建议。

67. B 收益登记册列出了计划的收益并且用来在项目集期间对收益的交付情况进行

判断及沟通。它包括了派生绩效指标和阈值在内的很多项，用来评估他们的成绩。

68．C 对国家的领空系统的升级由众多项目及持续的工作组成。如果这些项目以一种协调的方式来管理，那么你将会更好地控制他们并且将会获得更大的收益。

69．D 与你和工作室间的付款周期相比，你与你的分包商的付款周期要更长一些，这样来确保你将会有现金来支付你的承包商，而不需要借钱或从储蓄中取出支付。

70．D 很容易就做出相关方的缺席会有问题的假设，而这有可能是因为这些相关方对于项目的方向很有信心，所以才缺席。通过分析可以避免做出不正确的假设，比如，相关方的行为可能会导致糟糕的或者没有效率的决策。

71．B 问题升级流程应涵盖在治理计划中。有时项目集经理可能需要联系执行负责人或外部相关方，然后将信息提供给治理委员会。治理计划描述了在所有级别上，问题升级的目标期望，包括为了有效解决问题何时让相关方介入。

72．C 作为项目集经理，你负责指导启动活动并推进项目集的产出。这意味着你负责更新商业论证。在预算削减的情况下，机构不太会去争取该项目集，或者加入机构继续推动，这也将在投资组合中处于较低优先级。

73．A 因为绩效不佳或变更商业论证情况下项目集不再必要，这都可能导致项目集被取消。这是项目集绩效差的最终结果，因为市场上存在竞争对手的产品。

74．A 治理委员会批准质量计划，通过识别和应用交叉组件质量标准，来建立机制以确保项目集质量。

75．A 在项目集采购过程中，根据合同规定的项目或服务来编制合同管理计划。它用于合同管理。

76．B 项目集治理委员会负责确保项目集目标的实现，并为解决组织中的风险和问题提供支持。

77．B 项目集绩效报告包括项目集组件的总体进度，与项目集收益、资源使用相关的项目集状态，以确定项目集目标与收益是否能够达成。

78．B 影响力是影响他人的信念、行动、态度的技能，在相关方参与的谈判中非常有用。

79．B 领导力是贯穿在项目集经理工作中的，项目集经理和治理委员会存在协作关系。治理计划列出了目标、结构、角色、职责、政策和程序，以及后勤，来执行治理过程。

80．B 项目集B是质量驱动的，如战略所示，在必要时推迟进度计划作为权宜之计。它的竞争属性是卓越的品质，与组织的文化和环境相一致。

81．C 作为项目集财务监控的一部分，管理项目集基础设施上的花费很有必要。这些成本是不能忽视的，很有必要确保它们是在预期范围之内。

82．C 在收益交付阶段结尾之前，当一个组件已经准备好进行移交和收尾时，它将被审核以验证收益是否达成，并且对于任何剩余和继续的活动，有对应的转换安排。治理委员会成员和发起人执行本次最终审查。

83. B 项目管理办公室的形式多种多样，它们在不同领域为项目集经理提供支持，其中之一是，定义项目集质量标准和项目集组件质量标准。

84. D 虽然所有的职能都由治理委员会执行，通过项目集绩效支持，治理委员会分配资源，包括人员、预算和设施，以最优绩效来达成项目集目标。

85. B 项目集范围说明书，定义和评估项目集背景和框架。它确立了要采取的方向和必须完成的核心部分。相关方应核实和批准范围说明书。

86. D 项目集范围说明书是将来项目集决策的基础，并建立了项目集的预期。项目集相关方应确认批准该项目集范围说明书，并达成一致理解。当某相关方对于某特定产品、服务，或是项目集组件存在错误的理解时，这将显得尤为重要。

87. B 许多组织遵循的最佳实践是，定义适用于所有项目集的标准化监督和控制过程。治理委员会假设遵守这些过程。例如，已知项目集风险、应对计划和升级条件。

88. D 投资回收期可以通过初始固定投资除以估算项目集年度净现金流来计算。在这个例子中，项目集 D 的投资回收期是 2.5 年，所以应该选择 D。

89. D 该项目集主进度计划的草稿通常只标识子项目的顺序和起止日期。然后，在进度表中添加子项目的结果。

90. C 资源优先级排序是项目集经理的职责，以优化跨项目集的资源使用。项目集经理平衡项目集需求与可利用资源。

91. C 对于项目集和项目集组件，一些组织使用相同的治理委员会，另一些由项目集经理对治理功能责任。如果项目集经理担负此职责，需要考虑的因素包括项目集经理的经验、项目集复杂程度，以及组织管理项目集所需的协调努力程度。

92. A 成本偏差（CV）等于挣值（EV）减去实际成本（AC），即 $CV = EV - AC$。本题中为 €42 000 – €50 000 = –€8 000，相比于完工预算（BAC）是微不足道的。

93. B 治理委员会的这一决定是一个变更，因为现在大部分的工作将外包。项目集经理应更新角色和职责矩阵。

94. D 在进行前，应初步评估项目集，通过定义项目集目标、需求和风险，来确保该项目集与组织的战略计划、目标、优先事项和任务陈述保持一致。

95. C 在编制预算时，有必要编制所有可用的财务信息，并列出所有的收入和付款进度表（足够的细节）。这样，该项目集的成本可作为预算基准的一部分进行跟踪。

96. A 所有相关方应能及时收到相关项目集信息。当状态信息、成本信息、风险分析和其他相关信息被分发时，最好的做法是解决"设身处地（我能从中得到什么）"的问题。

97. D 知识管理是项目管理办公室（PMO）或企业项目管理办公室（EPMO）支持项目集经理的既定职能之一。

98. B 诸如人力资源、财务、技术和进度等项目集问题，需要进行识别。然后选择一个与项目集范围、约束和目标一致的行动计划，以实现该项目集收益。

99．C 作为选择标准，采用净现值（NPV），现在的一美元与一年后的一美元是不等值的。未来折现（高折扣率）越高，项目集的净现值越低。如果净现值较高，项目集的价值则高于其他项目集。此题组合 C 有最高的净现值。

100．B 建立项目集财务框架的目的在于评估该项目集整体财务环境，确定资金来源，并确定里程碑。关键输出是项目集财务框架，用于协调可用的资金、约束，以及如何付款。

101．A 当 PWBS（项目集工作分解结构）完成时，可以创建贴近实际的进度表，建立估算成本，以及组织项目集工作。

102．B 针对不确定性、风险识别、风险缓解和风险机会，项目集经理必须分析和更新收益实现和持续性计划，以确定是否需要采取纠正措施并传达给相关方。

103．C 这些活动由项目集经理和组件管理组织在整个过程中执行，包括收集、测量、传播绩效信息和评估项目集的趋势。

104．B 专注于从相关方群体征求意见反馈，关于他们对项目集的态度，以更好地了解组织文化、政治、关注点和整体项目集的影响。开放式问题有助于参与者相互交流，从而加深对项目集需求的理解。

105．D 知识产权（IP）是任何公司的命脉。将项目或项目组外包给承包商为承包商提供了处理和操作知识产权的机会。你必须绝对确认承包商有相应的保障措施来保护你的知识产权。

106．A 项目集质量控制包括监控组件和可交付成果，以确定它们是否满足质量要求，从而实现收益。此过程贯穿整个项目集周期。输出是一个已完成的质量检查清单。

107．A 作为项目集/项目管理的实践者，我们需要做出客观公正的决策和行动。在这种情况下，有必要采取纠正措施，避免出现利益冲突。

108．A 仪表盘通过使用红色（坏）、黄色（警告）、绿色（好）来突出并简要描述项目集的各方面状态。在项目集执行层面，这是个简单、易于解释、有用的沟通工具。呈现状态报告的方法有控制板、备忘录，以及给相关方做演示。

109．A 重要的是，不仅要从项目集的每个项目和整个项目集中，捕捉和记录知识资产，也要确保这些资产受到法律保护。对项目集经理而言，确保知识产权被捕获重用是在项目集收尾进行中的一个绩效指标。

110．D 收益登记册是一份最佳实践，可以很容易地转化为效益报告。它有助于向相关方报告收益、状态，同步沟通管理计划。

111．A 识别高层次风险是项目集启动中的一个绩效能力。需要准备一个这样的风险列表，作为该计划的一部分，分析任何项目并评估优势、劣势、机会和威胁。最初的风险评估是一项确定成功收益交付概率的活动。

112．D 这个阶段是项目集组件计划、整合和管理，以促进收益交付，包括组件的过渡和关闭。

113．D 项目集范围控制中，有许多关键活动包括创建一个管理范围变化的活动。这个过程的输出是更新 PWBS（项目集工作分解结构）。

114．B 项目集绩效报告汇总项目和非项目活动的所有绩效信息。这些报告汇总绩效数据，为相关方提供有关资源使用的信息，以确定是否该项目集目标和收益能够达成。

115．A 项目集呈现着变化，每个项目集的战略价值应该是明确的，受组织商业战略驱动。组织根据竞争性的属性确定战略方向，反过来，集中和定义项目集管理元素的内容。

116．D 这是典型的使用承包商的项目集。项目集团队需要把工作、法律和商业方面的报表与项目集流程结合起来，这样团队就可以用通用的流程来集成管理。验收标准应具有可比性并支持项目集过程。

117．C 对于识别、准备收益实现计划，建立收益类目是有用的。它们应该包含有形的和无形的收益，同风险规避放在一起。

118．A 在制定基准之前，需要制定收益实现计划及其度量标准。然后此基准作为通过该项目集的实施控制工具或机制来管理变化的收益和成本。许多关键任务的建议，包括制定一个战略，收集基准数据，如通过问卷调查、访谈、报告的形式。

119．B 在项目集交付管理中，明确地纳入项目集管理者权限范围内的变更请求，由项目集经理来批准或拒绝。

120．B 直属经理通常将资源分配给项目集和项目。对于项目集经理来说，向直属经理沟通人员绩效是非常重要的，可以作为薪酬审核、未来发展等的输入。

121．D SPI=EV/PV。此题即 0.86，这意味着你落后进度14%。这将难以恢复。治理委员会意识到不可能恢复和终止项目集，现在应该实施关闭项目集。

122．D 一个成功的项目集经理必须具备独特的综合素质，包括知识、技能和能力。领导力是与项目管理团队和职能经理一起工作，它被融入项目集经理工作中，贯穿在整个项目集周期中。

123．B 优先考虑收益交付是至关重要的，特别是对那些收益是增量交付的项目集。早期收益的证明也有助于确保资金继续项目集。在对收益进行优先级排序时，需要考虑的因素包括与战略的一致性、长短期的预期结果、可用资源的专业知识，以及成功的概率。

124．B 收益实现需要分析贯穿整个项目集中。此题场景是一个风险机会例子，如果获得治理委员会同意，将需要更新收益实现计划及维护计划。

125．C 风险配置文件是管理项目集风险最合适的方法，调整并监控风险的严重程度。风险配置可在政策声明中表达或在行动中得到提醒。

126．A 项目集管理支持活动可能包括解决项目集知识管理定位的工作和资源。在项目集过程中，应用知识管理将包括一系列有助于决策和参考的活动，如定期识别、存储和交付关键项目集知识。

127．D 在授权之前，需要开展大量的活动，来核实组件支持项目集的成果。每个组件需要一个启动请求。

128．B 人员分配的变更反映在项目集资源计划上。资源计划最初是资源计划活动的输出。

129．D 项目集章程包含相关方的想法和关注。它应该作为项目集沟通计划的初稿。

130．B　PWBS 包含其他事项，提供了一份绩效报告和跟踪的框架。

131．B 项目集应该与组织的长期目标有战略上的契合。在选择项目集时，这是要去考虑的方面。此题项目集 B 完全支持 5 个目标中的 4 个。

132．D 治理委员会建立了一个成功项目集最小可接受标准，以及监视这些标准的方法。

133．C 相关方参与要求项目集经理是个优秀的沟通者。他/她努力确保所有相关方的沟通得到充分记录，包括可能需解决的行动事项。

134．A 在项目集财务监控中，项目集经理需要积极确定造成预算基准变更的因素。另一个主动的例子是，识别组件的超支或未用完预算所带来的影响。如果一个子项目没有用完预算，项目集经理可以将资金调配到项目集其他地方。如果项目集已超支，项目集经理必须确定根本原因及对组件和整体项目集的影响。

135．A 治理结构基于众多因素而不同，其目的是监督和审查项目集进度和项目、非项目工作的收益交付。项目集发起人通常是在组织中具有高层级角色的执行人员。在许多组织中，项目集发起人是治理委员会的主席。

136．A 使用公共资金的项目集往往复杂、成本高、持续时间长。项目集经理需要对财务环境有一个全面的了解。

137．B 项目集管理应支持项目集组件的风险活动。应该对项目集组件的风险应对计划进行审查，以评估建议行动是否会对项目集风险反应产生更好或更坏的影响。这让响应机制能给多个子项目带来益处。因为对子项目风险和项目集层级的风险之间的联系进行管理，将为项目集和子项目都带来收益。

138．C 审计需要时间，结果必须录入文档。项目集管理团队负责实施质量要求的变更。作为审计的结果，应执行审计员的发现，出具质量保证变更申请。

139．B 阶段关口评审服务有多种不同目的。除了确保满足退出阶段和移动到下一阶段的要求的标准，它们还可以专注于项目集和其组成部分的战略与项目集和组织的预期目标保持一致。

140．A 与核心团队进行头脑风暴会议，对于识别潜在相关方、相关方角色，及其对项目集的意义，非常有用。

141．C 项目集发起人是负责提供项目集资源并确保项目集成功的个人。通常，项目集发起人是高层管理人员，负责定义组织和投资决策的方向。

142．D 竞争性分析或市场分析有助于帮助识别为潜在项目集带来组织收益。一个完善的商业论证将包括某一详略程度的分析，以及与现实或想象中的替代品的竞争情况。这些竞争会为最佳解决方案带来实质性的讨论。

143．A 资源需求和项目集资源计划将用于资源排序活动。作为要规划资源工作的项目集经理，在确定资源优先级排序的过程中，资源的可用性是一个关键的考量，关键资源应该被妥善利用，以便于可以多组件间分享。

144. B 一个常规的收益报告是达到既定收益而开展相关方沟通中的具有很重要的作用。它也有助于确保解决方案的所有权和相关商业领域内的收益，降低项目集团队"乐观"的报告内容带来的风险，还能使得收益报告也能用于常规管理报告。

145. A 质量管理遍布整个项目集管理。如项目集质量管理一切所述，在定义所有项目集管理活动、可交付产成果和服务时，都应该被考虑。推荐的做法是，项目集质量经理参与规划活动，如资源管理，以核实质量活动与控制得到了执行。不仅在项目集层级执行，在组件、子项目集、项目层面也要执行，即使是由分包商来执行也要执行。

146. C 沟通计划应该考虑文件与语言的差异。因此，正是在沟通计划中明确采用4 000通用英语词汇单词量。

147. C 根本原因是引发风险的基础条件与事件。项目集特定的风险活动包括决定项目集风险的首要原因，这可以通过不断细化与明确每一风险的定义和根据原因对风险进行分组得以实现。识别了根本原因后能够制订更加有效的风险应对方案。

148. A 一个风险触发因素是特定风险将要发生的信号。

149. D 项目集章程授权项目集经理使用组织的资源来执行项目集，并且将项目集与商业论证和组织的战略优先级相联系，也包括项目集治理的内容。

150. C 相关方问题与关注对项目集的方方面面都有可能会有影响。应用影响分析技术可以了解到相关方问题的紧迫性和可能性，这样便可以确定哪些风险会演变为项目集的风险。

151. B 在一应评价项目集目标时，职业道德是一个重要的方面。在本例中，学生的隐私是需要满足的职业道德之一。

152. A 一个有效的项目集管理信息系统在项目集管理和项目集治理中是重要的。它为保存项目集的信息及快速检索所需信息提供工具与机制。所提供的工具、技术、过程和流程既有自动的，也有手动的，它们都与项目集管理和项目组合优先级管理有关。

153. B 项目集需要收益维持计划。在本例中，将收益转移给新的项目集总监是重要的。有助于维持收益的一个方法是在准备这一计划的过程中就请这位新的项目集总监参与，并确保这位总监理解收益实现计划与最新的报告。

154. C 治理委员会批准项目集关闭的推荐意见，确保关闭的条件得以满足。而且关闭意见还要与当前的组织愿景和战略保持一致。

155. A 项目集经理必须要熟悉组织变更管理。他/她是变更的支持者，必须在项目集变更的事情上扮演核心沟通者的角色，无论此变更是积极的还是消极的。

156. A 项目集的目的是相比单独管理组件项目要获得更多的收益。这一场景说明的是项目集经理正在探索战略机会的发掘，寻求为公司最大化收益的变更。

157. D 项目集采购收尾包括在确保所有的可交付成果得以满意地完成后结束每一个

项目集的合同，应该准备合同关闭报告。

158．B 经验教训是一个项目集知识资产的合集。这个数据库应该在组件结束和项目集结束时定期更新。

159．A 项目集变更申请应该在项目集文档中更新。其中之一是更新项目集的治理计划。

160．D 收益审查能够在整个项目集中进行。这使得项目集团队能够审核收益战略的有效性，能基于经验教训进行变更，能通报相关方进展，能识别项目集更多的收益，能评估当前项目集整体的绩效，以及能为向外宣传项目集和宣布项目集的成功提供机会。

161．B 通过征询组织领导意见来评估组织在新产品中的能力，从而制定、确认和评估项目集目标。准备情况分析有助于建立项目集可带来的新的收益，确保资源可用，并且为排序需求而评估当前的状态。

162．C 因为项目集财务框架描述项目集资金流，所以在项目集定义阶段的早期，为了协调可用资金、确定制约因素并决定如何支付，创建项目集财务框架。项目集财务框架是一份高层级的初始计划。

163．C 资源平衡是一种显示在资源不能按计划提供的情况下进度所受影响的方法。这也是一种方法，通过识别、评审、平衡资源需求来优化项目集管理计划，从而获得效率并提升组件项目之间的生产力/协同效应。

164．A 项目经理的绩效根据他们根据项目计划执行项目的能力予以评价。这一方法能最大化他们对项目集目标的贡献。

165．D 每个项目集都应该按照变更管理计划管理变更。目的是控制范围、质量、进度、成本、合同、风险和回报。

166．A 在相关方管理中，很重要的是评估相关方识别的所有对项目集的风险，特别重要的是发起人识别的风险，因为发起人是项目集的倡导者，并且给项目集提供资源与资金。必要时，此评估也可纳入风险管理计划。

167．C 使命说明书是为了说明项目集存在的重要性和合理性，应根据相关方关注点和期待予以准备，以便于建立项目集的方向。

168．A 治理委员会会议是执行治理监督活动最常用的方式。按期举行审核会议，会前计划好日程与事项并会后记录决策能够促进治理过程的效果。

169．C 随着经验教训数据库的更新，如有经验教训，本活动的一个输出是 PMIS。PMIS 包括其他文件、数据和知识储备库。

170．C 项目集建立在可行的商业论证基础上，商业论证有初步的待实现收益清单

每个项目集都需要商业论证，其中有为项目集识别的收益。商业论证在项目集整个过程中都应被审核和更新，也应当被实现。这样人们才能致力于帮助项目集的全面成功。

## 12.2  PgMP®模拟试题二及参考答案

1. Finally both the Boeing 787 and the Airbus 380 are operational. Assume you are the Program Manager now for the Boeing 797.  You have reviewed all the lessons learned from the work done on the 787 as you are determined this time that the 797 will be in service before the scheduled date. However, the 797 uses new technology, and you have different subcontractors than those of the 787.  Your executive managers recently returned from the Paris Air Show and already have some orders, and you and your team are just identifying the various projects that will comprise this important program. You have been asked since you are the program manager to provide your sponsor and your Governance Board with regular updates on the status of the program's benefits, and you need to be able to measure the benefits that have accrued during each reporting period.  You decided to track the benefits in a_____

    A.  Benefits register               B.  Benefits realization report

    C.  Benefits control system      D.  Benefits monitoring system

1. 最终波音 787 和空中客车 380 飞机都投产运行。假设你现在是波音 797 项目的项目集经理。你在仔细回顾和审查了所有的来自已完成的波音 787 项目经验之后，你判断这次 797 项目将在计划的日期前投产。然而，这次 797 项目将采用多种新技术，而且将比 787 项目使用更多的分包商资源。你的高管经理刚刚从巴黎航空展参展返回同时带来了一批订单，此时你和你的团队正在识别组成这个重要项目集的项目。由于你是项目集经理，你必须按照要求定期向你的项目发起人和项目管理委员会汇报项目集的收益状态，同时你需要能够在每个汇报周内测量该项目集的累积收益。你将采取以下哪种方式跟踪项目集收益_____

    A.  收益登记册                B.  收益实现报告

    C.  收益控制系统              D.  收益监督系统

2. You are working to establish program management in your organization. You recognize since you are working in the Portfolio Management Office that there are many benefits to be attained if projects that are somehow related can be part of a program structure so through the program, more benefits can be attained than if they were managed separately. You recognize the importance to aligning program goals and benefits with long-term organizational goals. Therefore, you realize as the company embraces program management, you will need to hire people as program managers, or appoint people from within the organization, who have skills in_____

    A.  Leadership                B.  Organizational awareness

    C.  Political awareness        D.  Strategic visioning

2. 你正在忙于在你的组织中建立项目集管理规范。由于你就职于项目组合管理办公室，你已经意识到以下现象：当一些业务程度相关的项目作为项目集结构的一部分通过项目集的方式来统一管理时，他们将比分开的独立的单项目管理方式获取更大的项目收益。你已经充分意识到将项目集目标和收益与组织的长期目标相结合并使二者保持一致的重要性。因此，你已经意识到公司拥抱项目集管理，你需要招聘项目集经理，在组织中任命相关人员，这些人员必须具备以下哪种能力_____

    A. 领导力　　　　　　　　　　B. 组织意识

    C. 政治意识　　　　　　　　　　D. 战略愿景

3. Your organization has a defined career path in project and program management and you are now a program manager. Since you have your PMP®, when PMI announced the PgMP® certification, you asked if you could move into a program management position so you could gain the hours needed to qualify for this credential. This is your first program management job. Your program management plan now has been approved. Your emphasis now should be on_____

    A. Holding a kickoff meeting with your team

    B. Delivering intended benefits

    C. Chartering projects and appointing project managers

    D. Determining needed knowledge, skills, and competencies for potential team members

3. 你所在的组织中对项目和项目集管理人才发展通道有清晰的路线，现在你是一名项目集经理。你已经是一名 PMP®，当 PMI 发布 PgMP®认证时，你被要求考虑担任项目集管理专业人士以便你可以获取更多的项目集管理实践经验，这样可以申请相应的 PgMP®认证证书。这是你的第一个项目集管理工作。你的项目集管理计划现在被批准。目前你应该重点做以下哪项工作_____

    A. 与项目团队召开项目启动会

    B. 交付项目集计划收益

    C. 给不同的子项目授权并任命各个子项目的项目经理

    D. 考察潜在的团队成员并了解其必备的业务知识、技能及职业能力素质

4. You are working for pharmaceutical company, GenBioform, as program manager for the development of a breakthrough drug to inhibit the growth of cancer tumors and eliminate the need for chemotherapy or radiation treatments. Your CEO is determined that your company will be the first to get approval from the Food and Drug Administration (FDA) for this new drug. You have performed an in-depth analysis of stakeholders in your company and have identified the following key external stakeholders: consumer groups, oncologists, the FDA, and cancer patients. Your next step is to_____

    A. Finalize the results of your stakeholder identification and analysis by preparing a transition plan

B. Note stakeholder considerations in your program charter

C. Rank the stakeholders by importance and assign key team members to work with the top two

D. Ask your Marketing Department to perform an analysis of the competition

4. 你是 GenBioform 医药公司的一名项目集经理，你正在研发一款有重要突破性的药物，它将抑制癌细胞的生长，同时可以消除化疗和放射治疗。你们的 CEO 确认你们公司将会是第一个被 FDA（食品药品监督管理局）批准可以生产此种药物的单位。你已经对公司的相关方做了深入分析并识别了以下重要的外部相关方：消费者团队、肿瘤医师、FDA（食品药品监督管理局）、癌症患者。你接下来将怎么做_____

A. 通过移交计划最终确认识别和分析相关方的结果

B. 在项目集章程中备注相关方注意事项

C. 依据重要性对相关方进行排序并安排核心团队成员同优先级最高的两位进行沟通和工作

D. 安排市场部开展一次竞品分析

5. You are a newly hired program manager in your company and plan to use a number of contractors and serve as the system integrator on your program. Your Procurement Department suggested that the qualified vendor list be used to simplify the procurement process and pointed out one vendor that had performed well on a similar program in the past. The problem is that this vendor's company is owned by your cousin. You should_____

A. Use the vendor since the Procurement Director suggested the company based on past performance

B. Disclose this relationship to the Procurement Director and to your sponsor immediately

C. Suggest that since this vendor's firm is owned by your cousin that it is more appropriate to have a competitive process with a RFP

D. Use a competitive process with a RFP and do not include past performance work with your company as an evaluation criterion

5. 你是公司新招聘的项目集经理，现在正计划在你的项目集中使用一批分包商让他们担任你的系统集成商。公司采购部建议采用合资格的供应商以便减少采购的流程，并特别指出其中一家供应商在类似的项目集中表现良好。目前问题在于，这家公司的所有人是你的兄弟。此时你应该_____

A. 采用该供应商，因为采购总监基于该公司过去其他项目集的服务表现而给出了建议

B. 向采购部总监和项目发起人公开你们的关系

C. 由于该供应商的所有人是你的兄弟，因此建议公司通过 RFP（建议邀请书）形式引进其他竞争供应商流程

D. 通过 RFP（建议邀请书）形式引进其他竞争供应商流程同时不采用以往与公司合作的业务表现作为评价标准之一

6. You are working for pharmaceutical company, GenBioform, as program manager for the development of a breakthrough drug to inhibit the growth of cancer tumors and eliminate the need for chemotherapy or radiation treatments. Your CEO is determined that your company will be the first to get approval from the Food and Drug Administration (FDA) for this new drug. So far on your program, with its six projects, you have had a number of change requests, which is not surprising given the complexity of the program. At the program level, analysis of change requests involves identifying, documenting, and estimating the work the change would entail. As program manager, you also need to_____

A. Determine which components are affected

B. Meet with the program Governance Board for approval, rejection, or deferral of the request

C. Convene a meeting of the configuration control board

D. Maintain a change log for status

6. 你是 GenBioform 医药公司的一名项目集经理,正在研发一款有重大突破性的药物,它将抑制癌细胞的生长，同时也可以避免化疗和放射治疗。你们的 CEO 决定公司将会是第一个被 FDA（食品药品监督管理局）批准可以生产此种药物的单位。到目前为止，在你的项目集中有 6 个子项目，你已经收到一系列变更请求，由于项目集的复杂性，这些变更并不让人惊讶。在项目集层面，分析变更请求主要涉及识别、记录和估算变更需要承担的工作。作为项目集经理，你也需要_____

A. 确定哪些组件将受影响

B. 会见项目集治理委员会，获取通过、拒绝或者延迟变更的请求

C. 召集配置控制委员会，召开一次会议

D. 维护状态变更日志

7. The emphasis at your logistics company has always been to "do projects right". Therefore, your management established a Project Management Office, with the responsibility to develop a methodology that project managers would follow that was consistent across the organization. This has proven to be effective. Now the organization is doing the same for program management. Since it has been successful in "doing projects right" and is "doing programs right", the organization now has implemented portfolio management to ensure it is "doing the right programs and projects". The relationship between portfolio management to program management thus is_____

A. One comparable to a child-parent

B. Influenced by requirements

C. Focused on achieving planned outcomes

D. One that emphasizes management of issues and risks with an escalation process

7. 你在一家物流公司工作，公司的重点一直在强调"做正确的项目"。因此，管理层建立了项目管理办公室，其职责是制定一套整个组织的项目经理都能一致遵循的方法论，这个做法已经证明是行之有效的。目前，组织正在针对项目集管理做类似的工作。既然组织在"做正确的项目"方面已经拥有成功的经验，同时也正在落实"做正确的项目集"，因此组织开始实施项目组合管理来确保整个组织在"做正确的项目集和项目"。这样来看，项目组合和项目集管理的关系是_____

A. 可类比父子关系

B. 受需求的影响

C. 聚焦于实现计划的成果

D. 利用升级流程来强化问题和风险的管理

8. You are managing a systems integration program for your company, Globus Enterprises, which is under contract to the government of Moldova. This program includes a hardware systems project and an information systems project; other projects are expected to be added as the program progresses. Because this program will include numerous projects, you have decided to_____

A. Have each project use a distinct life cycle as defined by the program management office (PMO)

B. Define a common life-cycle model for the various projects

C. Deploy the program organization

D. Prepare the program management plans

8. 你正在负责管理公司（"阁乐葡"公司，一家和摩尔多瓦政府签订合同的企业）中的一个系统集成的项目集，其中包含一个硬件系统项目和一个信息系统项目。其他项目将根据项目集的进展逐步被添加进来。由于该项目集将包含许多项目，你必须决定做的是_____

A. 根据项目集管理办公室（PMO）所规定的，每个项目要使用独特的生命周期

B. 针对不同的项目，定义通用的生命周期模式

C. 部署项目集组织结构

D. 准备项目集管理计划

9. You have been appointed program manager for the closing phase of the systems integration program for Globus Enterprises, under contact to the government of Moldova. As the closing program manager, you must ensure that all administrative activities are complete. One best practice is to review the_____

A. Program work breakdown structure (PWBS)

B. Business case

C. Program management plan

D. Benefits management plan

9. 你被任命为项目集经理，负责"阁乐葡"公司的系统集成项目集收尾阶段的工作。该项目集是与摩尔多瓦政府签订合同进行合作的。作为收尾阶段的项目集经理，你必须确保所有的行政活动都完成。一个最佳实践是去审查_____

A. 项目集工作分解结构　　　　B. 商业论证

C. 项目集管理计划　　　　　　D. 收益管理计划

10. You are pleased to finally move into a program management position in your city, and as the program manager for the new wastewater treatment initiative you have now completed your program management plan. You have selected project managers and also a core team and have defined criteria to help you evaluate the various candidates. You are fortunate that you have worked with two of the people before on specific projects, but the others are new to you, and the team has not worked together previously as a team. As a program manager, you must be an effective leader. A key area of focus is_____

A. Ensuring task delivery　　　　B. Adding value to decision making

C. Setting directives and procedures　　D. Establishing program direction

10. 你很高兴最终到了你所在城市的项目集管理职位上工作。作为新的城市废水处理项目的项目集经理，你已经完成了项目集管理计划。你已挑选了项目经理和一支核心团队，并同时确定了帮助你评估各类候选人的标准。幸运的是你先前曾与其中的两个人在具体项目上共事过，但其他人对你来说都是新人，整个项目团队之前也没有合作过。作为项目集经理，你必须是一个高效的领导者。下面哪个是你需重点关注的领域_____

A. 确保任务交付　　　　　　　B. 为决策增值

C. 设置指令和程序　　　　　　D. 建立项目集方向

11. You are managing a program that comprises new systems application development and maintenance activities. These applications are critical to your company, CDE, as they involve access to proprietary data. The systems must be available to your clients on a 24/7/365 basis. Much of the work on you program will be outsourced as you have an aggressive schedule to meet; fortunately CDE has a qualified vendor list to simplify the acquisition process. This program has high visibility in CDE. You and your core team realize the high level of interest and have worked hard to identify the key stakeholders and determine their position toward your program. You have prepared your stakeholder engagement plan, and it has been approved by your sponsor and Governance Board. Now, the next step for you and your team is to_____

A. Provide guidelines for project-level stakeholder engagement

B. Prepare a stakeholder inventory

C. Ensure the stakeholder management plan supports CDE's strategic plan

D. Communicate to all stakeholders a need for change to the new systems applications

11. 你正在管理一个包括新系统应用开发和维护活动的项目集。因为涉及访问专利数据的权限，所以这些应用对你所在的 CDE 公司非常重要。该系统必须对客户全天候都可以访问使用。因为要实现一个很紧的进度，因此大部分项目集的工作都将外包。幸运的是，CDE 公司目前拥有一个合格的供应商清单，可以简化采购流程。该项目集在 CDE 公司内部高度被关注。你和你的核心团队意识到项目集涉及高层级的利益，因此努力去识别关键相关方，并确定他们对项目集的立场。你已经准备好了相关方参与计划，而且该计划已经被项目发起人和治理委员会批准。接下来对你和你的团队要做的是_____

A. 给项目层级的相关方参与提供指南

B. 准备相关方目录

C. 确保相关方的管理计划支持 CED 公司的战略计划

D. 与所有相关方沟通关于新系统应用的变更需求

12. On your new 797 program, you have a larger number of stakeholders than did your counterpart program manager on the 787. You are working actively to identify early all the key stakeholders and prepare and follow a stakeholder engagement plan. To date, you find the stakeholder's major interests are in the program's benefits. However, the program is progressing as planned. In your plans, you have decided to conduct an overall review of the program's benefits with the Governance Board during the_____

A. Execution phase                          B. Delivery of Program Benefits phase

C. Program Closing phase                   D. Program Setup phase

12. 在你的新 797 项目集中拥有更多数量的相关方，比你的 787 项目集经理同事还要多。你正在积极主动地尽早识别所有关键相关方，并准备和遵循相关方参与计划。目前，你发现相关方的主要利益是项目集的收益。项目集目前正在按照计划进行中。在你的计划中，你已经决定与治理委员会一起开展项目集整体收益的评审，应在什么阶段执行最合适_____

A. 执行阶段                                 B. 项目集收益交付阶段

C. 项目集收尾阶段                          D. 项目集建立阶段

13. As the manager of your company's natural gas distribution program, you are pleased to have this program as it is ranked number one in the company's portfolio. So far, you have five separate projects, and the program is scheduled to last four years. In order to gauge program quality, a powerful metric is_____

A. End user satisfaction

B. Benefit sustainment

C. Effectiveness of adherence to the program's quality policy

D. Cross-program inter-project quality relationships

13. 作为你公司的天然气管网的项目集经理，你非常高兴负责该项目集，因为它在公司的项目组合中排名第一。目前，你有 5 个独立的子项目，而且该项目集计划持续 4 年。为有效评估项目集的质量，以下哪一个是有力的指标_____

A. 终端用户的满意度      B. 收益维持

C. 遵循项目集质量政策的有效性   D. 跨项目集的项目之间的质量关系

14. Now that you have moved into this program management role in your manufacturing company, you realize your work really involves active involvement with stakeholders at a variety of levels. It is also compounded because on your program you have external stakeholders involved and need to spend time communicating with this group. Additionally, your Governance Board is extremely interested in your program and wants to meet more regularly than solely at phase-gate review sessions. They have requested these other meetings in order to_____

A. Ensure expected benefits are in line with the original business plan

B. Focus on alignment of the program and your projects in it with the organization's strategic plan

C. Determine if the level of risk still remains acceptable to your organization

D. Focus on ongoing performance and progress

14. 目前你已经被调到你所在制造业公司的项目集管理岗位。你意识到，你的工作在不同层级与相关方密切相关。而且情况也是非常复杂的，因为项目集中有许多外部相关方，需要花费大量时间和他们保持沟通。此外，你的治理委员会也非常关注你的项目集，并希望有更多的定期会面，而不仅仅是定期的项目阶段关口评审会。他们已经要求这些相关会议，目的是_____

A. 确保预期的收益与原来的商业计划保持一致

B. 聚焦于项目集及其项目与组织战略计划的一致性

C. 判断当前的风险等级仍在组织接受范围内

D. 关注持续的项目集绩效和进展

15. As a program manager in an aerospace organization, you are managing the next fighter plan. It is considered to be one that is high risk. It is going to require new technology, different types of scientific experts, a different manufacturing line, and new suppliers and subcontractors. Some members of the executive team, although they did approve the business case, are skeptical and believe that if the program does move ahead, and if it does not prove to be financially beneficial, it can jeopardize the reputation of the company in such a detrimental way that the company may not remain dominant in its field. This is why it is important in the early stages to_____

A. Prepare a program charter

B. Prepare a high-level scope statement

C. Develop a roadmap

D. Define standard measurement criteria

15. 作为一个航天行业公司中的项目集经理，你正在管理下一代战斗机的计划。这被认为是一个高风险的项目。它需要新科技、不同类型的科学家、不同的生产线，以及新的供应商和分包商。高管团队的部分成员虽然已经同意并批准了商业论证，但他们仍然对该项目集能否实际性地向前推进，以及能否证实有财务效益持怀疑态度。如果不顺利，那么将会对公司的声誉有损，并使公司无法在该领域保持优势地位。这就是为什么_____在项目早期阶段非常重要的原因。

    A. 准备项目集章程              B. 准备高层级的范围声明

    C. 开发路线图                     D. 定义标准的测量指标

16. As you work to propose a program to your Portfolio Review Board to develop a new colon cancer detecting approach that does not involve any pre-preparation work or after effects to patients, you want to also to identify high-level financial and non-financial benefits for this program. You also want to make sure the benefits are congruent with the funding goals for the program as the financial organization will not be a passive stakeholder. One business case driver for financial management that often is overlooked is_____

    A. Mission statements           B. Reducing risks

    C. Increasing efficiency         D. Streamlining administration

16. 你向项目组合管理审查委员会提议了一个项目集，目的是开发一种结肠癌检测方法。该方法不需要做任何前置准备，同时对病人也没有什么副作用。你希望识别出该项目集的财务和非财务的高层级收益。同时，你也想确保项目集收益与其融资目标相一致，因为出资组织不会是被动的相关方。商业论证中针对财务管理的常被忽视的一个驱动要素是_____

    A. 使命说明              B. 降低风险

    C. 提升效率              D. 精简管理

17. As the program manager for the landfill program for your county, you have assembled your program team. It consists of civil engineers, regulatory specialists, project managers, and environmental engineers. This program is considered to be a very large one that will take a number of years to complete to deliver the societal benefits as planned. You plan to add some key subject matter experts as required. You also will have contractors on your team. With the various contractors, you are considering_____

    A. Using your PMO

    B. Adding a specialist in contract management to the core team

    C. Using blanket purchase agreements

    D. Using fixed-price contracts with incentives for early completion

17. 作为你们县城的负责垃圾填埋项目集的项目集经理，你已组建你的项目集团队。

团队包括土建工程师、法规专家、项目经理和环境工程师。该项目集是一个非常大型的项目集，按计划它将耗时多年才能完成并产生社会效益。你也需要不同的分包商资源。针对不同类型的分包商，你将考虑_____

  A. 利用你的项目管理办公室

  B. 在核心团队中增加一名合同管理专家

  C. 使用一揽子采购协议

  D. 针对早期完成的分包商使用固定总价加激励的合同

18. Now that you have moved into this program management role in your manufacturing company, you realize your work really involves active involvement with stakeholders at a variety of levels. It is also compounded because on your program you have external stakeholders involved and need to spend time communicating with this group. Additionally, your Governance Board is extremely interested in your program and wants to meet more regularly than solely at phase-gate review sessions. While you have two projects in your program, the Manufacturing Director at your company, CCC, has requested that you add another project to your program. Criteria for initiating a project is contained in the_____

  A. Program management plan   B. Program business case

  C. Program charter      D. Governance plan

18. 既然你已经调到所在的制造公司的项目集管理岗位，你意识到你的工作在各种层级都与相关方密切相关。而且情况也是非常复杂的，这是因为在项目集中涉及许多外部相关方，需要花时间与其保持沟通。此外，治理委员会也非常关注你的项目集进展，并希望有更多的定期会议，而不仅仅是在阶段关口评审会议的碰面。现在项目集已经有两个项目，而制造总监 CCC 要求增加另一个项目到项目集中。启动一个项目的标准包含在以下哪项中_____

  A. 项目集管理计划     B. 项目集商业论证

  C. 项目集章程       D. 治理计划

19. As the program manager working to upgrade and integrate the back office components of your organization's systems, you have five projects in your program. You realize all programs, and projects, have risks associated with them, and some of the high-level risks are in your program charter. As you prepare a risk management plan, it is essential to define_____

  A. Risk profiles

  B. Market conditions

  C. Risk management consolidation

  D. How the risk may affect program success

19. 作为项目集经理，你的工作主要负责升级和集成组织系统的后台办公组件。项目集中有 5 个项目。你意识到所有的项目集和项目间都有关联的风险，并且一些高层级的风

险记录在你的项目集章程中。在你准备风险管理计划时，必须去定义_____

    A. 风险状况           B. 市场条件

    C. 风险管理的整合         D. 风险是如何影响项目集成功的

20. You are a program manager and are responsible for a major project to integrate the back office components of your organization's systems. You have five projects in your program. Quality is important to your company. A quality control measurement you plan to use is_____

    A. Number of defects       B. Number of workarounds

    C. Customer satisfaction surveys     D. Cost of quality

20. 你是一名项目集经理，主要负责集成你所在组织系统的后台办公组件。项目集有5个项目。质量对你的公司是非常重要的。你计划采用的质量控制度量是_____

    A. 缺陷数量           B. 权变措施的数量

    C. 客户满意度调查         D. 质量成本

21. You are the program manager to restructure your department within your government agency. The head of the agency informed your sponsor that she wants to change the scope of the program so you will be working to restructure the entire agency instead of just one department. The Agency Administrator felt this change would be beneficial as the Agency also has to undergo some funding cuts in the next three fiscal years. This represents a major change to your program. You decided before moving forward that your best course of action was to_____

    A. Inform your team and involve them in planning the next steps

    B. Meet with your program sponsor

    C. Convene a meeting of your Governance Board

    D. Meet with the Director of the Enterprise Program Management Office as obviously you now need additional resources for your program

21. 你在政府机关内担任项目集经理，负责重新组建你的部门。政府机关的领导通知你的项目集发起人，她希望变更项目及范围去重组整个机关，而不仅仅是一个部门。政府机关管理层认为这场变革将会让整个部门受益，因为机关内部未来3年将持续削减经费预算。这个将是项目集的一个主要变革方向。在决定朝这个方向努力之前你最好的做法是_____

    A. 通知你的团队成员并让他们参与到下面的行动计划中

    B. 会见你的项目集发起人

    C. 与治理委员会召开一次会议

    D. 会见公司 PMO 总监，因为很明显你需要增加额外的资源到项目集中

22. As the program manager for the systems integration program for Globus Enterprises, which is under contract to the government of Moldova, you have a number of projects in your program. First, your program includes a hardware systems project. Second, you have an

information systems project. Now, you recently added a software engineering project, and you plan to add a verification and validation project in the fourth quarter. Other projects also are on your roadmap. Your overall program success is measured in terms of_____

A. Benefits delivery

B. Earned value

C. Each project's adherence to its schedule

D. Products delivered according to specification

22. 你是作为 Globus 企业的系统集成项目集的项目集经理，该企业与摩尔多瓦（罗马尼亚一地区）政府有合同合作。项目集有一系列的项目。首先，你的项目集包含一个硬件系统项目；其次，还有一个信息系统项目。最近你增加了一个软件工程的项目，同时在第四季度计划添加一个验证和确认项目。其他项目也在你的路线图之中。整个项目集成功以哪个标准来测量_____

A. 收益交付　　　　　　　　　B. 挣值

C. 每个项目的执行是否符合进度　　D. 依据规格说明书交付产品

23. The roadmap is an important document used in program management. One key purpose of it is to_____

A. Use it as part of the program's business case

B. Evaluate through it your program's alignment to the strategic plan

C. Summarize the supporting infrastructure

D. Show internal details of components

23. 路线图是一个用于项目集管理的非常重要的文件。其重要目的之一是_____

A. 作为项目集商业论证的一部分

B. 通过路线图来评估你的项目集与战略计划的一致性

C. 汇总了支撑的基础架构

D. 展示了组件的内部详细信息

24. You met with the organizational leaders for your colon cancer detection program that does not involve any pre-preparation work or after effects to patients, and its business case was approved. You then were asked to take over sponsorship for a program for a long-time customer, which would be awarded to your company under contract, to develop drugs for use by people before undergoing a colon cancer detection program. Your company has never developed these types of drugs before, but your customer is convinced it will not be an issue. You do not wish to disappoint this customer. In this situation，you should_____

A. Proceed with the colon cancer detection program as its business case has been approved

B. Tell your customer you cannot take on this opportunity now because you are committed to another program

C. Meet with your organizational leaders

D. Diversify the portfolio and sponsor both programs

24. 你会见了你的结肠癌检测项目集的组织领导，该检测方法不需要任何的提前准备工作，也不会对病人产生任何检测副作用，而且商业案例已经被批准。假想你被要求接管一个长期赞助该项目集的客户，完成该项目集将会对你们公司带来很大的奖励，从而可以在你实施结肠癌检测项目集之前去开发被人们使用的药品。你们公司从来没有开发过这些药品，但是你们的客户确信这不是一个问题。你当然并不想让客户失望。在这种情形下，你应该_____

A. 执行该结肠癌检测项目集因为它的商业方案已经被批准

B. 告知你的客户你不能负责该项目集了，因为你已经承诺负责另一个项目集

C. 会见你的组织机构领导

D. 让项目组合和多样化，同时发起这两个项目集

25. At the last strategic planning meeting, the CEO set forth a three-year plan with a major goal to be the leading provider of portfolio, program, and project management training in your country; it still will offer general managerial and business analyst training. You are the program manager for this new initiative, and your program management plan has been approved. Resources are limited. To provide guidance to component managers, you decide to_____

A. Prepare a program resource plan

B. Set up a resource pool that is managed at the program level for the components

C. Prepare a staffing management plan

D. Set up a process so component managers can escalate any resource issues to you for prioritization

25. 在上次的战略计划会议上，CEO 设置了一个未来 3 年的主要发展目标，即成为你们国内在项目组合、项目集及项目管理培训行业的主要提供者；同时，也要成为通用项目管理和商业分析培训的提供者。你现在担任该项目的项目集经理，而且你的项目集管理计划已经被批准。资源是有限的。为了给各组件的项目经理提供指导，你决定_____

A. 准备一份项目集资源计划表

B. 在项目集层面为各个组件的项目建立一个资源池

C. 准备员工管理计划

D. 建立流程让各个组件经理人员可以将资源需求问题上诉给你，以排序资源优先级

26. You are the program manager to restructure your department within your government agency. The head of the agency informed your sponsor that she wants to change the scope of the program so you will be working to restructure the entire agency instead of just one department. The Agency Administrator felt this change would be beneficial as the Agency also has to undergo some funding cuts in the next three fiscal years. You now have acquired additional

resources for this major change and have re-structured your program. You realize, however, that with this change, you should have_____

A. Followed appropriate procedures and guidelines

B. An appropriate governance structure in place

C. Updated all your plans

D. Communicated with every stakeholder

26. 你在政府机关内担任项目集经理去负责重新组建你的部门。政府机关的主要领导通知你的项目集发起人，她希望变更项目及范围去重组整个机关而不仅仅是一个部门。政府机关管理层认为这个变革将会让整个部门受益，因为机关内部未来 3 年将持续削减经费预算。现在你已经为这个重大变更获取到了额外的资源，二期你重新调整了项目集组织架构。然而你意识到，在这种变更下，你应该_____

A. 遵循合适的程序和指导方案

B. 在适当的地方设置合适的项目治理架构

C. 更新你的所有计划

D. 和每个相关方沟通

27. You are managing a landfill program for your county. Your program team consists of civil engineers, regulatory specialists, project managers, and environmental engineers. You also have a number of internal and external stakeholders. Your client, the county executive, has informed you that your program must be completed no later than September 15, 2015, to comply with a regulatory mandate. You have prepared the program's master schedule, and the program dates for each component have been identified, which are_____

A. Constraints　　　　　　　　B. Assumptions

C. Dependencies　　　　　　　D. Schedule risks

27. 你正在负责你所在县城的一个垃圾填埋的项目集。你的项目集团队由土木工程师、法规专家、项目经理和环境工程师组成。该项目集有大量的内外部相关方。你的客户（县长）通知你，为了配合监管要求，你的项目集工作必须在 2015 年 9 月 15 日前完成。你已经准备了项目集主进度计划，而且针对各个组件的项目集日期已经确定，这些是_____

A. 制约　　　　　　　　　　　B. 假设

C. 依赖关系　　　　　　　　　D. 进度风险

28. When you were a project manager, you found the risk register to be an extremely useful tool. Now that you are a program manager, you ask your project managers to use a risk register, and you assign a member of your core program team to identify, analyze, and track program-level risks. You also need to_____

A. Conduct risk audits　　　　　B. Review residual risks

C. Track schedule risks　　　　 D. Track scope risks

28. 假设你是一名项目经理，你发现风险登记册是非常有用的工具。现在你是一名项目集经理，你要求项目经理都使用风险登记册，同时安排项目集核心团队成员去识别、分析和跟踪项目集级别的风险。你还需要做的是_____

A. 实施风险审计
B. 审查残余风险
C. 跟踪进度风险
D. 跟踪范围风险

29. You have been appointed program manager for the closing phase of Program CCC. As closing program manager, you must ensure that all administrative activities are complete. Sixty-two contracts were awarded during the life of this program. You contact the Contracts Department and a contracts specialist assists you. You need to_____

A. Review the contracts management plan
B. Make sure the contractors completed performance reports as stated in their contracts
C. Ensure payments were made
D. Review contract closure procedures

29. 你被任命为 CCC 项目集收尾阶段的项目集经理。作为收尾阶段项目集经理，你必须确保所有的行政活动被全部完成。在项目集周期中 62 个合同被奖励。你联系合同部门和一个合同管理专家去帮助你。你应该_____

A. 审核合同管理计划
B. 确保合同供应商绩效报告按照合同条款去执行完成
C. 确保付款工作已经完成
D. 审核合同收尾流程

30. Assume you are managing the reward loyalty operational activity for your airline. Members have been complaining about the difficulty of actually using an award, especially your elite members who tend to fly on your airline at least one million miles per year. You feel you will lose elite members to other airlines unless the program changes dramatically, and you believe it needs to offer more possible rewards in conjunction with free stays at leading hotels of the world and also free car rentals. You have received authority from your Portfolio Review Board to establish a new program to emphasize improvements in how rewards are to be handled. You now are in the Initiating process. The key output of it is_____

A. Identification of the program manager
B. The program charter
C. The benefits analysis plan
D. Feasibility studies

30. 假设你正在管理你的航线上忠诚度顾客奖励活动的项目。航空公司会员已经投诉反馈实际的里程奖励计划困难，尤其是每年在你们航线上飞行超过 100 万英里的精英会员。你已经感觉到你们如果不动态地调整该项目集，你们的航线将流失精英会员到达其他航空公司，同时你也认为需要给精英会员们提供更多可能的奖励，连同提供一些免费的业界著名酒店住宿和汽车租赁服务。你已经收到项目组合审核委员会授权去建立一个新的项

目集，重点强调提升 客户奖励计划时如何处理的。目前你正处于项目集工作启动阶段。它最重要的输出内容是_____

A. 识别项目集经理　　　　　　B. 项目集章程

C. 收益分析计划　　　　　　　D. 可行性研究

31. Assume you are the program manager to redesign the reward loyalty operational activity for your airline. Members have been complaining about the difficulty of actually using an award, especially your elite members who tend to fly on your airline at least one million miles per year. You feel you will lose elite members to other airlines unless the program changes dramatically, and you believe it needs to offer more possible rewards in conjunction with free stays at leading hotels of the world and also free car rentals. Therefore, you want to plan for success from the beginning of the program. This need means that the program manager requires which one of the following skills?_____

A. Facilitation　　　　　　　B. Political

C. Emotional intelligence　　　D. Conflict resolution

31. 假设你正在管理你的航线上忠诚度顾客奖励活动的项目。航空公司会员已经投诉反馈实际的里程奖励计划困难，尤其是每年在你们航线上飞行超过 100 万英里的精英会员。你已经感觉到你们如果不动态地调整该项目集，你们的航线将流失精英会员到达其他航空公司，同时你也认为需要给精英会员们提供更多可能的奖励，连同提供一些免费的业界著名酒店住宿和汽车租赁服务。于是你希望在项目集启动阶段就为项目成功做好规划。这个需求意味着该项目集经理需要以下哪个技能_____

A. 推动能力　　　　　　　　　B. 政治能力

C. 情商　　　　　　　　　　　D. 冲突解决能力

32. Assume that you have completed your program to re-design your organization's approach to how it works with other companies. Now that the process is in place and has been followed, it is time to close this program. You must transition the benefits of your program. This is demonstrated_____

A. According to strategic alignment

B. Through value delivery

C. By implementing required change efforts

D. By providing operational support as requested

32. 假设你已经完成了项目集，目的是重新设计你的组织如何去与其他公司工作的方式。现在这个流程已经到位并被遵循，而且是时间收尾项目集了。你必须转换你的项目集收益。这个将通过以下哪个来诠释_____

A. 与战略的一致性　　　　　　B. 通过价值交付

C. 通过实施所需变更的工作　　D. 通过提供所要求的运营支持

33. You are responsible for business development in your division, which is a subsidiary of a large defense contractor. Recently, you attended a conference and learned that many of your competitors are focusing on continuous improvement in the area of sales strategies and techniques and are conducting maturity assessments. When you returned to your office, you prepared a business case and recommended that such a program be initiated.  One of the criteria you used was_____

A.  Representatives from each business unit in the organization would participate in the program

B.  The program duration would be short because a maturity assessment typically can be conducted in three months

C.  It would be necessary to set up some specific projects as a result of the improvement plan from the maturity assessment, but these projects would be unique to each business unit

D.  The benefits that would accrue from the program would be independent of specific deliverables of the various associated projects

33. 你所在的事业部是一家大型国防承包商的子公司,你负责事业部的业务开发工作。最近你参加了一个会议并了解到许多竞争对手正关注销售战略和技术的持续提升,同时在实施成熟度评估。当你返回办公室后,你准备了一个商业论证并推荐发起一个项目集。你使用的一个评价标准是_____

A. 组织中每个业务单位的代表都参与该项目集

B. 该项目集周期会比较短,因为将在 3 个月内实施一个典型的成熟度评估

C. 为了支持成熟度评估的改进计划,有必要建立一些具体的项目,但这些项目对每个商业单元都是独一无二的

D. 项目集不断积累的收益,与各种不同关联项目的具体可交付成果无关

34.  Your company has established a program to manage the development of new pet food products, and you have been appointed manager of this program. One of your five projects has completed its deliverables successfully, and a transition request has been processed.  As the program manager, you should_____

A.  Reallocate the resources to the other four projects

B.  Update the resource plan

C.  Update the program roadmap

D.  Send the transition request to the program sponsor for approval

34. 你的公司已经设立了一个项目集,用来管理新宠物食品的开发。同时,你已经被任命为该项目集的经理。你的 5 位项目经理中的一个已经成功完成了项目的可交付成果,而且收益转换请求已经在执行过程中。作为项目集经理,你应该_____

A. 重新分配资源到其他 4 个项目中

B. 更新资源管理计划

C. 更新项目集路线图

D. 将收益转换请求发送给项目集发起人审批

35. You are the program manager for a program that is using multiple suppliers. Even though you have signed partnering agreements with each supplier, you know performance problems will surface, especially with this program because more than 75 percent of the work is being done by third-party suppliers. Also, your company has not worked with five of these suppliers in the past, and two are start-up companies. You have identified the various stakeholders on this program and classified them. As part of stakeholder analysis and planning you should document_____

A. The organizational culture and readiness for change

B. Affected individuals and organizations

C. Perceptions of program outcomes

D. Attitudes about the program and its sponsors

35. 你是一个正在使用多个供应商项目的项目集经理。即使你已经和每个承包商签订了合同协议，但是你知道分包商绩效表现问题将会浮现，尤其是因为 75%的项目集工作将被第三方供应商完成。而且你们公司还未和这 5 家供应商合作过，并且其中两家是新成立的公司。你需要识别该项目集的不同相关方并将其分类。作为相关方分析和计划，你应该说明_____

A. 组织文化和变化的敏捷性

B. 受影响的个人和组织

C. 项目集输出结果的认知

D. 对项目集和发起人的态度

36. Because of extreme droughts in Haddad, Jordan, water restrictions have been imposed.　Your company is awarded a contract to eliminate the need for these restrictions. The program includes a project to formulate and implement policies and procedures that ensure continuity of operations and performance of associated equipment. Another project will oversee improvements and modifications to existing treatment methods and facilities. A third project will design modifications to increase productivity and effectiveness. As program manager, you will manage, contract, and provide oversight for capital improvement projects. You will need various types of resources and a variety of office supplies. To assist in managing contracts, you should_____

A. Conduct inspections and audits

B. Use performance/earned value reports

C. Follow your procurement management plan

D.  Use written deviations

36.  在约旦哈达德地区，由于极其严重的干旱天气，水资源限制已经被提上日程。你的公司是被选为承包商去消除这些限制。该项目集包括一个制定和实施政策及流程的项目，确保运营的可持续性以及相关设备的性能良好。另外一个项目监督现有的治疗方法和设施的改善和修正效果。第三个项目则设计这些改进措施以便提升生产力和效率。作为项目集经理，你要管理合同，并资本改进项目的监督。你需要各种不同类型资源和多种办公用品。为了帮助你进行合同管理，你应该_____

A.  实施检查和审计
B.  使用绩效和挣值管理报告
C.  遵循采购管理计划
D.  使用记录的偏差

37.  You are the program manager for a program that is using multiple suppliers. Even though you have signed partnering agreements with each supplier, you know performance problems will surface, especially with this program because more than 75 percent of the work is being done by third-party suppliers. Also, your company has not worked with five of these suppliers in the past, and two are start-up companies. Many in your organization are interested in this program and especially how the integration efforts will be accomplished given the large number of suppliers involved.   It is important in this situation to ensure_____

A.  A contact change control system is in place
B.  A contract administrator is a member of your core team
C.  There is compliance with legal policies
D.  Key stakeholders have active involvement in the program at all times

37.  你是一个项目集经理，该项目集使用了多个供应商。即使你已经和每个承包商签订了合作协议，但是你知道分包商会有绩效问题，尤其是 75%的项目集工作将由第三方供应商完成。而且以前你们公司还没有与这 5 家供应商合作过，并且其中两家是新成立的公司。组织中由许多人对该项目集感兴趣，尤其感兴趣的是在大量的供应商参与下，如何完成集成工作。在这种情形下，下面最重要的是确保_____

A.  有合同变更控制系统
B.  合同管理员必须是你的核心团队中一员
C.  遵循法规政策
D.  关键相关方一直积极参与到项目集中

38.  As a program manager in the Department of the Interior, you are working on ways to ensure continued availability of water resources. You have a number of projects in your program, but you are particularly interested in the effect of earthquakes on water resources. You have appointed a manager for this project, and he has assembled an outstanding team that does impressive work. You have already determined your program's budget requirements for the next fiscal year; your Governance Board concurs with your financial analysis and includes your

requirements in the budget submitted to the Office of the Secretary. However, the Office makes 30 percent cuts across the board, thus forcing you to eliminate the earthquake analysis project. Your next step is to_____

A. Disband your team

B. Assign the project manager to another project so that he does not lose his job

C. Update your program plans as required

D. Make another attempt to secure funding for this project

38. 作为内政部的一名项目集经理,你正研究如何确保水资源的可持续性。你的项目集中有一系列项目,但是你特别感兴趣的是关于地震对水资源的影响。你安排了项目经理,而且他也组建了一支优秀杰出的团队并开展了卓有成效的工作。你已经确定了下一财年的项目集预算需求。治理委员会同意你的财务分析,并将你的需求纳入预算中提交给秘书处。然而,秘书处砍掉了你整整 30%的预算,迫使你不得不消除地震分析项目。你接下来要_____

A. 解散你的团队

B. 安排你的项目经理到其他项目,以避免其失业

C. 根据要求,更新你的项目集计划

D. 通过其他方式获取项目预算

39. Your program in the Department of Interior to ensure continued availability of water resources to the citizens of your country has a number of projects, now seven are under way, and unless there are no other budget cuts, you expect at least three more to be added. In most programs, there is a core infrastructure which is the_____

A. Governance Board

B. Program management team

C. Program management office

D. Program office

39. 你的国家正致力于确保让县城的居民有可持续性水资源的项目集拥有多个子项目,现在有 7 个项目正在进行中,而且如果预算上没有删减,你希望至少增加 3 个项目。在大多数项目集中,都有一个核心的设施,它们是_____

A. 项目集治理委员会　　　　　　　B. 项目集管理团队

C. 项目集管理办公室　　　　　　　D. 项目集办公室

40. As the manager of a major program in your company, you have access to various supporting resources. Your organization uses a balanced matrix organizational structure, and supporting resources come from a variety of functional departments. One member of your program team regularly prepares resource deviation reports. These reports are_____

A. Part of Resource Interdependency Management

B. Described in the resource plan

C. Helpful to determine if the program's benefits will be met

D. Used as part of Risk Monitoring and Control

40. 作为公司的一个主要项目集经理，你用权利去获取一些支持资源。你的组织使用的是平衡型矩阵组织结构，而且许多资源需要来自职能部门。你的一个项目集团队成员例行准备资源偏差报告。这些报告_____

A. 部分资源相互依赖性管理

B. 在资源计划中有描述说明

C. 有助于帮助确定项目集收益是否满足

D. 被用来作为风险监控的一部分

41. You have been appointed program manager to develop digital yo-yos. You are excited by this challenge, and when you learned of this possible opportunity, you decided to attain your PgMP® and also take a course on managing programs for best practices. This is your first time as a program manager, and this program is ranked number three in your organization. You are preparing a high-level program plan, which has a number of key purposes one of which is to_____

A. Demonstrate the value the program is to deliver

B. Justify the required resources

C. Serve as a reference to measure program success

D. Establish the relationship between program activities and expected benefits

41. 你被任命为项目集经理去负责开发一款数字溜溜球。面对这个挑战你充满兴奋之情，而且当你了解到这个可能的机会时，你决定要获取 PgMP®认证，同时通过参加项目集管理学习最佳实践。这是你第一次担任项目集经理，而且在你的组织中，这个项目集项目也排在第三重要的位置。你正在准备一份包含大量关键交付目标的高层级的项目集计划，那么其中一个是_____

A. 阐明该项目集将要交付的价值

B. 证明所需要的资源

C. 作为参考来衡量项目的成功

D. 建立起项目集活动和预期收益之间关系

42. As the program manager on the digital yo-yo program, you realize for success on this program, you need an outstanding team, and you have been negotiating for the best and the brightest people to manage the seven identified projects that will comprise the program and will be in your Program Management Office. It has been a difficult process working with the company's department managers to obtain needed resources. You know for success you also need_____

A. A determination of contractor resources for your use

B. Agreement among the team as to the program values

C. Standard measurement criteria

D. Risks identified by stakeholders

42. 作为数字溜溜球项目集经理，你意识到项目集如果需要成功，你需要一个杰出的项目团队，同时你已经在不断地和最优秀的人员洽谈并让他们来管理 7 个项目集子项目，他们将组成这个项目集，而且你将在项目集管理办公室工作。和公司的职能部门经理们沟通从而获取需要的资源是一个比较困难的过程。你明白想要项目集成功，你还需要_____

A. 一个独立自主的对承包商资源选择的决策权

B. 项目集团队之间对项目集价值的一致认可

C. 标准化的考核标准

D. 相关方的风险识别

43. You are a program manager in a global software company that uses virtual teams. Work is passed 24/7 from team members on one continent to those on another continent. Since this is a complex program with a significant amount of associated uncertainty, changes in program direction may be needed.  Recognizing this can occur on your program, you should_____

A. Use adaptive change

B. Provide consistent messages about changes to stakeholders

C. Set up an approach to facilitate timely decision making about needed changes

D. Follow your communications management plan

43. 你是一名采用虚拟团队的全球化软件公司的项目集经理。日常工作 7×24 小时持续开展，在全球不同地区的团队成员之间传递。这是一个有很大不确定性的复杂项目集，因此项目集方向可能有变更。意识到你项目集的上述问题，你应该_____

A. 使用适应性变更

B. 提供一致性的变更信息给项目集相关方

C. 建立一个实时快速决策的机制来制定一系列必要的变更

D. 遵循你的沟通管理计划

44. As the program manager for a new wastewater treatment initiative in your city, you must deliver both tangible and intangible benefits. You must also identify the interdependencies of the benefits delivered in various projects in your program. This means that you must map benefits to program outcomes. In terms of the benefits management life cycle, this is done during_____

A. Benefits identification　　　　　B. Benefits setup

C. Benefits analysis and planning　　D. Benefits delivery

44. 作为你们城市的一个新废水处理项目的项目集经理，你必须交付有形的和无形的项目集收益。你还必须要识别清楚不同的项目收益之间的相互依赖关系。这也意味着你必

须在项目集收益与项目集成果之间建立映射。根据项目集收益管理生命周期，这个将在哪个阶段实施_____

A. 收益识别阶段
B. 收益建立阶段
C. 收益分析和规划阶段
D. 收益交付阶段

45. You and your core team realize the high level of interest in your program and have worked hard to identify the key stakeholders and determine their position toward your program. You decided to use mapping to help develop a stakeholder matrix to put stakeholders into certain categories. One of the advantages of the mapping approach is that it_____

A. Can be done easily through brainstorming sessions

B. Shows the stakeholder's attitude toward the program

C. If done correctly, can promote stakeholder engagement

D. Visually shows the stakeholders' current and desired support and influence

45. 你和你的核心团队理解了你们项目集的高层级利益，而且已经着手努力去识别关键相关方并确定他们对项目集的立场。你决定使用映射关系去帮助你建立相关方矩阵，从而将项目集相关方划分到某些类别中。使用映射方法的一个优势是_____

A. 可以通过头脑风暴的形式轻松完成

B. 可以展示相关方对项目集的态度

C. 如果方法实施正确，它可以提升相关方的参与性

D. 可视化地展示相关方当前和期望的支持及影响

46. Before preparing your stakeholder engagement plan, you decided to conduct stakeholder analysis and planning. Your first step is to_____

A. Brainstorm the possible stakeholders to get a complete list of them

B. Evaluate the degree of support or opposition each stakeholder has regarding the program

C. Gain an understanding of expectations of program benefit delivery

D. Perform a detailed review of the Statement of Work and other key documents already completed

46. 在准备你的相关方参与计划之前，你决定实施相关方分析和规划。你的第一步是_____

A. 通过头脑风暴识别可能的相关方，从而制定一份完整的相关方清单

B. 评估每个相关方关于项目集上的支持或立场的程度

C. 获取关于项目集收益交付的期望的了解

D. 对已经完成的工作说明书和关键文件进行详细的审查

47. Your company is noted for its maturity and excellence in program management. It has received awards for program and project delivery. People seem dedicated to the success of the

company and in its management of programs and their projects, which is due to_____

    A.　Awareness of the influence of environmental enterprise factors

    B.　Use of a common program approach

    C.　A portal for sharing information

    D.　An up-to-date program management information system

47.　你的公司以其项目集管理成熟及卓越而闻名遐迩，并在项目集和项目交付领域获得了一些奖项。公司员工看起来愿意为公司的成功及其项目集和项目管理做出贡献，这是因为_____

    A.　事业环境因素影响的意识　　　　B.　通用项目集方法的应用

    C.　共享信息的门户　　　　　　　　D.　最新的项目集管理信息系统

48.　You are the program manager for a global Fortune 100 software company. The company has determined that it must pursue Cloud Computing, and it wants to use agile methods as it enters this market to speed the time to complete the Cloud Computing program and to develop a marketing campaign for it. You also know you will need to do extensive testing before the program is complete. One tool you should develop to help execute the program is a_____

    A.　Work authorization system　　　　B.　Issue and risk escalation process

    C.　Roadmap　　　　　　　　　　　　D.　Decision log

48.　你是一家全球财富 100 强软件公司的项目集经理。公司已决定必须开展云计算业务。因为刚进入该市场，公司希望采用敏捷的方法，目的是加速完成云计算项目集，并开展营销活动。你也清楚在该项目集完成之前，你们需要深入地测试。你需要开发的用于帮助你实施该项目集的工具是_____

    A.　工作授权系统　　　　　　　　　B.　问题和风险升级过程

    C.　路线图　　　　　　　　　　　　D.　决策日志

49.　You are the program manager for a global Fortune 100 software company. It has determined that it must pursue Cloud Computing, and it wants to use agile methods as it enters this market to speed the time to complete the Cloud Computing program and to develop a marketing campaign for it. You are responsible for ongoing management of program benefits. You must ensure that the program transition activities provide for continued management of benefits through the framework of_____

    A.　Ongoing operations

    B.　Transfer of the benefits to the customer

    C.　Program closure

    D.　Consolidation of the benefits

49.　你是一家全球财富 100 强软件公司的项目集经理。公司已经决定你们必须实现云计算，而且公司希望采用敏杰的方法作为其进入该市场去缩短时间加快完成云计算项目集，同时为他去开发一个营销策划互动。你正在负责持续的项目集收益管理工作。你必须确保项目集转换活动能够通过以下哪个框架提供持续性的收益管理_____

A. 持续运营
B. 将收益转移到过客处
C. 项目集收尾
D. 收益巩固

50. You are the legacy system conversion program manager in your company. You need to upgrade the company's business development/sales tracking system, which was developed in C++. You now have projects in your program to also upgrade the accounting/financial management system, interface them to the program management information system, and add a knowledge management system. You have a complex program. With these additional projects, you and your core team realize you need to prepare your stakeholder engagement plan. In developing this plan, you should_____

A. Analyze the stakeholder register

B. Determine how receptive the stakeholder is to communications from the program

C. Prioritize stakeholders in a matrix according to their ability to influence the program outcomes, either positively or negatively

D. Determine the degree of support or opposition the stakeholder has for the program's objectives

50. 你是你们公司遗产系统转换项目集的经理。你需要升级你们公司采用 C++语言开发的一套商业开发/销售跟踪系统。现在项目集中的项目也需要更新会计/财务管理系统，使它们与项目集管理信息系统对接，同时要增加一个知识管理系统。你的项目集是复杂的。加上这些额外的项目，你和你的核心团队认识到你们需要准备一份相关方参与计划。在开发这个计划时，你应该_____

A. 分析相关方登记册

B. 确定该项目集内的相关方以什么方式沟通更容易接受

C. 通过相关方对项目集成果的影响（影响或者是积极的，或者是消极的）能力来进行相关方优先级的排序

D. 确定相关方对项目集目标的支持和反对程度

51. You are the program manager for a program that is using multiple suppliers. Even though you have signed partnering agreements with each supplier, you know performance problems will surface, especially with this program because more than 75 percent of the work is being done by third-party suppliers. Also, your company has not worked with five of these suppliers in the past, and two are start-up companies. Today, one of the suppliers responsible for Project D informed you that it did not have sufficient financial capacity and resources to continue on the program and was going to declare Chapter 11 and file then for bankruptcy. Obviously, this change involves other projects on your program and the entire program's ability

to deliver its benefits on time. You have decided that the best course of action is to first_____

A. Call an immediate meeting with your program team

B. Contact the Procurement Department to obtain their services in obtaining another qualified supplier

C. Contact the suppliers with whom you have had positive working relationships in the past to see if they can take on this company's work

D. Follow the issue escalation process

51. 你是一个正在使用多个供应商项目的项目集经理。即使你已经和每个承包商签订了合同协议，但是你知道分包商会出现绩效问题，尤其是因为 75%的项目集工作是第三方供应商完成的。而且你们公司还未和 5 家供应商合作过，并且其中两家是新成立的公司。今天一个负责项目 D 的供应商通知你，他们没有充足的财务能力和资源去继续这个项目集，而且他们将要宣布申请破产保护。很明显，这个变更涉及项目集的其他项目，而且也涉及整个项目集按时交付收益的能力。你不得不决定接下来的最好行动是_____

A. 立即召集你的项目集团队开会

B. 联系采购部门获取他们的帮助以便获取其他合资格的供应商

C. 联系曾经和你一起工作的有良好供应商关系的其他供应商，然后考虑他们是否可以承接该公司负责的项目工作

D. 按照问题升级流程处理

52. As the manager for a water-gasification program that will provide potable sparkling mineral water from public water fountains in Garvey, England, you have leased some of the needed equipment. Unfortunately, you have found that on two of your projects, some of these leased resources did not meet specifications. The project managers on Projects A and D advised you of their concerns because they were concerned that overall program progress might be affected. You need to identify a course of action to best achieve program benefits, which means you need to_____

A. Perform an issues analysis　　　　B. Assess stakeholder risk tolerance

C. Conduct a risk audit　　　　　　　D. Manage program level issues

52. 作为一个水气化项目集项目的项目经理，该项目将从位于英格兰加维的公共水源泉水处取水并提供适用于饮用的水，你已经租赁了一些必要的设备。不幸的是，你发现在你的两个子项目上，一些租赁的资源并不满足规格要求。子项目 A 和 D 的项目经理们建议你关注他们的担忧，因为他们担心整个项目集项目进度将可能受到影响。你需要确定行动方案去获得最佳项目集收益，这意味着你需要_____

A. 开展一次问题分析　　　　　　　B. 评估相关方风险容忍度

C. 实施风险审计　　　　　　　　　D. 管理项目集级别的事项

53. Assume you are managing the next generation SMART car so it runs entirely on

ethanol rather than gasoline now that your country has ethanol stations in all major cities and on interstate highway systems. Your executives believe this type of SMART car will increase in popularity. Since there are a number of benefits associated with this new line of SMART cars, you decided to use a benefit register to track the benefits accrued by each of the projects in your program so your organization can realize them and then through its dealers be able to sustain them. As the program manager, you develop this benefits register during_____

A. Benefits identification

B. Benefits analysis and planning

C. Benefits transition

D. Benefits delivery

53. 假设你正在管理下一代智能汽车，它可以全部使用乙醇燃料代替汽油。现在在你们国家的主要城市和州际高速公路系统中已经有乙醇加油站。你的公司高官们相信这种类型的智能汽车需求量和受欢迎度都将快速增长。由于有大量的与这种新的智能汽车相关的利益，你决定使用一个利益登记册来跟踪项目集项目中积累的各种收益，因此你的组织能够识别他们而且通过其经销商能够维持收益。作为项目集经理，你在以下哪个阶段创建收益登记册_____

A. 收益识别阶段                    B. 收益分析和规划阶段

C. 收益转移阶段                    D. 收益交付阶段

54. You have successfully finished your new line of SMART cars, and they have been well received.  In all, you have four different models, all using ethanol and all with advanced safety measures. They also are environmentally efficient. Now that the cars are being purchased, to derive the optimal value from the work you and your team accomplished, as the program manager, you should_____

A. Conduct team satisfaction surveys

B. Plan the transition from program management to operations

C. Ask an independent party to contact end users to ensure the effectiveness of customer relationship management

D. Provide support to end users throughout the product life cycle

54. 你已经成功地完成了你的新智能汽车项目，而且它们已经被成功接受。整体而言，你拥有 4 款不同车型，全部采用乙醇同时带有高级安全措施。它们同时也是环保节能的。现在这些汽车已经被采购，你和你的项目集团队完成的工作将会产生最佳的价值，作为项目集经理，你应该_____

A. 开展团队满意度调查

B. 计划从项目集管理阶段向运营阶段转移

C. 安排独立第三方机构去联系终端用户来确保客户关系的有效管理

D. 在产品全生命周期内给客户提供支持

55. As the key member of your company's Program Selection Committee, you are responsible for deciding which programs to undertake. Your Committee meets on a quarterly basis and then selects new programs and projects as appropriate and also then rebalances the company's portfolio accordingly. As you consider the proposed business case for a new program and assess the suggestions of the other committee members, a key factor is_____

A. Constituent component identification and definition

B. Total available resources

C. Overall stakeholder interest

D. The project's feasibility study

55. 作为你们公司的项目集选举委员会重要成员，你们需要负责决策哪些项目集项目需要选择开展。你们的委员会满足按季度衡量，然后选择新的合适的项目集和项目，同时你们也需要对公司的项目组合项目进行再平衡管理。因此，你在考虑为一个新的项目集提供商业案例方案，同时评估其他委员会委员的建议，那么下面一个关键因素是_____

A. 组件组成识别和定义　　　　　B. 可利用资源总额

C. 全部相关方利益　　　　　　　D. 项目的可行性研究

56. You are the program manager for a program that is using multiple suppliers. Even though you have signed partnering agreements with each supplier, you know performance problems will surface, especially with this program because more than 75 percent of the work is being done by third-party suppliers. Also, your company has not worked with five of these suppliers in the past, and two are start-up companies. Many in your organization are interested in this program and especially how the integration efforts will be accomplished given the large number of suppliers involved. Given the extensive work being done by suppliers, you expect you will have more internal audits than usual on your program. Their specific timing should be_____

A. In your program's roadmap　　B. Set forth in an audit plan

C. Set forth in your program plan　D. In your program schedule

56. 你是一个正在使用多个供应商项目的项目集经理。即使你已经和每个承包商签订了合同协议，但是你知道分包商绩效表现问题将会浮现，尤其是因为75%的项目集工作将被第三方供应商完成。而且你们公司还未和这5家供应商合作过，并且其中两家是新成立的公司。你们组织中的许多人对该项目集非常感兴趣，尤其是考虑到大量的供应商参与，这些集成工作将如何被完成。考虑到大量的工作将由供应商完成，你希望在项目集内部，比一般的项目集将有更多的内部审计。它们的具体时间规划应该是_____

A. 在你的项目集的路标中

B. 在你的审计计划中阐明

C. 在你的项目集计划中阐明

D. 在你的项目集计划中

57. You are the program manager to restructure your department within your business unit. The head of the company informed your sponsor that she wants to change the scope of the program so you will be working to restructure the entire company instead of just one department. You prepared a stakeholder register as part of your planning efforts for the restructured program and then worked to_____

A. Assess the stakeholders' ability to influence strategic goals

B. Determine metrics to evaluate stakeholder participation in the program

C. Prioritize a list of stakeholders

D. Outline how stakeholders will be engaged in the program

57. 你在政府机关内担任项目集经理去负责重新组建你的部门。政府机关的主要领导通知你的项目集发起人，她希望变更项目及范围去重组整个机关而不仅仅是一个部门。你准备了一份相关方登记册作为你的项目及重组计划努力的一部分，然后你的工作是_____

A. 评估相关方对战略目标的影响能力

B. 确定指标用于该项目集中对相关方参与度的评价

C. 排列项目集相关方优先级

D. 概要列出项目集相关方将如何参与项目集

58. You are managing a program in your company, and you are following the phases articulated in the Project Management Institute's The Standard for Program Management. Assume you have prepared your benefit realization plan, and It was approved.  Now, you must concentrate on_____

A. Linking component activities to planned outcomes

B. Delivering benefits

C. Mapping the benefits to the program components

D. Establishing a program architecture

58. 你正在管理公司的一个项目集，同时你也在跟进各阶段性进展，各个阶段参照项目管理协会（PMI）的项目管理标准。假设你已经制订了项目集收益实现计划而且它已经被批准。那么现在你应该全神贯注于_____

A. 连接各组件活动来规划项目集的产出结果

B. 交付收益

C. 映射出项目集各组件收益

D. 建立起一个项目集架构

59. You are the program manager for a program that is using multiple suppliers. Even though you have signed partnering agreements with each supplier, you know performance problems will surface, especially with this program because more than 75 percent of the work is

being done by third-party suppliers. Also, your company has not worked with five of these suppliers in the past, and two are start-up companies. Many in your organization are interested in this program and especially how the integration efforts will be accomplished given the large number of suppliers involved.　Recently, your organization made a major change in its financial management policies and now is requiring a 10% retainage as part of each supplier's contract. This means that_____

A.　You require a person specializing in contracts and procurement management to be a member of your core team

B.　Suppliers are now a major stakeholder

C.　You need to actively work to rewrite each contract and then submit it to your Contracts Department

D.　A supplier engagement plan should be prepared

59.　你是一个正在使用多个供应商项目的项目集经理。即使你已经和每个承包商签订了合同协议，但是你知道分包商绩效表现问题将会浮现，尤其是因为 75%的项目集工作将被第三方供应商完成。而且你们公司还未和这 5 家供应商合作过，并且其中两家是新成立的公司。你们组织中的许多人对该项目集非常感兴趣，尤其是考虑到大量的供应商参与，这些集成工作将如何被完成。近期你的组织在其财务管理政策上做了重大改变，而且现在仍需要一笔 10%的保留金作为每一个供应商合同的一部分。这意味着_____

A.　你需要一位在合同和采购方面的专业人士作为你的核心团队成员

B.　供应商现在是主要的相关方

C.　你需要积极努力地工作去重写每个合同然后提交给你的合同管理部门

D.　一个供应商参与计划应该准备

60.　Assume that you are the program manager for a product to be delivered to an external customer, and you are now planning your program. This new product is to be completed in two years. So far, you have three projects in your program and plan to add several more as the program continues. You believe you have an excellent team with the key competencies to assist you in the program. You also are glad to have a Governance Board.　Conflicts, though, are program challenges, which means you should_____

A.　Actively listen

B.　Use a variety of approaches to lead the team

C.　Assume program ownership and take responsibility

D.　Leverage political dynamics to promote program goals

60.　假设你是一名项目集经理，负责将一款产品交付给外部客户，现在你在只做项目集计划。该新产品计划将在两年内完成。目前，在你的项目集中已经有 3 个子项目，而且你计划继续增加其他 7 个子项目到你的项目集中。你相信你拥有一个优秀的拥有核心胜任

能力的团队在项目中帮助你。你同时也很高兴有一个项目管理委员会。然而，冲突是项目集的重要挑战，这意味着你应该_____

A. 积极聆听

B. 采用各种方法去领导团队

C. 假定项目集所有权并承担责任

D. 利用行政权力杠杆去推动达成项目集目标

61. You are managing a program to produce the next generation of hurricane-, tornado-, and typhoon-resistant glass. Technical specialists in your company will support each of the projects in this program. Four projects are in process. Project A is fully staffed; Project B has about 75 percent of the staff members it needs; and Projects C and D are about to begin, but these two projects will require the services of several key specialists now working on Projects A and B. You tell Project Manager A that he must release two staff members to support Project C and three to support Project D. He uses resource leveling to analyze this change and tells you that the end date for Project A will need to be extended, as he will be understaffed. The program Governance Board and the executive sponsor agree to extend the schedule for Project A. The five specialists are released to the other projects. Your next step is to_____

A. Commend Project Manager A for his willingness to release these resources

B. Meet with the five people involved and tell them they must move to the new projects

C. Update the program-level documentation and records

D. Continue to prioritize resources as needed

61. 你正在管理一个生产下一代的能抵抗飓风、龙卷风和台风的玻璃材料的项目集。你的公司的技术专家将需要支持这个项目集中的每一个项目。项目集有 4 个项目正在进行之中。项目 A 配备了足够的人员；项目 B 配备了其所需要的 75%的工作人员；项目 C 和 D 即将开始，但这两个项目将需要当前正工作于项目 A 和 B 的几个关键的专家的服务。你告诉项目经理 A，他必须释放 2 名工作人员支持项目 C，并释放 3 名工作人员支持项目 D。项目经理 A 使用资源平衡分析这种变化，并告诉你由于人手不足项目 A 的结束日期将被推迟。项目集治理委员会和执行发起人同意了延长项目 A 的进度。5 位专家被释放到其他项目之中。你的下一步工作是_____

A. 对项目经理 A 愿意释放这些资源进行表扬

B. 会见所牵涉的 5 名专家，并告诉他们必须转移到新的项目

C. 更新项目集层次的文档和记录

D. 继续根据需要对资源进行优先处理

62. You are managing a program to produce the next generation of hurricane-, tornado-, and typhoon-resistant glass. Four projects are in process. Project A is fully staffed; Project B has about 75 percent of the staff members it needs; and Projects C and D are about to begin. Your

program team identifies several issues that force you to modify program requirements. Some changes are minor, but one issue requires a program scope change. Your next step is to_____

A. Involve the program's Governance Board in its resolution

B. Prepare a change request

C. Update the program management plan

D. Update the scope statement

62.　你正在管理一个生产下一代的能抵抗飓风、龙卷风和台风的玻璃材料的项目集。其中 4 个项目正在进行中。项目 A 配备了足够的人员；项目 B 配备了其需要工作人员的 75%；项目 C 和 D 即将开始。你的项目集团队识别出几个问题，迫使你修改项目集的需求。有些变化是无关紧要的，但有一个问题是需要项目集的范围变更。你的下一步工作是_____

A. 使项目集治理委员会来参与解决　　　B. 准备变更请求

C. 更新项目集管理计划　　　　　　　　D. 更新范围说明书

63.　You are the legacy system conversion program manager in your company. You need to upgrade the company's business development/sales tracking system, which was developed in C++. You now have projects in your program to also upgrade the accounting/financial management system, interface them to the program management information system, and add a knowledge management system. You have a complex program, and it now has increased risks with the variety of systems involved and the stakeholders who are used to these legacy systems and do not see the need to change. You also have three sponsors on this program. You should therefore update a number of the plans you have prepared with the first one to_____

A. Update your quality management plan

B. Update your schedule management plan

C. Update your financial management plan

D. Update your risk management plan

63.　你是公司的遗留系统（原有的系统）转换的项目集经理。你需要升级公司的业务发展/销售跟踪系统，并用 C++进行开发。现在，在你的项目集之中有一些项目也用来升级会计/财务管理系统，并将它们连接到项目集管理信息系统（PMIS），同时还添加一个知识管理系统。你面临一个复杂的项目集，并且由于涉及各种系统，以及相关方也习惯于使用这些遗留系统而并未意识到需要改变，现在已给项目集增添了风险。另外，在这个项目集中，你有 3 名发起人。因此，你应该对许多已经准备好的计划进行更新，第一个要做的是_____

A. 更新你的质量管理计划　　　　　　　B. 更新你的进度管理计划

C. 更新你的财务管理计划　　　　　　　D. 更新你的风险管理计划

64.　You are the developing your communications plan for your legacy system conversion program manager in your company. Compared to projects, this program is far more complex. It has a greater degree of uncertainty, and it will take longer to complete. Plus multiple vendors will be used.  As you develop this plan another concern is_____

  A.  You lack needed resources now for some of the new projects

  B.  New stakeholders will become known and addressed

  C.  You will be spending more time communicating with more groups

  D.  You realize you will require strong leadership skills to deal with the complexity of this program

64.  你正在为公司的遗留系统转换项目集经理制订沟通计划。与项目相比，项目集更为复杂。它有更大程度的不确定性，并且它将需要更长的时间来完成，再加上将使用多个供应商。当你制订这个沟通计划时，另外的问题是_____

  A.  你现在缺乏一些新项目所需要的资源

  B.  将要认识和处理新的相关方

  C.  你将花费更多的时间与更多的群体进行沟通

  D.  你意识到你需要很强的领导力来处理这个项目集的复杂性

65.  Assume you have just been named program manager to develop and manufacture a new drug designed to have fewer side effects than the existing ones on the marketplace to strengthen bones and help to minimize bone cancer. A number of benefits therefore will be associated with this program. You want to establish a program architecture in order to_____

  A.  Provide a process to determine the extent each benefit is achieved before the program closes

  B.  Describe how each benefit will be measured

  C.  Establish a performance baseline for the program

  D.  Map how the components will deliver outcomes to achieve the program's benefits

65.  假设你刚刚被任命为项目集经理，负责开发和制造一种新的药物，旨在增强骨骼并有助于减少骨癌发生，并比现有市场上的产品有更少的副作用。因此，将有许多与该项目集相关的收益。你希望建立一个项目集管理架构以用来_____

  A.  提供一个过程，以确定在项目集结束之前完成每项收益的程度

  B.  描述如何衡量每一项收益

  C.  为项目集建立一个绩效基准

  D.  描绘出组件将如何交付成果以实现项目集的收益

66.  Your company is a leader in the pharmaceutical industry. It has received approval from the Food and Drug Administration (FDA) for a new drug that will cure all glaucoma conditions. You are managing a process to upgrade the manufacturing process, and your CEO has given you an aggressive schedule, especially so the glaucoma drug can reach its numerous possible

patients. You have five projects in this program, and you are getting ready for your second gate review on it. Although it is cumbersome assembling all the required materials for these reviews, you know they are useful as they ensure_____

A. Expected benefits are in line with the benefits realization plan

B. Lessons learned are collected in order to prevent any future problems and improve overall processes

C. Alternatives can be uncovered when problems are identified

D. Processes and procedures are being used as designed

66. 贵公司是医药行业的领导者。它已获得了食品和药物管理局（FDA）的批准，获准用一种新的药物，将治愈所有患有青光眼的患者。你正在管理一个升级制造流程的过程，并且你的首席执行官（CEO）已经给你一个非常激进的进度表，尤其要将青光眼药物给众多潜在的患者使用。你在这个项目集中有 5 个项目，同时你正在准备你的第二个阶段关口评审。尽管收集所有需要的评审材料非常烦琐，然而你知道它们是有用的，因为它们能确保_____

A. 预期收益符合收益实现计划

B. 收集到经验教训，以防止任何未来的问题，并改进整体流程

C. 当识别出问题时，可以发现替代方案

D. 采用所计划或设计的过程及步骤

67. You are the program manager to restructure your department within your government agency. The head of the agency informed your sponsor that she wants to change the scope of the program so you will be working to restructure the entire agency instead of just one department. The entire agency basically is a stakeholder as everyone is concerned about the impact of the reorganization and the funding cuts that have been proposed. As the program manager, you need to_____

A. Use expert judgment

B. Bridge the gap between the current state and the to-be state

C. Demonstrate how the reorganization supports strategic goals

D. Hold meetings with affected groups to listen to their concerns and obtain their buy in to the program

67. 你是一名在你所在的政府机构内负责重组你所在部门的项目集经理。该机构负责人通知你的发起人，她想改变项目集的范围，因而你将致力于重组整个机构而不仅仅只是一个部门。因为每个人都在关注重组的影响，整个机构基本上可视为一名相关方，同时，已提出了资金削减的计划。作为项目集经理，你需要_____

A. 使用专家判断

B. 弥合当前状态与未来目标状态之间的差距

C. 展示重组能如何支持战略目标

D. 与受影响的小组举行会议，倾听他们的问题或顾虑，并获得他们对项目集的支持

68. As a program manager for Destruct, AB, a leading defense contractor, you must determine which components should be part of your program. Your program involves the development of the next generation parachute. It is to be completely safe, easy to deploy, and available in one year at a reasonable price. Your executives want it to be completed at the time of the next Paris Air Show. When you do this, you are working in the_____

A. Benefits planning

B. Pre-program preparations

C. Program initiation

D. Component identification

68. 作为一名领先的国防承包商 Destruct AB 的项目集经理，你必须确定哪些组件应该作为你项目集的一部分。你的项目集涉及下一代降落伞的发展。它应该是完全安全，易于部署的，并要在一年内以合理的价格提供。你的主管希望它在下一次巴黎航空展的时间点完成。当你做这些的时候，你正处于什么阶段_____

A. 收益规划

B. 项目集预先准备

C. 项目集启动

D. 组件识别

69. It is easy to focus primarily on the benefits programs will deliver to the organization and the deliverables the projects in each program will produce. Many organizations though do not have a clear understanding of all of the programs and projects that are under way, and many people do not want to disclose some "pet" program they are working on as they believe they are breakthrough initiatives for the company. However, assume you are in an organization that lacks such a list of all the work in progress, and your company needs such a list as the executives have mandated that a portfolio management process be followed. The executives plan to meet monthly to review the existing portfolio and determine whether or not new programs and projects should be added and others deferred or terminated. The overall objective is to ensure the_____

A. Programs and projects in the portfolio are focused on alignment to strategic objectives

B. The portfolio's strategy is one in which it focuses on preventing poor return on investments in the programs and projects that are pursued

C. Program and project inputs are emphasized along with direct program deliverables and metrics

D. The emphasis continues on the triple constraint as programs and projects to pursue are considered

69. 通常很容易将精力主要集中在项目集所提供给组织的收益，以及在每个项目集中的项目所产生的可交付成果。然而，许多组织对正在进行中的所有的项目集和项目没有一个清晰的理解，并且许多人不想公开透露一些他们正在努力地"宠爱"的项目集，

因为他们相信这些项目集是公司的突破性举措。然而，假设你所在的组织缺乏这样的一张包含所有工作状况的清单，而你的公司需要这样的一张由高层主管人员授权的清单，以及随后的投资组合管理过程。高层主管人员计划每月会面，以评审现有的投资组合，并确定新的项目集和项目是否应被添加，其他项目集和项目是否推迟或终止。总的目标是确保_____

 A.　在投资组合中的项目集和项目都聚焦于和战略目标的一致性

 B.　投资组合的战略是重点防止所进行的项目集和项目出现不良的投资回报

 C.　除了强调直接的项目集的可交付成果和指标外，还同时强调项目集和项目的投入

 D.　持续强调对所进行的项目集和项目的三重制约的考虑

70.　Assume you are working toward your doctoral degree in program management part-time as you work in your City government office that oversees all existing regulations and standards. You have suggested based on your studies that many of the existing projects to overhaul and review these regulations and standards might be better handled as a program since through a program the benefits from proposed projects can be coordinated more effectively especially if the benefits are interdependent. Intended interdependencies of benefits are stated in the_____

 A.　Program management plan  B.　Benefits management plan

 C.　Benefits realization plan  D.　Project management plan

70.　假设你正努力攻读项目集管理的博士学位，并在你的城市政府办公室兼职工作，负责监督所有现有的法规和标准。你认为根据你的研究，现有对法规和标准进行彻底检查和评审的项目，作为项目集来处理可能会更好，这次因为通过项目集，各种计划开展的项目收益能更有效地协同，尤其是如果收益之间是存在相互依赖关系的时候。预期的收益之间的相互依赖关系是在以下哪项之中进行说明_____

 A.　项目集管理计划  B.　收益管理计划

 C.　收益实现计划  D.　项目管理计划

71. Assume your suggestion to your City government to combine projects into programs in the regulations and standards area has been well received. After a meeting of the City's Commissioners, they appointed you as the program manager to oversee this work. You have decided as one of your first tasks to prepare a benefits register and will base it on the expected benefits as defined in the_____

 A.　Program charter  B.　Program business case

 C.　Program management plan  D.　Organization's strategic plan

71.　假设你所建议的市政府在法规和标准领域将各项目整合到项目集的方案已得到较好的采纳。在一次市政府委员会议之后，他们任命你作为项目集经理来监督这项工作。你已决定作为你的首要任务之一，就是先准备一个收益登记册，并将其建立于预期收益的基

础上，该预期收益定义在_____

A. 项目集章程      B. 项目集商业论证

C. 项目集管理计划      D. 组织的战略规划

72. You are the program manager for a new product development program for Company AAA. This product will serve to make sure that consumers will be able to wash all types of clothing through use of your product, and therefore, they no longer will need to spend money at dry cleaning establishments. To complete your program successfully, you have identified five projects. You also will require some specialized resources that are always in demand in your organization; therefore, you meet with members of your core team and subject matter experts to_____

A. Assign roles and responsibilities

B. Determine reporting relationships

C. Prepare a staffing management plan

D. Prepare a program resource plan

72. 你是 AAA 公司的一个新产品开发项目集的项目集经理。该产品将用于确保消费者将能够通过使用你的产品来洗涤所有类型的服装，因此，他们不再需要花钱在干洗店。要成功实现你的项目集，你已经确定了 5 个项目。你还将需要一些专业的资源，这些资源在你的组织中总是被不断需要；因此，你会见你的核心团队的成员和主题专家，从而____

A. 分配角色和职责      B. 确定报告关系

C. 准备人员管理计划      D. 准备项目集资源计划

73. You are the program manager for a new product development program for Company AAA. This product will serve to make sure that consumers will be able to wash all types of clothing through use of your product, and therefore, they no longer will need to spend money at dry cleaning establishments. To complete your program successfully, you have identified five projects. You want to assess the likelihood of achieving these planned outcomes so you decide to_____

A. Use trend analysis      B. Prepare a forecast

C. Conduct a benefit audit      D. Conduct a risk review

73. 你是 AAA 公司的一个新产品开发项目集的项目集经理。该产品将用于确保消费者将能够通过使用你的产品来洗涤所有类型的服装，因此，他们不再需要将钱花在干洗店。要成功实现你的项目集，你已经确定了 5 个项目。你想评估实现这些计划的成果的可能性，因而你决定_____

A. 使用趋势分析      B. 准备预测

C. 进行收益审计      D. 进行风险评审

74. Your organization is embarking on an international program to update all processes

now used in portfolio, program, and project management to ensure they are useful and are not responsible for bureaucratic overhead.　It this situation, it is useful to_____

A. Appoint the program manager from outside of headquarters given its global nature

B. Ensure each location is represented on the Governance Board

C. State that the vision for the program is standardized processes in the three areas to promote common understanding

D. Recognize the need to address cultural, socioeconomic, and political differences

74. 你的组织正在开始着手一个国际化的项目集，要更新在投资组合、项目集和项目管理中当前所使用的全部过程，以确保这些过程都是有用的，并且不会由此带来官僚开销。在这种情况下，非常有用的是_____

A. 任命来自总部外部的、带有全球化特征的项目集经理

B. 确保每个位置都在治理委员会中有相应代表

C. 说明项目集的愿景是在 3 个领域的标准化过程，以促进共同理解

D. 认识到需要解决文化、社会经济和政治上的差异

75. As the program manager in your company responsible for establishing a culture of portfolio management, you were fortunate to be assigned early so you could participate in the development of the program's charter. Your program management plan and the other key subsidiary plans have been approved.　As you are working to provide oversight on the program and its four components, you realize a new component is needed to integrate the efforts of the existing components. This is needed because_____

A. There are resource prioritization issues that are causing existing components to miss scheduled milestones

B. You are using earned value and now are at 15% into your program and forecasts show your schedule and budget targets will not be met

C. You must continually escalate issues and risks to the Governance Board for resolution

D. The components are producing deliverables as planned, but their benefits are not being realized successfully

75. 作为贵公司的项目集经理，你负责建立投资组合管理的文化，很幸运地你被较早地得以任命，这样你就可以参与该项目集章程的制定。你的项目集管理计划和其他关键附属计划已被批准。由于你正在工作于为项目集及其 4 个组件提供监督，你认识到需要一个新的组件来整合现有组件的工作。这是有必要的，因为_____

A. 存在资源优先级的问题，从而导致现有的组件错过预定的或计划的里程碑

B. 你正在使用挣值，你的项目集现在是在 15%，预测显示你的进度和预算目标将无法满足

C. 你必须将问题和风险不断地升级至治理委员会来进行决议

D. 组件正在按计划生成可交付成果，但它们的收益并没有被成功地实现

76. Working with a small core team, you completed your program management plan and the other key subsidiary plans and also prepared a master schedule. As your company follows the PMI Program Management Standard for guidance, you know lessons learned are useful but should be organized effectively in order that they_____

A. Assist in preparing the final program report and in overall program transition

B. Serve as a useful reference for other program and project managers

C. Provide data for use in quickly responding to stakeholder requests for additional program information

D. Serve as a reference for the program manager for program information and documentation accessibility

76. 与一个小核心团队合作，你完成了你的项目集管理计划和其他的关键附属计划，并准备了一个主进度计划。由于你的公司以 PMI 项目集管理标准作为指导，你知道经验教训是有用的，但它们要被有效地加以组织，以使得它们_____

A. 协助准备最终的项目集报告和协助进行整个项目集的转移

B. 为其他项目集和项目经理提供一个有用的参考

C. 为快速响应相关方对额外的项目集信息的请求提供所使用的数据

D. 为项目集经理提供可访问的项目集信息和文档的参考

77. You are the program manager for a program that is using multiple suppliers. Even though you have signed partnering agreements with each supplier, you know performance problems will surface, especially with this program because more than 75 percent of the work is being done by third-party suppliers. You also have a large number of internal stakeholders who are actively involved or interested in your program. To help your stakeholders have a common understanding of the high-level expectations for the program, you should provide stakeholders with information contained in the_____

A. Stakeholder engagement strategy    B. Business case

C. Benefits transition plan    D. Program management plan

77. 你是在一个项目集中使用了多个供应商的项目集经理。即使你已经与每一个供应商签署了合作协议，你知道绩效问题将浮出水面，特别是这个项目集中，因为超过 75% 的工作正在由第三方供应商所完成。你也有大量的内部相关方，他们积极参与或对你的项目集感兴趣。为了帮助你的相关方对该项目集的高层期望有一个共同的理解，你应该为相关方提供信息，这些信息包含在_____

A. 相关方参与策略    B. 商业论证

C. 收益转移计划    D. 项目集管理计划

78. You are sponsoring a new program to be implemented at the beginning of the

corporation's fiscal year. This program is to design the next generation refrigerator that also can serve as a dishwasher and a stove with an oven so there is only one large appliance in one's home. It will use state-of-the-art technology but will be offered at an affordable price. The new appliance is to be designed to be attractive and also not to require much space. As the validity of the business case was assessed to also help develop the charter, you prepared_____

A. An analysis of the expected benefits from the program

B. A feasibility study

C. An analysis of competing efforts under way in the corporation

D. A SWOT analysis

78. 你正在发起一个新的项目集，其将在公司的财政年度开端予以实施。这个项目集是设计下一代冰箱，同时也可以作为一个洗碗机和一个烤箱炉，因为该产品将成为在家里的唯一的大型设备。它将使用最先进水平的技术，另一方面也将提供一个能负担得起的价格。新设备被设计为具有吸引力的，也不需要太多的空间。由于对商业论证的有效性进行评估也有助于制定章程，因此你准备进行_____

A. 对项目集预期收益的分析

B. 可行性研究

C. 在公司中正在进行的竞争工作的分析

D. SWOT 分析

79. You are the contract program manager to restructure a department in a government agency. The head of the agency informed your sponsor that she wants to change the scope of the program so you will be working to restructure the entire agency instead of just one department. The Agency Administrator felt this change would be beneficial as the Agency also has to undergo some funding cuts in the next three fiscal years. Since most everyone is involved to some extent, there is extreme resistance to change, and many key stakeholders have been going directly to the Administrator and not to you since your firm has never worked with this agency before as to why their department should not be part of the reorganization. You and your team are striving to gain the support of all stakeholders, both positive and negative. You decide to_____

A. Actively use your stakeholder register

B. Use a questionnaire to get everyone in the agency involved in the process

C. Conduct interviews with the heads of each of the departments and support offices

D. Re-evaluate your stakeholder engagement plan

79. 你是一名合同项目集经理，负责为一个政府机构重组一个部门。该机构负责人通知你的发起人，她想改变项目集的范围，因而你将致力于重组整个机构，而不仅仅是一个部门。该机构管理者认为这种变化将是有益的，因为该机构还必须在未来接下来的 3 个财政年度进行一些资金削减。由于大多数人都会在某种程度上对变化存在过激的抵抗，而且许多关键相关方都已直接和机构管理者联系而不是和你联系，这是因为你的公司之前从未与该机构合作过，因此要考虑到为什么他们所在的部门不应是重组的一部分。你和你的团队正在努力获得所有相关方的支持，包括正面的和负面的。你决定_____

    A. 积极使用你的相关方登记册

    B. 用问卷调查的方法让每个人都参与到这个过程中

    C. 与各部门和支持办公室的负责人进行面谈

    D. 重新评估你的相关方参与计划

80. Your company is a leader in the pharmaceutical industry. It has received approval from the Food and Drug Administration (FDA) for a new drug that will cure all glaucoma conditions. You are managing a process to upgrade the manufacturing process, and your CEO has given you an aggressive schedule, especially so the glaucoma drug can reach its numerous possible patients. You have five projects in this program, and you are getting ready for your second gate review on it. Your Governance Board is one that is extremely proactive, and it also holds a number of periodic health checks on your program in between these gate reviews. This is because_____

    A. They want further involvement than just a possible four meetings during the life cycle

    B. They want to determine if the level of risk associated with this program remains acceptable especially given the lengthy regulatory process

    C. They want to assess performance against the strategic direction of the organization

    D. They want to assess performance against expected benefits and sustainment

80. 贵公司是医药行业的领导者。它已获得了食品和药物管理局（FDA）的批准，获准用一种新的药物，将治愈所有患有青光眼的患者。你正在管理一个升级制造流程的过程，并且你的首席执行官（CEO）已经给你一个非常激进的进度表，尤其要将青光眼药物给众多潜在的患者使用。你在这个项目集中有 5 个项目，同时你正在准备你的第二个阶段关口评审。你的治理委员会非常积极主动，它也在这些阶段关口评审之间对你的项目集开展许多定期健康检查。这是因为_____

    A. 他们希望进一步的参与，而不只是在生命周期参与可能的 4 次会议

    B. 他们想确定与此项目集相关的风险水平是否仍然可接受，特别是考虑到漫长的监管过程

    C. 他们想评估对于组织的战略方向的绩效

    D. 他们想评估对于预期收益和收益维持的绩效

81. Your stakeholder engagement plan now is complete. As you prepared this plan, you recognized that some stakeholders' interests needed special consideration. However, with this plan you now have_____

    A. An in-depth understanding of the organization's environment

B. A detailed strategy for effective stakeholder engagement

C. A method to communicate program benefits to affected stakeholders

D. A way to balance the impact of negative or resistant stakeholders with those who view the program positively

81. 你的相关方参与计划现在完成了。当你准备这个计划时，你认识到一些相关方的利益需要特别的考虑。然而，有了这个计划，你现在具备_____

A. 对组织环境的深入了解

B. 有效的相关方参与的详细策略

C. 将项目集收益与受影响的相关方进行沟通的方法

D. 一种平衡消极或抵抗的相关方与那些积极对待项目集的相关方之间的影响的方法

82. You are the program manager to set up one integrated system in your company that provides a single point of entry that is easy to use rather than the numerous legacy systems that now exist. You have people who are actively interested and strong supporters of this program, and others are resistors as no one really likes change. You have prepared a stakeholder register. This register_____

A. Shows information distribution methods

B. May require access restrictions

C. Becomes the basic document used to prepare the communications plan

D. Sets forth a stakeholder engagement strategy

82. 你是在你的公司中负责建立一个集成系统的项目集经理，负责提供一个简单使用的切入点而不是提供现存的众多的遗留系统。一些人对该项目集积极感兴趣并是强烈的支持者，而其他人是抵抗者，这些人没有人能真正地喜欢改变。你已经准备了一个相关方登记册。这个登记册_____

A. 显示信息发布方法

B. 可能需要访问限制

C. 成为准备沟通计划的基础文档

D. 阐述了相关方参与策略

83. You are responsible for a major systems integration program that involves converting customer relationship management software, supplier management software, human resources software, and telecom systems from legacy systems to an integrated platform. Your program management plan has been approved. Because of poor performance on two of the projects and by associated vendors, you needed to implement a number of preventive actions and workarounds. You have had to implement a number of change requests. A best practice to follow is to_____

A. Ensure they are ones you can approve or reject

B.   Consult the Governance Board for assistance because the performance of these projects may be such they should be terminated

C.   Establish an integrated change control process

D.   Set up Change Control Boards for each project and at the program level

83. 你负责一个重大的系统集成项目集，其中包括将客户关系管理软件、供应商管理软件、人力资源软件和电信系统从遗产系统转换到一个集成平台。你的项目集管理计划已被批准。由于其中两个项目及相关厂商的绩效表现不佳，你需要实施一些预防措施和解决方法。你必须实施多个变更请求。接下来的最佳实践是_____

A.   确保他们是你可以批准或拒绝的人

B.   咨询治理委员会的协助，由于这些项目的绩效表现可能不佳，因而它们应该被终止

C.   建立一个集成的变更控制流程

D.   为每个项目及在项目集层级设置变更控制委员会

84.   You are responsible for a major systems integration program that involves converting customer relationship management software, supplier management software, human resources software, and telecom systems from legacy systems to an integrated platform. You prepared a program risk response plan. Because of poor performance on two of the projects and by associated vendors, you needed to implement a number of preventive actions and workarounds. However, this program is long and complex, and changes are inevitable. You have described the scope, limitations, expectations, and business impact of the program along with a description of each project and its resources, but now you need to_____

A.   Set up a scope change control system

B.   Update the scope statement

C.   Focus on preparing and following a change management plan

D.   Establish metrics to track adherence to the scope management plan

84. 你负责一个重大的系统集成项目集，其中包括将客户关系管理软件、供应商管理软件、人力资源软件和电信系统从遗产系统转换到一个集成平台。你准备了一个项目集风险应对计划。由于其中两个项目及相关厂商的绩效表现不佳，你需要实施一些预防措施和解决方法。然而，这个项目集是漫长而复杂的，而且变化是不可避免的。你已经描述了该项目集的范围、限制、期望和商业影响，以及对每个项目及其资源的描述，但现在你需要_____

A.   建立范围变更控制系统

B.   更新范围说明书

C.   专注于准备和跟踪一个变更管理计划

D.   建立指标，严格跟踪范围管理计划

85. You are the program manager for a new accounting system that will affect more than 500 accounting professionals in 10 locations. You have a core team of five people, and your preliminary schedule shows that in month 13, the transition of your system to the users will begin. This aggressive schedule recently was made even more difficult as every program in your company will have a five percent budget cut; this means it will be even harder for you to get the key subject matter experts you need when you need them. You have a Governance Board for your program. It is important before you submit a recommendation to formally close the program to the Board that you_____

A. Ensure the members of the operations group are actively involved in the program from the start

B. Provide extensive job aids to the people who will be responsible for running the program once it is completed

C. Document your final lessons learned after you submit a performance report

D. Ensure conditions for closure are satisfied

85. 你是一个新的会计系统的项目集经理，该系统将影响在 10 个不同地方的、超过 500 人的会计专业人员。你有一个 5 人的核心团队，而且你的初步计划显示，你的系统将在第 13 个月开始移交给用户。这一挑战性的计划最近变得更加困难，这是因为你的公司中的每个项目集都将有 5%的预算削减；这意味着当你需要关键主题专家（SME）的时候，将变得更难以得到。你有一个针对项目集的治理委员会。重要的是，在你提交建议给治理委员会正式关闭项目集之前，你需要_____

A. 确保运营工作组的成员自启动以来积极参与该项目集

B. 一旦项目集完成，为那些将负责运营该项目集的人提供广泛的工作帮助

C. 在你提交绩效报告后记录你的最终的经验教训

D. 确保项目集收尾的条件得到满足

86. You have numerous stakeholders, both internal and external as your program involves members of the public. You also are using five different vendors. Different stakeholders have different areas of interest at different times and may be positive toward the program or negative. You have decided you should_____

A. Use a stakeholder impact and issue tracking and prioritization tool

B. Work with a mentor to update your own negotiation and influencing skills as you work with negative stakeholders on this program

C. Conduct another stakeholder analysis to make sure you have a greater understanding of the culture of the organization

D. Set up specific channels of communications

86. 你有众多的相关方，包括你的项目集所涉及的内部的和外部的公众成员。你还使

用了 5 个不同的供应商。不同的相关方，在不同的时间，有不同的兴趣领域，并且可能是积极的或消极的。你已经决定了你应该_____

A. 使用对相关方的影响和问题进行跟踪和优先处理的工具

B. 由于你在项目集中与消极的相关方一起工作，因此你与一位导师合作，更新谈判和影响技能

C. 进行另一种相关方分析，以确保你对组织文化有更深入的理解

D. 建立特定的沟通渠道

87. You have been appointed as manager for a new program in your organization. This program will receive $250,000 as an initial investment; $175,000 at the beginning of year 2; $150,000 at the beginning of year 3; and $125,000 at the beginning of year 4. The program will start with a core team of seven senior managers; three project managers will be added during year 2, and two more project managers during year 3. While you work on this program, it is essential to ensure you can_____

A. Identify and evaluate integration opportunities and needs

B. Set up a PMO for overall support, especially in administrative requirements

C. Focus in your planning first on a bottom-up approach and then integrate it with a top-down approach

D. First address the program's vision and justification

87. 在你的组织中，你被任命为一名新的项目集经理。该项目集将获得 25 万美元作为初始投资；17.5 万美元在第 2 年的年初；15 万美元在第 3 年的年初；12.5 万美元在第 4 年的年初。该项目集启动之初包括一个 7 名高管组成的核心团队；将在第 2 年期间增加 3 名项目经理，并在第 3 年增加 2 名以上的项目经理。当你在这个项目集上工作的时候，必不可少的是要确保你能够_____

A. 识别和评价整合的机会和需求

B. 建立 PMO 的全面支持，尤其是在行政的及管理的需求方面

C. 专注于你的计划首先采用一个自下而上的方法，然后把它与一个自上而下的方法相结合

D. 首先解决项目集的愿景和合理性

88. Wanting to make sure that existing lessons learned from every project and program undertaken in your organization are actually captured and used, you have received approval from your Portfolio Selection Committee to establish a program in knowledge management for your services company. The purpose is not only to record these lessons learned in an easily accessible fashion but to also make sure they are used by future program and project managers. You have identified four projects so far that will be part of this program. You recognize for this program to have visibility among the executives of your company that the mission, vision, and

strategic fit of the program must be aligned with the organization's objectives. This is done as part of the_____

A. Pre-Program Preparations  B. Program Initiation

C. Program Strategy Alignment  D. Benefits Identification

88. 要确保在你的组织中的每一个项目和项目集中的现有的经验教训能被实际地捕获和使用，你已收到投资组合选择委员会的批准，建立一个你的服务公司在知识管理方面的项目集。目的不仅是以容易访问的方式来记录这些经验教训，也要确保它们能被未来的项目集和项目经理所使用。到目前为止你已经确定了 4 个项目，其将是该项目集的一部分。你认识到这个项目集在你的公司的管理人员之中具备可见性，项目集的使命、愿景和战略适配必须与组织的目标相一致。这被完成并作为以下哪个阶段的一部分_____

A. 项目集预先准备  B. 项目集启动

C. 项目集战略一致性  D. 收益识别

89. You are the program manager for a new accounting system that will affect more than 500 accounting professionals in 10 locations. You have a core team of five people, and your preliminary schedule shows that in month 13, the transition of your system to the users will begin. You have a Governance Board for your program. Possible members of your Governance Board were first identified_____

A. As a section in the governance plan

B. At the time the business case was developed

C. As part of the program management plan

D. At the end of the program formulation

89. 你是一个新的会计系统的项目集经理，该系统将影响在 10 个不同地方的、超过 500 人的会计专业人员。你有一个 5 人的核心团队，而且你的初步计划显示，你的系统将在第 13 个月开始移交给用户。你有一个项目集的治理委员会。治理委员会的可能成员首先被确定_____

A. 作为治理计划中的一部分  B. 在制定商业论证的时候

C. 作为项目集管理计划的一部分  D. 在项目集形成阶段结束时

90. Rarely have hurricanes reached the northern states of the United States until the past two years. People were not equipped to deal with them. You are the program manager to help ensure people are prepared. Your company won a government contract and developed a business case for the program that was approved quickly. You have a Governance Board set up, but in the last three meetings, the Chief Information Officer or a substitute from IT did not attend. You have defined metrics to monitor performance of stakeholders in your program in the_____

A. Communications plan  B. Stakeholder engagement strategy

C. Stakeholder engagement plan  D. Stakeholder register

90. 直到过去的两年，很少有飓风能到达美国北部各州。人们没有装备来对付它们。你是一名帮助确保人们完成准备应对飓风的项目集经理。贵公司赢得了一个政府合同，并制定了一个商业论证，该项目集很快被批准。你建立了一个治理委员会，但在过去的 3 次会议上，首席信息官（CIO）或来自 IT 部门的替代者没有出席。你已定义了指标以监督在你的项目集中的相关方的绩效，这些指标处于如下哪项之中_____

A. 沟通计划
B. 相关方参与策略
C. 相关方参与计划
D. 相关方登记册

91. As you plan your program, so far you have identified three projects, and you are to complete it in six months. It is especially important to identify the program's resource requirements and prepare a resource plan. A useful tool and technique to use is_____

A. Capacity planning

B. Resource assignment matrix

C. Resource breakdown structure

D. Program management information system

91. 当你规划你的项目集的时候，到目前为止，你已经确定了 3 个项目，并且你要在 6 个月之内完成它。特别重要的是要确定项目集的资源需求并准备一个资源计划。一个有用的工具和技术是_____

A. 容量规划
B. 资源分配矩阵
C. 资源分解结构
D. 项目集管理信息系统

92. Working on an internal program to restructure your company so it is more customer facing is a major challenge. No one ever likes reorganizations, and many people fear they will lose their jobs as a result of your program. However, it has relied on its existing customer base for its 20 year life, and a new focus is part of the company's strategic plan to attract new customers and enter new markets. As you plan your program, so far you have identified three projects, and you are to complete the reorganization in six months. You are determined to control expenditures to stay within your budget. Therefore. you are focusing on the need to_____

A. Identify opportunities to return funds back to the company

B. Completing the program ahead of schedule

C. Avoid use of contingency and management reserves

D. Monitor costs reallocation impact and results between components

92. 你工作于一个内部的项目集，需要重组你的公司，因此需要更多地面向客户是一个重大的挑战。没有人喜欢重组，许多人担心他们会因为你的项目集而失去工作。然而，它已对现有的客户群依赖了 20 年，新的重点是吸引新客户进入新市场，并作为公司的战略计划的一部分。当你规划你的项目集的时候，到目前为止，你已经确定了 3 个项目，并

且你要在 6 个月之内完成重组。你决定控制支出保持在你的预算之内。因此，你专注于需要_____

A. 确定机会，以将资金返还给公司

B. 将进度提前以完成项目集

C. 避免使用应急和管理储备

D. 监控在组件之间进行成本再分配的影响和结果

93. Your company is a leader in the pharmaceutical industry. It has received approval from the Food and Drug Administration (FDA) for a new drug that will cure all glaucoma conditions. Although demand for the product is high, your company has many other drugs to manufacture. You are managing a process to upgrade the manufacturing process, and your CEO has given you an aggressive schedule. Many people who have responsibility for other drugs in your company are concerned that once your manufacturing upgrade program is complete, the production of the glaucoma drug will be given preferential treatment, and their products will not be produced in sufficient quantities. You and your team realize you have a large number of stakeholders, and many of them are negative toward your program. This means you need to foster use of_____

A. Leadership skills  B. Management skills

C. Strategic visioning skills  D. Political skills

93. 贵公司是医药行业的领导者。它已获得了食品和药物管理局（FDA）的批准，获准用一种新的药物，将治愈所有患有青光眼的患者。虽然对该产品的需求很迫切，但贵公司也有许多其他的药品要生产。你正在管理一个升级制造流程的过程，并且你的首席执行官（CEO）已经给你一个非常有挑战性的进度表。令你的公司中许多负责其他药物的人担心的是，一旦你的制造升级项目集得以完成，青光眼药物的生产将被给予优待，而他们的产品将无法生产出足够数量。你和你的团队意识到你有大量的相关方，并且他们中的许多人对你的项目集是消极的。这意味着你需要促进使用_____

A. 领导技能  B. 管理技能

C. 战略愿景规划技能  D. 政治技能

94. On your program, you and your team realize you have a large number of stakeholders. Of course you require a number of interpersonal skills, but the most important one is_____

A. Leadership skills  B. Communications skills

C. Strategic visioning skills  D. Political skills

94. 在你的项目集上，你和你的团队意识到你有大量的相关方。当然，你需要一些人际交往技能，但最为重要的技能是_____

A. 领导技能  B. 沟通技能

C. 战略愿景规划技能  D. 政治技能

95. Working on your glaucoma program, you have received approval from the Food and

Drug Administration (FDA) for a new drug that will cure all glaucoma conditions. Although demand for the product is high, your company has many other drugs to manufacture. You are managing a process to upgrade the manufacturing process, and your CEO has given you an aggressive schedule Many people who have responsibility for other drugs in your company are concerned that once your manufacturing upgrade program is complete, the production of the glaucoma drug will be given preferential treatment, and their products will not be produced in sufficient quantities. You and your team realize you have a large number of stakeholders; many seem to be negative toward your program. Given this situation, your best course of action should be to_____

    A. Focus on customer expectations

    B. Proceed according to your program management plan

    C. Establish buy-in from stakeholders to ensure program success

    D. Escalate this issue to your Governance Board to seek assistance in dealing with these stakeholders

95. 贵公司是医药行业的领导者。它已获得了食品和药物管理局（FDA）的批准，获准用一种新的药物，将治愈所有患有青光眼的患者。虽然对该产品的需求很迫切，但贵公司也有许多其他的药品要生产。你正在管理一个升级制造流程的过程，并且你的首席执行官（CEO）已经给你一个非常有挑战性的进度表。令你的公司中许多负责其他药物的人担心的是，一旦你的制造升级项目集得以完成，青光眼药物的生产将被给予优待，而他们的产品将无法生产出足够数量。你和你的团队意识到你有大量的相关方，并且他们中的许多人对你的项目集是消极的。考虑到这种情况，你最好的行动路线应该是_____

    A. 专注于客户的期望

    B. 按照你的项目集管理计划进行

    C. 赢得相关方的支持，以确保项目集的成功

    D. 将问题升级到你的治理委员会，以寻求协助处理这些相关方

96. You have three projects that comprise your program. Your aggressive schedule recently was made even more difficult as every program in your company will have a five percent budget cut; this means it will be even harder for you to get the key subject matter experts (SME) you need when you need them. You have a Governance Board for your program. Today, you had your regularly scheduled status meeting with Project Manager A. He told you he needed a key SME earlier than anticipated because of a new technological risk that had occurred. You were able to negotiate for this SME by meeting later with Project Manager C and getting the SME reassigned for two months to Project A. This was handled appropriately by Project Manager A as he_____

    A. Immediately reported the problem to you

B.　Followed the issue escalation process

C.　Realized that the SME was on Project Manager C's team and notified you accordingly

D.　Asked Human Resources where he might locate a SME before contacting you

96.　你的项目集由 3 个项目所组成。你的挑战性的计划最近变得更加困难，这是因为你的公司中的每个项目集都将有 5% 的预算削减；这意味着当你需要关键主题专家（SME）的时候，将变得更难以得到。你有一个针对项目集的治理委员会。现在，你已经与项目经理 A 就定期进度状态进行了会面。他告诉你他要早于预期地需要一名关键 SME，这是因为一个新的技术风险已经发生了。你可以随后与项目经理 C 进行会谈，就该 SME 进行协商，使得将该 SME 重新分配 2 个月的时间给到项目 A。项目经理 A 对此进行了适当的处理，这是因为他_____

A.　立即向你报告了问题

B.　遵循问题升级流程

C.　意识到 SME 在项目经理 C 的团队中，并给你相应的通知

D.　在联系你之前，他请求可能要使用一名 SME 的人力资源

97.　You were appointed program manager early in your program's life cycle, and you are leading the development of the benefits realization plan. You are working in benefits analysis and planning, which is important in that you are_____

A.　Establishing the program's performance baseline

B.　Establishing processes to measure progress against the benefits plan

C.　Creating tracking and communications processes

D.　Defining the program's critical success factors

97.　在你的项目集生命周期的早期，你被任命为项目集经理，并且你领导收益实现计划的制订。你在进行收益分析和规划的工作，这是很重要的，因为你正在_____

A.　建立项目集的绩效基准

B.　建立对收益计划的进展进行衡量的过程

C.　创建跟踪和沟通过程

D.　定义项目集的关键成功因素

98.　You are meeting with your company's Program Selection Committee. Because your company has limited resources, you are selecting one of two programs to undertake. The return on investment (ROI) and payback periods for the programs are basically identical, so the major factor in making your decision is_____

A.　The balance between cost and benefit

B.　The ability to realize benefits before the program is complete

C.　Whether the business benefits are easily quantifiable

D.　Extrinsic versus intrinsic benefits

98. 你与你公司的项目集选择委员会进行会面。由于你公司拥有有限的资源，所以你正在从两个项目中选其一开展工作。这些项目集的投资回报率（ROI）和投资回收期基本上是相同的，因此你制定决策的主要因素是_____

   A. 成本与收益之间的平衡

   B. 在项目集完成之前，实现收益的能力

   C. 业务收益是否容易量化

   D. 外在与内在的收益

99. As you work as the program manager to establish Centers of Excellence in your global company on every continent except Antarctica, you have a large number of stakeholders who are interested in your program. You also have 12 different projects and know others will be added as the program continues. Your team, therefore, is a large virtual one, and you hold conference calls regularly, rotating the times in which they are held so no one is always inconvenienced. You also do a lot of traveling to the various sites. You realize you as well as your project managers must be excellent in_____

   A. Communicating                     B. Understanding cultural differences
   C. Distributing consistent messages  D. Actively engaging stakeholders

99. 你作为一名项目集经理，要在你的全球化公司中的每个大陆板块（南极洲除外）建立卓越中心，你拥有大量的相关方，他们对你的项目集感兴趣。你也有 12 个不同的项目，并知道随着项目集的绩效进行，其他人也会不断加入。因此，你的团队是一个很大的虚拟团队，而且你定期举行电话会议，轮换他们参加会议的时间，使得大家都很方便。你也前往了大量的不同的地点。你意识到你和你的项目经理必须具备在以下哪方面的优秀表现_____

   A. 沟通                     B. 理解文化差异
   C. 发布一致的消息           D. 积极争取相关方

100. You are the legacy system conversion program manager in your company. Your Governance Board recognizes the importance of improving other projects in this upgrade so there is an integrated system for all applications in your company. You now have projects in your program to also upgrade the accounting/financial management system, interface them to the program management information system, and add a knowledge management system. You have a proactive Governance Board, which can assist in_____

   A. Managing quality across the life cycle

   B. Ensuring you have the most competent people assigned to your program

   C. Enabling you to use a benchmarking forum with other organizations that have done similar programs

   D. Providing you with direct access to the senior executives in your company as needed.

100. 你是你公司的遗留系统（原有的系统）转换的项目集经理。你的治理委员会认识到在这个升级过程中改善其他项目的重要性，因而在你的公司中的所有的应用需要具有一个集成的系统。现在，在你的项目集中的有些项目也需要升级会计/财务管理系统，并将它们连接到项目集管理信息系统，同时添加一个知识管理系统。你有一个积极的治理委员会，它可以帮助_____

A. 跨整个生命周期的质量管理

B. 确保将最有能力的人分配到你的项目集

C. 使得你利用标杆管理论坛，和开展类似项目集的其他组织一起讨论

D. 必要的时候使得你能直接接触公司的高级管理人员

101. Assume that your organization specializes in programs to handle conferences for government agencies. Each conference tends to attract about 800 to 1,000 people throughout the country in different locations. Each conference is a separate program as it involves different agencies, subject matter, themes, and speakers. Your company handles all the logistical requirements and basically is transparent to the agencies for which it works. Most of your programs, therefore, are initiated as a result of_____

A. Alignment with the company's mission statement

B. The business case

C. A decision to bid on a contract

D. The desire to remain competitive in the field

101. 假设你的组织的项目集专门负责处理政府机构会议。每次会议往往吸引约800~1 000 人，分布在整个国家的不同地点。每次会议都是一个单独的项目集，因为它涉及不同的机构、主题、议题和发言人。你的公司要处理所有的后勤需求，而且对所工作的机构基本上要保持透明。因此，你的大多数项目集的启动是作为如下哪项的结果_____

A. 与公司使命的陈述保证一致

B. 商业论证

C. 投标该合同的决策

D. 在该领域保持竞争力的要求

102. In each of these conferences, the program sponsor has important responsibilities as this person has primary responsibility for securing finances and ensuring the program delivers its intended benefits. The sponsor is identified_____

A. When the business case for the program is presented

B. Before program initiation

C. In the program initiation

D. In the pre-program preparations process

102. 在这些会议的每次会议之中，项目集发起人承担重要的责任，因为这个人主要

负责保证财务状况的安全，并确保该项目集能提供其预期的收益。该发起人在以下哪个阶段被确定_____

A. 当提出该项目集的商业论证时 B. 在项目集启动之前

C. 在项目集启动阶段 D. 在项目集预先准备过程

103. Assume that your organization specializes in programs to handle conferences for government agencies. You are the program manager for an upcoming conference on portfolio management for government agency representatives. This conference is expected to attract about 200 people as each agency will send at least five people to it, many of whom will be political appointees. You realize as you plan this program, with your five identified projects in it thus far, that changes are inevitable. In your program planning, you want to include an approach to communicate scope changes. This should be included as part of your_____

A. Integrated Change Control Plan B. Scope Management Plan

C. Communications Management Plan D. Scope Control Plan

103. 假设你的组织的项目集专门负责处理政府机构会议。你是一名即将召开的、为政府机构代表服务的投资组合管理会议的项目集经理。这次会议预计将吸引约 200 人，每个政府机构将至少 5 人参加，其中许多人是政府官员。你意识到你规划这个项目集的时候，到目前为止已确定了其中的 5 个项目，而且变化也是不可避免的。在你的项目集规划中，你想要包含一个沟通范围变更的方法。这应该包含在以下哪项之中并作为其中的一部分_____

A. 整合的变更控制计划 B. 范围管理计划

C. 沟通管理计划 D. 范围控制计划

104. Program governance covers systems and methods by which program and its strategy are defined, authorized, and monitored. It conducts periodic reviews of the program in delivering its benefits enabling the organization to assess the viability of the program and the organization's strategic plan and the level of support needed to achieve program goals. The structure for your Governance Board and its meeting schedules are part of the_____

A. Overall governance framework

B. Gate review requirements established by the Enterprise Program Management Office

C. Governance plan

D. Program management plan

104. 项目集治理涵盖了定义、授权和监控项目集及其战略的系统和方法。它对项目集在交付收益方面进行定期评审，使得组织能评估该项目集和组织战略计划的可行性，以及评估完成项目集目标所需要的支持水平。你的治理委员会的结构和它的会议时间表是如下哪项的一部分_____

A. 整体治理框架

B.　由企业项目集管理办公室所建立的阶段关口评审要求

C.　治理计划

D.　项目集管理计划

105.　Assume you are working for a dry foods company. For the past five years, every one of your projects in this company has met its goals in terms of being on schedule, within budget, and meeting its specifications. However, your company finds that even though its projects are meeting its goals, overall the company is not meeting its strategic goals and objectives. You were asked to meet with the executive team to discuss your opinions as to what is occurring in the company as you are an experienced and successful project manager. You pointed out that you felt the basic problem was_____

A.　The projects should be managed as a program

B.　The projects were defined in too narrow a fashion

C.　The organization's strategic goals would change, but the project managers were not aware of the changes

D.　The organization requires a Program Management Office

105.　假设你在一家干货食品公司工作。在过去的 5 年里，你在这家公司的每一个项目都符合其目标，按时、在预算范围内并满足范围说明书。然而，你的公司发现，即使项目是符合目标的，总体而言，公司未达到其战略目的和目标。作为一名有经验的和成功的项目经理，你被要求与执行团队会面，就你的公司究竟发生了什么进行意见讨论。你指出，你觉得基本的问题是_____

A.　项目应该作为一个项目集来管理

B.　项目被定义在太窄的领域和方式内

C.　该组织的战略目标会发生变化，但项目经理们没有意识到变化

D.　组织需要一个项目集管理办公室

106.　You are managing a complex training program in your company. It has a number of component projects plus some ongoing work especially in logistical areas. Your team consists of instructional system design specialists who support the program on a full-time basis. For each training project, you need the services of subject-matter experts (SMEs) to complement the instructional designers. Assume that you met today with the manager of Functional Unit C in your company, and she agreed to release two chemists to support Project D in your program. You now need to_____

A.　Meet with Project Manager D and inform him that you have acquired the needed SMEs

B.　Transition the SMEs to the program position

C.　Determine how this assignment can benefit the SMEs in their career path

D.　Update the program resource plan

106. 在你的公司内部，你正在管理一个复杂的培训方面的项目集。它有一些组件项目，加上一些正在进行的、主要是在后勤领域的工作。你的团队由教学系统设计专家所组成，他们全职支持这个项目集。对于每个培训项目，你需要主题专家（SME）的服务，来补充教学设计师。假设你今天与公司的功能单元 C 的经理进行了会谈，她同意释放 2 名化学专家以支持你的项目集中的项目 D。你现在需要_____

A. 会见项目经理 D，并通知他你已经获得了所需的 SME

B. 将 SME 转移到项目集的位置

C. 确定如何委派，使其在他们的职业生涯中获益于 SME

D. 更新项目集资源计划

107. You have a complex program. Thus far, you have passed gate 3 and are executing your program. Because the executing phase in the life cycle will last over a year, your Governance Board is holding periodic performance reviews with you and your team on a bi-monthly basis. The Governance Board has assumed responsibility for compliance with organizational reporting and control functions. An example is_____

A. Benefit transition

B. Strategic and operational assumptions

C. Quality criteria and standards

D. Code of conduct compliance

107. 你有一个复杂的项目集。到目前为止，你已经通过了第三个关口，并正在执行你的项目集。因为项目集生命周期中的执行阶段会持续一年以上，你的治理委员会将与你和你的团队定期进行绩效评审，按照每双月的周期进行。公司治理委员会承担了负责组织报告和控制功能方面的合规性的职责，例如_____

A. 收益转移

B. 战略的和运营层面的假设

C. 质量准则和标准

D. 行为守则

108. In managing a program, you terminated three contracts that supported your projects. One of the contractors went bankrupt, and the other two were unable to deliver as promised. You now are preparing your final report as your program is ready for closure. In it these problems show_____

A. The need to conduct contractor performance reviews

B. The importance of following documented contract closure procedures

C. A major area of improvement

D. Why contractual terms and conditions need to be revised

108. 在管理一个项目集时，你终止了支持你的项目的 3 个合同。其中 1 个承包商破产了，另外 2 个也无法兑现承诺。由于你的项目集准备收尾，你现在正在准备最终报告。在该项目集中，这些问题表明_____

A. 进行承包商绩效评审的必要性

B. 遵循书面合同收尾程序的重要性

C. 一个重要的改进领域

D. 为什么需要修订合同条款和条件

109. Assume that you just finished a meeting with your Program's Governance Board. It was not a stage_gate review but was a more informal health check as several of the key stakeholders were concerned that a key milestone had been missed, and an incremental benefit from the program now would be delayed. They also were concerned that missing this milestone may lead to missing future milestones. Unfortunately, you are not using earned value on your program, but when you prepared your benefits realization plan, you did include a number of metrics that you and your core team have been tracking. To ensure continual realization of the intended benefits and to reassure your stakeholders and the Governance Board members that the program is not in trouble, you and your team have used which of the following techniques before taking corrective action_____

A. Delphi technique
B. Decision trees
C. Brainstorming
D. Causal analysis

109. 假设你刚刚完成了一个与项目集治理委员会的会议。该会议不是一个阶段关口评审，但是它是一个较为非正式的健康检查，正如几个关键的相关方所担心的，一个关键的里程碑已经失败，并且从该项目集获得的增量收益现在将被推迟。他们还担心这一里程碑的失败可能会导致未来的更多里程碑的失败。不幸的是，你并没有在你的项目集中使用挣值，但是当你准备好了你的收益实现计划时，你确实包括了一些你和你的核心团队一直在跟踪的度量指标。为了确保持续实现预期收益，并消除你的相关方和治理委员会成员对于项目集存在问题的疑虑，你和你的团队在采取纠正行动之前已经使用了以下哪种技术_____

A. 德尔菲法
B. 决策树
C. 头脑风暴
D. 因果分析

110. You are the program manager for a new accounting system that will affect more than 500 accounting professionals in 10 locations. You have a core team of five people and your preliminary schedule shows that in month 13, the transition of your system to the users will begin. This aggressive schedule recently was made even more difficult as every program in your company will have a five percent budget cut; this means it will be even harder for you to get the key subject matter experts you need when you need them. You have set up a stakeholder register

and are using it to_____

    A.  Provide an inventory of how each type of stakeholder will be impacted the program

    B.  Provide a way to make sure the key stakeholders remain engaged in the program

    C.  Show how best to manage the impacts of the program on stakeholders

    D.  Report and distribute program deliverables and formal and informal communications

110.　你是一个新的会计系统的项目集经理，该系统将影响 10 个不同地方的、超过 500 人的会计专业人员。你有一个 5 人的核心团队，而且你的初步计划显示，你的系统将在第 13 个月开始移交给用户。这一挑战性的计划最近变得更加困难，这是因为你的公司中的每个项目集都将有 5%的预算削减；这意味着当你需要关键主题专家（SME）的时候，将变得更难以得到。你已建立了一个相关方登记册并使用它来_____

    A.  提供一个每个类型的相关方将如何影响项目集的清单

    B.  提供一种方法，以确保关键的相关方保持参与该项目集

    C.  展示如何最佳地管理项目集对相关方的影响

    D.  报告和分发项目集可交付成果，以及正式和非正式的沟通

111.　You and your team have prepared your stakeholder register for your organizational change program. In preparing it, you and your team found which of the following techniques to be the most useful_____

    A.  Nominal group technique        B.  Organizational analysis

    C.  Interviews                    D.  Open-ended questions

111.　你和你的团队已经为你的组织变革项目集准备好了相关方登记册。在准备的过程中，你和你的团队发现以下哪一项技术是最有用的_____

    A.  名义小组技术              B.  组织分析

    C.  访谈                     D.  开放式问题

112.　Programs need to be funded to the degree noted in the approved program plan for success in realizing their benefits. Funding should be provided consistently with program needs and organizational priorities, which may be defined in the organization's portfolio management process. This responsibility is one that is handled by the_____

    A.  Portfolio manager          B.  Program sponsor

    C.  Governance Board         D.  Finance Department

112.　为成功实现收益，要按照已批准的项目集计划所注明的资助程度来对项目集进行资助。资金应随着项目集的需要和组织的优先事项而连续地予以提供，这些优先事项可能在组织的投资组合管理过程中定义。以上职责是由以下哪项来负责管理_____

    A.  投资组合经理           B.  项目发起人

    C.  治理委员会            D.  财务部

113.　You are the program manager to restructure your entire government agency. Since no

one likes change, you are holding meetings every two weeks that are recorded and made available to everyone in the Agency as to your progress. You are requesting comments from people throughout the Agency after each meeting. You feel these meetings can better help you understand the urgency and probability of stakeholder-related risks so basically you are_____

A. Updating your stakeholder register

B. Updating your communications log

C. Striving to focus on risks as opportunities

D. Conducting a program impact analysis

113. 你是一名负责重组你所在的整个政府机构的项目集经理。由于没有人喜欢改变，于是你每两周举行会议，根据你的进展，将会议记录下来并提供给机构中的每个人。你要求在每次会议后，整个机构的人要提供意见。你觉得这些会议可以更好地帮助你了解与相关方相关的风险的紧迫性和发生概率，因此从根本上说你是在_____

A. 更新相关方登记册　　　　　　B. 更新沟通日志

C. 努力专注于将风险转化为机会　D. 进行项目集影响分析

114. Working in portfolio management and helping program sponsors prepare the business case for new programs in your chemical company, you want to make sure each program supports at least one of the objectives in your company's five year strategic plan. You encourage one program sponsor to meet with the strategic planners to make sure there is alignment and also to make sure the strategic planners do not expect any major changes in the next three years, the proposed length of the sponsor's program. One best practice is to prepare a high-level roadmap and continue to use it during the program. However, a disadvantage of the roadmap is_____

A. People believe it is the program's schedule

B. It is difficult to keep its information current and relevant

C. It typically is not possible to balance the timing of program demands with resource availability

D. It is hard to use it to provide senior and program managers with a view of the programs in the portfolio over time

114. 你正在从事投资组合管理的工作，并在你的化学公司中帮助项目集发起人准备新项目集的商业论证，你想要确保每个项目集均支持公司的 5 年战略计划中的至少一个或以上的目标。你促使一名项目集发起人和战略规划人员会谈，以确保一致性，并确保战略规划者在未来 3 年内不期望任何重大变化，3 年的时间正好是发起人的项目集所计划的长度。一个最佳实践是准备一个高级别的路线图，并在项目集期间持续使用它。然而，路线图的一个缺点是_____

A. 人们相信它是项目集的进度表

B. 很难保持其信息是流动的和有关联性的

C. 它通常不能平衡项目集需求的及时性与资源的可用性

D. 很难用它来为高管和项目集经理提供一个历经较长时间的在投资组合中的项目集的视图

115. Working as the program manager for Guenther, Germany's water-alleviation program, you have an outstanding core team of five subject matter experts and a Program Management Office to support you. So far, you have three projects in your program. As you create your program work breakdown structure (PWBS), decomposition is useful to identify program deliverables and related work. The decomposition process is complete when_____

A. Each phase of the program life cycle has been detailed

B. The program manager has the desired level of control

C. The work packages of the various projects in the program have been identified

D. Verifiable products, services, or results from each project have been determined

115. 作为负责德国 Guenther 的水资源缓解项目集的一名项目集经理，你有一个优秀的核心团队，其中有 5 名主题专家，并且也有项目集管理办公室的支持。到目前为止，在你的项目集中你有 3 个项目。在你创建项目集工作分解结构（PWBS）时，分解工作是有助于确定项目集的可交付成果及相关工作。该分解过程是在什么情况下完成的_____

A. 项目集生命周期的每个阶段得以细化

B. 项目集经理所需的控制层级

C. 项目集中的各种项目的工作包已被确定

D. 每个项目之中的可核查的产品、服务或结果已被确定

116. Continuing to work on your water-alleviation program in Guenther, Germany, you and your team now have prepared your program's work breakdown structure. This turned out to be a far more difficult process than you imagined because in the past, you had templates you could use to assist you in preparing the PWBS. However, you and your team completed it. The next step is to_____

A. Organize the work                    B. Prepare the program schedule

C. Develop cost estimates               D. Prepare a scope management plan

116. 你继续工作在德国 Guenther 的水资源缓解项目集，你和你的团队现在准备好了项目集工作分解结构（PWBS）。在过去，你有模板可以用来帮助你准备 PWBS。这是一个超出你想象的非常困难的过程。然而，你和你的团队已经完成了它。下一步是_____

A. 对工作进行组织                        B. 准备项目集进度表

C. 制定成本估算                          D. 准备范围管理计划

117. You are pleased to be the program manager for Guenther, Germany's water alleviation program. So far, you have three projects in your program. Six months after your plan was

approved, Guenther issued some new regulations, and you requested approval and received it to add a new project to address regulatory compliance. However, this project is consuming extensive time, and it affects other initiatives under way in the organization. Your best approach is to_____

A.  Request additional resources and reprioritize some that now support the other projects

B.  Suggest to the Governance Board that this project be moved from your program to be a distinct program

C.  Conduct a quality assurance audit to determine the extent of compliance with the new regulations

D.  Reprioritize resources to the regulatory project and acquire the services of a qualified vendor to support the other projects

117.  你非常乐意成为德国 Guenther 水资源缓解项目集的项目集经理。到目前为止，在你的项目集中有 3 个项目。在你的项目集被批准了 6 个月后，Guenther 颁布了一些新的规定，你要求批准和接收这些规定并添加一个新项目以解决监管合规性。然而，这个项目已经消耗了大量的时间，并且它影响到在组织中正在进行的其他行动计划。你最好的方法是_____

A.  请求额外的资源，并对当前正支持其他项目的一些资源变更优先顺序

B.  向治理委员会建议将这个项目从你的项目集中移走，成为一个独特的项目集

C.  进行质量保证审计，以确定符合新规定的程度

D.  重新优化针对监管项目的资源的优先顺序，并获得一个合格的供应商的服务来支持其他的项目

118.  As the program manager for Guenther, Germany's water alleviation program, you have many challenges. So far, you have three projects in your program. One challenge of course is the aggressive schedule you must meet and the high priority of this program in your company's portfolio. You also have a number of technical SMEs on your program, who seem to want to really work on technical topics in a functional environment. Also, as program manager you must work with stakeholders at all levels as well as with your team and your Governance Board.  Your flexibility in managing this program is limited by_____

A.  Communication channels       B.  Constraints

C.  Assumptions                          D.  Benefits analysis

118.  作为负责德国 Guenther 的水资源缓解项目集的一名项目集经理，你有很多的挑战。到目前为止，在你的项目集中有 3 个项目。当然，一个挑战是你必须满足有挑战性的进度表，并使得这个项目集在你的公司的投资组合中保持高优先级。你的项目集中也有一些技术主题专家（SME），他们看起来想要在功能环境中能真正地解决技术问题。此外，

作为项目集经理，你必须与所有层次的相关方，以及与你的团队和你的治理委员会进行合作。你管理这个项目集的灵活性受到如下哪方面的限制_____

    A. 沟通渠道                  B. 制约因素

    C. 假设                          D. 收益分析

119. For Guenther, Germany's water-alleviation program, you have many challenges. Fortunately, you have assembled your core team and have a PMO. You also have met individually with your key stakeholders. You regularly communicate with your program sponsor. So far, you have three projects in your program. Your core team uses earned value at the program package level. Your cost performance index (CPI) is at 0.67, although the schedule performance index (SPI) is at 0.88. Your team recognizes the cost overrun and the fact that you are only 15 percent into the program. The team revises the Estimate at Completion, and you present the revision to your Governance Board. The Estimate at Completion is_____

    A. A forecast                  B. A trend

    C. Atypical                    D. An inappropriate technique at this time

119. 负责德国 Guenther 的水资源缓解项目集，你有很多的挑战。幸运的是，你已经组建了你的核心团队并且也有一个 PMO。你也已经单独会见了你的关键相关方。你经常与你的项目集发起人沟通。到目前为止，在你的项目集中有 3 个项目。你的核心团队在项目集工作包级别使用挣值。虽然进度绩效指数（SPI）是 0.88，但你的成本绩效指数（CPI）只有 0.67。你的团队认识到成本超支，并且事实上你只有 15% 的工作进入了项目集。团队修改了完工估算（EAC），同时你向治理委员会提交了该修订方案。该完工估算（EAC）是_____

    A. 预测                    B. 趋势

    C. 非典型性的              D. 在这个时候是一种不适当的技术

120. You have been managing Guenther, Germany's water alleviation program for three years. Fortunately, you have had an outstanding core team and have a PMO. Your project managers have diligently completed their projects, and their deliverables have been accepted by the City. Now, the program is officially complete, as all deliverables have been accepted by the City. Your next step is to_____

    A. Prepare your closure report

    B. Archive your program records

    C. Meet with the sponsor for a closure review

    D. Obtain a signed final acceptance from the customer

120. 你一直管理德国 Guenther 的水资源缓解项目集有 3 年的时间了。幸运的是，你有一个优秀的核心团队并有一个项目集管理办公室（PMO）。你的项目经理们已经在努力完成他们的项目，他们的可交付成果已经被该城市所接受了。现在，因为所有的可交付成

果已被该城市所接受，该项目集已正式完成。你的下一步是_____

 A.　准备收尾报告

 B.　归档项目集记录

 C.　与发起人会面进行一次收尾评审

 D.　从客户处获得最终的签字验收

121. You are the director of your telecommunications company's enterprise project management office (PMO). Your company has more than 200 projects under way, and you are considering managing some of them as a program. It took about six months to even determine how many projects were in process as many people felt if they described every project they worked on, their "pet" project that they felt would really benefit the company might be canceled. Obtaining the trust of the project professionals was a major challenge, but you believe you have an inventory now of all the project work. As you move into program management, which of the following is best suited to manage as a program?_____

 A. Conducting a training class in program management

 B. Providing product support to a recently introduced cellular phone

 C. Developing the next-generation cellular phone and related products

 D. Preparing a marketing campaign to introduce the next phone when it is developed

121. 你是一家通信公司企业项目管理办公室的负责人。你的公司有 200 多个项目将要实施，你现在正在考量将其中一些项目作为项目集来管理。由于许多人觉得如果对他们所工作的每个项目加以描述，他们感觉对公司真正有收益的所最"宠爱"的项目就有可能被取消，因此花费了近 6 个月的时间才确定所开展的项目的数量。获得项目专业人员的信任将是一项重大的挑战，但是你相信你已经具备了目前所有项目工作的清单。当你准备要进行下一步的项目集管理时，以下哪一项最适合作为项目集来加以管理_____

 A.　在项目集管理中举办培训课程

 B.　为最新引入的手机提供产品支持

 C.　开发下一代蜂窝手机和相关产品

 D.　当手机开发完成后，为其准备相应的营销活动

122. Leading organizations in diverse fields have noted the importance of governance for effective programs and to ensure programs are completed successfully as defined by their business case. To begin to establish governance processes, the first step is to_____

 A. Prepare a governance plan

 B. Follow processes established by the Enterprise PMO

 C. Define governance goals for each program

 D. Have a sponsor organization

122. 各个领域的领导组织结构已经声明了治理对于有效项目集的重要性，以及能够

保证项目集能够像他们在商业论证中所定义的一样成功完成。要开始建立一个治理过程，第一步是_____

A. 准备一个治理计划
B. 遵循企业 PMO 所建立的流程
C. 为每一个项目集定义治理目标
D. 有一个发起人组织

123. You are managing a program to develop a new source of energy to use in the tropics when solar power is not available. Working with your core program team and your Governance Board, you identify a number of component projects. However, several other key projects are under way in your company, and resources will be difficult to acquire for a new program. In determining whether you will use internal or external resources, you should consider_____

A. When the resources will be needed

B. Your ability to negotiate with functional managers for the needed staff

C. Previous work by the staff as a successful team

D. The need to advertise for the open positions

123. 你正在管理一个项目集，此项目集致力于在热带地区当太阳能不可用的时候，开发使用新的能源。与核心项目集团队和治理委员会一起工作的时候，你识别出若干组件项目。然而，公司中几个其他关键项目正在进行，并且相关资源很难调用到新的项目集。在决定是否要使用内部或者外部的资源时，你应该考虑_____

A. 何时需要这些资源

B. 对于必不可少的职员，你同职能经理协调的能力

C. 成功团队的成员的前期工作

D. 需要为开放职位进行宣传

124. You are managing a program to develop a new source of energy to use in the tropics when solar power is not available. Working with your core program team and your Governance Board, you identify a number of component projects. You also have identified some non-project activities. Analysis of program costs must be performed, although some overlook the need to consider the non-program/non-project cost activities. You are, however, analyzing them on your program as you believe doing so is a best practice for program and project managers. Accordingly, they_____

A. Should be tracked outside the program's budget

B. Ensure costs are within expected parameters

C. Are part of earned value

D. Are an expense to be consumed by the program

124. 你正在管理一个项目集，此项目集致力于在热带地区当太阳能不可用的时候，开发使用新的能源。与核心项目集团队和治理委员会一起工作的时候，你识别出若干组件项目。你还识别到一些非项目的活动。必须完成对项目集成本的分析，虽然可以忽略对一

些非项目集/非项目的成本活动的考虑，然而，你在项目集中还是对它们加以分析，这是由于你认为这样做对项目集经理和项目经理是一个最佳实践。因此，它们_____

A. 应该在项目集预算之外加以跟踪　　B. 确保成本在期望值内

C. 是挣值的一部分　　　　　　　　D. 是用于项目集开支的一项费用

125. Assume you have sponsored a program to develop a new stent for coronary patients that is based on new laser technology and that will only take 30 minutes from the time the patient actually enters the hospital. Then, the patient will be able to be discharged and resume normal activities as if nothing happened. The patient will not experience any side effects from this new approach. You have obtained approval from your Executive Committee to develop this program in more detail so you are now in the initiating process. Once the charter is approved_____

A. The program's financial framework is prepared

B. A draft communications management plan is prepared

C. The program is linked to the ongoing work and strategic priorities

D. A high-level plan for components is prepared

125. 假设你已经发起了一个基于新的激光技术给冠心病病人开发新支架的项目集，此项目集实际上只需要 30 分钟就可以使病人入院。然后，病人就能出院并且恢复正常活动，就好像什么都没发生。在这种新的方式下将不会对病人产生任何副作用。你已获得执行委员会的批准，以制定该项目集的细节，因此你现在正在启动过程。一旦项目集章程被批准，那么_____

A. 项目集的财务框架是准备好的

B. 沟通管理计划的草稿是准备好的

C. 项目集已关联到正在进行中的工作和战略优先事项

D. 组件的高级别计划是准备好的

126. Assume your company has a new program to develop a new stent for coronary patients that is based on new laser technology and that will only take 30 minutes from the time the patient actually enters the hospital. Then, the patient will be able to be discharged and resume normal activities as if nothing happened. The patient will not experience any side effects from this new approach. As a project manager, when you prepared your schedule, you focused on identifying activities on your critical path and managing them aggressively. Now you are the program manager. Your focus now is on_____

A. Estimating program activity duration

B. Using a critical chain to incorporate buffers and manage drum resources that affect your component projects

C. Identifying interdependences among the constituent projects

D. Performing "what if " analyses to ensure that the key stakeholders' expectations for program deliverables are met

126. 假设你已经发起了一个基于新的激光技术给冠心病病人开发新支架的项目集，此项目集实际上只需要 30 分钟就可以使病人入院。然后，病人就能出院并且恢复正常活动，就好像什么都没发生。在这种新的方式下将不会对病人产生任何副作用。作为一个项目经理，你准备好了你的预定计划，专注于识别在关键路径上的活动，并积极地管理它们。现在，你是一个项目集经理，你现在要专注于_____

    A. 估算项目集活动的持续时间

    B. 使用关键链来合并各缓冲区和管理影响你的组件项目的各种资源

    C. 识别出所组成的各个项目之间的相互依赖关系

    D. 执行"假设"分析来确保满足关键相关方对项目集交付成果的期望

127. Recently, a member of your core team on your program for the next generation air traffic control system in your country obtained his Risk Management Professional credential from the Project Management Institute. While you and your core team spent time early in the program preparing a risk management plan, which was approved by your Governance Board, and you have been maintaining a program risk register, this core team member felt you and the other team members needed to perform another in depth session identifying risks given that the program had slightly changed direction during the past year and had added one more project than planned. Also, the Administrator of your government agency resigned to take a position in industry, and the new Administrator is more risk adverse, especially where new technology is involved. You have a choice of different technologies to employ. As you considered each one in terms of possible risks, you and your team used which of the following techniques to best make a recommendation to the Administrator and the core team in terms of overall program benefits_____

    A. Sensitivity analysis

    B. Modeling through Monte Carlo simulation

    C. Decision-tree analysis

    D. Risk urgency analysis

127. 最近在你们国家下一代空中交通管制系统的项目集核心团队中的某一个成员从项目管理协会获得了他的风险管理专业证书。在项目集早些时候，你和你的核心团队准备了一个风险管理计划，且已经获得治理委员会的批准，并且你已经在维护一个项目集风险登记册，该名核心团队成员认为在过去的几年中，项目集已经稍微地偏离了方向，并且比预期计划多加入了不止一个项目，你和其他团队成员需要更深入地探讨并重新识别风险。同时，政府机构的管理人员已经辞职并到企业任职，新的政府管理人员是一项更不利的风险，尤其是涉及新技术。你可以选择不同的技术来加以使用。当你考虑到每一个可能的风险时，在整体项目集收益方面，最好将以下哪一项技术推荐给政府管理人员和项目集核心

团队_____

  A. 敏感分析

  B. 蒙特卡洛仿真建模

  C. 决策树分析

  D. 风险紧迫性分析

128.　In developing your benefit realization plan for this air traffic control upgrade system, you and your core team set it up in order that you would have specific metrics in place to help monitor the actual realization of the benefits throughout the program. The plan includes both tangible and intangible benefits of this major program. While the tangible benefits are easy to monitor, you now are finding the intangible benefits to be a challenge. One approach that has been useful to you so far is to use_____

  A. Business value measurement

  B. Total cost of ownership

  C. Cost of quality

  D. Trend analysis

128.　你正在为空中交通管制升级系统制订收益实现计划，你和你的核心团队设立此计划是为了在项目集中你可以有具体的指标来帮助监控贯穿整个项目集的收益的实际实现。该计划同时包括这个重大项目集的有形和无形的收益。监控有形的收益较为容易，你现在发现监控无形的收益将成为一个挑战。到目前为止，对你有用的一个方法是_____

  A. 商业价值度量

  B. 所有权总成本

  C. 质量成本

  D. 趋势分析

129.　In your role as program manager for your country's food safety department to ensure the safety of imported food in your country, you are facing a number of challenges. It seems as if more imported food is arriving rather than producing the food domestically. Many of the food products are totally new to your country. You lack the needed number of inspectors who have expertise in some of the exotic food that now is being imported, and you are implementing a Hazard Analysis Critical Control Program approach as part of this important program. You realized you needed a Governance Board to assist in ensuring your program continued to meet the Department's strategic objectives. Your sponsor agreed and assisted you in preparing a governance plan and also obtained commitments from senior level executives in the Department to be Board members. As you worked on your plan, you realized a key activity that occurs within governance is_____

  A. Resource prioritization

  B. Issue management

  C. Risk response planning

  D. Transition planning

129.　你是一个国家食品安全部门的项目集经理，要保证国家进口食品的安全，你面对着很多挑战。这个项目集似乎更多是在进口食品而不是在国内自主生产食品。很多食品对于你的国家来说非常的新颖。在当前进口的一些国外的食品中，你缺乏一定数量的具有专业知识的检测员，同时你实施了一个危害分析关键控制程序方法作为这个重要项目集的一部分。你意识到你需要一个治理委员会来协助保证你的项目集能够持续满足国家主管部门的战略目标。你的发起人同意并协助你准备一个治理计划，同时也获得国家主管部门的高管的承诺，他们将成为治理委员会的成员。当你按照你的计划工作时，你意识到在治理中有一个关键的活动是_____

A. 资源优先级　　　　　　　　B. 问题管理
C. 风险响应计划　　　　　　　D. 移交计划

130. You are a member of your company's Program Selection Committee, which is deciding which program to pursue in consideration of the company's limited resources. Your company prides itself on time to market as an attribute that distinguishes it from its competitors in the automobile parts field. Each program has prepared a business case addressing its strategy, organization, process, metrics and tools, and culture. Proposed Program A will eliminate features if necessary in a trade-off situation; Proposed Program B will delay its schedule if necessary; Proposed Program C has a flexible structure to ensure innovative features at a minimum cost; and Proposed Program D will focus on technical, cost, and schedule in its metrics. Which program should be selected?_____

A. Program A　　　　　　　　B. Program B
C. Program C　　　　　　　　D. Program D

130. 你是公司的项目集选择委员会的成员，项目集选择委员会基于对公司有限的资源的考虑来决定执行哪个项目集。公司引以为傲的是其快速的上市时间，使其可以在汽车零部件领域中的众多竞争者中脱颖而出。每一个项目集都准备了一份商业论证，包括项目集的战略、组织、过程、度量、工具及文化。所建议的项目集 A，在权衡大局的情况下必要时将去掉一些功能；所建议的项目集 B，必要时会延迟进度；所建议的项目集 C，具有一个灵活的架构可以在成本最小的情况下确保创新功能；对于所建议的项目集 D，专注于项目集在技术、成本、进度方面的指标。应该选择哪一个项目集_____

A. 项目集 A　　　　　　　　B. 项目集 B
C. 项目集 C　　　　　　　　D. 项目集 D

131. No one likes to prepare cost estimates since almost every estimate turns out not to be accurate even if you have outstanding historical information to help you in this process and organizational templates. However you have prepared your estimate and financial management plan. Your next step is to_____

A. Publish this cost estimate

B. Prepare the budget baseline

C. Determine program financial metrics

D. Have component managers prepare component cost estimates

131. 没人会喜欢成本估算，因为几乎每个估算都不精确，即使在这个过程中你有非常棒的历史信息和结构性的模板。但是，你不得不准备你的估算和财务管理计划，下一步

你应该_____

   A. 公开成本估算

   B. 准备预算基准

   C. 确定项目集财务度量标准

   D. 让各组件级的经理准备组件级的成本估算

132. You realize since your company recently merged with a competitor, and there is a revised strategic plan that for your program to continue to be in alignment, you need to add a new project. To do so, you require approval from your Governance Board, and the Board's approval generally requires_____

   A. Highlighting any possible risks

   B. Ensuring compliance with existing program processes and procedures

   C. Ensuring communication of critical component-related information to stakeholders

   D. Confirming the business case for the new project

132. 你发现因为公司最近和一个竞争对手进行合并，并且发现你的项目集需要有一份修订的战略计划，从而持续保持一致性，你需要增加一个新的项目。为此，你要求得到治理委员会的批准，治理委员会的批准通常要求_____

   A. 强调任何可能的风险

   B. 确保当前项目集的过程和程序的合规性

   C. 确保同相关方进行与关键的组件相关的信息的沟通

   D. 确认对新项目的商业论证

133. You are managing a program to build your country's new embassy, consulate, residences, and other facilities in the Republic of Sarsmania. It will be the largest construction project on the Isthmus of Rak, requiring more than 50 subcontractors working on 20 projects. To have ownership of subcontractor selection, the selection process criteria must be defined_____

   A. At the program level

   B. At the project level

   C. By professionals in the construction business working with the program manager

   D. By local Sarsmanian officials working with the program team

133. 你正在管理你所在的国家在萨尔斯曼尼亚共和国的新的大使馆、领事馆、住宅和其他设施一个项目集，这将是在 Rak 海峡区域最大的基建项目，要求多于 50 多个子承包商并工作在 20 个项目上。为了获得对子承包商选择的所有权，对于选择过程标准的定义一定要_____

   A. 基于项目集级别

   B. 基于项目级别

   C. 在基建业务方面的专业人士同项目集经理一起工作

D. 萨尔斯曼尼亚本地政府官员同项目集经理一起工作

134. Managing a program to improve the services of your city government to elderly people, you have six projects in progress. Your program is to be completed in two years. Project Manager B met with you today and requested a change to the scope of her project. She noted that this scope change also affected Projects A and E, which is why she is escalating it to you. The next step should be to_____

A. Convene a meeting of all six project managers to discuss the ramifications of this change

B. Analyze the change request

C. Ask a member of your core team to analyze the change request and determine its impact in terms of overall program benefits

D. Meet with your Governance Board to inform them of this change and receive their authorization to implement it

134. 你正在管理一个提高市政府对老年人的服务质量的项目集，你有 6 个项目在进展中。你的项目集将在两年内完成。项目经理 B 今天与你会面并且提出一个她的项目范围的变更请求。她提到这个项目范围同样影响到了项目 A 和项目 E，这也是为什么他要把这个问题升级提交给你。下一步应该_____

A. 召集 6 个项目经理一起讨论这个变更的影响

B. 分析该变更请求

C. 要求一名核心团队的成员分析该变更请求，并且确定此变更给整个项目集收益所带来的影响

D. 同治理委员会会面，通知他们此次变更，获取他们的授权来实施变更

135. Rarely have hurricanes reached northern states in the United States until the past two years. You are a contractor to the government to manage a program to help people prepare should a hurricane occur. As you are the program manager, you want to keep all of your stakeholders apprised of your process on this program and want to obtain information from them to better understand their concerns relative to your program so you used_____

A. Interviews　　　　　　　　　B. Focus groups

C. Questionnaires　　　　　　　D. Organizational analysis

135. 在过去两年很少有飓风会到达美国北部各州。你是一个政府承包商，管理着一个帮助人们准备应对飓风的项目集。作为项目集经理，你想要保持所有相关方知晓你的项目集的各个过程，并且想要从他们获得信息以便于更好地了解他们在你的项目集中的关注点，因此你使用_____

A. 访谈　　　　　　　　　　　B. 焦点小组

C. 调查问卷　　　　　　　　　D. 组织分析

136. On your program you and your team prepared a detailed stakeholder register. You also used a variety of methods to better understand stakeholder concerns about your program. However as the program manager, a best practice to follow is to_____

A. Establish a balance between people who have negative views about the program and those who are advocates

B. Work diligently with stakeholders that have been identified as program resistors to better understand there issues

C. Prepare a stakeholder inventory to help classify stakeholder groups who are affected positively and negatively

D. Prepare a stakeholder management strategy

136. 在你的项目集中，你和你的团队准备了一个详细的相关方登记册。你同时也使用了一系列方法来更好地了解相关方关于你的项目集的关注点，但是作为项目集经理，接下来的最佳实践是_____

A. 在对于项目集持有消极观点和积极观点的人之间建立一个平衡

B. 尽力地同已识别出的被视为项目集抵抗者的相关方进行接触，从而更好地了解他们的问题

C. 准备一份相关方清单，将相关方划分为有积极影响和消极影响的不同分组

D. 准备相关方管理策略

137. You are a member of your insurance company's Program Selection Committee, which is considering a number of possible programs to pursue. Each one has identified benefits that will support your company's overall strategic plan. Program A is estimated to cost $100,000 to implement and will have annual net cash inflows of $25,000; Program B is estimated to cost $250,000 to implement, with annual net cash inflows of $75,000; Program C is estimated to cost $300,000 to implement, with annual net cash inflows of $80,000; and Program D is estimated to cost $500,000 to implement, with annual net cash inflows of $225,000. You should recommend that your company select_____

A. Program A　　　　　　　　B. Program B
C. Program C　　　　　　　　D. Program D

137. 你是保险公司的项目集选择委员会的一名成员，项目集选择委员会正在考量一系列可能要开展的项目集。每一个已经完成收益识别的项目集都能支持公司整体的战略计划。项目集 A 实施的估算成本为 100 000 美元，年净现金流为 25 000 美元；项目集 B 实施估算成本为 250 000 美元，年净现金流为 75 000 美元；项目集 C 实施估算成本为 300 000 美元，年净现金流为 80 000 美元；项目集 D 实施估算成本为 500 000 美元，年净现金流为 225 000 美元；你应该推荐公司选择_____

A. 项目集 A　　　　　　　　B. 项目集 B

C. 项目集 C          D. 项目集 D

138. You are managing a program, BBB, for your manufacturing firm. You have five projects in your program (three were under way before the program officially began). While some contracts will be ones at the program level, some have been awarded already at the project level on the existing projects. The best approach to follow for these existing contracts is to_____

　A. Conduct regular supplier performance reviews

　B. Have one provider that supports several projects

　C. Have service level agreements

　D. Have the project managers report procurement results to the program manager

138. 你正在为你的制造企业管理一个项目集 BBB。在你的项目集中有 5 个项目（在项目集正式开始之前有 3 个已经在进行）。有些合同将成为在项目集级别的合同，而当前已有的项目在项目级别就已经签订合同。接下来对当前已有的合同最好的处理方法是_____

　A. 执行定期的供应商绩效审查　　　B. 让一个供应商支持多个项目

　C. 有一个服务水平协议　　　　　　D. 让项目经理汇报采购结果给项目集经理

139. You have just received approval from your Executive Team to begin to develop the next generation of stealth shield aircraft. You prepared a business case, which the Executive Team accepted, and it showed you could achieve a payback on your investment in this new program within three years. You received approval to begin to initiate this program. Now, you are preparing estimates of cost and_____

　A. Schedule          B. Scope

　C. Risk          D. Benefits

139. 你已经获得领导团队的批准来开展下一代隐形盾飞行机项目集。你准备好了领导团队接受的商业论证，商业论证显示在你的调研中，这个新的项目集可以在 3 年内获得投资回报。你获得批准，可以启动此项目集。现在，你准备进行成本和以下哪项的估算_____

　A. 进度          B. 范围

　C. 风险          D. 收益

140. You have been the program manager for an aerospace company on its stealth shield aircraft program now for five years and officially closed the program. However, your product support team monitors the product from a reliability and availability-for-use perspective and compares it with the expected performance, which was predicted when the product was developed. The team cites a need to improve reliability and uncovers various anomalies in the software system. Your best approach in this situation is to_____

　A. Use project management to perform the upgrade

　B. Contact the client and all stakeholders immediately

C. Support this new problem independently of the program through an operations function in the company

D. Relinquish the product support function to the client

140. 你已经是一家航空公司的项目集经理，在其隐形盾飞行机项目集中工作 5 年之久并已经正式关闭此项目集。但是，当产品开发完成后，你的产品支持团队按照预期基于可靠性和实用前景监控产品，并且同预期的性能做比较。支持团队在软件系统中引用一个需求，用来改善可靠性和未覆盖到的各种异常情况。这种情况下最好的办法是_____

A. 使用项目管理来执行升级

B. 马上联系客户和所有相关方

C. 在公司中通过运营职能来支持将此问题独立于项目集

D. 此产品支持功能不开放给客户

141. You are the manager for a wind-energy program that will last for eight years. You identify a number of component projects and expect to add others as the program proceeds, especially since this program will last such a long time. Although you have fully staffed your program team, you realize that some of your core team members and project managers will leave the organization or your program for other opportunities. You have decided to facilitate the development of your team members and in doing so perhaps turnover will be minimal. A best practice to follow is_____

A. Set up a succession program for career advancement

B. Support coaching

C. Support mentoring

D. Set up a 360 degree performance evaluation system

141. 你是一个将要持续 8 年之久的风能项目集的经理。你识别出很多组件项目，并预料随着项目集进行而要添加其他组件，尤其是因为该项目集将要持续这么长时间。虽然你的项目集团队人员配备齐全，但是你意识到一些核心团队的成员和项目经理会离开组织或者你的项目集去寻求其他机会。你已经决定推动团队成员的发展，这样做也许可以将人员流失率保持在较低水平。以下要遵守的最佳实践是_____

A. 建立一系列的职业发展计划　　B. 支持教练

C. 支持指导　　D. 建立一个 360°绩效评价系统

142. On your program you have a large number of stakeholders, many of whom are not supporters. To listen to their concerns as you work with these stakeholders over this large and complex program, you should_____

A. Follow your stakeholder engagement strategy

B. Update your stakeholder register

C. Use an issue log

D. Update your communications plan

142. 在你的项目集中，你有大量的相关方，其中很多人不是支持者，在这个庞大而复杂的项目集中，倾听这些相关方的关注点成为你和他们合作的一部分。你应该_____

A. 遵循相关方争取策略　　　　B. 更新相关方登记册

C. 使用问题日志　　　　　　　D. 更新沟通计划

143. You are a member of your energy services company's Program Selection Committee, which is considering a number of possible programs to pursue. Each one has identified benefits that will support your company's overall strategic plan. You have the following data on four possible programs. You may select only one because of resource limitations.

| Program A NPV at | Program B NPV at | Program C NPV at | Program D NPV at |
|---|---|---|---|
| 5% = 3,524 | 5% = 2,201 | 5% = 6,400 | 5% = 3,055 |
| 10% = 2,901 | 10% = 2,254 | 10% = 3,275 | 10% = 2,857 |
| 15% = 1,563 | 15% = 1,632 | 15% = 1,679 | 15% = 1,125 |

Note: NPV = net present value.

You should recommend that your company select_____

A. Program A　　　　　　　　B. Program B

C. Program C　　　　　　　　D. Program D

143. 你是一个能源服务公司项目集选择委员会的成员，正在考量一系列可能要开展的项目集。每一个项目集都识别出支持公司整体战略计划的收益，如下为 4 组可能的项目集的数据，由于资源限制你可能只能选择一个，你将会推荐公司选择_____

| 项目集 A 净现值（NPV） | 项目集 B 净现值（NPV） | 项目集 C 净现值（NPV） | 项目集 D 净现值（NPV） |
|---|---|---|---|
| 5% = 3 524 | 5% = 2 201 | 5% = 6 400 | 5% = 3 055 |
| 10% = 2 901 | 10% = 2 254 | 10% = 3 275 | 10% = 2 857 |
| 15% = 1 563 | 15% = 1 632 | 15% = 1 679 | 15% = 1 125 |

注：NPV=净现值。

A. 项目集 A　　　　　　　　B. 项目集 B

C. 项目集 C　　　　　　　　D. 项目集 D

144. Assume you are the program manager to implement enterprise resource planning software in all the agencies in your province. This program would be difficult if it were limited to only one agency, but it is especially hard because you have 17 agencies in the province, and each one has its own legacy system that it uses. You will have to have a separate project for each agency as well as projects for training, implementation, and maintenance. This program

thus will span several years and budget cycles. Before the budget is baselined, you must_____

    A. Add program overhead costs

    B. List income and payment schedules

    C. Determine component payment schedules

    D. Update the program management plan

144. 假设你是项目集经理，将要对你所在省份的所有经销商实施企业资源计划软件。如果仅限于 1 个经销商，这个项目集将会很难实施，但是在该省你有 17 个经销商，每个经销商都在使用其自己的遗留系统，这就会更加困难。你不得不为每个经销商开展各自分开的项目，并进行培训、实施和维护。这个项目集因此将跨越数年和数个预算周期。在制定预算基准之前，你必须_____

    A. 添加项目集的管理费用

    B. 列出收入和支出进度

    C. 决定组件支出进度

    D. 更新项目集管理计划

145. Quality is essential in IT projects especially in complex ones such as enterprise resource planning software development and implementation. A quality management plan contains_____

    A. Standard templates

    B. A schedule for planned quality assurance audits

    C. Checklists

    D. A method to handle change requests from quality assurance and control results

145. 在 IT 项目中质量至关重要，尤其在复杂项目中，例如企业资源计划软件开发和实施。一个质量管理计划包含_____

    A. 标准模板

    B. 质量保证审计计划的进度表

    C. 检查清单

    D. 从质量保证和控制的结果中处理变更请求的方法

146. Assume you are the program manager to implement enterprise resource planning software in all the agencies in your province. This program would be difficult if it were limited to only one agency, but it is especially hard because you have 17 agencies in the province, and each one has its own legacy system that it uses. The executive director of your program Governance Board suggests that you explore local consulting firms for additional resource support. The best document to use to identify potential sellers is the_____

    A. Request for information　　　　B. Invitation to bid

    C. Contract terms and conditions　　D. Contract statement of work

146. 假设你是项目集经理，将要对你所在省份的所有经销商实施企业资源计划软件。如果仅限于 1 个经销商，这个项目集将会很难实施，但是在该省你有 17 个经销商，每个经销商都在使用其自己的遗留系统，这就会更加困难。你的项目集治理委员会的执行主任建议你利用本地咨询公司以寻求额外的资源支持。用来识别潜在卖家的最好的文档是_____

A. 信息请求　　　　　　　　　B. 投标邀请书

C. 合同条款与条件　　　　　　D. 工作的合同声明

147. Introducing program management to your electric company has been a challenge but is finally being embraced as executives to team members now are seeing that using programs can produce more benefits to the company and its customers than if projects were managed in a standalone way. One approach that has been useful to you in your role of leading this culture change in the electric company has been to prepare a benefits realization plan and to get it signed off by your sponsor, members of the Governance Board, and other key stakeholders. Your company also uses the balanced scorecard approach, and your benefits realization plan considered it when you developed it so the benefits are aligned to the scorecard.  One benefit that is often overlooked is_____

A. Cost of quality　　　　　　B. New income

C. Competitive advantage　　　D. Risk avoidance

147. 将项目集管理方法引入你所在的电力公司是一项挑战，但高层管理人员看到使用项目集比独立管理项目可以给公司和客户带来更多收益，最终接受了此方式。一种在电力公司中有效地倡导文化变革的方法是准备好收益实现计划，并且获得发起人、治理委员会成员和其他关键相关方的签字批准。你公司也使用了平衡计分卡的方法，当你制订收益实现计划时也考虑了此方法，因此这些收益同平衡计分卡是一致的。一种通常容易被忽视的收益是_____

A. 质量成本　　　　　　　　　B. 新收入

C. 竞争优势　　　　　　　　　D. 风险规避

148. One of the first programs you managed at your electric company, DDD, was for a city in Draeger, New York. The purpose was to reduce the numerous power outages so that if a power outage occurred, residents in Draeger would only lose power momentarily until a backup system could be deployed to provide time for on-site personnel to arrive at the location and diagnose the problem and provide corrective action. When you prepared your benefits realization plan for this program early on, one of the items you included in it was_____

A. Review sessions to be held on a periodic basis by citizens of Draeger

B. Methods to maximize citizen satisfaction in the program delivery

C. Ways to ensure all stages of the program are managed in a way to satisfy the use of the program's outputs

D.　Overall business requirements, including scope and limitations

148. 你在电力公司管理的第一个项目集 DDD,是为纽约德尔格地区的全体居民服务。目的是减少长时间的停电,万一停电了,在德尔格的居民也只是短暂地停电,部署的备份系统可以提供缓冲时间,直到驻场工程师到达事故发生地诊断问题并开展纠正行动。当你早期为这个项目集准备收益实现计划时,其中应该包含_____

A.　面向德尔格居民定期举行评审会议

B.　在交付项目集时使居民满意度最大化方法

C.　确保对项目集所有阶段的管理能满足对项目集的各种输出的整合利用

D.　整体业务需求,包括范围和限制

149.　Researchers have noted the emergence of corporate program management and note that its processes must be structured to coordinate and manage the multiple components that together contribute to business value and organizational structure. It therefore is clear that being a program manager is different from being a project manager as required competencies as a program manager are significantly different. As the business case for a program is being prepared, a performance competency for the program manager is_____

A.　Marketing

B.　Political awareness

C.　Aligning program objectives with strategic goals

D.　Preparing a benefits realization plan

149.　研究人员已经注意到公司项目集管理的出现,并且注意到项目集的过程必须是以结构化的方式来协调和管理多个共同有助于商业价值和组织架构的组件。因此,对一个项目集经理的能力要求明显不同于一个项目经理,当项目集的商业论证准备好后,项目集经理的一个能力表现是_____

A.　市场

B.　政治意识

C.　保持项目集目标和战略目标的一致性

D.　准备收益实现计划

150.　Your organization receives an award for the construction of a new courthouse complex in the state capital of State A. Your company is located in State B, approximately 1,000 miles away, and has never worked in State A. You plan to use a number of contractors and to hire local people to support the program team. From time to time, you will need cranes. To facilitate acquiring these cranes, you should_____

A.　Purchase the cranes　　　　　　　B.　Develop a qualified seller list

C.　Issue an Invitation for Bid　　　　　D.　Issue a Request for Proposals

150.　你的组织在 A 州的首府获得一个新法院建筑群的基建项目,你的公司在 B 州,离 A 州大概有 1 000 英里远，并且你的组织从来没有在 A 州工作过。你计划使用一些承包商，并雇用本地人来支持这个项目集团队。随着时间的推移，你需要起重机。为推动能获取这些起重机，你应该_____

A. 购买起重机　　　　　　　　B. 开发一个合格卖家清单

C. 发起一个投标邀请　　　　　D. 发起一个报价书请求

151. Your organization receives an award for the construction of a new courthouse complex in the state capital of State A. Your company is located in State B, approximately 1,000 miles away, and has never worked in State A. You plan to use a number of contractors and to hire local people to support the program team. From time to time, you will need cranes. However, you always have some type of risks whenever you use contactors. Therefore, it is important as a best practice to_____

A. Only use contractors on the qualified seller list

B. Perform a site visit to each contractor's headquarters to demonstrate to its leaders the importance of your program

C. Have each contractor prepare a monthly performance report

D. Manage risk in accordance with the risk management plan

151. 你的组织在 A 州的首府获得一个新法院建筑群的基建项目，你的公司在 B 州，离 A 州大概有 1 000 英里远，并且你的组织从来没有在 A 州工作过。你计划使用一些承包商，并雇用本地人来支持这个项目集团队。随着时间的推移，你需要起重机，但是不管你何时使用承包商通常都存在一定的风险，因此，作为最佳实践最重要的是_____

A. 只使用在合格卖家清单中的承包商

B. 到每一个承包商的总部去参观，并给其领导层展示你的项目集的重要性

C. 为每一个承包商准备月度绩效报告

D. 根据风险管理计划来管理风险

152. Assume this is the first time you are managing a program. You have had success in your company in project management, and you are on a career path that now leads to program management. On your program, you want to apply some of the successful best practices you used on your projects, recognizing the differences between programs and projects and their greater complexity. However, since you have been in project management for so long now in this company (17 years), you also know that_____

A. You need to prepare a comprehensive WBS for the program that includes the work of the projects

B. You want to build your program schedule only after all the project schedules are complete

C. You recognize the importance of qualifying and quantifying all possible risks

D.　You realize project stakeholders are also program stakeholders

152.　假设你是第一次管理一个项目集，你在你的公司已经有成功的项目管理经验，你的职业生涯路径现在转向项目集管理，在你的项目集中，你想要应用一些在你之前的项目中已经成功使用的最佳实践，但意识到项目集和项目之间的区别，以及项目集更加复杂。既然你已经在公司中管理项目这么长时间（17 年），你同样知道_____

A.　你需要给项目集准备一个包含各项目工作的综合的工作分解结构

B.　你想要构建的项目集进度表，只能是在完成所有项目进度表之后

C.　你意识到对所有可能风险进行定性和量化的重要性

D.　你意识到项目相关方同样是项目集相关方

153.　You are managing a program that comprises new systems application development and maintenance activities. The program has been under way for three years. One of the projects has completed its deliverables, and its benefits have been realized.  However approval by your Governance Board is required, and their review generally includes_____

A.　Ensuring communications of closure to stakeholders

B.　Reviewing your program issues register

C.　Verifying customer acceptance of deliverables

D.　Reviewing compliance with quality assurance plans

153.　你正在管理一个包含新系统应用开发和维护活动的项目集，此项目集已经进行了 3 年，其中一个项目已经完成了可交付成果，并且实现了收益。然而，还需要取得治理委员会的批准，他们的审查通常包括_____

A.　确保同相关方的紧密沟通　　　　B.　审查项目集的问题登记册

C.　核实可交付成果的客户验收　　　D.　审查质量保证计划的合规性

154.　In your organization, the program Governance Board has assumed organizational responsibilities that its programs are prepared for audits that may be required or desired.  These audits_____

A.　Are part of the quality assurance function

B.　Should be documented in the master schedule

C.　Should be included in the roadmap

D.　Focus on management processes

154.　在你的组织中，项目集治理委员会假设组织负责按照要求或者期望对项目集准备进行审计，这些审计_____

A.　是质量保证功能的一部分　　　　B.　应该记录在主要进度表中

C.　应该包含在路线图中　　　　　　D.　专注于管理过程

155.　In determining whether it is better to use program management or project management, the culture of the organization should be considered.  Your organization is considering implementation of program management, and you are leading a team to recommend this approach to your CEO and other members of the executive team. One of your arguments for the change is that the organization's culture has transitioned so that it is now characterized by_____

A. A specialist level of business expertise

B. A strong connection between execution output and strategic objectives

C. A lower dependency between cross-discipline specialties in the organization

D. Less need for a time-to-money improvement

155. 在决定使用项目集管理或者项目管理哪一项更好时，组织的文化应该被考虑进来。你的组织正在考虑实施项目集管理，你带领你的团队建议公司的 CEO 和其他执行团队的成员使用这个方法。这一管理方式变化的理由之一就是组织文化的转变，因此组织文化现在的特征是_____

A. 具有专业水平的业务专业知识

B. 在执行层面的输出和战略目标之间强大的连接关系

C. 组织中交叉领域专家之间较低的相互依赖关系

D. 不太需要提升效率

156. You are managing a program that comprises new systems application development and maintenance activities. These applications are critical to your company, CDE, as they involve access to proprietary data. The systems must be available to your clients on a 24/7/365 basis. Much of the work on you program will be outsourced as you have an aggressive schedule to meet; fortunately CDE has a qualified vendor list to simplify the acquisition process. This program has high visibility in CDE and is a major change to the organization. Therefore, CDE's CEO decided to serve as the executive director of the program and chairs each meeting of your program's Governance Board. Before Board meetings are held to review program performance, your Board members have asked you to submit_____

A. Benefit realization reports          B. Estimate to complete data

C. To-complete performance index data          D. Financial reports

156. 你正在管理一个包含了新系统应用开发和维护活动的项目集，这些应用对 CDE 公司很关键，因为他们涉及要访问专有数据。对于客户来讲，该系统必须全天候对客户可用。项目集之中的很多工作都要外包，这是因为你要满足紧凑的进度要求。幸运的是，CDE 公司有一个合格的供应商清单可以简化收购的流程。这个项目集对 CDE 公司高度可见，并且对组织来说是一个重大的变更，因此，CDE 公司的 CEO 决定作为项目集的执行主任并出席项目集治理委员会的每次会议。在治理委员会举行会议并对项目绩效进行审查之前，治理委员会成员要求你提交_____

A. 收益实现报告          B. 完工估算数据

C. 将要完成的绩效指标数据          D. 财务报告

157. Now that you have moved into this program management role in your manufacturing company, you realize your work really involves active involvement with stakeholders at a variety of levels. It is also compounded because on your program you have external stakeholders involved and need to spend time communicating with them. It seems as if each time you pass a stage_gate review, the number of stakeholders increase, or people who lacked interest in the program now are interested. Therefore, the primary skill to best engage stakeholders_____

A. Negotiation
B. Conflict management
C. Communications
D. Influencing

157. 你在一家制造公司，现在你要开始进行项目集管理，你意识到工作中实际上需要使得不同级别的相关方积极参与进来。这也很复杂，因为在你的项目集中你涉及外部的相关方，并且需要花费时间同他们进行沟通。看上去好像每通过一次阶段关口评审，相关方的数量都在增长，或者在项目集之中之前没有利益关系的人变成了利益相关方，因此，能最佳地争取相关方的主要技能是_____

A. 谈判
B. 冲突管理
C. 沟通
D. 影响

158. One of the project managers in your program has told you that although he did a thorough job of risk management planning, a new risk has emerged that has major negative ramifications for the project. This risk could also affect another project in the program, as it involves a lack of critical resources. Another project manager tells you that he will need this same resource on his project, although he did not consider it during resource planning. In this situation, you should_____

A. Implement your contingency reserve to hire needed resources to support these projects

B. Propose a solution to these risks escalated by the project managers

C. Ask each project manager to revise the risk register to add these risks and to use a workaround

D. Revise your program work breakdown structure accordingly, because this risk shows that a key planning package is missing

158. 你项目集的其中一个项目经理告诉你虽然他已经做了全面的风险管理计划，但是还是发生了一个新的风险，并且对项目产生了很大的负面影响。因为牵涉缺少关键的资源，这个风险可能影响到该项目集的另一个项目。另一个项目经理告诉你他在项目中需要同样的资源，然而他在资源计划中没有考虑到这一点。在这种情况下，你应该_____

A. 使用应急储备，将需要的资源提供给这些项目
B. 针对项目经理所报告上升的风险提出相应的解决方案
C. 要求每一个项目经理修订风险登记册，在其中增加这个风险并且使用替代方案

D. 修订项目集工作分解结构，因为这个风险显示出一个关键计划包的丢失

159. You are a member of your organization's Program Selection Committee. The company's strategic plan includes five major goals, which are all weighted equally. Goal 1 is to fall within the time-to-market window; Goal 2 is to reduce operational costs; Goal 3 is to differentiate the products from others on the market; Goal 4 is to deliver the highest-quality product; and goal 5 is to promote economic sustainability. At the next committee meeting, you will consider four programs and recommend one. Program A partially supports goal 1, fully supports goals 2–4, and does not support goal 5;Program B fully supports goals 1, 3, 4, and 5, but does not support goal 2;Program C fully supports goals 1 and 2, partially supports goals 3 and 4, but does not support goal 5;Program D partially supports goals 1, 2, and 5, and fully supports goals 3 and 4.  With this information, which program will you recommend?_____

A. Program A                         B. Program B

C. Program C                         D. Program D

159.  你是组织项目集选择委员会的成员。公司的战略计划包括 5 项主要的目标，且权重都一样。目标 1 是要在上市窗口期内完成；目标 2 是减少运营成本；目标 3 是产品要区别于市场上其他产品；目标 4 是交付高质量的产品；目标 5 是促进经济可持续发展。在下一次委员会会议时，你将会考虑 4 个项目集并且推荐其中一个。项目集 A 部分支持目标 1，全力支持目标 2、3、4，但是不支持项目 5；项目集 B 全力支持目标 1、3、4 和 5，但是不支持项目 2；项目集 C 全力支持目标 1 和目标 2，部分支持目标 3 和目标 4，但是不支持目标 5；项目集 D 部分支持目标 1、2 和 5，全力支持目标 3 和目标 4。在如上信息中，你将推荐哪一个项目集_____

A. 项目集 A                           B. 项目集 B

C. 项目集 C                           D. 项目集 D

160. You are managing a complex program to develop the next-generation submarine. It is planned to replace the existing non-nuclear submarines in your country with nuclear weapons. It is estimated to take about nine years to complete as you will be using new technology now not available in your country. The program includes a number of projects, and you plan to use subcontractors extensively. You also plan contracts for services or for insurance to protect the program. For these contracts, you need to_____

A. Use qualified seller lists

B. Document the relevant parties' responsibilities regarding risk

C. Prepare a contract administration plan

D. Prepare component cost estimates

160.  你在管理开发下一代潜艇的复杂项目集，这个项目集计划使用核武器代替国家当前的非核潜艇，这个项目集因为要使用当前在国家中没有的新技术，所以预计要花费 9

年的时间完成。项目集包括很多项目，你计划广泛地使用子承包商的形式，你还在计划一些服务合同或者保护项目集的保险合同。对于这些合同，你需要_____

　　A．使用合格的卖家清单　　　　　　B．书面记录相关方对于风险的责任

　　C．准备一个合同管理计划　　　　　D．准备组件级的成本估算

161.　It is a challenge to effectively exchange information among all program stakeholders. This is one reason why the program manager must have excellent communications skills. Managing information on programs may become a formidable task in itself. To assist in this key area, the Governance Board may_____

　　A．Establish a standard reporting process

　　B．Set up a knowledge management system

　　C．Set up a program management information system

　　D．Protect intellectual property

161.　在所有项目集相关方之中有效地交换信息是一个挑战，这就要求项目集经理要有优秀沟通技能的一个原因。管理项目集的信息也许本身就是一个艰巨的任务。为能够在此关键领域提供帮助，治理委员会可以_____

　　A．建立一个标准的汇报流程　　　　B．设立一个知识管理系统

　　C．设立一个项目集管理信息系统　　D．保护知识产权

162.　Your organization recently conducted an Organizational Project Management Maturity Assessment (OPM3®). The assessment results and the improvement plan showed much work needed to be done in the area of portfolio management. It was especially apparent that many projects, and almost every program, lacked a defined business case that had been prepared by the sponsor and then approved and authorized by leadership. After receiving the reports from the OPM3® assessor, you held a focus group of program sponsors to determine why business cases were not regularly prepared. It turned out many of the people in the focus group lacked an understanding of the benefits of preparing one. You explained that the primary benefit is to_____

　　A．Establish alignment with strategic goals

　　B．Provide a perspective on how best to execute the program

　　C．Determine how the program will help the organization meet its business and strategic goals

　　D．Make the portfolio process more effective

162.　你的组织最近进行了组织项目管理成熟度评估。评估结果和改进计划显示，在投资组合管理领域有很多工作需要做。组织中缺少一份由发起人准备的并后续由领导批准和授权的明确定义的商业论证，这在很多项目和几乎所有的项目集之中显现得尤为突出。在收到 OPM3®评估员的报告后，你举行了一个项目集发起人的焦点小组会议，讨论为什么商业论证没有按时准备好，结果是在焦点小组中很多人对准备商业论证的好处缺乏理

解，你解释主要的好处是_____

    A. 建立同战略目标的一致性

    B. 提供一个如何最佳实行项目集的视角

    C. 决定项目集如何帮助组织满足其商业和战略目标

    D. 使投资组合过程更加有效

163. Your organization announces that funds in all areas will be cut by 10 percent. Even though you are still in the planning stages and your program is a high priority for your company, your program is not exempt from the budget cuts. Management has also mandated certain delivery dates that will be hard to meet with the budget cuts. As you decide which program components should be handled internally and which should be outsourced, you consider the_____

    A. PWBS                     B. Program scope statement

    C. Make-or-buy analysis        D. Qualified seller lists

163. 你的组织声明在所有领域的资金都要砍掉 10%。即便你的项目集仍处在计划阶段，而且你的项目集在公司中有很高的优先级，你的项目集也不能在这次预算削减中幸免。管理部门还在预算缩减的情况下强制了某个交付日期，因此你要决定哪些项目集组件应该内部处理，哪些应该外包，你的考虑是_____

    A. PWBS                     B. 项目集范围说明书

    C. 自制或外购分析           D. 合格的卖家清单

164. Assume that your program for The Bronx, New York is in its final stages. The purpose was to reduce the numerous power outages so that if a power outage occurred, residents in The Bronx would only lose power momentarily until a backup system could be deployed to provide time for on-site personnel to arrive at the location and diagnose the problem and provide corrective action. Recently, there was a power outage in one part of the City. The new power station's backup capability was available in less than two minutes. It is now time to close this program and transition it to ongoing operations. Before doing so, a best practice is to_____

    A. Review the program's scope statement

    B. Conduct a customer satisfaction survey

    C. Review the quality assurance plan

    D. Review the benefits realization plan

164. 假设你在纽约的布朗克斯区的项目集进行到了最后阶段。项目集的目的是减少长时间的停电以便于万一发生停电，在布朗克斯区的居民也只是短暂地停电，部署的备份系统提供缓冲时间，直到驻场工程师到达事故发生地诊断问题并开展纠正行动。最近，在该地区的某地停电了，新电站的备份能力能将停电时间缩短到少于两分钟，现在，项目集可以关闭并移交至日常运营。在这样做之前，一个最佳实践是_____

    A. 评审项目集的范围说明书        B. 实行一个客户满意度调查

C. 评审质量保证计划　　　　　　　D. 评审收益实现计划

165. In determining whether to pursue a program, it is important to assess goals and objectives. In your new product development organization, of the triple constraint, quality and scope are the dominant. This does not imply the schedule and budget are not important, but given that the programs must achieve regulatory approval, quality dominates in the company. Quality goals that are too low may lead to customer and end-user dissatisfaction, whereas goals that are too high may result in a high cost to the business. Therefore, it is important to consider_____

    A. Market needs and expectations　　　B. The value proposition

    C. Cash-flow management　　　　　　D. Risk analysis and assessment

165. 在决定是否开展一个项目集时，最重要的是评估其目的和目标。在你的新产品开发的组织中，三重约束之中的质量和范围占主导地位。但这并不是说进度和预算不重要，而是说项目集一定要获得监管部门的批准，在公司内保证质量优先。质量目标过低会导致客户和最终用户的不满意，但是质量目标过高也可能会导致业务上成本太高。因此，最重要的是考虑_____

    A. 市场需求和期望　　　　　　　　　B. 价值定位

    C. 现金流管理　　　　　　　　　　　D. 风险分析和评估

166. As part of your procurement management plan for this new product development program, you have explicitly stated the actions that you and your program team can take on its own and those that require involvement by or should be deferred to the Procurement or Contracting Department. As you prepare your procurement management plan, the best practice is to optimize procurements to meet program objectives and deliver benefits. To do so you need to_____

    A. Address commonalities and differences across components

    B. Review your resource management plan

    C. Use pre-negotiated contracts and blanket purchase agreements

    D. Direct procurements to be centralized at the program level

166. 作为新产品开发项目集的采购管理计划的一部分，你明确地声明，你和你的项目集团队可以自行采购，并确定要求由采购部门或承包部门参与或延期解决的事项。随着你准备好你的采购管理计划，最佳实践是通过优化采购来满足项目集目标及交付收益。要做到这些，你需要_____

    A. 解决不同组件之间的共性和差异

    B. 评审你的资源管理计划

    C. 使用预先协商合同和一揽子采购协议

    D. 在项目集层面实行集中采购

167. You are Company A's program manager for the development of an online banking system for your community bank. One of its objectives is to make sure all transactions are secure. You have a large team supporting you as program manager, and you have four projects thus far. Two of the project managers are new to your company and lack familiarity with the company's standard program management procedures. Because time and quality are of the essence in this program, you are need to make sure these two project managers understand what must be done to comply with the various procedures. Your best approach to do so is through_____

A. One-on-one meetings each day

B. Developing an on-line training system to show all the various procedures to follow

C. Using mentoring

D. Using skills in creative thinking

167. 你是 A 公司为社区银行开发网络银行系统的项目集经理。其中一个目标是确保所有的交易是安全的。作为项目集经理你有庞大的团队做支撑，迄今为止你已经有 4 个项目。其中两个项目经理是新加入公司的，对公司的标准项目及管理流程不是很熟悉，因为时间和质量是这个项目集的必要属性，你需要确保这两个项目经理能理解在各种程序下必须做些什么。你的最佳方法是通过_____

A. 每天的一对一的会议

B. 开发在线培训系统来展示所有需要遵循的程序

C. 使用指导

D. 使用创造性思维的技能

168. You are Company A's program manager for the development of an online banking system for your community bank. One of its objectives is to make sure all transactions are secure. You have a large team supporting you as program manager, and you have four projects thus far. Two of the project managers are new to your company and lack familiarity with the company's standard program management procedures. You have set up a change management plan as you know programs involve change and with this program and its four projects, changes will occur. You especially want to use it to help control_____

A. Benefits　　　　　　　　　B. Issues

C. Quality　　　　　　　　　D. Human resources

168. 你是 A 公司为社区银行开发网络银行系统的项目集经理。其中一个目标是确保所有的交易是安全的。作为项目集经理你有庞大的团队做支撑，迄今为止你已经有 4 个项目。其中两个项目经理是新加入公司的，对公司的标准项目及管理流程不是很熟悉。你已经建立了一个变更管理计划，因为你知道项目集涉及变更，也知道在该项目集及其 4 个项目中会发生变更。你特别期望使用它来控制_____

A. 收益　　　　　　　　　　B. 问题

C. 质量　　　　　　　　　　　　D. 人力资源

169. Assume you are sponsoring a proposed program. You have identified tangible benefits such as a one year payback period, a high return on investment, and an increase in productivity by 25 percent. Some of the intangible benefits that you have identified include an increase in employee morale with retention of intellectual property. You also believe it will contribute to knowledge sharing. You are getting ready to present your business case to the Portfolio Review Board. Before doing so, you want to make sure it has been completed properly so you first should_____

A. Present a cost/benefit analysis

B. Describe the business opportunity and product, service, or result that you are proposing

C. Identify the Key Performance Indicators

D. Describe the high-level risks if the program is approved

169. 假设你正在发起一个项目集。你已经识别到了有形的收益，例如一年的投资回报期、高投资回报和提高 25%的生产效率。你也已经识别到一些无形的收益，包括知识产权的留存、员工士气的提高。同时，你相信这也会对知识共享有贡献，你正准备把你的商业论证展现给投资组合评审委员会。在这样做之前，你想要确保你的商业论证已经正确完成，因此你首先需要_____

A. 展示成本/效益分析

B. 描述你所建议的商业机会和产品，服务或者结果

C. 识别关键绩效指标

D. 描述出如果项目集批准之后的高级别风险

170. The organization is new to program management but has been a leader in program management. A new CEO was appointed, who used program management extensively in his previous organization. He has set up programs and Governance Boards. The Governance Board is a first step and it should_____

A. Establish policies and procedures

B. Provide training in program management

C. Determine the knowledge, skills, and competencies of existing project managers to manage programs

D. Provide the link to portfolio management

170. 组织刚开始使用项目集管理，但是一直倡导项目集管理。现在任命了一个新的 CEO，其在之前的组织中习惯于广泛地使用项目集管理。他已经建立了项目集和治理委员会。治理委员会是第一步，它应该_____

A. 建立政策和流程

B. 在项目集管理中提供培训

C. 决定当前项目经理管理项目集的知识、技术和能力

D. 提供与投资组合管理的联系

# PgMP®模拟试题二参考答案

1. A 收益登记册是由收益的识别建立起来，同时收益登记册的维护贯穿整个项目集过程。它被用来量化和沟通收益交付，在其他方面，它也包含目标日期和收益成就的里程碑。

2. D 项目集经理需要一个知识、技能和胜任力的组合能力。战略愿景和计划是两个关键技能，它需要调整项目集目标与组织的长期目标和收益。项目集经理也必须要安排不同子项目的项目计划使之与项目集目标和收益相协调。

3. B 当项目集管理计划被批准后，项目集收益交付阶段开始。在此阶段，目标是去计划，管理和整合各个组件来促进交付预期收益。

4. B 非常推荐适当采用开展市场调查研究的方法去识别潜在的相关方，他们可能对项目集感兴趣或者影响你的整个项目集及各个子项目。项目集章程应该描述相关方的考量点，包含一个最初有效的策略让他们积极参与进来。

5. B 在《项目管理协会（PMI）道德和专业行为规范》中，公平是一项必须遵守的准则。在第 4.3.3 条中，这种情形很容易被认为会产生利益冲突，供应商并没有意识到基于个人考虑，其中一个是裙带关系。

6. A 在项目集范围管理中，项目集经理必须要确定哪些组件将由于请求范围的变更而受到影响，并需要相应地更新项目集分解结构（PWBS）。

7. B 当组织管理其项目组合时，项目集将受到许多组合需要的影响，需要细化为需求，然后再转化为项目集的范围、可交付成果、预算和进度。

8. C 在项目集准备阶段，当项目集管理计划通过审核和批准，项目集组织已经部署，一个最初的计划小组建立用来开展项目集管理计划，这意味着该阶段的结束。

9. B 商业论证和当前的组织目标被用于判断项目集完成的成功标准。

10. D 实质性的领导力对于管理多个项目集生命周期内的多个子项目是必需的。项目集领导力需要建立项目集方向，识别内部互相依赖性、沟通需求、跟踪进展、制定决策，以及处理冲突事件的同时包含其他重要任务。

11. A 当相关方参与计划文档阐明相关方将如何参与整个项目集时，项目集经理也需要给各个单项目组件的相关方和项目集中的部分非项目工作参与提供指导大纲方针。

12. C 在项目集收尾阶段，所有的项目集工作已经全部完成，同时项目集收益正在累积。在该阶段，项目集经理的关键活动就是当项目集移交的时候，与治理委员会一起审查项目集的收益状态。

13. A 质量控制贯穿整个项目集。确保项目组件和项目集实现质量需求从而实现充

足的收益 是非常重要的。终端客户满意度被认为是衡量项目集的一个关键标准。

14．D 除了关口审查之外，项目治理委员会更趋向于一些非正式的"周期性健康检查"过程去评估正在进行的项目集绩效和进度，尤其是项目集收益的实现和维护。

15．D 当所有的答案都与启动阶段活动相关联时，标准的检查对成功监控项目集状态是非常必要的，这将会给予与项目集相关的高等级风险和一些重点相关方更多关注。

16．B 降低风险是商业论证的驱动要素之一，其目的是财务控制，以及与外部需求（如企业报告和强制性审计）相一致。

17．A 项目管理办公室在项目集支持方面具有重要职能，尤其是对一些大型、复杂的项目集来说，提供合同和采购方面的支持是很正常的。

18．D 项目集组件启动标准是项目集治理计划的一部分，而且组件初始的关口审查是在其启动阶段进行的。治理委员会通常基于其商业计划，来批准组件的启动。

19．A 在准备项目集风险管理计划时，定义项目集所涉及的组织风险概况是必要的，目的是构建管理项目集风险的最合适方法、调整风险敏感度，以及监督风险临界点。

20．C 在项目集质量控制阶段，确定项目级所交付的收益、产品或服务对终端用户的适用性是非常必要的。因此，项目集经常使用客户满意度调查作为质量控制度量的标准。

21．C 项目集治理活动贯穿于整个项目集生命周期。其中一个目的就是建立并监督实施管理项目集变更的政策。对于重大变更，应咨询治理委员会如何处理这些变更。

22．A 项目集的成功是由实现项目集的需求和收益的程度来衡量的。

23．C 路线图服务于项目集管理中大量的功能。另外，它提供了一个高层级的关于支持基础设施和组件的计划。

24．C 遇到冲突的原因是项目集具有竞争性。你应该毫不犹豫地与你所在组织的领导沟通。因为客户的请求受限于其经验资历，与组织背景不一致。

25．A 虽然在资源规划过程中准备项目集资源计划时，但它是整个项目集应对资源需求的计划。根据题意，现在项目集管理计划已被批准，你正在排列资源使用的优先级。项目集资源计划通常描述了稀缺资源的使用情况，以及哪个组件使用该资源的优先级。

26．B 项目集治理架构能够确保项目集目标和目的与项目集战略的目标保持一致。项目集的原始治理架构可能不再适应急剧性的变化。不同的相关方现在可能需要被邀请加入作为项目集管理委员会的一员，也包括项目集发起人。

27．A 制约限制了项目集管理团队的选择。一旦确定了高层级的项目集主进度，那么每个组件的日期也被确定下来。这些日期将用于开发各个组件的进度计划，而且是每个组件团队的制约。

28．C 在项目集进度控制方面，延误和机会都应该识别并用于风险管理。这意味着项目集进度风险应该作为风险管理活动的一部分来跟踪。

29．C 在项目集采购收尾阶段，关闭所有的合同是必须的。这项目工作将在确认所有可交付成果全部圆满完成，所有的付款工作已经被完成，而且没有任何突出的合同问题之后执行。

30．B 项目集章程的批准至关重要，因为它正式授权项目集的开始。

31．A 项目集经理们需要大量的人际关系技能。为了推动项目集进展，一个重要的元素就是在项目集开始阶段就去制订成功计划。里程碑计划可以被放在高层级的项目集计划中，它可以比较容易地满足需要，目的是在项目团队中，早期的成功可以被引导营造一种后续成功的氛围。

32．B 当组织、社区，或者其他项目集受益者能使用项目集收益时，价值才被交付。

33．A 这个内部的项目集被当作一种变革的催化剂。横跨多个不同业务部门的参与者强烈期盼资源能够共享。而且，成熟度评价本身是一个典型的实施过程，而不是一蹴而就的。它需要时间去实施不同的建议，每一个建议又是一个具体的项目，依赖其他项目去创造一系列收益。

34．C 收益转换请求的过程是完成项目集路线图更新的过程。这些更新反映了通过或不通过的决策，同时批准了影响项目集主要里程碑、范围、主要阶段时点的变更请求。

35．D 相关方分析和计划是在相关方参与计划准备之前进行的。在其他的要点之中，相关方参与态度是需要考虑的，相关方已经识别了项目集参与态度而且相关方是项目集发起人。

36．B 项目集经理要保持项目集采购管理的透明化以此来确保项目集预算被合理使用去交付项目集收益。一个输出就是使用绩效指数和挣值报告去帮助完成该角色任务。

37．C 治理委员会通常负责项目集的汇报和控制。其职责之一是确保遵循公司政策与法规。这个案例包含了很多供应商，更要注重这一点。

38．C 预算削减、组织财年和预算规划周期都可能影响项目集和项目。如果它们影响了你的项目集，作为项目集经理，你有责任再次检查和更新你的项目集计划。规划是持续迭代的活动，这个活动是伴随着竞争性优先级假设的验证和制约的解决而进行的。

39．C 对大多数项目集而言，项目集管理办公室是项目集基础设施的重要部分。项目集基础设计开发包括 PMO 多项目集工作和项目集组件的管理及协调工作的支持。

40．C 项目集绩效报告包含识别资源，确定项目集收益是否满足。同时，总结项目组件的绩效状态和项目集收益。

41．C 项目集计划有许多目标，它是一个文档记录参考，在项目集过程中，项目集管理团队将评估它的成功；它包含成功的指标，评价方法和成功的定义。

42．C 在每一个项目集过程中，对于成功的标准化考核标准必须被定义用于所有的一致性项目。它通过分析整个过程中的相关方期望和需求来达到管理和把控项目集的目的。

43．A 虽然项目集管理计划和路线图将展示意图的项目集方向和收益，但整个组件的情况可能并不清晰。项目集经理应该在整个收益交付阶段进行监督，判断是否需要为了适度的集成或者通过适应性变更来重新规划。

44．C 在收益分析和计划阶段，收益连同衍生和排序的组件、衍生的收益指标，以及确立的收益实现计划一起，被导入项目集计划中。

45．D 映射和绘图是一个非常实用的相关方识别工具，可用于分析相关方并将其分成不同的类别。它形象地代表所有相关方之间关于项目集的当前和期望的支持和影响。

46．C 相关方分析和计划的目的之一是了解相关方对项目集收益交付的期望。当相关方分析和规划完成之后，这个结果便是相关方参与计划。

47．B 项目集方法定义了项目集如何实现其目标和收益；共同的项目集方法可以带向重复性的项目集成功。

48．C 应用路线图有许多目的，其中一个是，把它一个价值工作，去帮助管理执行中的项目集，同时用于评估项目集取得具体收益的进展。

49．A 即使项目集生命周期结束之后，收益管理允许组织从其投资中去实现和维持相应的收益。项目集经理要确保这个是在组织中持续运行的框架下完成的。

50．A 完成相关方争取计划是为了勾画出如何使项目集相关方参与到项目集中。应该分析相关方登记册，从而帮助理解项目集运行所处的环境。

51．D 在这种情形下，应使用问题升级流程向上反馈问题到治理委员会，并让其参与到决策中，就如同按照治理计划中所陈述的。

52．D 被关注的问题将可能影响项目集。通过定义和选择一系列的与项目集范围、约束条件和实现项目集收益的目标，管理项目集级别的问题，例如涉及人力资源管理、财务、技术，以及项目集计划等。

53．A 收益登记册是在收益识别阶段准备的，而且它是被持续维护和更新的，直到转换收益或者项目集过早地结束的时候。

54．B 通过收益维持，持续维持活动会被转化为运营或者后面的项目集。项目集经理和组件经理们将在项目集期间为项目集持续经营制订计划。一个方面是去规划产品的转换或者考虑项目集从项目集管理到运营的支撑能力。

55．B 资源、资金、设备和人力这些都会在所有组织中被限制。在选择项目集时，必须要考虑项目集可用的总资源，它将是成功实施项目集所需要的。资源评估应该被包含在基本的商业案例之中。

56．B 项目管理委员会负责创建审计组织，制订具体的项目集计划，以用于项目集审计工作。

57．C 当相关方登记表被准备后，相关信息被获取用于更好地了解组织文化、政治和关于项目集及它的整体影响关注点。从这个信息角度，一份相关方优先级清单将被准备，用于帮助聚焦于对项目集至关重要的人和组织上的参与努力。

58．B 当收益实现计划被准备后，关注点将转移到交付定义在项目集计划中的预期收益。

59．B 在该情形下，供应商是一个主要相关方，尤其是因为你组织中变更策略和流程步骤。他们需要关于变更的沟通，而且他们将需要和项目集经理，以及他/她的团队互动沟通，从而让他们不再成为消极的相关方。

60. A 项目集经理需要强有力的沟通能力。一个重要的沟通原则是积极聆听，要理解和响应相关方。密切关注演讲者，同时确认有一个清晰地理解演讲者的关注点，表现出同情他人的观点，这样是非常重要的。

61. A 项目集经理负责管理单个组件的管理人员和核心团队成员。因此，项目集经理对这些个人的表现进行了评价。在这种情况下，项目经理 A 应该被予以表扬，因为他所释放的这些资源将促进团队参与，并有助于实现对项目集目标的更大的承诺。

62. B 在项目集范围控制中的一个关键活动是建立一个变更管理活动。第一步是捕获请求的范围变更，接着是作为变更管理活动的一部分的政策和程序。

63. D 重要的是评估风险，识别相关方，包括发起人，然后将他们纳入风险管理计划。

64. B 在项目集的层次准备一个沟通计划比在项目的层次要困难得多。要认识和处理新的相关方，并且新的组件也将被添加。由于项目集需要更长的时间来完成，许多相关方将随着新的相关方的加入而离开项目集。使用多个供应商也增加了要考虑的相关方的数量。

65. D 项目集架构通过确定组件之间的关系和管理组件所包含在项目集之中的规则，从而定义出组件的结构。

66. A 阶段关口评审对项目集就一些质量和战略相关的标准进行评估，包括预期收益是否符合收益实现计划。

67. B 项目集经理是变革拥护者。他/她需要缩小在"当前"状态和"未来"状态的期望愿景之间的差距，从而显示出对当前状态的理解，并能够描述出收益将随组织移动到"未来"状态而不断积累。

68. C 在项目集启动阶段，项目集组件被定义并被配置，用来交付项目集。这个阶段可能还包括一个针对所有组件的高级别规划。

69. A 组合管理涉及创建、管理和评估一个战略计划的投资组合的过程，专注于提供持久的结果和收益。目标是投资组合与战略目标保持一致，只批准那些能支持业务目标的组件。如果战略方向发生变化，投资组合也要被重新审视。

70. C 收益实现计划确定了业务收益，并记录了实现它们的计划。它包括预期的收益的相互依赖关系，这些收益通过项目集之中的不同项目而实现交付。它确定了所需的组织的过程和系统，包括这些过程和系统的变化，以及如何和何时转移到将要发生的运营状态上（新的安排）。

71. B 收益登记册是在收益实现过程中建立的，并使用项目集的商业论证来制定，因为商业论证是项目集所预计提供的价值，以及为实现这些价值所需的资源的正式声明。

72. D 项目集资源计划被准备来作为资源规划的一种输出。为了执行项目集及其组件，必须确定出所需的资源，它们何时被需要，以及所需要的数量。

73．B 预测是项目集绩效监测和控制的一部分。它们使项目经理和相关方能评估实现所计划的成果的可能性。

74．D 虽然项目集经理必须确定整体项目集管理的最佳方法，但这是一个全球化的项目集，因此，为了有效地解决文化、社会经济、政治和环境的差异，有必要量身定制项目集管理的活动、过程和接口。

75．D 在组件的监督和整合的过程中，不同的组件在不同的时间产生收益。项目集经理接收状态信息，并使用这些信息来将组件集成到项目集活动中。在许多情况下，项目集经理可以启动一个新的组件来进行集成工作，尤其是如果组件正生产出可交付成果。另外，在没有协同交付时，这些组件的收益就无法实现。

76．D 项目管理支持活动可能包括处理项目集的知识管理的工作。通过组织这些项目集管理信息，并将其用作一种参考信息，这使项目集经理确保重要的项目集信息和文档能被很容易地访问和提供给那些需要它的人，并且它可以帮助支持决策。

77．B 为了帮助相关方建立项目集收益的共同期望，项目集经理为相关方提供了项目集章程和商业论证的信息，其中概括了依赖关系、风险和收益的细节。

78．D 环境分析被用来评估商业论证和项目集计划的有效性。SWOT 分析是进行环境分析的类型之一，并且 SWOT 分析为制定章程和项目集计划提供相应信息。

79．B 鉴于这一项目集的规模，它在一定程度上几乎影响到该机构的每个人，问卷调查是一个征求相关方反馈的关键方法，从而对组织的文化有更好的理解。

80．D 阶段关口评审并不能代替定期的绩效评审，定期的绩效评审是用来评估针对预期结果，以及用来评估在长期实现和维持项目集收益的所需要的绩效。

81．B 相关方争取计划显示了在项目集期间如何争取相关方。当该计划得以完成时，项目集经理就有了一个详细的策略，从而为项目集提供有效的相关方争取。

82．B 相关方登记册应该是易于被项目集团队所访问的，但它可能包含政治的、引人注意的敏感信息。因此，项目集经理可能需要创建对其进行访问和审查的限制。

83．A 变更请求在项目集及其组件中是常见的。项目集经理必须确保他/她所能够批准或拒绝的变更是在权限范围之内，并且其作为项目集交付管理的一部分。

84．B 项目集范围控制是必要的，因为随着项目集发展要确保其成功地完成，同时范围变更可能来源于诸多方面。输出的结果是一个更新的项目集范围说明书。

85．D 在提交收尾的建议之前，必须满足授权收尾的条件，同时收尾的建议也必须与组织的愿景和战略相一致。

86．A 相关方的问题和关注点应该被予以跟踪直至其得到解决和闭环。使用一个工具来记录、优先处理并跟踪这些问题和相关方利益，从而可以帮助确保相关方所关注的事项得到妥善解决。

87．A 在战略项目集管理中，一旦已经获得对项目集的组织的领导，并获得对启动该项目集的授权，然后确定和评估整合的机会和需求就是非常必要的。这些整合工作的范围包括从人力资本、人力资源需求和技能集，到项目集及其运营活动之内的设施、财务、资产、流程和系统，从而对整个组织的收益进行调整和整合。

88. B 对项目集的论证、愿景和战略适配的声明是包括在项目集章程内并作为其中的一部分，这是在项目集启动阶段得以制定的。项目集章程提供了对向前推进开展项目集或者根据检查内容大纲对生命周期进行规划的授权。

89. D 在项目集形成阶段结束时，治理结构得以描述，在项目集章程中对相关方的考虑也完成了准备。项目集的项目发起人和项目经理也得以指派。

90. C 积极地进行相关方争取的工作，需要通过指标来衡量相关方争取活动的绩效，例如会议出席和沟通计划的落实。这些指标是相关方争取计划的一部分，除此之外，它还描述了如何有效地争取项目集中的相关方。

91. D 衡量资源可用性的一种常用方法是咨询项目集管理信息系统（PMIS）。它有助于在早期识别资源问题，以及有助于资源分配活动。项目集经理对资源的可用性和分配进行分析，确保资源没有过量使用。如果项目集想取得成功，必须解决资源限制的问题。

92. D 许多活动在项目集的财务监督和控制中被执行。通过监控在项目集组件之间进行成本再分配的影响和结果，项目集经理正在积极和努力控制成本保持在预算基准之内。

93. D 虽然在项目集中需要一些关键的人际交往技能，项目集经理必须认识到每个项目集相关方期望的动态人力方面，并进行相应的管理。他/她必须利用组织的政治动力，以促进与相关方建立关系的项目集目标。

94. B 虽然项目集管理需要一个由技术技能、时间管理技能和良好基础人员技能所构成的特定技能集，但是沟通是最重要的能力。项目集经理需要具有强有力的沟通技能来处理与所有的相关方团队成员、发起人、管理人员、职能经理、客户、供应商、公众和其他相关方的关系。

95. C 所有相关方的利益都是重要的。作为项目集经理，重要的是要启动、参与并保持有效的相关方关系来管理该项目集，并达到预期的收益。积极的相关方参与是必要的，从而建立和维持不间断的项目集支持。

96. B 在治理计划中所描述的问题升级流程分为两个层次，其中之一是在组件团队和项目集管理团队之间。

97. A 除了准备收益实现计划之外，还有大量关键活动在收益分析和计划阶段加以执行。其中之一就是建立项目集的绩效基准，以及和关键相关方沟通项目集的绩效指标。

98. A 制定项目集的商业论证是用来评估项目集在成本和效益之间的平衡。它可以是高层次的或者细化的，其中包含用于评估项目集的目标和约束的参数。

99. A 沟通技能是通用管理技能的一部分，并且是项目集经理和项目经理的必要技能。项目集经理需要具备强大的沟通技能，从而有效地与相关方在各个层级进行沟通。

100．A　在许多项目集中，重要的是，要在项目集的层级确保项目集质量。项目集经理准备由治理委员会所批准的质量计划。质量计划通过确定和应用跨组件的质量标准，从而建立了确保项目集质量的机制。

101．B　项目集的商业论证及项目集章程是组织领导考虑许可和授权项目集的关键输入。

102．C　在项目集启动阶段，选择发起人来监督项目集，保证财务状况健康并确保项目集提供预期的收益。

103．B　在项目集范围规划中，一旦确定了范围，则需要准备一个范围管理计划，以管理、记录和沟通范围变更。

104．C　治理计划包含几个部分，其中包括治理计划的结构和会议日程。这个计划可能作为项目集管理计划中的一部分。它描述了执行治理策略的目标、结构、角色和职责、政策、程序和后勤工作。

105．C　组织面临众多的复杂性和挑战，这导致其战略目的和目标的不断变化，但通常一个项目集经理距离组织的过程太远而不知道这些变化，或者缺乏经验、能力和技能去理解为什么目标已经改变及其对项目的影响。

106．D　内部的人员配备包括识别现有人才所处职位的任职资格情况，为获得他们的服务与他们的管理人员进行谈判，然后将他们转移到项目集的工作之中。在资源优化期间，项目集工作人员的分配预计会发生变化，并将其反映到更新的项目集资源计划之中。

107．B　治理委员会承担有如下职责，在许多情况下，要确保项目集符合标准化的报告和控制过程并适用于所有的项目集。一个例子是符合战略和运营层面的假设。通常假设是不正确的。由于这些假设可以转化为战略或运营领域的风险，因此要对这些假设进行评审。

108．C　这些承包商的问题表明需要一个重要的改进领域，以防止未来的、类似的问题出现。改进领域是在项目集的最终报告中所讨论的相应条款。

109．D　因果分析是一种用来提供一些事情为何发生的真正原因的技术，然后针对重点的变更活动而采取纠正行动。它强调根本原因，并经常使用因果关系图。

110．D　相关方登记册在整个项目集中所被使用，因为它列出了所有的相关方，并用于报告、分发程序集的可交付成果，进行正式和非正式的沟通。它是项目集相关方识别过程的主要输出。

111．A　与项目集团队和其他相关方开展头脑风暴会议对于准备相关方登记册是有用的。名义小组技术是头脑风暴的一种形式，允许在场的每个人都能不间断地讨论想法，并使所有参与者都能积极参与。

112．C　项目集的资金通常是通过预算过程予以提供的，该过程由负责监督多个项目集的治理委员会所控制。其目的是确保资金的提供方式与可能在项目组合管理中所定义的项目集和组织的优先事项保持一致。

113. A 由于相关方列表及他们对该项目集的态度将发生改变，相关方争取在项目集之中是一个连续的活动。在这些会议的每次会议之后，相关方登记册都应该被更新。而且，它应该经常被引用，并由项目集经理和团队进行评估，并根据需要进行更新。

114. B 高层的项目集路线图或框架可以为项目集的定义、规划和执行设置一个基准。它是动态变化的，并随投资组合管理过程而准备或更新。它的一个缺点是需要相关的准则，许多组织缺乏保持其信息的流动性和关联性。

115. B 项目集工作分解结构（PWBS）不代替项目集的每个项目的工作分解结构（WBS）。从项目集的角度来看，PWBS 应该分解到项目集经理所需要控制的层次，这通常对应到组件项目的 WBS 的最开始的一个或两个层次。

116. D 一旦项目集范围被确定和被描述出来，那么范围说明书和 PWBS 就已准备好了，下一步是准备范围管理计划。它可以用于管理、记录和沟通范围的变化。

117. B 涉及合规性的项目集是由于立法、法规或合同义务而发起的。这种情况是需要创建一个新项目集的一个例子，因为即使新法规它本身不是一个战略性的举措，组织也必须对该新法规予以执行。

118. B 约束是限制项目团队的选择的因素；通常情况下，它们会影响计划、成本、资源或项目集可交付成果。它们是一个项目集之中所普遍存在的部分，其可能会限制行动。

119. A 完工估算是一种预测技术；它也是对完成活动、项目集工作包或控制账户的剩余工作的一种估算。它是来自项目集财务监测和控制的一个输出。

120. C 通过和发起人一起进行评审，从而获得对项目集的正式接受是很重要的。该项目集在取得治理委员会或发起人的接受收尾（项目集已经实现其目标）之后而被正式关闭。

121. C 下一代蜂窝手机和相关产品的开发是最适用于作为一个项目集来进行管理的，项目集将以一种协调的方式对大量的项目进行管理，相比在可能情况下的单独管理能获得更大的收益和控制。

122. D 在组织中建立治理要求一个发起人组织去实施治理过程，然后启用组织去监控项目集的目的和目标来保证它们满足组织需要。

123. A 资源的可用性应该作为项目集资源计划的一部分。相较于其他事情，其表明了需要完成项目目的和可交付成果的人员、资产、材料或者资本资源时的可用性，是决定要不要进行采购的一项关键因素。

124. B 管理项目集公共建设的开支是很有必要的，以便于保证这些花销在期望的参数值内，并且没有对预算基准和必须的纠正行动造成影响。

125. C 当项目章程被批准后，项目集被正式授权可以开始，项目章程的批准也使项目集和组织中正在进行的工作和战略优先事项产生了关联。

126. C 作为一个项目集经理，你必须保证在构成的各项目之间的内部依赖关系能够正确地反映出来，并在项目集进度表中对其正确管理，然而项目经理专注在项目进度的具体活动。内部和外部的依赖关系是该过程的一个关键的输入。项目集进度表包括呈现出项目集输出的组件里程碑，或分享出组件和其他组件之间的相关性。

127．C　决策树分析是用于当某些未来场景或者结果不确定时，帮助选择可用的替代解决方案。其有助于组织识别替代活动的相对价值。在项目集管理中，对于某些不确定性、风险识别、风险转移和风险机会，决策树分析是有助于分析和更新收益实现计划和收益维持计划的一种有用技术。

128．A　商业价值度量在整体收益度量中是有用的，尤其是在无形收益的度量上。这种方法能持续地测试出项目集相对于商业战略和目标的无形收益，从而确保商业战略和目标是健壮的、有重大意义的。即使是对于人员规模与商业目标的一致性，在某种程度上也是可度量的。

129．B　问题上升是在治理内发生的一种活动。娴熟地跟踪、管理和解决项目集级别的和内部组件的问题有助于提高治理的有效性。

130．A　项目集 A 如果有必要会在权衡折中的情况下去掉某些功能。这是进度驱动的，并且是能支持该公司快速上市的能力属性，因此其合乎该组织的文化和环境。

131．C　在制订项目集财务管理计划时，项目集的财务管理计划是一个关键的输出。然而，其他输出是项目集资金进度、组件支出进度、项目集运营成本和项目集财务度量标准。由于这些度量标准是用于衡量项目集效益，所以它们是必要的。

132．C　在大部分组织中，治理委员会批准各独立组件的启动。治理委员会的批准包括一些关键的活动，其中之一就是同关键相关方对关键组件相关的信息进行沟通。这样的沟通对于相关方争取和支持是必要的。

133．A　为了使所有基建活动在项目集级别达到一致性，作为项目集的买方或者所有者，对于有关子承包商和他们的选择，以及绩效的职责，应当在项目集级别予以定义。

134．B　作为项目集范围控制的一部分，应该创建一个变更管理活动来处理范围变更。在变更请求被接受后，下一步就是要对其进行评估或者分析。

135．B　相对于通过个人访谈或者调查问卷，焦点小组是非常有用的，能提供对项目集影响的更为深刻的理解；焦点小组提供相关方小组对于项目集的态度的反馈，并且提供沟通方法和减轻影响的方式。

136．A　在相关方登记册准备好之后，相关方的关注点就能得以更好的理解，由项目集经理建立一种平衡来减轻对项目集持有消极观点的相关方的影响，并鼓励项目集的积极拥护者对项目集予以积极支持。

137．D　投资回报周期可以用项目集的初始固定的投资除以估计的每年的净现金流。在这个例子中，项目集 D 的投资回报周期是 2.2 年，应该选择 D。

138．D　在项目集采购管理中，许多合同的管理和收尾是由各组件来处理的。合同交付成果、需求、截止时间、成本和质量的细节也都是在组件级别予以处理的。

139．B　范围、资源和成本的估算是在项目集启动阶段予以准备的。由于项目集要同其他项目集比较以确定其优先级，因此这些研究要尽早确定，以评估组织执行该项目集的能力。

140. A 当项目集结束时，交付的收益必须是可维持的。也许有必要的是，要保证持续的产品支持，通过对产品生命周期后期的管理来增加价值。在产品生命周期中，项目管理经常用于对产品进行升级。

141. C 对项目集经理来说，指导是一项关键的个人能力，鼓励并促进团队成员的职业发展。它不用于教练和其他事情，它鼓励项目集经理对于团队成员的绩效和团队发展表现出真实兴趣。

142. C 相关方会议主要服务于两个主要目的：沟通项目集状态、听取相关方的问题和顾虑。这些问题和顾虑随后在问题日志中予以记录，排列优先级排序，并进行跟踪以帮助理解所提供的反馈。

143. C 在使用净现值（NPV）作为选择标准时，对于货币的时间价值的考虑是基于以下事实，即 1 年之后的 1 美元的价值要低于现在 1 美元的价值。未来的价值换算成现在的价值时贴现地得越多（也就是说贴现率越高），那么项目集的 NPV 就越低。如果 NPV 越高，那么项目集的估值就越高。在这种情况下，你应该选择项目 C。

144. A 虽然项目集成本的主要部分是归因于组件和承包商所完成的工作，但是直到将项目集管理费用添加到最初的预算数字中之前，预算基准还不能最终生效。

145. C 核对单包含在项目集质量计划之中，核对单对于保证条目的完整是非常有用的，同时也可以在质量保证和质量控制中使用。

146. A 信息请求用于帮助组织能够规划需求和识别合格的卖家，从而及时地支持项目集采购。

147. D 收益可以分为有形收益和无形收益，然而风险规避应该考虑为一种深层次的收益，因为很多情况下，风险规避可以作为驱动一项变更的主要力量。

148. C 收益实现计划定义了每一个收益、关联假设，并决定每一个收益如何实现。相较于其他计划，收益实现计划应该确保对项目集所有阶段的管理能满足对项目集的各种输出的整合利用，因为通过项目集进行管理的目标是为了保证相对于各项目以单独的方式管理，有更多的收益。

149. C 能力可以是基于个人或者基于绩效，在项目集的早期阶段，项目集经理必须保证项目集目标和组织战略目标的一致性，从而最佳地实现商业价值。为达到这种一致性，组织和商业战略也必须进行评估。

150. B 项目集经理协商和敲定项目集层面的政策和协议。合格卖家清单可以促进采购过程，因为采购文档可以发送给预期的卖家来评估收益，并看看他们是否愿意提供建议书或者报价单。

151. D 使用承包商是一种转移风险的方式，但是，所有的风险需要根据风险管理计划来管理以便保证收益的实现。

152. D 相关方登记册识别出相关方及他们的角色和职责。每一个组件项目同样也要在项目集的级别来考虑相关方，争取得到其支持，项目相关方同样是项目集相关方，因为项目相关方的不满意能给整个项目集的相关方的接受标准带来负面影响。

153. A 通过治理委员会所批准的典型需要是关闭或转移一个项目集组件。治理委员会对已完成的一系列活动转移或收尾的建议进行评审。评审事项之一是确保与项目集级别的相关方进行了沟通，确保组件已做好关闭的准备，以便于相关方同意该组件已经满足要求并已给项目集交付收益。

154. D 审计可能是由组织内部的或外部的人员来执行的。项目集审计专注于项目集财务，管理过程和实践，项目集质量和项目集文档。

155. B 组织文化是项目集管理成功的一个重要部分。如果高管们将发展工作视为战略而不是战术来关联到商业的成功上，那么建议采用项目集管理。

156. D 状态报告、财务报告和资源偏差报告是提交给治理委员会的报告的例子，这些报告帮助治理委员会成员在其能力范围内监控项目集进展，强化组织评估状态的能力，以及与组织的控制相一致的能力。

157. C 沟通是争取相关方的主要工具，谈判、冲突管理和影响也很重要，但是沟通对项目集经理来说是最重要的能力。

158. B 作为项目集经理，你必须解决你的项目经理们所上升的风险。当风险未被解决时，项目集经理要保证风险在组织中逐级上升直到风险被解决。上升的方式可以作为风险管理计划的一部分，并作为各职权层级制定决策的一部分。

159. B 项目集应该具备能适应组织的长期目标的战略。在这个例子中，项目集 B 完全支持 5 个目标中的 4 个。

160. B 在项目集级别，项目集采购过程负责进行必要的协商和敲定各种不同协议和奖励合同，用来支持项目集的各种项目组件和其他正在进行的工作。如果这些协议涉及保护项目集的保险或者服务，那么相关方对于潜在风险的责任必须予以书面记录并纳入合同和项目集文档之中。

161. C 项目治理为项目集管理提供支持。治理委员会支持项目集管理的能力的可能方式是通过建立一个项目集管理信息系统，该系统能收集、评估、报告和分析有关项目集管理的信息。

162. C 有很多原因可以阐明为什么需要准备商业论证，其中主要的原因是来回答如下关键问题："这个项目集如何帮助我们的公司满足其商业和战略目标？"商业论证中会包含对于项目集所有的关键信息。于是，商业论证被用于从成本、收益和商业风险的角度来评估项目集投资的可行性，并且一旦准备好商业论证，就可以为项目集计划和执行提供愿景指南。

163. A 在项目集采购计划中，一些技术（例如自制或外购决策、PWBS）可以协助项目集经理制订采购管理计划，确定采购标准，并决定是否有必要更新项目集的财务计划或者更新预算。

164. D 收益实现计划,较于其他计划而言,应该保证项目集交付其预期的收益。收益实现计划在治理委员会转移收益之前的收益交付阶段进行评审。实际交付效益相对于在计划之中的预期收益的情况应该予以定期评估。

165. A 理解客户和最终用户的期望是要求具备市场知识的,这样的知识有助于制定项目集商业论证,因为这些知识提供的信息(例如市场规模、市场细分和销售潜力等)都有助于提高项目集和组织获得成功的可能性。

166. A 较早的和清晰的计划对成功地制订项目集采购计划是至关重要的。项目集经理统观所有组件来制订采购管理计划,以优化目标和收益交付。通过解决不同组件之间的共性和差异,就可以决定对于项目集的最佳采购方式。

167. C 指导可以有效地应用于以下场景,即用于模拟这 2 名项目经理所应该遵循的合适行为,尤其是当他们要学习各种各样的标准过程加以使用的时候。随着他们获得信心,随着他们不需要你更多地主动参与的时候,指导关系应该予以改变,变得更加非正式和更多地采用咨询的方式。

168. C 项目集的变更应该根据变更管理计划来进行管理,以便于控制范围、质量、进度、成本、合同、风险和奖励。

169. B 在商业论证进入细节之前,首先定义出商业机会,然后同组织战略目标相关联,并展示和项目集相关的收益,最后描述成本/收益分析和其他财务收益、无形效益,以及风险及复杂性。

170. D 项目集治理委员会负责很多支撑功能。它通过提供组织培训支持项目集管理,尤其是在项目集管理的角色、职责、技能、能力和竞争力方面。由治理委员会所发起的培训使得培训专注于组织的具体实践和需要,从而确保那些重要的项目集能够做好履行相应职责与角色的准备。

# PgMP®报考流程指南

整个 PgMP®报考流程分为 7 步，分别是：

（1）注册信息（Registration）。

（2）填写材料（Application）。

（3）报名缴费（Submit Payment）。

（4）小组评估（Panel Review）。

（5）笔试（Exam）。

（6）多方评估（MRA）。

（7）考试结果（Exam Result）。

在上述 7 步中最重要的就是第二步——填写材料，尤其是项目集经验描述的填写，是很有技巧的。如果这部分的材料填写不当，很可能导致初审和小组评估环节不通过，直接影响认证考试的报名成功。因此，报考流程指南也着重解析这一部分。下面我们会逐一来解析流程步骤，助你顺利报考。

## A.1 注册信息（Registration）

### 1. PgMP®考试的基本要求

PgMP®考试的基本要求如表 A-1 所示。

A-1 PgMP®考试的基本要求

| 教育背景 | 项目管理经验要求 | 项目集管理经验要求 |
| --- | --- | --- |
| 高中毕业 | 最少 4 年（6 000 小时）不重合的项目管理经验 | 最少 7 年（10 500 小时）不重合的项目集管理经验 |
| 或者 | | |
| 大学本科或以上 | 最少 4 年（6 000 小时）不重合的项目管理经验 | 最少 4 年（6 000 小时）不重合的项目管理经验 |

注："项目管理经验"是指项目管理五大过程组的工作经验；"项目集管理经验"是指每个项目集至少包含 2 个拥有共同的战略目标且共享项目集预算的项目。

## 2. 注册 PMI 用户

- 要先登录 PMI 网站( http://www.pmi.org/ ),才能在线申请 PgMP®考试或修改 PgMP®申请信息。
- 如果以前曾经申请过 PMP®，则应该有 PMI 网站用户名与密码，无需重新注册。
- 如果没有，则新申请成为 PMI 网站用户，并保存好用户名和密码。

# A.2　填写材料（Application）

## 1. 填写项目

需填写的项目包括以下内容，其中认证要求最为复杂，后面我们会着重解析。

- 联系地址、邮件、电话。
- 受教育信息。
- 认证要求（项目管理经验、项目集管理经验、经验总结）。
- 可选填信息、证书信息、协议等。

## 2. 注意事项

- 一旦开始填写申请材料，则不能取消，但可以保存。在提交申请材料前可以随时修改。
- 申请人有 **90** 天的时间来完成申请材料的填写并提交（自申请材料开始填写算起）；
- 在申请人提交申请材料后，PMI 会在 **10 个工作日内**，审核申请材料的完整性（ Application Completeness Review，材料完整性初审），并通知相关结果。只要在初审通过后，才可以进行缴纳认证费、材料审查与小组评估等后续环节。
- PMI 主要通过邮件与你沟通，告知申请的各个步骤、结果与进展，请务必添加发件人域名为 pmi.org 到你的邮件系统的白名单（告诉邮件系统来自 pmi.org 的邮件均不是垃圾邮件）或者添加 customercare@pmi.org 至你的邮件系统的白名单，以确保收到来自 PMI 的邮件。

## 3. 填写步骤

- **选择 PgMP®认证周期的确定方式**。通常有两个选项——Option A 和 Option B，其中 Option A 表示自动确定 PgMP®的认证周期，同时调整 PMP®认证周期与 PgMP®认证周期一致；Option B 表示与 PgMP®认证周期与 PMP®证书的认证周期一致。无论哪种情况，PMP®与 PgMP®的认证周期最终都将调整为一致，并共享 PDU 积分。以后同时拥有 PMP®和 PgMP®证书的朋友将同时续证。**一般建议选择 Option A**。
- **填写联系信息与教育背景**（**Contact & Education Information**）。请注意：电子邮件一定要填写正确。电子邮件是以后 PMI 与申请人联系的主要手段。
- **认证要求**（**Requirements**）填写。

■ 认证要求建议：

➢ 可以将自己的工作经历梳理一下，一般情况，至少分隔成 3 个阶段，且 3 个阶段时间上不重叠。

一是工程师阶段（建议至少 2 年，即大学本科或硕士毕业到刚开始担任项目经理阶段）；

二是项目经理阶段（至少 4 年，48 个月）；

三是项目集经理阶段（至少 4 年，48 个月，本科学历以上申请者）。

➢ 项目经理阶段所管理的项目作为项目管理经验信息填入申请材料里，将项目集经理阶段所管理的项目集中作为项目集管理经验信息填入申请材料里。

➢ 所有项目（包括项目管理经验中的项目和项目集下的子项目）不得重复，不允许出现在同一个项目集中，同时担任项目集经理和子项目经理的情况。

■ 认证要求说明：通过这个显示页面，申请人可以查看项目管理经验（月份数）、项目集管理经验（月份数）、项目集经验总结、经验证明人等条件的填写完成情况。

■ 项目管理经验填写：

➢ 共需 48 个月，6 000 小时的项目管理经验。可以填写多个项目（不限项目数）的管理经验。

➢ 每个项目需要登记一个证明人（上级、客户、发起人或者高管层等）。

➢ 距离申请日超过 15 年的项目管理经验不计月份（填写过去 15 年内你管理的项目）。截止申请日仍未结束的项目，项目管理经验算到申请日为止。

➢ 填写的项目不能是你管理的项目集（在项目集管理经验处填写）下的子项目。

➢ 如果在某个月份同时管理多个项目，项目管理经验（月份数）只能算一个月，不能累计计算。

■ 项目集管理经验填写：

➢ 共需 48 个月，6 000 小时的项目集管理经验（本科以上学历申请者，本科以下学历需要 72 个月，10 500 小时经验）。可以填写多个项目集的管理经验。

➢ 记录 6 000 小时的项目管理工作时长。管理小时数按 5 个项目集管理领域（战略项目集管理、项目集生命周期管理、收益管理、相关方管理、项目集治理）分别填写。对于某个项目集，并不是每个领域都要填写管理小时数，但是所有项目集的管理小时数汇总的时候，5 个项目集管理领域必须都包含有小时数。

➢ 48 个月的项目集管理经验与 6 000 小时的项目集管理工作时长两个数据要同时满足。每个项目集需要登记一个证明人。

➢ 每个项目集至少登记两个拥有共同的战略目标且共享项目集预算的子项目，并记录子项目的相关信息。子项目的起止时间要在项目集的起止时间范围之内。

> 距离申请日超过15年的项目集管理经验不计月份。截止申请日仍未结束的项目集，项目集管理经验算到申请日为止。如果在某个月份同时管理多个项目集，项目集经验只能算一个月，不能累计计算。

# A.3 报名缴费（Submit Payment）

如在国内考试，则缴费须在中国国际人才交流基金会（原国家外专局培训中心）开始报名网站（http://exam.chinapmp.cn/）报名。

# A.4 小组评估（Panel Review）

认证费缴纳完成后，PMI 会通知申请者邮寄申请资料做抽查（Audit），然后再启动小组评估（Panel Review），小组评估由人工进行，相对严格。只有小组评估通过后才能预约笔试。如果小组评估最终没有通过，PgMP®认证流程将终止，PMI 也会退回部分考试费。

**1. 抽查（Audit）**

请于收到 PMI 抽查通知之后，立即准备并邮寄抽查所需材料到 PMI，以避免耽误后续的小组评估和笔试预约。

抽查所需材料包括：
- PMI 申请时所填写的学位与学历证书复印件 + 英文翻译。
- 项目集经验审查表（打印之后填写完整）。

材料邮寄注意事项：
- 2 份材料分别装在 2 个信封里（A4 大信封），每个信封都不需要封口，只需拆好即可。装项目集经验审查表的信封封口处要签上证明人的名字（拼音）。
- 如果你的项目集经验证明人不是同一人，那么项目集经验就要分别装在不同的信封里，封口处让相对应的证明人签字。
- 请务必于 PMI 规定日期前用 UPS 或是 DHL（速度快）邮寄到 PMI，地址详见项目集经验证明最后一页。

**2. 小组评估（Panel Review）**

小组评估没有通过的常见原因如下：
- 经验描述没有反映出项目集相关的经验，如下例：

Responses did not address all of the major component elements required for one or more of the experience summary questions. Responses did not thoroughly explain the method or approach used to perform the program management functions in one or more of the experience summary questions. In addition, responses did not provide specific examples demonstration candidate's role as a program manager.

- 经验描述的方法与项目集不相关，如下例：

Responses did not thoroughly explain the method or approach used to perform the program management functions in one or more of the experience summary questions. Responses were tactical in nature and/or limited to "textbook" explanation of topics.

确保小组评估一次性通过最好的办法是严格按照本书附录 B 关于项目集经验认真地填写。请参考项目集管理经验的正反例，认真填写。

## A.5　笔试（Exam）

小组评估顺利通过后，即可收到获得参与笔试资格的邮件通知，请按照邮件通知的要求到相应考点，按时参加笔试。

## A.6　多方评估（MRA）

多方评估在最初的 PgMP®认证考试中存在，但目前已取消。在材料填写的时候，会请你填写 MRA 评估人（Reference）的信息，说明如下：

- 系统会自动将申请在填写项目管理经验与项目集管理经验时的证明人汇总显示出来作为 MRA 评估人。
- 申请人可以增加、删除和修改这些评估人。
- MRA 评估人至少 12 人，且至少包含 1 位申请人的上司、4 位平级同事、4 位直接下属，其他 3 位可以任选。

## A.7　考试结果（Exam Result）

多方评估通过后一个月左右申请者将收到 PgMP®证书，同时在 PMI 网站也可查询到 PgMP®证书持有者的情况。

# PgMP®项目集经验描述技巧

## B.1 项目集思维

项目集经理是一个更对接战略的角色,因此要**更多从战略层面思考**,切记不要停留在**战术层面思考**,填写经验描述时也要秉承这一原则。具体来说有以下 3 种重要思维:

- **战略匹配**:项目集经理负责在组织战略目标和商业目标的背景下协调管理多个相关项目。这些项目涉及跨部门、组织、地理区域和文化的复杂活动。项目集经理在相关方的各个层面建立信任、和谐关系,保持各相关方的沟通,这也包括与组织外部相关方的联络与沟通。
- **收益导向**:项目集经理启动和管理项目集,在此过程中分配给项目经理相应资源,并负责项目的最终绩效结果,确保项目集的最终成功。项目集经理要不断确保项目集活动与组织战略和商业目的相一致。项目集经理负责决定、协调各个项目之间的资源共享,以使整个项目集获得收益。
- **治理决策**:项目集经理应具有在复杂的事业环境因素下做出决策的能力,而且这种决策需要在共同的治理结构下确保风险的可控与决策的合理性。同时,项目集经理应拥有财务管理、政治敏感性、领导力、跨文化沟通、谈判和冲突解决等方面的高级技巧。

## B.2 项目集经验填写介绍

- 填写 5 个项目集管理经验总结,分别对应 5 个项目集绩效领域:项目集战略一致性、项目集生命周期管理、项目集收益管理、项目集相关方参与、项目集治理。
- 每个项目集管理经验的描述方向可以有 2 个(选择项 A 与选择项 B),请选择其中任意一个来有针对性地介绍你的项目集管理经验与经历。请务必清晰理解每个选择项的含义，并有针对性地做出描述。

- 每个项目集管理经验不少于 300 个英文单词，最多可填写 350 个英文单词（1 000 个字符）。

## B.3　经验描述填写技巧

- 经验描述需提供实例，证明你的角色是一名项目集经理，切忌"教科书式"的描述，但也要平衡字数要求，做到言简意赅。
- 经验描述中，需解释你做项目管理工作时所用到的具体方法，这些方法要与项目集思维一致。
- 经验描述会被小组评估的评估人书面阅读，请务必保持英语语句通顺、文字简洁，避免单词有误的低级错误。
- 建议先在 Word 中写好后，一是至少润色 1~2 遍，二是检查拼写是否都正确（可以用 Word 的拼写检查功能），三是核对字数和内容无误后，再复制到在线的申请表中，确保万无一失。

## B.4　经验描述正反例解析

### 1. 正例一（该示例选择 B）

*Question*

*Experience Summary #2: Benefits Realization*

*A.  Defined and monitored benefits realization measurement criteria*

*B.  Identified opportunities that resulted in optimized program benefits*

×××　is one joint venture company by Germany ××× and Shanghai Electronics. This program was implemented in Shanghai plant which was built in 1950s. and it consists of 4 independent but related projects, namely OMEGA PUMP R&D, Process definition & Investment planning, Plant re-layout, lean production support.

As the large-scale Investment program, the major benefits delivered incrementally during the program life cycle: 1.OMEGA Pump production localization; 2.Plant layout update3.Lean production implement On regular weekly review meeting, I discovered that there is one issue raised by Warehouse department, which is they are confusing about the lean production requirement, and some materials are not available when needed.

After detail investigation on this topic, I found that it is the first time warehouse team heard about lean production and the way of managing warehouse still laid on mass production management warehouse, with only record in - out. I think it is one threat to program success, so I made one set of plan to update the warehouse record system to support Program including employee training.

After 2-3 months efforts, the efficiency of logistics and warehouse improved a lot. The respond time for logistics shortened 30%, and warehouse scrap rate decrease from 10% to 0.5%. This improvement not effecting this program, but also effect all productions on going. And also fit with the strategic plans for future program.

评价：该示例有具体的项目集方法、过程，详细介绍了如何利用项目集管理来进行商业目标的达成，有数据、有思路。

## 2. 正例二（该示例选择 A）

*Question*

*Experience Summary #1: Strategic Program Management*

*A. Developed program justification and business case in alignment with the organization's strategic plan*

*B. Monitored the business environment, program goals, and benefits realization plan in order to ensure the program remains aligned with the organization's strategic objectives.*

I am currently in building a continuous staff welfare platform,which is closely related to the needs of the employees, welfare services. The original GAT1.0 had many problems, the visual effect is obsolete, the user experience is poor,unable to meet the needs of the internal information management business and welfare corporate customers, and competitors had brought new products,we can not accept the loss of customers, so it is necessary to develop a new platform to enhance the user experience and increase the number of customers.

Based on above background, I am assigned with a high level business case to further assess the opportunity to increase the number of customers our products development. First, I collect historical information in the organizations database, such as actual cost information, supply chain, customer delivery, yearly demand information, and also previous project benefit. Second, I do the feasibility analysis to verify the cost reduction feasibility, from financial, technical and operational etC.  view.

After that, SWOT analyze to refer strengths, weaknesses and opportunities. After above analyzing, I justify that GAT2.0 is feasible to achieve the target of increasing the number of customers through continuous development and delivery of sub projects such as Enterprise management center, Applications management, Personal center, Care mall.

The benefits of this program are as following:

(1) Our customers will increase about 30% within a year after this paltform released to the

market;

(2) Our technology will make our technology in advance of the competitor at least 6 months;

(3) It will bring us more incomes. I prepare program charter based on above assessment and include above business case analyzing. I discuss a lot with program steering committee, which includes high level management team and the sponsors.

To develop GAT2.0 is quite important for our company. Finally, this program is approved by company program steering committee. I move ahead of this program.

评价：该示例同样详细解释了项目集过程，遵循项目集思路，其中包括商业论证、可行性研究、SWOT 分析、收益评估等环节，确保项目集与组织战略一致。言之有物，语言明了。

### 3. 反例一（该示例选择 B）

*Question*

*Experience Summary #1: Strategic Program Management*

*A. Developed program justification and business case in alignment with the organization's strategic plan*

*B. Monitored the business environment, program goals, and benefits realization plan in order to ensure the program remains aligned with the organization's strategic objectives.*

First of all, XXX machine is the No.1 program for MESNAC for short period, and we need a totally new design from all those we had made. So we face a lot of technical problems at the beginning. The second challenge is that our technical engineers are sent from the United States and Brazil, and they spoke different languages—English and Portuguese. However, our technical engineers can ONLY speak a little English and can rarely speak Portuguese, and a lack of confidence to talk about their own design idea for building the machine at the right beginning and ONLY followed GY's theory, which put us in a negative position. Those are the three big problem in program management.

I defined some other risks in program management which might influence the strategic objectives.

(1) The complexity has a impact on the deadline or delivery of the TBR.

(2) The huge amount of work is a burden to our personnel.

(3) The determination of delivery date is difficult.

(4) Too much safety requirement to the machine add financial burden to MESNAC

To solve all these problems, I update my plan for the program regularly with GY partners. Every morning at 9 o'clock, we had a morning meeting to review the problems we left the last day. To solve the communication problems, I encouraged all our staff to talk to foreign partners and discuss questions by themselves in whatever way that can make it including making gesture and showing around the machine. That made it much easier than just language communicating. Only after several weeks, communication problem was not a real problem. In order to make the delivery time, I arranged out staff 3 shifts a day, morning shift, middle shift and night shift. It turned out that it was a great way and it released our working burden and also improved working efficiency. As for the financial problem, I talked to the sales manager and gave a final determination to that.

评价：该示例的内容与"选择 B：监督商业环境、项目集计划、收益实现计划，目的是与组织战略一致"的要求没有明显的关联，只是在简单堆积做了什么事情，而这些事情也看不出有任何的项目集管理的思路、过程和方法的应用，故应以此为戒。

4．反例二（该示例选择 B）

*Question*

*Experience Summary #4: Governance*

*A. Established and adapted the program governance model*

*B. Identified and evaluated risks and their impact on the program objectives throughout the program*

Risk management is significant for ××× program. At the beginning of the project, I prepared the risk management plan and I provide some ways for managing them.

I carry on some conference to discuss the potential risks and the way to solving them. All members of conference are active at the meeting. Only after several turns, we collect more than 100 risk issues. They we make schedule and regularly review them just in case.

Every day, I will check out the risk register with both our own personnel and foreign partners and update every day. It is very common for the big machine to fail once or two. For every time, I will assign personnel to check out where is the risk and discuss how to fix it. We never let any small risk go and that's why we can finally get the achievement.

Due to the risk plan, it informed us that something need to be checked and it served as a warning. By keeping record of each risk and finding out who should be responsible for the risk, I improve staff's initiative and sense of responsibility.

评价：该示例的内容没有举出任何实例，只是列举了任务，显得空洞无物，也很难看出选项 B "对项目集目标的影响"，故应以此为戒。

# PgMP<sup>®</sup>术语表

术语表中的许多词语，为了符合项目集管理的背景，可能比词典中的定义更广，有些情况下还具有不同的含义。

**采购管理计划 Procurement Management Plan**：项目或项目集管理计划的组成部分，说明项目团队将如何从执行组织外部获取货物和服务。

**发起人 Sponsor**：为项目、项目集或项目组合提供资源和支持的个人或团体，负责为成功创造条件。

**范围管理计划 Scope Management Plan**：项目或项目集管理计划的组成部分，描述将如何定义、制定、监督、控制和确认范围。

**风险管理计划 Risk Management Plan**：项目、项目集或项目组合管理计划的组成部分，说明将如何安排与实施风险管理活动。

**相关方 Stakeholder**：能影响项目、项目集或项目组合决策、活动或结果的个人、群体或组织，以及会受或自认为会受项目、项目集或项目组合决策、活动或结果影响的个人、群体或组织。

**绩效域 Performance Domain**：由个人所承担的，为了解决某一具体项目集管理的聚焦领域，按照标准的、代表完整的知识要素和活动来衡量的一组任务与能力。

**阶段关口评审 Phase-Gate Reviews**：在阶段末所做的评审，其评估结果是决定进入下阶段、调整后进入或结束该项目或项目集。

**进度管理计划 Schedule Management Plan**：项目或项目集管理计划的组成部分，建立编制、监督和控制项目或项目集的活动。

**路线图 Roadmap**：按时间顺序展现项目集的预期发展方向，以图形化方式描绘项目集主要里程碑与决策点之间的依赖关系，同时传递业务战略与项目集工作之间的连接。

**商业论证 Business Case**：用于验证项目集交付收益的经济可行性研究文档。

**事业环境因素 Enterprise Environmental Factors**：团队不能直接控制的，将对项目、项目集或项目组合产生影响、限制或指导作用的各种条件。

**收益 Benefit**：为发起组织及项目集预期受益者提供具有实用性的行动、行为、产品或服务的结果。

**收益管理计划 Benefits Management Plan**：定义创造、最大化并维持项目集收益过程的文档说明。

**收益维持 Benefits Sustainment**：为确保项目集交付的结果及改进的持续产生，由项目集收益接收组织在项目集结束后实施的持续性的维护活动。

**项目 Project**：为创造独特的产品、服务或成果而进行的临时性工作。

**项目管理 Project Management**：将知识、技能、工具与技术应用于项目活动，以满足项目的要求。

**项目集 Program**：经过协调管理以获取单独管理所无法取得收益的一组关联的项目、子项目集和项目集活动。

**项目集财务管理 Program Financial Management**：识别项目集资金来源与资源，整合项目集组件预算，编制项目集总体预算，并控制项目集与组件整个生命周期内成本的相关活动。

**项目集财务框架 Program Financial Framework**：关于如何协调可用资金，并决定资金限制和分配的高层面的初始计划。

**项目集采购管理 Program Procurement Management**：运用必要的知识、技能、工具与技术来获得用以满足整体项目集和组成项目/组件需求的产品和服务。

**项目集定义 Program Definition**：对提议项目集在执行后将要实现的边界、范围、目标及收益进行解释的文档。

**项目集发起人 Program Sponsor**：组织内负责为项目集提供财务资源的高级管理人员。

**项目集范围管理 Program Scope Management**：定义、制定、监督、控制和确认项目集范围的活动。

**项目集风险 Program Risk**：不确定事件或条件，一旦发生，会对项目集造成积极或消极影响。

**项目集风险登记册 Program Risk Register**：记录风险、风险分析结果及风险应对计划的文档。

**项目集风险管理 Program Risk Management**：主动识别、监督、分析、接受、减轻、避免或回避项目集风险。

**项目集相关方 Program Stakeholders**：积极参与项目集，或者其利益受项目集正面或负面影响的个人或组织。

**项目集相关方参与 Program Stakeholder Engagement**：捕捉相关方需求、期望，取得并维持相关方支持，以及减轻或疏通相关方的阻力。

**项目集沟通管理 Program Communications Management**：及时并恰当地产生、收集、分发、存储、检索和最终处置项目集信息的必要活动。

项目集管理 Program Management：将知识、技能、工具和技术应用于项目集，以满足项目集要求并获取单独管理这些项目时无法获取的收益与控制。

项目集管理办公室 Program Management Office：对与项目集相关的治理过程进行标准化，促进共享资源、方法论、工具与技术的管理结构。

项目集管理计划 Program Management Plan：管理项目集所需的一整套文档。

项目集管理信息系统 Program Management Information Systems：用于收集、整合并沟通有效管理一个或多个组织项目集关键信息的工具。

项目集活动 Program Activities：项目集内开展的一系列任务与工作。

项目集绩效衡量标准 Program Performance Metrics：用以评估和提升项目集管理过程效率、效用和结果的一套衡量标准。

项目集经理 Program Manager：机构、组织或公司内负责领导、指导和实施项目集的个人。

项目集启动 Program Initiation：定义项目集、筹集资金、为交付项目集收益将进行的工作而准备项目集环境的项目集活动。

项目集生命周期管理 Program Life Cycle Management：管理与项目集定义、收益交付及收尾相关的全部项目集活动。

项目集收尾 Program Closure：从移交项目集收益到维持该收益，以及释放和处置项目集资源的必要的项目集活动。

项目集收益交付 Program Benefits Delivery：项目集执行过程中开展的能产生收益实现计划中定义的期望收益的工作。

项目集团队/团队成员 Program Team/Team Members：直接参与项目集或其组件活动的个人。

项目集战略一致性 Program Strategy Alignment：与业务战略和组织目标和目的的整合和开发、确保运营和绩效与组织既定目标和目的一致相关的项目集活动。

项目集章程 Program Charter：定义提议项目集范围及目的，并呈交治理层以获取批准、投资和授权的文档。

项目集整合管理 Program Integration Management：在项目集内为整合、统一、协调、调整多个组件和活动所实施的项目集活动。

项目集质量保证 Program Quality Assurance：与定期评估项目集整体质量、为该项目集符合相关质量政策及标准带来信息相关的活动。

项目集质量计划 Program Quality Plan：项目集管理计划的组成部分，描述如何执行组织的质量政策与标准。

项目集质量控制 Program Quality Control：一种监控具体项目集可交付成果和结果，以验证是否满足质量要求的手段。

项目集治理 Program Governance：发起组织用以监督、管理并支持其项目集的体系与方法。

**项目集治理计划 Program Governance Plan**：描述可用于监督、管理、支持给定（既定）项目集的体系和方法的文档，并描述特定个人的责任以确保及时、有效地利用这些体系和方法。

**项目集主进度计划 Program Master Schedule**：交付项目集收益所必需的，逻辑上连接组件、里程碑和高层面活动的进度模型的输出。

**项目集资源管理 Program Resource Management**：为保证项目集收益交付而确保项目组件所需全部资源（包括人力、设备、材料等）到位而开展的项目集活动。

**项目经理 Project Manager**：由执行组织委派，领导团队实现项目目标的个人。

**项目组合 Portfolio**：为实现战略目标，把项目、项目集、子项目组合和运营工作按照一组的方式来进行管理。

**项目组合管理 Portfolio Management**：为实现战略目标而对一个或多个项目组合进行的集中管理。

**执行发起人 Executive Sponsor**：机构、组织或公司内对经授权的项目集活动的成功负有责任的高级管理人员。

**执行组织 Performing Organization**：其成员最直接参与项目或项目集工作的企业。

**制约因素 Constraint**：对执行项目、项目集、项目组合或过程有影响的限制性因素。

**质量管理计划 Quality Management Plan**：项目或项目集管理计划的组成部分，描述将如何实施组织的质量政策。

**治理管理 Governance Management**：提供稳定的、可重复的决策框架来控制组织、机构和公司内的资本投资的项目集管理职能。

**治理委员会 Governance Board**：在授权范围内批准和支持项目集建议，并对项目集实现其既定目标的进展实施监控和管理的评审与决策团体。

**子项目集 Subprogram**：作为另一个项目集的组成部分而被管理的一个项目集。

**组件 Components**：组成项目集的单个项目或非项目工作活动。